T0155980

Lecture Notes in Computer Science 13759

Founding Editors

Gerhard Goos

Juris Hartmanis

Editorial Board Members

Elisa Bertino, *Purdue University, West Lafayette, IN, USA*

Wen Gao, *Peking University, Beijing, China*

Bernhard Steffen ⓘ, *TU Dortmund University, Dortmund, Germany*

Moti Yung ⓘ, *Columbia University, New York, NY, USA*

The series Lecture Notes in Computer Science (LNCS), including its subseries Lecture Notes in Artificial Intelligence (LNAI) and Lecture Notes in Bioinformatics (LNBI), has established itself as a medium for the publication of new developments in computer science and information technology research, teaching, and education.

LNCS enjoys close cooperation with the computer science R & D community, the series counts many renowned academics among its volume editors and paper authors, and collaborates with prestigious societies. Its mission is to serve this international community by providing an invaluable service, mainly focused on the publication of conference and workshop proceedings and postproceedings. LNCS commenced publication in 1973.

Leopoldo Bertossi · Guohui Xiao
Editors

Reasoning Web

Causality, Explanations and Declarative Knowledge

18th International Summer School 2022
Berlin, Germany, September 27–30, 2022
Tutorial Lectures

 Springer

Editors
Leopoldo Bertossi
SKEMA Business School
Montreal, Canada

Guohui Xiao
University of Bergen
Bergen, Norway

ISSN 0302-9743   ISSN 1611-3349 (electronic)
Lecture Notes in Computer Science
ISBN 978-3-031-31413-1   ISBN 978-3-031-31414-8 (eBook)
https://doi.org/10.1007/978-3-031-31414-8

This Springer imprint is published by the registered company Springer Nature Switzerland AG
The registered company address is: Gewerbestrasse 11, 6330 Cham, Switzerland

Preface

The "Reasoning Web School" (RW) traditionally takes place in the late Summer, in Europe, as an event hosted under the umbrella of the "Declarative AI" conference. In 2022, Declarative AI was organized by the Technical University of Berlin, Germany. It was held online due to anticipated mobility restrictions caused by the Covid-19 pandemic. Still, it was a successful event that was attended by over one hundred participants.

The program contained eight three-hour courses, given over four days. We were fortunate to have excellent speakers and course subjects. The broad, but not exclusive theme of RW 2022 was "Reasoning in Probabilistic Models and Machine Learning". The courses were as follows:

1. João Marques-Silva (IRIT, CNRS, Toulouse, France).
   "Logic-Based Explainability in Machine Learning".
2. Sudeepa Roy (Duke University, USA) and Babak Salimi (University of California, San Diego, USA).
   "Causal Explanations and Fairness in Data".
3. Joohyung Lee (Arizona State University, USA).
   "Statistical Relational Extensions of Answer Set Programming".
4. Emanuel Sallinger (Technical University of Vienna, Austria & Oxford University, UK).
   "Vadalog: Its Extensions and Business Applications".
5. Meng Wang (South East University, China) and Ningyu Zhang (Zhejiang University, China).
   "Cross-Modal Knowledge Discovery, Inference, and Challenges".
6. Guy Van den Broeck (University of California, Los Angeles, USA).
   "Reasoning with Tractable Probabilistic Circuits".
7. Giuseppe Marra (Katholieke Universiteit Leuven, Belgium).
   "From Statistical Relational to Neural Symbolic Artificial Intelligence".
8. Stefan Pabst and Cassandra Hunt (RelationalAI Inc., USA).
   "Building Intelligent Data Apps in Rel using Reasoning and Probabilistic Modelling".

We are grateful to all the speakers who made possible a successful RW School 2022. Recordings of the presentations can be found online, at https://www.youtube.com/playlist?list=PLNbok10XIASfBCzgo_KUslIaSD06UUdNc .

Following tradition, the speakers were invited to submit a chapter for the RW Lecture Notes volume that is usually published in the Tutorial Series of the Springer Lecture Notes in Computer Science. Chapters were submitted for the first five courses above. They form the core of the current volume. All the chapters received at least one anonymous review, which provided feedback and recommendations in relation to readability and contents.

On this occasion, we are also including an additional, initial chapter on explanations in AI written by L. Bertossi. This chapter is written in a style that fits well with those with their origin in the RW courses. (Actually, it is based on a similar short course given in 2022 at the SKEMA Business School.) It can also be seen as an introduction and a motivation for the subjects that are treated more deeply in the three subsequent chapters.

We are grateful to the Scientific Advisory Board for their contribution of ideas to shape the School Program. We are particularly thankful to Mantas Simkus, who shared with us his experience with the organization of RW. We also appreciate much help received from Adrian Paschke (T. U. Berlin, Germany), Theodoros Mitsikas (National U. of Athens, Greece), and Kumas Manas (T. U. Berlin, Germany) for their logistic and operational support. For their contribution to the editorial process, we are also very grateful to Maria Vanina Martinez (U. de Buenos Aires, Argentina), Miguel Romero (U. Afolfo Ibañez, Chile), and Ali Emani (Brock University, Canada).

Last, but not the least, we appreciate the traditional and valuable support from Springer for the publications of the lecture notes.

September 2022

Leopoldo Bertossi
Guohui Xiao

Organization

General Chair of "Declarative AI 2022"

Adrian Paschke — Technical University of Berlin, Germany

Web Chair

Theodoros Mitsikas — National Technical University of Athens, Greece

Reasoning Web Chairs

Leopoldo Bertossi — SKEMA Business School, Canada
Guohui Xiao — University of Bergen, Norway

Scientific Advisory Board

Reinhard Pichler — Technical University of Vienna, Austria
Vanina Martinez — Universidad de Buenos Aires, Argentina
Ivan Varzinczak — University of Artois, France
Alexey Ignatiev — Monash University, Australia
Pablo Barcelo — P. Catholic University of Chile, Chile
Mantas Simkus — Technical University of Vienna, Austria

Contents

Attribution-Scores and Causal Counterfactuals as Explanations in Artificial Intelligence

Leopoldo Bertossi[✉]

SKEMA Business School, Montreal, Canada
leopoldo.bertossi@skema.edu

Abstract. In this expository article we highlight the relevance of explanations for artificial intelligence, in general, and for the newer developments in *explainable AI*, referring to origins and connections of and among different approaches. We describe in simple terms, explanations in data management and machine learning that are based on attribution-scores, and counterfactuals as found in the area of causality. We elaborate on the importance of logical reasoning when dealing with counterfactuals, and their use for score computation.

1 Introduction

The search for explanations belongs to human nature, and as a quest, it has been around since the inception of human beings. Explanations, as a subject, have been investigated in Artificial Intelligence (AI) for some decades, and also, and for a much longer time, in other disciplines, such as Philosophy, Logic, Physics, Statistics. Actually, the explicit study of explanations can be traced back to the ancient Greeks, who were already concerned with *causes* and *effects*. Nowadays, a whole area of artificial intelligence (AI) has emerged, that of *Explainable AI* (XAI). It has become part of an even larger area, *Ethical AI*, that encompasses other concerns, such as fairness, responsibility, trust, bias (better, lack thereof), etc.

Research done under XAI has become diverse, intensive, extensive, and definitely, effervescent. Accordingly, it is difficult to keep track of: (a) the origins of some popular approaches to explainability; and (b) the new methodologies, and the possible connections, similarities and differences among them. It is also the case that AI has become of interest for many stakeholders, and most prominently, for people who may be affected by developments in AI and by the use of AI-based systems. It has also become a subject of investigation or discussion for people who do not directly do research, system development or applications inside AI. This has contributed to a certain degree of confusion about what exactly falls under AI, and the role of XAI within AI.

L. Bertossi—Member of the Millennium Institute for Foundations of Data Research (IMFD, Chile).

Consistently with these observations, in this work we will revisit, in intuitive and simple terms, some "classic" approaches to explanations that have been introduced and investigated in AI, and have been established in it for some time. We will also discuss newer approaches to explanations that have emerged mainly in the context of Machine Learning (ML), and have become best examples of Explainable AI. One of our goals is to make clear that explanations have been investigated in AI much before this "new wave" of XAI arrived [51], and that the new methods build (or can be seen as building) upon older approaches. We also discuss in more detail the place of XAI in AI at large.

Motivated by our own recent research, we describe some approaches to XAI that are based on assigning numerical scores to elements of an input to an AI system, e.g. an ML-classifier, that give an account of their relevance with respect to the outcome obtained from the system for that particular input. Instead of providing all the mathematical and algorithmic background, we use concrete examples to convey the main ideas and issues. Technical details can be found in the provided bibliographic references.

We end this article with a general discussion of the role of reasoning in XAI as it has been traditionally understood in AI. In general, the current approaches do not explicitly appeal to reasoning, nor are they extended with any kind of logical reasoning. We argue in favor of extending these newer approaches with reasoning capabilities, in particular, with counterfactual reasoning, which has to do with exploring, analyzing and comparing, usually hypothetically, different alternative scenarios. This form of reasoning is at the basis of causal explanations, and other areas of computer science.

This is not an exhaustive survey of explanation methods, nor of XAI. Recent surveys that cover XAI can be found, e.g. in [15, 28, 50, 51]. This expository article can be taken as an invitation and a basis for a broader discussion around explanations, and explainable AI; and also as a motivation to explore some subjects in more detail.

2   The Role of Explanations in AI

Explanations are an important part of Artificial Intelligence (AI), and we can clearly identify a couple of fundamental reasons for this:

(A) Searching for explanations for external phenomena, observed behaviors, etc., and providing them, are important manifestations of human intelligence, and as such, they become natural subjects of investigation in AI.

(B) AI systems themselves provide results of different kinds, and they require explanations, for humans and AI systems as well.

The former direction has been investigated in AI and more traditional disciplines, as already mentioned above. The second direction is much newer, because AI systems used at large are also much newer. The "older" kind of explanations can be used and adapted for this second purpose, but also some new forms of explanations, that can be more *ad hoc* for different kinds of AI systems, have been introduced and investigated in the last few years. Let us consider a simple example, for the gist.

Example 1. Consider a client of bank who is applying for loan. The bank will process his/her application by means of an AI system that will decide if the client should be given the loan or not. In order for the application to be computationally processed, the client is represented as an *entity* describing him/her, say $e = \langle john, 18, plumber, 70K, harlem, 10K, basic \rangle$, that is, a finite record of *feature values*. The set of features is $\mathcal{F} = \{Name, Age, Activity, Income, Debt, EdLevel\}$.

The bank uses a *classifier*, $\mathcal{C}$, that is an AI system that may have been learned on the basis of existing data about loan applications. There are different ways to build such a system. After receiving input e, $\mathcal{C}$ returns a *label*, *Yes* or *No* (or 0 or 1). In this case, it returns *No*, indicating that the loan request is rejected. The client (or the bank executive) asks *"Why?"*, and would like to have an explanation. The issues are: (a) What kind of explanation? (b) How could it be provided? (c) From what? $\square$

These kinds of motivations and applications are typical of *Explainable AI* (XAI) these days, and of explainable machine learning, in particular. Actually, the whole area has become part of a larger one, usually called *Ethical AI*, which includes concerns such as transparency, fairness, bias, trust, responsibility, etc., that should be taken into account when the use of AI systems may affect stakeholders. I's no wonder that these issues are being discussed and investigated in other disciplines, such as Law, Sociology, Philosophy; and others that are more directly affected by the use of AI systems, e.g. Business, Medicine, Health, etc. Some countries have already passed new legislation forcing AI systems affecting users to provide guarantees of an ethical behaviour [16]. *Explainability and interpretability* of AI systems are part of this picture.

Some claim that ethical AI research is *not part of* AI, but *about* AI. The fact that an increasing number of people who work in this area do not do actual AI research, does not make the area less AI. It is part of AI for several reasons, among them: (a) AI systems should be extended with the capability to provide explanations, and the extended systems would become also AI systems; (b) the individual subjects that fall under ethical AI are developed on a scientific and technical basis by AI researchers, who understand, model and implement explanations; (c) as already mentioned, explanation finding and giving are intelligent human activities worth of investigation under AI; (d) explanations become additional resources for AI system building, e.g. one can (automatically) learn from explanations; etc.

3   Some Classical Models of Explanation

In this section, we will briefly introduce and discuss some approaches to explanations that have been proposed and investigated in the context of AI, actually for a few decades by now. Some of them fall in the area of AI called *model-based diagnosis* [61], in that the explanation process relies on the use of a mathematical model of a system under observation, e.g. a logical or a probabilistic model. We will use a running example to illustrate different approaches.

3.1 Consistency-Based Diagnosis

If we are confronting a system that is exhibiting an unexpected or abnormal behavior, we want to obtain a *diagnosis* for this, i.e. some sort of explanation. Diagnoses are obtained from a model of the system, possibly extended with some additional knowledge. In the following, we briefly describe the approach to diagnosis proposed by Ray Reiter [56], usually called *consistency-based diagnosis* (CBD).

Example 2. Consider the very simple Boolean circuit in Fig. 1, with an *And*-gate, A, and an *Or*-gate, O. The input variables are a, b, c, the intermediate output variable for A is x, and the final, output variable is d; all of them taking values 0 or 1. The intended meaning of the propositional variable a is "input a is true" (or takes value 1), etc.

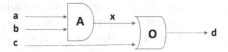

Fig. 1. A Boolean circuit

From a conceptual point of view, this could be a *binary classifier*, for which an input entity **e** is represented by a record of binary values for a, b, c. The classifier computes the output d, which becomes the binary label assigned to **e**. Now, assume we observe the following behavior:

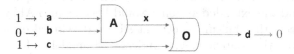

Fig. 2. A malfunctioning Boolean circuit

According to the laws of propositional logic, we should obtain $x = 0$ and $d = 1$, which is not the case here. We ask: *Why? What is wrong?* Or more specifically, *What is a* diagnosis *for the abnormal behavior of the circuit?* □

A more general question now is: *What is a diagnosis?* Diagnoses have to be characterized. Since we are adopting a model-based approach, we need a model.

In our example, a logical model of the circuit, when it works properly, is the set of propositional formulas

$$\{(x \longleftrightarrow (a \wedge b)), (d \longleftrightarrow (x \vee c))\}. \tag{1}$$

However, our circuit at hand, by working abnormally, is *not* modeled by these formulas.

Furthermore, notice that the *observation, Obs*, represented by the formula: $a \wedge \neg b \wedge c \wedge \neg d$, indicating that a and c are true, b is false, and d is true, is mutually inconsistent with the ideal model above, that is, there is no assignment of truth values to the propositional variables that makes the combination true. From their combination we cannot logically obtain any useful information, because everything is entailed by an inconsistent set of propositional formulas. We may want instead *a model that allows failures, or abnormal behaviors.* From such a model, we could try to obtain explanations for those abnormal behaviors.

A better, more flexible model that allows failures, and specifies how components behave under normal conditions is as follows:

$$\mathcal{M} = \{\neg AbA \longrightarrow (x \leftrightarrow (a \wedge b)), \neg AbO \longrightarrow (d \leftrightarrow (x \vee c))\}. \tag{2}$$

The first formula says *"When A is not abnormal, it works as an And-gate"*, etc. Here, AbA and AbO are new propositional variables. This is a "weak model of failure" in that it specifies how things behave under normal conditions only, but not under abnormal ones. This is a typical (but non-mandatory) form models take under CBD [21]. The model assumes that the only potentially faulty components are, in this case, the gates (but not the wires connecting them), a modeling choice. Now gates could be abnormal (or faulty), and $\{Obs\} \cup \mathcal{M}$ is a perfectly consistent logical model.

Notice that when one specifies, in addition, that the gates are not abnormal, we have:

$$\{Obs\} \cup \mathcal{M} \cup \{\neg AbA, \neg AbO\} \text{ is inconsistent,} \tag{3}$$

as before. So, something has to be abnormal. It is through *consistency restoration* that we will be able to characterize and compute diagnoses.

Notice that making gate O abnormal in (3) restores consistency, that is, in contrast to (3),

$$Obs \cup \mathcal{M} \cup \{\neg AbA, \underline{AbO}\} \text{ is consistent.}$$

We are underlying the change we made. More precisely, and by definition, $\{abO\}$ is a diagnosis. Similarly, $D' = \{abO, abA\}$ is a diagnosis, because making every gate abnormal also restores consistency:

$$Obs \cup \mathcal{M} \cup \{\underline{AbA}, \underline{AbO}\} \text{ is consistent.}$$

We may consider D as a "better" diagnosis than D', because it makes fewer assumptions, is more informative by providing narrower and more focused diagnosis. D is a *minimal diagnosis* in that it is not set-theoretically included in any other diagnosis. It is also a *minimum diagnosis* in that it has a minimum cardinality. As expected, different preference criteria could be imposed on diagnosis.

3.2   Abduction

Abduction is a much older approach to obtaining a *best* explanation for an observation at hand. It can be traced back to Aristotle, and, more recently, to the work by the Philosopher C.S. Peirce [54]. Abductive diagnosis has been extensively investigated in AI, and has become one of the classic approaches to explanations [46,55,61].

For the gist, and at the risk of simplifying things too much, a typical example provides the following simple model (a propositional logical theory): *Covid19* → *Breathlessness*. Now, we observe (for a patient): *Obs*: *Breathlessness*. In the light of the only information at hand, that provided by the model, we may "infer" *Covid19* as an explanation. However, this is not classical inference in that we are using the implication backwards. So, *Covid19* is being *abduced* from the model and the information (as opposed to classically inferred or deduced), in the sense that:

$$\{\underline{Covid19}\} \cup \{Covid19 \ \rightarrow \ Breathlessness\} \models Obs, \qquad (4)$$

which defines *Covid19* as an abductive explanation. Here, the symbol $\models$ denotes classical logical consequence.[1] Of course, if the model becomes more complex, this sort of *backward reasoning* in search for explanations that support implications (via forward reasoning), becomes much more complex and computationally costly. As expected, one may consider additional preference criteria on abductive explanations, most typically some sort of minimality condition.

Example 3 (Example 2 cont.). Consider the same circuit and observation, in this case $Obs' = \{\neg d\}$, which we would like to entail with additional information provided by abducible facts. We cannot expect to obtain $\{\underline{abO}\} \cup \mathcal{M} \cup \{a \wedge \neg b \wedge c\} \models \neg d$, with $\mathcal{M}$ as in (2), which is only a weak model of failure. Actually, the entailment does not hold since $\{abO\} \cup \mathcal{M} \cup \{a \wedge \neg b \wedge c\} \cup \{d\}$ is a consistent theory.

However, if we change the model in order to specify failures, e.g. with $\mathcal{M}' = \{a \wedge b \wedge AbA \rightarrow \neg x, x \wedge AbO \rightarrow \neg d, c \wedge AbO \rightarrow \neg d\}$, we do obtain $\{\underline{abO}\} \cup \mathcal{M}' \cup \{a, \neg b, c\} \models \neg d$, as expected. It is common, but not mandatory, to use abduction with implicational models [24]. $\square$

Abduction has found its way into XAI, most prominently, to provide explanations for results from classification models. They are usually called *sufficient explanations*: A (hopefully minimal) set of abducible facts that are sufficient to entail the observed label [4,34,45].

3.3   Actual Causality and Responsibility

We can use the running example to illustrate the notion of *actual causality* [29,30].

---

[1] If some other non-classical logic is used instead, $\models$ has to be replaced by the corresponding entailment criterion [23].

Example 4 (Example 2 cont.). Consider the same circuit as in Fig. 2, and the same model as in (2), for which we had in (3):

$$\{a, \neg b, c\} \cup \mathcal{M} \cup \{\neg AbA, \neg AbO\} \cup \{\neg d\} \text{ is inconsistent,}$$

which is logically equivalent to:

$$\{a, \neg b, c\} \cup \mathcal{M} \cup \{\neg AbA, \neg AbO\} \models d. \tag{5}$$

In this setting, we will play a *counterfactual* game consisting in hypothetically changing variables' truth values, to see if the entailment in (5) changes. Before proceeding, we have to identify the *endogenous* variables, those on which we have some control, and the *exogenous variables* we have as a given. This choice is application dependent. In our case, it is natural to consider a, b, c as exogenous, and x, d, abA, abO as endogenous. Here, the *interventions* are the hypothetical changes of non-abnormalities into abnormalities, to see if implication in (5) changes as a result. (The interventions are also application dependent).

Switching $\neg abO$ into AbO, does invalidate the previous entailment:

$$\{a, \neg b, c\} \cup \mathcal{M} \cup \{\neg AbA, \underline{AbO}\} \not\models d.$$

For this reason (and by definition), we say that "abO is a *counterfactual cause*" (for the observation).

However, when we switch abA: $\{a, \neg b, c\} \cup \mathcal{M} \cup \{\underline{AbA}, \neg AbO\} \models d$. The entailment still holds. Accordingly, AbA is *not* a counterfactual cause. For this candidate, an extra counterfactual change, a so-called *contingent* change, is necessary: $\{a, \neg b, c\} \cup \mathcal{M} \cup \{\underline{AbA}, \underline{AbO}\} \not\models d$. Had abO not been already (and alone) a counterfactual cause, AbA would have been called (by definition) an *actual cause with contingency set* $\{abO\}$. So, AbA is neither a counterfactual nor an actual cause.[2]   □

Actual causality provides *counterfactual explanations* to observations. In general terms, they are "components" of a system that are a cause for an observed behavior. Counterfactual causes are actual causes with an empty contingency set. Accordingly, counterfactual causes are *strong* causes in that they, by themselves, explain the observation. Actual (non-counterfactual) causes are *weaker* causes, they require the company of other components to explain the observation.

Readers who are more familiar with causality based on *structural models* [53,58] may be missing them here. Actually, the diagnosis problems can be cast in those terms too. A purely logical model, as in the previous examples, does not distinguish causal directions, or between causes and effects. They can be better represented by a structural model that takes the form of a (directed) *causal network*.

Example 5 (Example 4 cont.). The following causal network represents our diagnosis example, or better, our possibly faulty circuit.

---

[2] Example 7 will show an actual cause that is not a counterfactual cause.

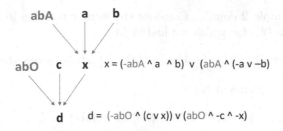

Fig. 3. Causal Network

Here, abA, abO are endogenous variables, which can be subject to counterfactual interventions, which, in this case, amount to making AbA and AbO true or false. Variables x and d are endogenous, and have *structural equations* associated to them, as shown in Fig. 3, capturing the circuit's logic. They are unidirectional, so as the edge directions. Contrary to the weak model of failure in (2), the equations specify the behaviour also under abnormality conditions. □

Actual causality has been extended with the quantitative notion of *responsibility* [18]. Causes are assigned a numerical score that captures their causal strength. The score takes into account, for endogenous variables, if it is an actual cause or not; and, in the positive case, its contingency sets (CSs).

Example 6 (Example 4 cont.). The responsibility score for an endogenous variable takes into account, in this case, is defined (for the endogenous variables) as follows:

$$Resp(abO) \quad := \quad \frac{1}{1 + |\Gamma|} = \frac{1}{1+0} = 1,$$

with Γ a minimum-cardinality CS for abO.

$$Resp(abA) \quad := 0\,.$$

The first case is due to the fact that abO is a counterfactual cause, and then, has the maximum responsibility, 1. The second case is due to the fact that abA is not an actual cause.[3] □

Actual causality has been applied to provide explanations in the context of relational databases [6,47,48]. There, the observation is a query result, and one wants to unveil the causes, inside the database, in the form of, say, database tuples or attribute values in them, for the query to be true (or returning a particular answer). Also, responsibility scores can be assigned to tuples or their attribute values.

Example 7. Consider the relational database instance D:

---

[3] Less "trivial" cases will be shown in Example 7.

R	S
$\langle c,b \rangle$	$\langle a \rangle$
$\langle a,d \rangle$	$\langle b \rangle$
$\langle b,a \rangle$	$\langle c \rangle$
	$\langle d \rangle$

The conjunctive query $\mathcal{Q}$: $\exists x \exists y (S(x) \wedge R(x,y) \wedge S(y))$ posed to D is true because join can be satisfied with the database tuples in different ways. For example, the tuples $S(c), R(c,b), S(b)$ jointly satisfy the query condition.

We want to identify tuples as actual causes for the query to be true. If the tuple $S(b)$ is deleted, the particular instatiation of the join just mentioned above becomes false. However, the query is still true, jointly via the tuples $S(a), R(a,d)$, $S(d)$; or the tuples $S(b), R(b,a)$, $S(a)$. In order to falsify the query, some of these tuples have to be deleted as well. There are different combinations, but a minimum deletion is that of $S(a)$. In more technical terms, in order for $S(b)$ to be an *actual cause* for the query to be true, it requires a *contingency set* of tuples to be further deleted. In this case, $\{S(a)\}$ is a minimum-size contingency set, of cardinality 1. Accordingly, $S(b)$ is an actual cause with *causal responsibility* $Resp(S(b)) = \frac{1}{1+1} = \frac{1}{2}$. Notice that if we just delete $S(a)$, the query is still true. A condition on contingency sets for an actual cause is that its deletion alone does not falsify the query; it has to be combined with the cause candidate at hand.

If we, instead, had the following database D' here below, tuple $S(b)$ would be a

R	S
$\langle c,b \rangle$	$\langle a \rangle$
$\langle a,d \rangle$	$\langle b \rangle$
$\langle b,b \rangle$	$\langle c \rangle$

counterfactual cause in the sense that it does not require any additional contingent deletion to falsify the query. The empty set is a minimum-size contingency set for it,

and its responsibility becomes 1, the maximum responsibility.

Tuple $S(c)$ has $\{R(b,b)\}$ as a minimum contingency set, but not $\{S(b)\}$ that alone can falsify the query. We have $Resp(S(c)) = \frac{1}{2}$. □

The examples above shows similarities between CBD and actual causality, in that in both cases we try to make changes with the purpose of possibly seeing a different outcome. In fact, a precise connection for the particular case of databases was established in [6], and the connection was appropriately exploited. We give a simple example for the gist.

Example 8 (Example 7 cont.). Instead of performing interventions directly on the data-base, and in relation to the query at hand, we can build a CBD problem.

The first observation is that the conjunctive query $\mathcal{Q}$: $\exists x \exists y (S(x) \wedge R(x,y) \wedge S(y))$ can be transformed into an *integrity constraint*, κ: $\neg \exists x \exists y (S(x) \wedge R(x,y) \wedge S(y))$, actually a *denial constraint* that prohibits the satisfaction of the query join (the conjunction). It holds that $\mathcal{Q}$ is satisfied by D iff κ is violated by D, which would be considered the faulty behavior. Accordingly, we specify a system that may not be working as normal, in the sense that the IC can be violated (under abnormal conditions). The main component of the diagnosis model is the formula:

$$\forall x \forall y (\neg Ab_S(x) \land \neg Ab_R(x,y) \land \neg Ab_S(y) \longrightarrow \neg(S(x) \land R(x,y) \land S(y))). \quad (6)$$

Here, we have introduced one auxiliary abnormality predicate for each database predicate. This formula says that when the tuples are not abnormal, they do not participate in the violation of the IC κ. In other words, under the normality assumptions, the database behaves as intended (or normal), i.e. satisfying the IC, which in this case, amounts to not making the query true.

For example, the tuples $S(c), R(c,b), S(b)$ in D jointly satisfy the non-negated join on the RHS of (6). In order to make (6) true, at least one of $Ab_S(c)$, $Ab_R(c,b)$, $Ab_R(b)$ has to be true. The rest continues as with Example 2. The tuples whose associated abnormality atoms become true are, by definition, the actual causes for the query to be true.   □

In the database context, actual causality was also connected with abductive diagnosis for Datalog queries [7].

4   Attribution Scores in Machine Learning

In machine learning, in situations such as that in Example 1, actual causality and responsibility have been applied to provide *counterfactual explanations* for classification results, and scores for them. In order to do this, having access to the internal components of the classifier is not needed, but only its input/output relation.

Example 9 (Example 1 cont.). The entity

$$e = \langle \text{john}, 18, \text{plumber}, 70K, \text{harlem}, 10K, \text{basic} \rangle \quad (7)$$

received the label 1 from the classifier, indicating that the loan is not granted.[4] In order to identify counterfactual explanations, we intervene the feature values replacing them by alternative ones from the feature domains, e.g. $e_1 = \langle \text{john}, \underline{25}, \text{plumber}, 70K, \text{harlem}, 10K, \text{basic} \rangle$, which receives the label 0. The counterfactual version $e_2 = \langle \text{john}, 18, \text{plumber}, \underline{80K}, \underline{\text{brooklyn}}, 10K, \text{basic} \rangle$ also get label 0. Assuming, in the latter case, that none of the single changes alone switch the label, we could say that Age = 25, so as Income = 70K with contingency Location = harlem (and the other way around) in e are (minimal) counterfactual explanations, by being actual causes for the observed label.

We could go one step beyond, and define responsibility scores: $Resp(e, \text{Age}) := 1$, and $Resp(e, \text{Income}) := \frac{1}{2}$ (due to the additional, required,

---

[4] We are assuming that classifiers are *binary*, i.e. they return labels 0 or 1. For simplicity and uniformity, but without loss of generality, we will assume that label 1 is the one we want to explain.

contingent change). This choice does reflect the causal strengths of attribute values in **e**. However, it could be the case that only by changing the value of Age to 25 we manage to switch the label, whereas for all the other possible values for Age (while nothing else changes), the label is always *No*. It seems more reasonable to redefine responsibility by considering an average involving all the possible labels obtained in this way.   □

The direct application of the responsibility score, as in [6,47], works fine for explanation scores when features are *binary*, say taking values 0 or 1, [11,12]. However, when features have more than two values, it makes sense to extend the definition of the responsibility score.

4.1   The Generalized *Resp* Score

In [8], a generalized *Resp* score was introduced and investigated. We describe it next in intuitive terms, and appealing to Example 9.

1. For an entity **e** classified with label $L(\mathbf{e}) = 1$, and a feature $F^\star$, whose value $F^\star(\mathbf{e})$ appears in **e**, we want a numerical responsibility score $Resp(\mathbf{e}, F^\star)$, characterizing the causal strength of $F^\star(\mathbf{e})$ for outcome $L(\mathbf{e})$. In the example, $F^\star =$ Salary, $F^\star(\mathbf{e}) =$ 70K, and $L(\mathbf{e}) = 1$.
2. While we keep the original value for Salary fixed, we start by defining a "local" score for a fixed contingent assignment $\Gamma := \bar{w}$, with $F^\star \notin \Gamma \subseteq \mathcal{F}$. We define $\mathbf{e}^{\Gamma,\bar{w}} := \mathbf{e}[\Gamma := \bar{w}]$, the entity obtained from **e** by changing (or redefining) its values for features in Γ, according to $\bar{w}$.
   In the example, it could be $\Gamma = \{\text{Location}\}$, and $\bar{w} := \langle \text{brooklin} \rangle$, a contingent (new) value for Location. Then, $\mathbf{e}^{\{\text{Location}\},\langle \text{brooklin} \rangle} = \mathbf{e}[\text{Location} := \text{brooklin}] = \langle \text{john}, 25, \text{plumber}, 70K, \underline{\text{brooklin}}, 10K, \text{basic} \rangle$.
   We make sure (or assume in the following) that $L(\mathbf{e}^{\Gamma,\bar{w}}) = L(\mathbf{e}) = 1$ holds. This is because, being these changes only contingent, we do not expect them to switch the label by themselves, but only and until the "main" counterfactual change on $F^\star$ is made.
   In the example, we assume $L(\mathbf{e}[\text{Location} := \text{brooklin}]) = 1$. Another case could be $\mathbf{e}^{\Gamma',\bar{w}'}$, with $\Gamma' = \{\text{Activity}, \text{Education}\}$, and $\bar{w}' = \langle \text{accountant}, \text{medium} \rangle$, with $L(\mathbf{e}^{\Gamma',\bar{w}'}) = 1$.
3. Now, for each of those $\mathbf{e}^{\Gamma,\bar{w}}$ as in the previous item, we consider all the different possible values v for $F^\star$, while the values for all the other features are fixed as in $\mathbf{e}^{\Gamma,\bar{w}}$.
   For example, starting from $\mathbf{e}[\text{Location} := \text{brooklin}]$, we can consider $\mathbf{e}'_1 := \mathbf{e}[\text{Location} := \text{brooklin}; \underline{\text{Salary} := 60K}]$ (which is the same as $\mathbf{e}^{\text{Location},\langle \text{brooklin} \rangle}[$ Salary $:= 60K]$), obtaining, e.g. $L(\mathbf{e}'_1) = 1$. However, for $\mathbf{e}'_2 := \mathbf{e}[\text{Location} := \text{brooklin}; \underline{\text{Salary} := 80}]$, we now obtain, e.g. $L(\mathbf{e}'_2) = 0$, etc.
   For a fixed (potentially) contingent change $(\Gamma, \bar{w})$ on **e**, we consider the difference between the original label 1 and the expected label obtained by further

modifying the value of $F^\star$ (in all possible ways). This gives us a *local* responsibility score, local to $(\Gamma, \bar{w})$:

$$Resp(\mathbf{e}, F^\star, \underline{\Gamma, \bar{w}}) := \frac{L(\mathbf{e}) - \mathbb{E}(\ L(\mathbf{e}') \mid F(\mathbf{e}') = F(\mathbf{e}^{\Gamma, \bar{w}}), \forall F \in (\mathcal{F} \smallsetminus \{F^\star\}\ )}{1 + |\Gamma|}$$

$$= \frac{1 - \mathbb{E}(\ L(\mathbf{e}^{\Gamma, \bar{w}}[F^\star := v]) \mid v \in Dom(F^\star)\ )}{1 + |\Gamma|}. \tag{8}$$

This local score takes into account, so as the original responsibility score in Sect. 3.3, the size of the contingency set Γ.

We are assuming here that there is a probability distribution over the entity population $\mathcal{E}$. It could be known from the start, or it could be an empirical distribution obtained from a sample. As discussed in [8], the choice (or whichever distribution that is available) is relevant for the computation of the general *Resp* score, which involves the local ones (coming right here below).

4. Now, generalizing the terms introduced in Sect. 3.3, we can say that the value $F^\star(\mathbf{e})$ is an *actual cause* for label 1 when, for some $(\Gamma, \bar{w})$, (8) is positive: at least one change of value for $F^\star$ in $\mathbf{e}$ changes the label (with the company of $(\Gamma, \bar{w})$).

When $\Gamma = \emptyset$ (and then, $\bar{w}$ is an empty assignment), and (8) is positive, it means that at least one change of value for $F^\star$ in $\mathbf{e}$ switches the label by itself. As before, we can say that $F^\star(\mathbf{e})$ is a *counterfactual cause*. However, as desired and expected, it is not necessarily the case anymore that counterfactual causes (as original values in $\mathbf{e}$) have all the same causal strength: $F_i(\mathbf{e}), F_j(\mathbf{e})$ could be both counterfactual causes, but with different values for (8), for example if changes on the first switch the label "fewer times" than those on the second.

5. Now, we can define the global score, by considering the "best" contingencies $(\Gamma, \bar{w})$, which involves requesting from Γ to be of minimum size:

$$Resp(\mathbf{e}, F^\star) := \max_{\Gamma, \bar{w} : |\Gamma| \text{ is min.\&8)} > 0} Resp(\mathbf{e}, F^\star, \Gamma, \bar{w}). \tag{9}$$

This means that we first find the minimum-size contingency sets Γ's for which, for an associated set of value updates $\bar{w}$, (8) becomes greater that 0. After that, we find the maximum value for (8) over all such pairs $(\Gamma, \bar{w})$. This can be done by starting with $\Gamma = \emptyset$, and iteratively increasing the cardinality of Γ by one, until a $(\Gamma, \bar{w})$ is found that makes (8) non-zero. We stop increasing the cardinality, and we just check if there is another $(\Gamma', \bar{w}')$ that gives a greater value for (8), with $|\Gamma'| = |\Gamma|$. By taking the maximum of the local scores, we have an existential quantification in mind: there must be a good contingency $(\Gamma, \bar{w})$, as long as Γ has a minimum cardinality.

With the generalized score, the difference between counterfactual and actual causes is not as relevant as before. In the end, and as discussed under Item 4. above, what matters is the size of the score. Accordingly, we can talk only about "counterfactual explanations with responsibility score r". In Example 9, we could say "$\mathbf{e}_2$ is a (minimal) counterfactual for $\mathbf{e}$ (implicitly saying that it switches the label), and the value 60K for Salary is a counterfactual explanation with responsibility $Resp(\mathbf{e}, \mathsf{Salary})$". Here, $\mathbf{e}_2$ is possibly only one of those counterfactual entities that contribute to making the value for Salary a counterfactual explanation, and to its (generalized) $Resp$ score.

The generalized $Resp$ score was applied for different financial data [8], and experimentally compared with a simpler version of responsibility, and with the $Shap$ score [43], all of which can be applied with a black-box classifier, using only the input/output relation. It was also experimentally compared, with the same data, with a the FICO-score [17] that is defined for and applied to an open-box model, and computes scores by taking into account components of the model, in this case coefficients of nested logistic regressions.

The computation cost of the $Resp$ score is bound to be high in general since, in essence, it explicitly involves in (8) all possible subsets of the set of features; and in (9), also the minimality condition which compares different subsets. Actually, for binary classifiers and in its simple, binary formulation, $Resp$ is already intractable [12]. In [8], in addition to experimental results, there is a technical discussion on the importance of the underlying distribution on the population, and on the need to perform optimized computations and approximations.

4.2   The *Shap* Score

The *Shap* score was introduced in explainable ML in [43], as an application of the general *Shapley value* of *coalition game theory* [59], which we briefly describe next.

Consider a set of players $\mathcal{S}$, and a *wealth-distribution function* (or *game function*), $\mathcal{G}\colon \mathcal{P}(\mathcal{S}) \to \mathbb{R}$, that maps subsets of $\mathcal{S}$ to real numbers. The Shapley value of player $p \in \mathcal{S}$ quantifies the contribution of p to the game, for which all different coalitions are considered; each time, with p and without p:

$$Shapley(\mathcal{S}, \mathcal{G}, p) := \sum_{S \subseteq \mathcal{S} \setminus \{p\}} \frac{|S|!(|\mathcal{S}| - |S| - 1)!}{|\mathcal{S}|!} (\mathcal{G}(S \cup \{p\}) - \mathcal{G}(S)). \quad (10)$$

Here, $|S|!(|D| - |S| - 1)!$ is the number of permutations of $\mathcal{S}$ with all players in S coming first, then p, and then all the others. In other words, this is the *expected contribution* of p under all possible additions of p to a partial random sequence of players, followed by random sequences of the rest of the players.

The Shapley value emerges as the only quantitative measure that has some specified properties in relation to coalition games [57]. It has been applied in many disciplines. For each particular application, one has to define a particular and appropriate game function $\mathcal{G}$. Close to home, it has been applied to assign scores to logical formulas to quantify their contribution to the inconsistency of a knowledge base [32], to quantify contributions to the inconsistency of a database [42], and to quantify the contribution of database tuples to making a query true [40,41].

In different application and with different game functions, the Shapley value turns out to be computationally intractable, more precisely, its time complexity is $\#P\text{-}hard$ in the size of the input, c.f., for example, [40]. Intuitively, this means that it is at least as hard as any of the problems in the class $\#P$ of problems about counting the solutions to decisions problems (in NP) that ask about the existence of a certain solution [52,63]. For example, SAT is the decision problem asking, for a propositional formula, if there exists a truth assignment (a solution) that makes the formula true. Then, $\#SAT$ is the computational problem of counting the number of satisfying assignments of a propositional formula. Clearly, $\#SAT$ is at least as hard as SAT (it is good enough to count the number of solutions to know if the formula is satisfiable), and SAT is the prototypical NP-complete problem, and furthermore, $\#SAT$ is $\#P$-hard, actually, $\#P$-complete since it belongs to $\#P$.[5] As a consequence, computing the Shapley value can be at least as hard as computing the number of solutions for SAT; a clear indication of its high computational complexity.

As mentioned earlier in this section, the *Shap* score is a particular case of the Shapley value in (10). In this case, the players are the features F in $\mathcal{F}$, or, more precisely, the values $F(\mathbf{e})$ they take for a particular entity $\mathbf{e}$, for which we have a binary classification label, $L(\mathbf{e})$, we want to explain. The explanation comes in the form of a numerical score for $F(\mathbf{e})$, reflecting its relevance for the observed label. Since all the feature values contribute to the resulting label, we may conceive the features values as players in a coalition game.

The game function, for a given subset S of the features, is the *expected (value of the) label* over all possible entities whose values coincide with those of $\mathbf{e}$ for the features in S:

$$\mathcal{G}_{\mathbf{e}}(S) := \mathbb{E}(L(\mathbf{e}') \mid \mathbf{e}' \in \mathcal{E} \text{ and } \mathbf{e}'_S = \mathbf{e}_S), \tag{11}$$

where $\mathbf{e}'_S, \mathbf{e}_S$ denote the projections of $\mathbf{e}'$ and $\mathbf{e}$ on S, resulting in two subrecords of feature values. We can see that the game function depends on the entity at hand $\mathbf{e}$.

With the game function in (10), we obtain the *Shap* score for a feature value $F^\star(\mathbf{e})$ in $\mathbf{e}$:

$$Shap(\mathcal{F}, \mathcal{G}_{\mathbf{e}}, F^\star) := \sum_{S \subseteq \mathcal{F} \setminus \{F^\star\}} \frac{|S|!(|\mathcal{F}| - |S| - 1)!}{|\mathcal{F}|!} [\mathbb{E}(L(\mathbf{e}'|\mathbf{e}'_{S \cup \{F^\star\}} = \mathbf{e}_{S \cup \{F^\star\}})$$
$$- \mathbb{E}(L(\mathbf{e}')|\mathbf{e}'_S = \mathbf{e}_S)]. \tag{12}$$

Example 10 (Example 9 cont.). For the fixed entity $\mathbf{e}$ in (7) and feature $F^\star =$ Salary, one of the terms in (12) is obtained by considering $S = \{\text{Location}\} \subseteq \mathcal{F}$:

$$\frac{|1|!(7-1-1)!}{7!} \times (\mathcal{G}_{\mathbf{e}}(\{\text{Location}\} \cup \{\text{Salary}\}) - \mathcal{G}_{\mathbf{e}}(\{\text{Location}\}))$$
$$= \tfrac{1}{42} \times (\mathcal{G}_{\mathbf{e}}(\{\text{Location}, \text{Salary}\}) - \mathcal{G}_{\mathbf{e}}(\{\text{Location}\})),$$

with, e.g., $\mathcal{G}_{\mathbf{e}}(\{\text{Location}, \text{Salary}\}) = \mathbb{E}(L(\mathbf{e}') \mid \mathbf{e}' \in \mathcal{E}, \text{Location}(\mathbf{e}') = \text{harlem}$, and Salary$(\mathbf{e}') = 70\text{K})$, that is, the expected label over all entities that have the same values as $\mathbf{e}$ for features Salary and Location. Then, $\mathcal{G}_{\mathbf{e}}(\{\text{Location}, \text{Salary}\}) -$

---

[5] Another $\#P$-complete problem is $\#Hamiltonian$, about counting the number of Hamiltonian cycles in a graph. Its decision version, about the existence of a Hamiltonian cycle, is NP-complete.

$\mathcal{G}_e(\{\text{Location}\})$ is the expected difference in the label between the case where the values for Location and Salary are fixed as for **e**, and the case where only the value for Location is fixed as in **e**, measuring a local contribution of **e**'s value for Salary. After that, all these local differences are averaged over all subsets S of $\mathcal{F}$, and the permutations in which they participate.   □

We can see that, so as the *Resp* score, *Shap* is a *local* explanation score, for a particular entity at hand **e**. Since the introduction of *Shap* in this form, some variations have been proposed. So as for *Resp*, *Shap* depends, via the game function, on an underlying probability distribution on the entity population $\mathcal{E}$. The distribution may impact not only the *Shap* scores, but also their computation [8].

4.3   Computation of the *Shap* Score

Boolean classifiers, i.e. propositional formulas with binary input features and binary labels, are particularly relevant, *per se* and because they can represent other classifiers by means of appropriate encodings. For example, the circuit in Fig. 1 can be seen as a binary classifier that can be represented, on the basis of (1), by means of the single propositional formula $((a \wedge b) \vee c)$ that, depending on the binary values for a, b, c, also returns a binary value.

Boolean classifiers, as logical formulas, have been extensively investigated. In particular, much is known about the satisfiability problem of propositional formulas, *SAT*, and also about the *model counting* problem, i.e. that of counting the number of satisfying assignments, denoted *#SAT*. In the area of *knowledge compilation*, the complexity of *#SAT* and other problems in relation to the syntactic form of the Boolean formulas have been investigated [19,20,27]. Boolean classifiers turn out to be quite relevant to understand and investigate the complexity of *Shap* computation.

The computation of *Shap* is bound to be expensive, for similar reasons as for *Resp*. For the computation of both, all we need is the input/output relation of the classifier, to compute labels for different alternative entities (counterfactuals). However, in principle, far too many combinations have to go through the classifier. Actually, under the *product probability distribution* on $\mathcal{E}$ (which assigns independent probabilities to the feature values), even with an explicit, open classifier for binary entities, the computation of *Shap* can be intractable.

In fact, as shown in [8], for Boolean classifiers in the class *Monotone2CNF*, of negation-free propositional formulas in conjunctive normal form with at most two atoms per clause, *Shap* can be *#P*-hard. This is obtained via a polynomial reduction from *#Monotone2CNF*, the problem of counting the number of satisfying assignments for a formula in the class, which is known to be *#P*-complete [63].[6] For example, if the classifier is $(x_1 \vee x_2) \wedge (x_2 \vee x_3)$, which belongs to *#Monotone2CNF*, the entity $\mathbf{e}_1 = \langle 1, 0, 1 \rangle$ (with values for x_1, x_2, x_3, in this

---

[6] Interestingly, the decision version of the problem, i.e. of deciding if a formula in *Monotone2CNF* is satisfiable, is trivially tractable: the assignment that makes all atoms true satisfies the formula.

order) gets label 1, whereas the entity $\mathbf{e}_2 = \langle 1,0,0 \rangle$ gets label 0. The number of satisfying truth assignments, equivalently, the number of entities that get label 1, is 5, corresponding to $\langle 1,1,1 \rangle$, $\langle 1,0,1 \rangle$, $\langle 0,1,1 \rangle$, $\langle 0,1,0 \rangle$, and $\langle 1,1,0 \rangle$.

Given that $Shap$ can be $\#P$-hard, a natural question is whether for some classes of open-box classifiers one can compute $Shap$ in polynomial time in the size of the model and input. The idea is to try to take advantage of the internal stricture and components of the classifier -as opposed to only the input/output relation of the classifier- in order to compute $Shap$ efficiently. We recall from results mentioned earlier in this section that having an open-box model does not guarantee tractability of $Shap$. Natural classifiers that have been considered in relation to a possible tractable computation of $Shap$ are decision trees and random forests [44].

The problem of tractability of $Shap$ was investigated in detail in [2], and through other methods also in [64]. They briefly describe the former approach in the rest of this section. Tractable and intractable cases were identified, with algorithms for the tractable cases. (Approximations for the intractable cases were further investigated in [3]). In particular, the tractability for decision trees and random forests was established, which required first identifying the right abstraction that allows for a general proof, leaves aside contingent details, and is also broad enough to include interesting classes of classifiers.

In [2], it was proved that, for a Boolean classifier L (identified with its label, the output gate or variable), the uniform distribution on $\mathcal{E}$, and $\mathcal{F} = \{F_1, \ldots, F_n\}$:

$$\#SAT(L) = 2^{|\mathcal{F}|} \times \left(L(\mathbf{e}) - \sum_{i=1}^{n} Shap(\mathcal{F}, G_{\mathbf{e}}, F_i) \right). \tag{13}$$

This result makes, under the usual complexity-theoretic assumptions, impossible for $Shap$ to be tractable for any circuit L for which $\#SAT$ is intractable. (If we could compute $Shap$ fast, we could also compute $\#SAT$ fast, assuming we have an efficient classifier.) This excludes, as seen earlier in this section, classifiers that are in the class $Monotone2CNF$. Accordingly, only classifiers in a more amenable class became candidates, with the restriction that the class should be able to accommodate interesting classifiers. That is how the class of *deterministic and decomposable Boolean circuits* (dDBCs) became the target of investigation.

Each $\vee$-gate of a dDBC can have only one of the disjuncts true (determinism), and for each $\wedge$-gate, the conjuncts do not share variables (decomposition). Nodes are labeled with $\vee, \wedge$, or $\neg$ gates, and input gates with features (propositional variables) or binary constants. An example of such a classifier, borrowed from [2], is shown in Figure 4, which has four (input) features, and an a gate that returns the output label (the $\wedge$ at the top). For a counterexample, the BC $((a \wedge b) \vee c)$ for Fig. 1 is decomposable, but not deterministic.[7]

Model counting is known to be tractable for dDBCs. However, this does not imply (via (13) or any other obvious way) that $Shap$ is tractable. It is also the

---

[7] It could be transformed into a dDBC, but this would make the circuit grow. The transformation cost is always a concern in the area of knowledge compilation. For

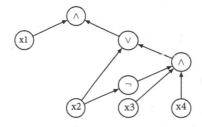

Fig. 4. A decomposable and deterministic Boolean classifier

case that relaxing any of the determinism or decomposibility conditions makes model counting #P-hard [3], preventing *Shap* from being tractable.

It turns out that *Shap* computation is tractable for dDBCs (under the uniform or the product distribution), from which we also get tractability of *Shap* for free for a vast collection of classifiers that can be efficiently compiled into (or represented as) dDBCs; among them we find: Decision Trees (even with non-binary features), Random Forests, Ordered Binary Decision Diagrams (OBDDs) [14], Deterministic-Decomposable Negation Normal-Forms (dDNNFs), Binary Neural Networks (e.g. via OBDDs) [60], etc.

For the gist, consider the binary decision tree (DT) on the LHS of Fig. 5. It can be inductively and efficiently compiled into a dDBC [3, appendix A]. The leaves of the DT become labeled with propositional constants, 0 or 1. Each node, n, is compiled into a circuit $c(n)$, and the final dDBC corresponds to the compilation, $c(r)$, of the root node r, in this case, $c(n7)$ for node $c7$. Figure 5 shows on the RHS, the compilation $c(n5)$ of node $n5$ of the DT. If the decision tree is not binary, it is first binarized, and then compiled [3, sect. 7].

Abductive explanations have for dDNNF-Boolean circuits have been investigated in [33].

5   Counterfactual Reasoning

As we saw in the preceding sections, counterfactuals are at the basis of the responsibility score. It is captured in (8) that some counterfactual interventions may not change the label of a feature value. However, for a feature value to have a non-zero responsibility, there must be at least one counterfactual intervention on that value that changes the label. In the case of *Shap*, all counterfactuals are implicit and taken into account in its computation.

Independently from their participation in the definition and computation of attribution scores, counterfactuals are relevant and informative *per se* [65]. Assuming they satisfy some minimality condition, they tell us what change of

---

some classes of BCs, a transformation into another class could take exponential time; sometimes exponential on a fixed parameter, etc. [1, 26].

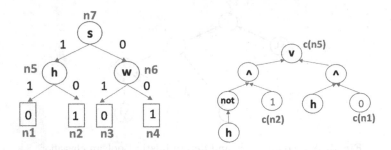

Fig. 5. A decision tree and part of its compilation into an dDBC

feature values may change the label, pointing to the relevance of the original values for the label at hand. Furthermore, in many situations we would like to know what we could do in order to change the label, e.g. granting a loan instead of rejecting it. If those changes can be usefully made in practice, we are talking about *actionable counterfactuals*, or counterfactuals that are *resources* [35,36,62,65]. In the ongoing example, changing the age, and then waiting for seven years to get the loan, may not be feasible. Nor changing the name of the applicant from john to elon. However, slightly increasing the salary might be doable. We may also want to compare two alternative counterfactuals, or ask about the existence of one with a particular property, e.g. a particular value for a feature, etc.

Working with and analyzing counterfactuals can be made easier and more understandable if we can *reason* about them under a single platform that includes (or interacts with) the classifier, and the score computation mechanisms, for a particular application. By reasoning we mean, among other tasks, the *logical specification* of counterfactuals, the *entailment* of counterfactuals, their analysis, and obtaining them and their properties. Counterfactual reasoning has been investigated from a logical point of view [22]. If we want to put counterfactual reasoning in practice, we need the right logics and their implementations.

We have recently argued in favor of using *answer-set programming* (ASP) for this task [10]. ASP is a form of logic programming that has several advantages for the kind of problems we are confronting [13], among them: (a) It has the right-expressive power and computational complexity since it can be applied to solve complex combinatorial problems. (b) Through its non-monotonic negation, and associated predicate minimality, it allows to represent the (common sense) inertia or persistence of objects and their properties unless they are explicitly changed (intervened in our case). (c) Logical disjunction allows to specify several alternative counterfactual candidates at once. (d) One can pose queries to obtain results from reasoning (c.f. below). (e) Its *possible worlds semantics* for the specification leads to multiple models corresponding to equally multiple counterfactuals, with different properties. (f) A *cautious* and a *brave query answering semantics* that allow asking what is true *in all* or *in some* models, respectively.

(g) There are implementations of ASP that can interact with external classifiers.

In essence, one can specify the underlying logical setting, e.g. some classes of classifiers, the possible interventions that lead to counterfactuals, properties such as actionability and other properties that may force counterfactuals "to make sense", minimality conditions on counterfactuals, and the computation of (some) attribution-scores that are based on counterfactuals. ASPs also allow for score aggregations, for more global and higher-level explanations.

We have used ASP, in particular the *DLV* system and its various extensions [39], to specify counterfactuals for causality in data management [9] and for explanations in ML [11,12], including the computation of the simple responsibility score.[8] However, if we want to compute scores that are defined in terms of of expected values, e.g. *Resp* or *Shap*, over probability distributions other than easily specifiable and computable ones, it may be necessary to resort to probabilistic extensions of ASP [5,31,37,38].

Counterfactual reasoning on the basis of ASPs is best seen as *query-driven*. One can pose all kinds of queries about counterfactuals, for which having a cautious and a brave semantics comes handy. Typical queries request counterfactual with a particular property, e.g. that changes, or does not change a particular feature value; or counterfactuals that exhibit (or avoid) a particular combination of feature values; or pairs of counterfactuals that differ in a pre-specified manner. Queries may ask if a particular feature value is never changed in a (preferred kind of) counterfactual; or about the existence of good counterfactuals that do not change more than a certain number of feature values; or whether there are "similar" counterfactuals with different labels (according to a specified notion of similarity), etc. C.f. [10–12] for concrete examples. One can also compare counterfactual entities with pre-specified *reference entities* for obtaining *contrastive explanations* [36,49].

Specifying actionable counterfactuals is only one way to convey relevant *application domain knowledge* into the definition of counterfactuals. A logical specification allows for much more than that, including the adoption of a *domain semantics*. We started this section recalling that, in principle, all counterfactuals are considered for the computation of attribution scores. However, it would be much more natural, useful, and possibly also more efficient, to consider and compute counterfactuals that conform to the domain semantics, which can be specified through logical rules and constraints, in such a way that only those are brought into a score computation [12]. For example, since the age of an individual (represented as an entity) never decreases, changing it by a lower value may not make much sense in most applications. Similarly, some combinations of values may not make sense, e.g. Age = 6 and MaritalStatus = married.

---

[8] It is worth mentioning that ASP and *DLV* have been used to specify and compute model-based diagnoses, both in their abductive and consistency-based formulations [25].

Considering that counterfactuals are at the very basis of causality, it is not surprising to see that they are playing a prominent role in Explainable AI. However, they have also found applications in Fairness in AI. C.f. [58] and references therein.

Acknowledgements. Part of this work was funded by ANID - Millennium Science Initiative Program - Code ICN17002. The author is a Professor Emeritus at Carleton University, Ottawa, Canada; and a Senior Universidad Adolfo Ibáñez (UAI) Fellow, Chile. Comments by Paloma Bertossi on an earlier version of the article are much appreciated.

References

1. Antoine Amarilli, A., Capelli, F., Monet, M., Senellart, P.: Connecting knowledge compilation classes width parameters. Theory Comput. Syst. **64**, 861–914 (2020)
2. Arenas, M., Barcelo, P., Bertossi, L., Monet, M.: The tractability of SHAP-scores over deterministic and decomposable boolean circuits. In: Proceedings of AAAI (2021)
3. Arenas, M., Barcelo, P., Bertossi, L., Monet, M.: The tractability of SHAP-scores over deterministic and decomposable boolean circuits. Extended version of AAAI 2021 paper. arXiv:2104.08015 (2021)
4. Arenas, M., Pablo Barcelo, P., Romero, M., Subercaseaux, B.: On computing probabilistic explanations for decision trees. In: Proceedings of NeurIPS (2022)
5. Baral, C., Gelfond, M., Rushton, N.: Probabilistic reasoning with answer sets. Theory Pract. Logic Program. **9**(1), 57–144 (2009)
6. Bertossi, L., Salimi, B.: From causes for database queries to repairs and model-based diagnosis and back. Theory Comput. Syst. **61**(1), 191–232 (2017)
7. Bertossi, L., Salimi, B.: Causes for query answers from databases: datalog abduction, view-updates, and integrity constraints. Int. J. Approximate Reasoning **90**, 226–252 (2017)
8. Bertossi, L., Li, J., Schleich, M., Suciu, D., Vagena, Z.: Causality-based explanation of classification outcomes. In: Proceedings of 4th International Workshop on "Data Management for End-to-End Machine Learning" (DEEM) at ACM SIG-MOD/PODS, pp. 6:1–6:10 (2020)
9. Bertossi, L.: Specifying and computing causes for query answers in databases via database repairs and repair programs. Knowl. Inf. Syst. **63**(1), 199–231 (2021)
10. Bertossi, L.: Score-based explanations in data management and machine learning: an answer-set programming approach to counterfactual analysis. In: Šimkus, M., Varzinczak, I. (eds.) Reasoning Web 2021. LNCS, vol. 13100, pp. 145–184. Springer, Cham (2022). https://doi.org/10.1007/978-3-030-95481-9_7
11. Bertossi, L., Reyes, G.: Answer-set programs for reasoning about counterfactual interventions and responsibility scores for classification. In: Katzouris, N., Artikis, A. (eds.) ILP 2021. LNCS, vol. 13191, pp. 41–56. Springer, Cham (2022). https://doi.org/10.1007/978-3-030-97454-1_4
12. Bertossi, L.: Declarative approaches to counterfactual explanations for classification. Theory Pract. Log. Program. (2020). https://doi.org/10.1017/S1471068421000582, arXiv:2011.07423
13. Brewka, G., Eiter, T., Truszczynski, M.: Answer set programming at a glance. Commun. ACM **54**(12), 92–103 (2011)

14. Bryant, R.E.: Graph-based algorithms for boolean function manipulation. IEEE Tran. Comput. **C-35**, 677–691 (1986)
15. Burkart, N., Huber, M.F.: A survey on the explainability of supervised machine learning. J. Artif. Intell. Res. **70**, 245–317 (2021)
16. Chatila, R., et al.: Trustworthy AI. In: Braunschweig, B., Ghallab, M. (eds.) Reflections on Artificial Intelligence for Humanity. LNCS (LNAI), vol. 12600, pp. 13–39. Springer, Cham (2021). https://doi.org/10.1007/978-3-030-69128-8_2
17. Chen, C., Lin, K., Rudin, C., Shaposhnik, Y., Wang, S., Wang, T.: An interpretable model with globally consistent explanations for credit risk. arXiv:1811.12615 (2018)
18. Chockler, H., Halpern, J.Y.: Responsibility and blame: a structural-model approach. J. Artif. Intell. Res. **22**, 93–115 (2004)
19. Darwiche, A., Marquis, P.: A knowledge compilation map. J. Artif. Intell. Res. **17**, 229–264 (2002)
20. Darwiche, A.: On the tractable counting of theory models and its application to truth maintenance and belief revision. J. Appl. Non-Classical Log. **11**(1–2), 11–34 (2011)
21. de Kleer, J., Mackworth, A., Reiter, R.: Characterizing diagnoses and systems. Artif. Intell. **56**(2–3), 197–222 (1992)
22. Eiter, T., Gottlob, G.: On the complexity of propositional knowledge base revision, updates, and counterfactuals. Artif. Intell. **57**(2–3), 227–270 (1992)
23. Eiter, T., Gottlob, G.: The complexity of logic-based abduction. J. ACM **42**(1), 3–42 (1995)
24. Eiter, T., Gottlob, G., Leone, N.: Abduction from logic programs: semantics and complexity. Theor. Comput. Sci. **189**(1–2), 129–177 (1997)
25. Eiter, T., Faber, W., Leone, N., Pfeifer, G.: The diagnosis frontend of the DLV system. AI Communun. **12**(1–2), 99–111 (1999). Extended version as Tech. Report DBAI-TR-98-20, TU Vienna, 1998
26. Ferrara, A., Pan, G., Vardi, M.Y.: Treewidth in verification: local vs. global. In: Sutcliffe, G., Voronkov, A. (eds.) LPAR 2005. LNCS (LNAI), vol. 3835, pp. 489–503. Springer, Heidelberg (2005). https://doi.org/10.1007/11591191_34
27. Gomes, C.P., Sabharwal, A., Selman, B.: Model counting. In: Handbook of Satisfiability, pp. 993–1014. IOS Press (2009)
28. Guidotti, R., Monreale, A., Ruggieri, S., Turini, F., Giannotti, F., Pedreschi, D.: A survey of methods for explaining black box models. ACM Comput. Surv. **51**(5), 1–93 (2018)
29. Halpern, J., Pearl, J.: Causes and explanations: a structural-model approach. Part I: causes. Br. J. Philos. Sci. **56**(4), 843–887 (2005)
30. Halpern, J.: Actual Causality. MIT Press, Cambridge (2016)
31. Hahn, S., Janhunen, T., Kaminski, R., Romero, J., Rühling, N., Schaub, T.: Plingo: a system for probabilistic reasoning in Clingo based on LP MLN. In: Proceedings of RuleML+RR, pp. 54–62 (2022)
32. Hunter, A., Konieczny, S.: On the measure of conflicts: shapley inconsistency values. Artif. Intell. **174**(14), 1007–1026 (2010)
33. Huang, X., Izza, Y., Ignatiev, A., Cooper, M.C., Asher, N., Marques-Silva, J.: Tractable explanations for d-DNNF classifiers. In: Proceedings of AAAI, pp. 5719–5728 (2022)
34. Ignatiev, A., Narodytska, N., Marques-Silva, J.: Abduction-based explanations for machine learning models. In: Proceedings of AAAI, pp. 1511–1519 (2019)
35. Karimi, A.-H., von Kügelgen, B.J., Schölkopf, B., Valera, I.: Algorithmic recourse under imperfect causal knowledge: a probabilistic approach. In: Proceedings of NeurIPS (2020)

36. Karimi, A.-H., Barthe, G., Schölkopf, B., Valera, I.: A survey of algorithmic recourse: contrastive explanations and consequential recommendations. ACM Comput. Surv. **55**(5), 95:1–95:29 (2023)
37. Lee, J., Yang, Z.: LPMLN, weak constraints, and P-log. In: Proceedings of AAAI, pp. 1170–1177 (2017)
38. Lee, J., Yang, Z.: Statistical relational extension of answer set programming. In: Bertossi, L., Xiao, G. (eds.) Reasoning Web. Causality, Explanations and Declarative Knowledge. LNCS, vol. 13759, pp. 132–160. Springer, Cham (2023)
39. Leone, N., et al.: The DLV system for knowledge representation and reasoning. ACM Trans. Comput. Log. **7**(3), 499–562 (2006)
40. Livshits, E., Bertossi, L., Kimelfeld, B., Sebag, M.: Query games in databases. ACM SIGMOD Rec. **50**(1), 78–85 (2021)
41. Livshits, E., Bertossi, L., Kimelfeld, B., Sebag, M.: The shapley value of tuples in query answering. Log. Methods Comput. Sci. **17**(3), 22:1–22:33 (2021)
42. Livshits, E., Kimelfeld, E.: The shapley value of inconsistency measures for functional dependencies. Log. Methods Comput. Sci. **18**(2), 20:1–20:33 (2022)
43. Lundberg, S., Lee, S.-I.: A unified approach to interpreting model predictions. In: Proceedings of NIPS, pp. 4765–4774 (2017)
44. Lundberg, S.M., Erion, G., Chen, H., DeGrave, A., Prutkin, J., Nair, B., Katz, R., Himmelfarb, J., Bansal, N., Lee, S.-I.: From local explanations to global understanding with explainable AI for trees. Nat. Mach. Intell. **2**(1), 56–67 (2020)
45. Marques-Silva, J.: Logic-based explainability in machine learning. In: Bertossi, L., Xiao, G. (eds.) Reasoning Web. Causality, Explanations and Declarative Knowledge. LNCS, vol. 13759, pp. 24–104. Springer, Cham (2023)
46. Marquis, P.: Extending abduction from propositional to first-order logic. In: Jorrand, P., Kelemen, J. (eds.) FAIR 1991. LNCS, vol. 535, pp. 141–155. Springer, Heidelberg (1991). https://doi.org/10.1007/3-540-54507-7_12
47. Meliou, A., Gatterbauer, W., Moore, K.F., Suciu, D.: The complexity of causality and responsibility for query answers and non-answers. In: Proceedings of VLDB, pp. 34–41 (2010)
48. Meliou, A., Gatterbauer, W., Halpern, J.Y., Koch, C., Moore, K.F., Suciu, D.: Causality in databases. IEEE Data Eng. Bull. **33**(3), 59–67 (2010)
49. Miller, T.: Contrastive explanation: a structural-model approach. Knowl. Eng. Rev. **36**(4), 1–24 (2021)
50. Minh, D., Xiang-Wang, H., Fen-Li, Y., Nguyen, T.N.: Explainable artificial intelligence: a comprehensive review. Artif. Intell. Rev. **55**, 3503–3568 (2022)
51. Molnar, C.: Interpretable machine learning: a guide for making black box models explainable, (2020). https://christophm.github.io/interpretable-ml-book
52. Papadimitriou, P.: Computational Complexity. Addison-Wesley (1994)
53. Pearl, J.: Causality: Models, Reasoning and Inference, 2nd edn. Cambridge University Press, Cambridge (2009)
54. Peirce, C.S.: Collected papers of Charles Sanders Peirce. In: Hartsthorne, C., Weiss, P. (eds.) vol. 2. Harvard University Press (1931)
55. Poole, D., Mackworth, A.K.: Artificial Intelligence. Section 5.7, 2nd edn. Cambridge University Press (2017)
56. Reiter, R.: A theory of diagnosis from first principles. Artif. Intell. **32**(1), 57–95 (1987)
57. Roth, A.E.: The Shapley Value: Essays in Honor of Lloyd S. Shapley. Cambridge University Press, Cambridge (1988)

58. Roy, S., Salimi, B.: Causal inference in data analysis with applications to fairness and explanations. In: Bertossi, L., Xiao, G. (eds.) Reasoning Web. Causality, Explanations and Declarative Knowledge. LNCS, vol. 13759, pp. 105–131. Springer, Cham (2023)
59. Shapley, L.S.: A value for n-person games. Contrib. Theory Games **2**(28), 307–317 (1953)
60. Shi, W., Shih, A., Darwiche, A., Choi, A.: On tractable representations of binary neural networks. In: Proceedings of KR, pp. 882–892 (2020)
61. Struss, P.: Model-based problem solving. In: Handbook of Knowledge Representation, chap. 4, pp. 395–465. Elsevier (2008)
62. Ustun, B., Spangher, A., Liu, Y.: Actionable recourse in linear classification. In: Proceedings of FAT, pp. 10–19 (2019)
63. Valiant, L.G.: The complexity of enumeration and reliability problems. SIAM J. Comput. **8**(3), 410–421 (1979)
64. Van den Broeck, G., Lykov, A., Schleich, M., Suciu, D.: On the tractability of shap explanations. In: Proceedings of AAAI, pp. 6505–6513 (2021)
65. Verma, S., et al.: Counterfactual explanations and algorithmic recourses for machine learning: a review. arXiv:2010.10596 (2022)

Logic-Based Explainability in Machine Learning

Joao Marques-Silva(✉) 📵

IRIT, CNRS, Toulouse, France
`joao.marques-silva@irit.fr`

Abstract. The last decade witnessed an ever-increasing stream of successes in Machine Learning (ML). These successes offer clear evidence that ML is bound to become pervasive in a wide range of practical uses, including many that directly affect humans. Unfortunately, the operation of the most successful ML models is incomprehensible for human decision makers. As a result, the use of ML models, especially in high-risk and safety-critical settings is not without concern. In recent years, there have been efforts on devising approaches for explaining ML models. Most of these efforts have focused on so-called model-agnostic approaches. However, all model-agnostic and related approaches offer no guarantees of rigor, hence being referred to as non-formal. For example, such non-formal explanations can be consistent with different predictions, which renders them useless in practice. This paper overviews the ongoing research efforts on computing rigorous model-based explanations of ML models; these being referred to as formal explanations. These efforts encompass a variety of topics, that include the actual definitions of explanations, the characterization of the complexity of computing explanations, the currently best logical encodings for reasoning about different ML models, and also how to make explanations interpretable for human decision makers, among others.

Keywords: Explainable AI · Formal explanations · Automated reasoning

1 Introduction

Recent years witnessed remarkable advancements in artificial intelligence (AI), concretely in machine learning (ML) [49,143,217,222]. These advancements have triggered an ever-increasing range of practical applications [142]. Some of these applications often impact humans, with credit worthiness representing one such application, among many others [116]. Unfortunately, the most promising ML models are inscrutable in their operation, with the term *black-box* being often ascribed to such ML models. Black-box ML models cause distrust, especially when their operation is difficult to understand or it is even incorrect, not to mention situations where the operation of ML models is the likely cause for events with disastrous consequences [82, 104, 183], but also the case of unfairness and bias [292, 334]. (The issues caused by AI systems are illustrated by an ever-increasing list of incidents [6, 252].) Moreover, recent work argues [53] that Perrow's framework of normal accidents [284] (which has been used to explain the occurrence of catastrophic accidents in the past) also applies to AI systems, thereby conjecturing that such (catastrophic) accident(s) in AI systems should be expected in the near future. Motivated by this state of affairs, but also by recent regulations and recommendations [115, 156, 277], and by existing proposals of regulation of AI/ML systems [7, 116, 338], there is a pressing need for building trust into the operation of ML models. The demand for clarifying the operation of black-box decision making has motivated the rapid growth of research in the general theme of *explainable AI* (XAI). XAI can be viewed as the process of aiding human decision makers to understand the decisions made by AI/ML systems, with the purpose of delivering trustworthy AI. The importance of both trustworthy AI and XAI is illustrated by recent guidelines, recommendations and regulations put forward by the European Union (EU), the United States government, the Australian government, the OECD and UNESCO [7, 30, 31, 93, 115–117, 156, 157, 273, 277, 338], among others. Motivated by the above, there have been calls for the use of formal methods in the verification of systems of AI and ML [315], with explainability representing a key component [242]. There have also been efforts towards developing an understanding of past incidents in AI systems [251–253, 285, 360, 361].

Well-known explainability approaches include so-called model-agnostic methods [235, 301, 302] and, for neural networks, approaches based on variants of saliency maps [263, 309, 322]. Unfortunately, the most popular XAI approaches proposed in recent years are marred by lack of rigor, and provide explanations that are often logically unsound [170, 180, 272]. (One illustrative example is that of an explanation consistent both with a declined bank loan application and with an approved bank loan application [242].) The drawbacks of these (non-formal) XAI approaches raise important concerns in settings that impact humans. Example settings include those referred to as *high-risk* and *safety-critical*[1]. The use of unsound explainability methods in either high-risk or safety-critical could evidently have catastrophic consequences. (And there are unfortunately too many examples of bugs having massive economic cost, or that resulted in the loss of lives [3, 39, 133, 223, 254, 311].)

A more recent alternative XAI approach offers formal guarantees of rigor, it is logic-based, and it is in most cases based on efficient automated reasoning tools. This document offers an overview of the advancements made in the general field of *formal explainability* in AI (FXAI).

---

[1] The definition of *high-risk* in this proposal is aligned with recent EU documentation [116]. Concrete examples include the management and operation of critical infrastructure, credit worthiness, law enforcement, among many others [116]. Some authors refer to *high-stakes* when addressing related topics [304]. By safety-critical, we take the meaning that is common in formal methods [211], namely settings where errors are unacceptable, e.g. where human lives are at risk. There is growing interest in deploying ML-enabled systems in safety-critical applications (e.g. [91]).

A Brief History of FXAI. The recent work on formal explainability in machine learning finds its roots in the independent efforts of two research teams [178, 320][2]. The initial goals of this earlier work seemed clear at the outset: to propose a formal alternative to the mostly informal approaches to explainability that were being investigated at the time. Nevertheless, the experimental results in these initial works also raised concerns about the practical applicability of formal explanations. However, it soon became clear that there was much more promise to formal explainability than what the original works anticipated. Indeed, we claim that it is now apparent that formal explainability represents an emerging field of research, and one of crucial importance. A stream of results in recent years amply support this claim [11–13, 19, 21, 22, 24–29, 38, 40, 60–62, 65, 66, 84, 85, 96–99, 101, 122, 145, 163–168, 170–172, 174, 177–180, 185, 186, 186, 187, 189–192, 219, 232, 233, 237, 239, 240, 242, 272, 297, 298, 319–321, 354, 355, 362, 367, 368]. Among these, several results are significant. It has been shown that computing one explanation is tractable for a number of classifiers [84, 99, 165, 166, 186, 187, 239, 240]. Different duality results have been obtained [177, 179], which relate different kinds of explanations. Practically efficient logic encodings have been devised for computing explanations for a number of families of classifiers [28, 170, 172, 174, 180, 191]. Compilation approaches for explainability have been studied in a number of recent works [96, 97, 99, 101, 320, 321]. A number of computational complexity results, that cover the computation of one explanation but also other queries, have been proved [25, 166, 174, 191, 240]. Different explainability queries have been studied [25, 29, 166]. The size of formal explanations have been addressed by considering probabilistic explanations [22, 189, 190, 354, 355]. The effect of input constraints on explainability, that restrict the points in feature space to consider, has been studied in recent works [145, 367]. The use of surrogate models for computing formal explanations of complex models has been proposed [66]. Formal explanations have been applied in different application domains [237]. Furthermore, initial links between explainability and fairness, robustness and model learning have been uncovered [171, 179]. Given the above, the purpose of this document is to offer an account of what we feel have been the most important results in this novel field of research, up until the time of writing.

Main Goals. The paper aims to offer a high-level comprehensive overview of the emerging field of formal explainability. The paper starts by covering existing formal definitions of explanations. One class of explanations answers a **Why?** question; these are referred to as abductive explanations. Another class of explanations answers a **Why not?** question; these are referred to as contrastive explanations. Then, the paper builds on the rigorous definitions of explanations to

---

[2] It should be noted that efforts towards explaining the operation of systems of artificial intelligence (AI) can be traced back to at least the late 70s [331], with follow up work since then [14–16, 111, 118, 119, 128, 175, 283, 308, 313, 317, 332]. Nevertheless, the interest in formalizing explanations is documented in much earlier work [153]. A distinctive aspect of recent work is not only the focus on ML models, namely classifiers, but also the research on novel topics, e.g. contrastive and probabilistic explanations, which we will define later.

study how formal explanations can be computed in practice, highlighting some of the algorithms used. The paper uses running examples to illustrate how such explanations are computed in practice. Moreover, the paper also overviews families of classifiers for which computing one explanation is tractable. These include decision trees and naive bayes classifiers, among several others. Furthermore, the paper summarizes recent progress along a number of lines of research, which aim at making formal explainability a practical option of choice. Concrete examples of lines of research include: i) answering a growing number of explainability queries, e.g. enumeration of explanations; ii) computing probabilistic explanations, which trade-off explanation size for rigor; iii) taking into account input constraints and distributions, since not all inputs may be possible for an ML model; and also iv) approximating complex ML models with simpler models, which are easier to explain. The paper also overviews a number of additional topics of research in the general area of formal explainability. Since the paper aims at offering a broad overview of the field, some more technical aspects are omitted, and left to the existing references.

Additional Goals. This document also takes the opportunity to deconstruct a number of misconceptions that pervade Machine Learning research. One unfortunately common misconception is that logic is inadequate for reasoning about ML models. This paper, but also a growing list of references (see above), offer ample evidence that this is certainly not the case. For example, formal explanations for random forests [191] were shown to be more efficient to compute than those obtained with heuristic methods. Another common misconception is that computationally hard (e.g. NP-hard, D^P-hard, etc.) problems are *intractable*, and so large-scale problems cannot be solved in practice. By now, there are more than two decades of comprehensive experimental evidence that attests to the contrary [55,131]. In many practical settings, automated reasoners are often (and sometimes most often) remarkably efficient at solving computationally hard problems of very large scale [131,342,343]. Boolean satisfiability (SAT) solvers (but also mixed integer linear programming (MILP) solvers) are prime examples of the progress that has been observed in improving, sometimes dramatically, the practical efficiency of automated reasoners [55,57,58,81,212][3]. The bottom line is that some of these computational problems may be intractable in theory, but in practice that is hardly ever the case [131,343]. Another quite common misconception is the existence of so-called interpretable models, e.g. decision trees, lists and sets, but even linear classification models. For example, some of the best known model agnostic (and so non-formal) explainability approaches [235,301]

---

[3] It should be clarified that SAT, MILP and SMT automated reasoners and their variants solve their target problems *exactly*, provided such reasoners are given enough time [55,57,58,81,212]. Nevertheless, these automated reasoners should not be confused with the burgeoning field of exact exponential and parameterized algorithms [90,125]. The former, i.e. automated reasoners, are without exception extensively validated and evaluated in practical settings, being applied to large-scale problem-solving [55,81]; regarding the latter, decades of research have resulted in significant theoretical advances, but these have not been matched by practical impact.

learn a simple *interpretable* model as the explanation for a more complex model. Some other authors propose the use of interpretable models as the explanation itself [262,304,305], specially in high-risk and safety-critical settings. There is by now comprehensive evidence [166,174,186,187,239] that even these so-called interpretable models can provide explanations that are *arbitrarily* redundant. Therefore, even so-called interpretable models ought to be explained with the methods described in this paper[4].

Organization. The paper is organized in two main parts. The first part introduces a number of well-established topics. Section 2 introduces the definitions and notation used throughout the paper. Section 3 introduces the formal definitions of explanations that have been studied in recent years. Based on the proposed definitions of explanations, Sect. 4 studies algorithms for the computation of explanations. In addition, as shown in Sect. 5, for some families of classifiers, there are polynomial-time algorithms for computing one explanation. The rest of the document covers the second part of the paper, and targets topics related with ongoing research. Thus, this second part is presented with less detail. Section 6 goes beyond computing one explanation, and delves into explainability queries, that include enumeration of explanations and deciding feature inclusion in explanations. Section 7 addresses the size of explanations, and proposes *probabilistic explanations* as a mechanism to reduce explanation size. Section 8 overviews approaches for accounting for input constraints and distributions. Section 9 overviews work on approximating complex ML models with surrogate (or distilled) simpler models, which are easier to explain. Section 10 summarizes a number of additional topics of research. Finally, Sect. 11 identifies some directions of research, and concludes the paper.

2   Preliminaries

Computational Complexity. The paper addresses a number of well-known classes of decision and function (or search) problems. For decision problems, these include P, NP, D^P, Σ_2^p, among others. For function problems, we will also consider standard classes, including FP, FNP, among others. (The interested reader is referred to a standard reference on computational complexity [23].)

2.1   Logic Foundations

Throughout this section, we adopt notation and definitions from standard references [45,55,67,81,87,281].

---

[4] More importantly, the growing evidence on the need to explain "interpretable" models [166,174,187,187,239] justifies wondering, in hindsight, about the practical relevancy of learning (quasi-)optimal interpretable models [4,5,10,17,18,32,33,43, 51,52,78,105,106,136–138,161,162,173,181,196,220,228,238,255,271,275,276,280, 306,312,314,318,346–349,352,353,356,358,365,366].

2.1.1   Propositional Logic and Boolean Satisfiability

This section studies the decision problem for propositional logic, also referred to as the Boolean Satisfiability (SAT) problem [55]. (The presentation follows standard references, e.g. [55,87,210].) SAT is well-known to be an NP-complete [83] decision problem, with algorithm implementations that can be traced to the early 1960s [102,103].

Syntax – Well-Formed Propositional Formulas. We consider a set of propositional atoms $X = \{x_1, \ldots, x_n\}$ (these are also most often referred to as boolean variables), and associate an index with each atom, i.e. i with x_i, $i = 1, \ldots, n$, represented as the set $\mathfrak{X}$. A (well-formed) propositional formula, or simply a formula, is defined inductively as follows:

1. An atom x_i is a formula.
2. If φ is a formula, then $\neg\varphi$ is a formula. (The logic operator $\neg$ is referred to as negation.)
3. If φ_1 and φ_2 are formulas, then $\varphi_1 \vee \varphi_2$ is a formula. (The logic operator $\vee$ is referred to as disjunction.)
4. If φ is a formula, then (φ) is a formula.

A literal is an atom x_i or its negation $\neg x_i$. We can use additional logic operators, defined in terms of the basic operators above. Well-known examples include:

1. $\varphi_1 \wedge \varphi_2$ represents the formula $\neg(\neg\varphi_1 \vee \neg\varphi_2)$. (The logic operator $\wedge$ is referred to as conjunction.)
2. $\varphi_1 \rightarrow \varphi_2$ represents the formula $\neg\varphi_1 \vee \varphi_2$. (The logic operator $\rightarrow$ is referred to as implication.)
3. $\varphi_1 \leftrightarrow \varphi_2$ represents the formula $(\varphi_1 \rightarrow \varphi_2) \wedge (\varphi_2 \rightarrow \varphi_1)$. (The logic operator $\leftrightarrow$ is referred to as equivalence. Also, we use $\rightarrow$ in the definition for simplicity, and could just use the initial logic operators.)

Parentheses are used to enforce precedence between operators. Otherwise, the precedence between operators is: $\neg, \wedge, \vee, \rightarrow, \leftrightarrow$. A clause is a disjunction of literals. A term is a conjunction of literals. For both clauses and terms, we will disallow having either clauses or terms defined using an atom and its negation, or repetition of literals. This is formalized as follows. Given $A, B \subseteq \mathfrak{X}$, with $A \cap B = \emptyset$, a clause is defined by,

$$\omega_{A,B} \triangleq (\vee_{i \in A} x_i \vee \vee_{i \in B} \neg x_i)$$

and a term is defined by,

$$\tau_{A,B} \triangleq (\wedge_{i \in A} x_i \wedge \wedge_{i \in B} \neg x_i)$$

when clear from the context, we will drop the subscript from $\omega_{A,B}$ and $\tau_{A,B}$. $\mathbb{W}$ denotes the set of all possible clauses defined on the set of atoms X. Similarly, $\mathbb{T}$ denotes the set of all possible terms defined on the set of atoms X. A conjunctive normal form (CNF) formula is a conjunction of clauses. A disjunctive normal form (DNF) formula is a disjunction of terms.

To simplify some of the subsequent definitions in this section, clauses and terms will also be viewed as sets of literals, each CNF formula as a set of clauses, and each DNF formula as a set of terms.

Semantics – Assignments and Valuations. An assignment is any point in $\mathbf{u} \in \{0,1\}^n$. (Throughout, we associate 0 with both **false** and $\bot$, and 1 with both **true** and $\top$.) The actual value ascribed to a propositional formula is derived from the assignment of propositional values to the formula's atoms. Each such complete assignment is referred to as an *interpretation*. Given a formula φ, and an assignment $\mathbf{u} \in \{0,1\}^n$, the valuation of φ given $\mathbf{u}$ is represented by $\varphi^{\mathbf{u}}$, and it is defined inductively as follows:

1. $\varphi^{\mathbf{u}} = 1$ if $\varphi = x_i$ and $u_i = 1$ or $\varphi = \neg x_i$ and $u_i = 0$.
2. $\varphi^{\mathbf{u}} = 0$ if $\varphi = x_i$ and $u_i = 0$ or $\varphi = \neg x_i$ and $u_i = 1$.
3. $\varphi^{\mathbf{u}} = \neg(\psi^{\mathbf{u}})$, if $\varphi = \neg \psi$.
4. $\varphi^{\mathbf{u}} = \psi_1^{\mathbf{u}} \vee \psi_2^{\mathbf{u}}$, if $\varphi = \psi_1 \vee \psi_2$.
5. $\varphi^{\mathbf{u}} = (\psi^{\mathbf{u}})$, if $\varphi = (\psi)$.

Clearly, for any $\mathbf{u} \in \{0,1\}^n$, $\varphi^{\mathbf{u}} \in \{0,1\}$. Also, it is plain to extend the semantics to the other logic operators: $\wedge, \rightarrow, \leftrightarrow$. A propositional formula φ can also be viewed as representing a boolean function that maps $\{0,1\}^n$ to $\{0,1\}$. The same symbol will be used to refer to both formula and function, i.e. $\varphi : \{0,1\}^n \rightarrow \{0,1\}$. Given some assignment $\mathbf{u} \in \{0,1\}^n$, it is the case that $\varphi(\mathbf{u}) = \varphi^{\mathbf{u}}$.

Given a formula φ, $\mathbf{u} \in \{0,1\}$ is a *model* of φ if it makes φ **true**, i.e. $\varphi^{\mathbf{u}} = 1$. A formula φ is *satisfiable* or *consistent* (represented by $\varphi \nvDash \bot$) if it admits a model; otherwise, it is *unsatisfiable* or *inconsistent* (represented by $\varphi \vDash \bot$).

Practical reasoners for the SAT problem represent a success story of Computer Science [131,342]. Modern conflict-driven clause learning (CDCL) SAT reasoners routinely decide formulas with millions of variables and tens of millions of clauses [55, Chapter 4]. (This success hinges on the paradigm of learning clauses from search conflicts [247,248].) Furthermore, SAT reasoners are the underlying engine used to achieve significant performance gains in different areas of automated reasoning, including different boolean optimization problems [55, Chapters 23, 24, 28], answer-set programming [134], constraint programming [278], quantified boolean formulas [55, Chapters 30, 31], but also for reasoners for fragments of first order logic [55, Chapter 33] and theorem proving [132,213,214,351]. SAT reasoners are often publicly available and their performance improvements are regularly assessed[5]. There exist publicly available toolkits that streamline prototyping with SAT reasoners. At the time of writing, the reference example is PySAT [176].

It should be noted that the high performance reasoners mentioned above most often require logic formulas represented in CNF (or in clausal form). There are well-known, efficient, procedures for converting arbitrary (non-clausal) logic formulas into clausal form [286,336]. Given a propositional formula φ, defined on a set of propositional atoms X, $\psi = [\![\varphi]\!]$ is the *clausification* of φ, such that ψ

---

[5] http://www.satcompetition.org/.

is defined on a set of atoms $X \cup A$, where A denotes additional auxiliary atoms. One important result is that φ and ψ are *equisatisfiable*, i.e. φ is satisfiable iff ψ is satisfiable. Encodings are detailed further in Sect. 2.1.3.

Entailment and Equivalence. Given two formulas φ and τ, we say that τ *entails* φ, denoted by $\tau \vDash \varphi$, if,

$$\forall(\mathbf{u} \in \{0,1\}^n).\ [\tau^{\mathbf{u}} \rightarrow \varphi^{\mathbf{u}}]$$

which serves to indicate that any model of τ is also a model of φ. We say that $\varphi_1 \equiv \varphi_2$ iff $\varphi_1 \vDash \varphi_2$ and $\varphi_2 \vDash \varphi_1$.

Let $\tau_{A,B}$ and $\tau_{C,D}$ be terms, with both A, B and C, D representing disjoint pairs of subsets of $\mathfrak{X}$. Then, we have that,

Proposition 1. $\tau_{A,B} \equiv \tau_{C,D}$ *iff* $A = C$ *and* $B = D$.

Proposition 2. *If* $\tau_{A,B} \vDash \tau_{C,D}$ *and* $\tau_{A,B} \not\equiv \tau_{C,D}$, *then* $C \subseteq A$, $D \subseteq B$, *and* $C \subsetneq A$ *or* $D \subsetneq B$.

Clearly, similar results can be stated for clauses.

Example 1. The terms $x_1 \wedge \neg x_2 \wedge x_3$ and $x_1 \wedge \neg x_2$ are represented, respectively, by $\tau_{A,B}$ and $\tau_{C,D}$, with $A = \{1,3\}$, $B = \{2\}$, $C = \{1\}$ and $D = \{2\}$. It is the case that $x_1 \wedge \neg x_2 \wedge x_3 \vDash x_1 \wedge \neg x_2$. As can be concluded, $C \subsetneq A$ and $D \subseteq B$. ◁

Prime Implicants and Implicates. Let φ represent a propositional formula, and let $\tau_{A,B}$ represent a term. $\tau_{A,B}$ is a *prime implicant* of φ if,

1. $\tau_{A,B} \vDash \varphi$.
2. For any other term $\tau_{C,D}$, such that $\tau_{A,B} \vDash \tau_{C,D}$ and $\tau_{A,B} \not\equiv \tau_{C,D}$, then $\tau_{C,D} \not\vDash \varphi$.

Whenever the first condition holds (i.e. $\tau_{A,B} \vDash \varphi$), then we say that $\tau_{A,B}$ is an *implicant* of φ.

Example 2. Consider the terms $\tau_{A,B} = x_1 \wedge x_2$ and $\tau_{C,D} = x_1$. (Note that $A = \{1,2\}, B = \emptyset, C = \{1\}, D = \emptyset$.) Let $\varphi = (x_1 \wedge x_2 \wedge x_3) \vee (x_1 \wedge x_2 \wedge \neg x_3)$. Clearly, for any assignment $\mathbf{u} \in \{0,1\}^3$ to x_1, x_2, x_3, if $x_1 = x_2 = 1$, then $\tau_{A,B} = 1$ and also $\varphi = 1$, independently of the value of x_3. Hence, $\tau_{A,B} \vDash \varphi$. However, $\tau_{C,D} \not\vDash \varphi$, in that there are assignments $\mathbf{u}$ to x_1, x_2, x_3 such that $\tau_{C,D}^{\mathbf{u}} = 1$ but $\varphi^{\mathbf{u}} = 0$. For example, whenever $x_2 = 0$, then φ takes value 0, and that is not necessarily the case with $\tau_{C,D}$. Proving that $\tau_{A,B}$ is a prime implicant of φ would apparently require proving that any term with literals that are a proper subset of $\tau_{A,B}$ are not implicants of φ. As discussed below, in practice one can devise more efficient algorithms. ◁

For completeness, we also mention prime implicates. Let φ be a propositional formula, and let $\omega_{A,B}$ be a clause. $\omega_{A,B}$ is a *prime implicate* of φ if,

1. $\varphi \vDash \omega_{A,B}$.
2. For any other clause $\omega_{C,D}$, such that $\omega_{C,D} \vDash \omega_{A,B}$ and $\omega_{A,B} \neq \omega_{C,D}$, then $\varphi \nvDash \tau_{C,D}$.

Whenever the first condition holds (i.e. $\varphi \vDash \omega_{A,B}$), then we say that $\omega_{A,B}$ is an *implicate* of φ.

A well-known result (which can be traced to [307]) is that, for a propositional formula φ, prime implicants are minimal hitting sets (MHSes) of the prime implicates and vice-versa[6]. This result is at the core of recent algorithms for enumerating prime implicants and implicates of a propositional formula φ [288].

Given a propositional formula φ and a term τ, with $\tau \vDash \varphi$, a prime implicant π, with $\tau \vDash \pi$, can be computed with at most a linear number of calls to an NP oracle [68,288,337]. (The same observations apply to the case of prime implicates.) In Sect. 4, we will revisit some of these results when computing formal explanations.

Reasoning About Inconsistency. In many situations, there is the need to reason about inconsistent formulas [246]. For example, we may be interested in explaining the reasons of inconsistency, but we may also be interested in identifying which clauses to ignore (or equivalently to remove from the formula) so as to restore consistency[7]. The general setting is to consider a set of clauses $\mathcal{B}$. $\mathcal{B}$ represents some background knowledge base, and so it is assumed to be consistent. We say that $\mathcal{B}$ contains the *hard* clauses (or in general the hard constraints). A clause is hard when it cannot be removed (from the set of clauses) to recover consistency. Furthermore, we also consider a set clauses $\mathcal{S}$, such that $\varphi_{\mathcal{B},\mathcal{S}} = \mathcal{B} \cup \mathcal{S} \vDash \bot$, and $\varphi_{\mathcal{B},\mathcal{S}}$ is the formula (or set of constraints) we want to reason about. The clauses in $\mathcal{S}$ represent the *soft* clauses (or constraints), and these can be removed to restore consistency. (In the rest of this document, we will just refer to φ, being implicit that φ is characterized by the background knowledge $\mathcal{B}$ and by the soft clauses $\mathcal{S}$.)

Definition 1 (MUS). *Let* $\varphi = \mathcal{B} \cup \mathcal{S}$ *be an inconsistent set of clauses (or constraints), i.e.* $\varphi \vDash \bot$. $\mathcal{M} \subseteq \mathcal{S}$ *is a* Minimal Unsatisfiable Subset *(MUS) if* $\mathcal{B} \cup \mathcal{M} \vDash \bot$ *and* $\forall_{\mathcal{M'} \subsetneq \mathcal{M}}, \mathcal{B} \cup \mathcal{M'} \nvDash \bot$.

Informally, an MUS provides some irreducible information that suffices to be added to the background knowledge $\mathcal{B}$ to attain an inconsistent formula; thus, an MUS represents an explanation for the causes of inconsistency. Alternatively, one might be interested in correcting the formula, removing some clauses to achieve consistency.

Definition 2 (MCS). *Let* $\varphi = \mathcal{B} \cup \mathcal{S}$ *be an inconsistent set of clauses (*$\varphi \vDash \bot$*).* $\mathcal{C} \subseteq \mathcal{S}$ *is a* Minimal Correction Subset *(MCS) if* $\mathcal{B} \cup \mathcal{S} \setminus \mathcal{C} \nvDash \bot$ *and* $\forall_{\mathcal{C'} \subsetneq \mathcal{C}}, \mathcal{B} \cup \mathcal{S} \setminus \mathcal{C'} \vDash \bot$.

---

[6] Recall that a set $\mathcal{H}$ is a *hitting set* of a set of sets $\mathcal{S} = \{S_1, \ldots, S_k\}$ if $\mathcal{H} \cap S_i \neq \emptyset$ for $i = 1, \ldots, k$. $\mathcal{H}$ is a minimal hitting set of $\mathcal{S}$, if $\mathcal{H}$ is a hitting set of $\mathcal{S}$, and there is no proper subset of $\mathcal{H}$ that is also a hitting set of $\mathcal{S}$.

[7] This paragraph aims at brevity. However, there are recent up-to-date treatments of these topics [246].

With each MCS $\mathcal{C}$, one associates a Maximal Satisfiable Subset (MSS), given by $\mathcal{S} \setminus \mathcal{C}$.

Example 3. Let $c_1 = (x_1)$, $c_2 = (x_2)$, $c_3 = (x_3)$, $c_4 = (\neg x_1 \vee \neg x_2)$, and $c_5 = (\neg x_1 \vee \neg x_3)$. Moreover, let $\varphi = \mathcal{B} \cup \mathcal{S}$, with $\mathcal{B} = \{c_4, c_5\}$ and $\mathcal{S} = \{c_1, c_2, c_3\}$. Hence, it is simple to conclude that an example of an MUS is $\{c_1, c_2\}$, an example of an MCS is $\{c_1\}$, and an example of an MSS is $\{c_2, c_3\}$.   ◁

Let MUS, be a predicate, MUS $: 2^\mathcal{S} \to \{0, 1\}$, such that $\text{MUS}(\mathcal{M}) = 1$ iff $\mathcal{M} \subseteq \mathcal{S}$ is an MUS of $\varphi = \mathcal{B} \cup \mathcal{S}$. Moreover, let MCS, be a predicate, MCS $: 2^\mathcal{S} \to \{0, 1\}$, such that $\text{MCS}(\mathcal{C}) = 1$ iff $\mathcal{C} \subseteq \mathcal{S}$ is an MCS of $\varphi = \mathcal{B} \cup \mathcal{S}$. Furthermore, we define,

$$\mathbb{MU}(\varphi) = \{\mathcal{M} \subseteq \mathcal{S} \mid \text{MUS}(\mathcal{M})\} \tag{1}$$

$$\mathbb{MC}(\varphi) = \{\mathcal{C} \subseteq \mathcal{S} \mid \text{MCS}(\mathcal{M})\} \tag{2}$$

Moreover, there exists a well-known (subset-)minimal hitting set relationship between MUSes and MCSes:

Proposition 3. *Given $\varphi = \mathcal{B} \cup \mathcal{S}$, and $\mathcal{M} \subseteq \mathcal{S}$, $\mathcal{C} \subseteq \mathcal{S}$, then*

1. $\mathcal{M}$ is an MUS iff it is a minimal hitting set of the MCSes in $\mathbb{MC}$;
2. $\mathcal{C}$ is an MCS iff it is a minimal hitting set of the MUSes in $\mathbb{MU}$.

The MHS relationship between MUSes and MCSes was first demonstrated in the context of model-based diagnosis [300] and later investigated for propositional formulas in clausal form [56]. As immediate from the original work [300], the MHS relationship applies in general to systems of constraints, where each is represented as a first-order logic statement.

Example 4. For the formula from Example 3, it is immediate to conclude that,

$$\mathbb{MU}(\varphi) = \{\{c_1, c_2\}, \{c_1, c_3\}\}$$
$$\mathbb{MC}(\varphi) = \{\{c_1\}, \{c_2, c_3\}\}$$

Moreover, one can observe that each MUS is an MHS of the MCSes, and that each MCS is an MHS of the MUSes.   ◁

Complexity-wise, deciding whether a set of clauses is an MUS is known to be D^P-complete [281, 282]. It is also well-known that an MUS can be computed with at most a number of calls to an NP-oracle that grows linearly with the number of clauses in the worst-case [79]. MUSes and MCSes are tightly related with optimization problems [246]. For example, if each soft constraint is assigned a unit cost, then solving the maximum satisfiability problem (MaxSAT) corresponds to finding a maximum cost MSS [55, 264]. Under the assumption of a unit cost assigned to each clause, then an MCS can be computed with a logarithmic number of calls to an NP-oracle, e.g. by solving (unweighted) MaxSAT. (If non-unit costs are assumed, then a worst-case linear number of calls to an NP-oracle is required.) However, in practice there are more efficient algorithms that may require in the worst-case a number of calls to an NP-oracle larger than logarithmic [241,256,257]. There have been very significant improvements in the practical performance of MaxSAT solvers in recent years [55, Chapters 23, 24, 28]. A number of solvers for MaxSAT and related problems are publicly available[8].

Quantification Problems. It is often of interest to quantify some of the variables in a propositional formula (by default it is assumed that all variables are existentially quantified). This is achieved by using two more logic operators, namely $\forall$ for universal quantification and $\exists$ for existential quantification. QBF (Quantified Boolean Formulas) is the problem of deciding whether a quantified propositional formula is true or false. The problem of deciding QBF is PSPACE-complete [23]. In this paper, we will briefly study quantified problems with two levels of quantifier alternation, concretely $\exists\forall$, which is a well-known Σ_2^P-complete decision problem. There have been very significant improvements in the practical performance of QBF solvers in recent years [55, Chapters 30, 31]. A number of solvers for QBF are publicly available[9].

Logic-Based Abduction. Abductive reasoning can be traced to the work of C. Peirce [152], with its first uses in artificial intelligence in the early 1970s [266,287]. Logic-based abduction can be viewed as the problem of finding a (minimimum or minimal) subset of hypotheses, which is consistent with some background theory, and such that those hypotheses are sufficient for some manifestation. A propositional abduction problem (PAP) is represented by a 5-tuple $P = (X, \mathcal{H}, \mathcal{M}, \mathcal{T}, \varsigma)$ [175,308]. X is a finite set of atoms. $\mathcal{H}$, $\mathcal{M}$ and $\mathcal{T}$ denote propositional formulas representing, respectively, the set of hypotheses, the set of manifestations, and the background theory. ($\mathcal{H}$ is further constrained to be a set of clauses.) ς is a function that associates a cost with each clause of $\mathcal{H}$, $\varsigma : \mathcal{H} \to \mathbb{R}_0^+$. Given the background theory $\mathcal{T}$, a set $\mathcal{E} \subseteq \mathcal{H}$ of hypotheses is an explanation (for the manifestations) if: (i) $\mathcal{E}$ entails the manifestations $\mathcal{M}$ (given $\mathcal{T}$), i.e. $\mathcal{T} \wedge \mathcal{E} \vDash \mathcal{M}$; and (ii) $\mathcal{E}$ is consistent (given $\mathcal{T}$), i.e. $\mathcal{T} \wedge \mathcal{E} \nvDash \bot$. The propositional abduction problem is usually defined as computing a minimum cost (or cardinality minimal) explanation for the manifestations subject to the background theory. Moreover, one can consider explanations of (subset-)minimal cost. The complexity of logic-based abduction has been studied in the past [74,111]. There are also recent practical algorithms for propositional abduction [175,308].

The computation of a prime implicant of some propositional formula φ, defined on atoms X, can be formulated as a problem of abduction. Let $\mathbf{u}$ be an assignment to the atoms of φ, such that $\varphi^{\mathbf{u}} = 1$. Given $\mathbf{u}$, construct the set $\mathcal{H}$ of hypotheses as follows: if $u_i = 1$, then add x_i to $\mathcal{H}$, otherwise add $\neg x_i$ to $\mathcal{H}$. We let $\mathcal{T} = \emptyset$ and $\mathcal{M} = \varphi$. Given the definition of $\mathcal{H}$, then a (subset-)minimal set $\mathcal{E} \subseteq \mathcal{H}$ is a prime implicant if, (i) $\mathcal{E} \vDash \varphi$; and (ii) $\mathcal{E} \nvDash \bot$. Observe that, by

---

[8] https://maxsat-evaluations.github.io/ and http://www.cril.univ-artois.fr/PB16/ http://www.satcompetition.org/2011/ (MUS track).
[9] http://www.qbflib.org/.

hypothesis, condition (ii) is trivially satisfied. Hence, a prime implicant of φ (given $\mathcal{H}$) is a subset-minimal set of literals $\mathcal{E} \subseteq \mathcal{H}$ such that $\mathcal{E} \vDash \varphi$.

In practice, when φ is non-clausal, deciding entailment is somewhat more complicated. In these cases, and as mentioned earlier, most often one needs to clausify φ, so that it can be reasoned about. A difficulty with efficient clausification procedures is that these introduce auxiliary variables. As a result, we need to follow a different approach for computing a prime implicant.

Let $\psi = [\![\varphi]\!]_{\mathcal{V}}$ be the propositional clausal representation of φ, given some logic theory $\mathcal{V}$, which uses additional auxiliary atoms represented as set A. (Section 2.1.3 details further the use of logic encodings.) We distinguish an auxiliary propositional atom $t \in A$, such that $t = 1$ for the assignments to X and A which satisfy ψ (and so φ). In this new setting, we let $\mathcal{T} = \psi$ and $\mathcal{M} = (t)$. Given a (consistent) set of literals $\mathcal{H}$, representing a satisfying assignment to the atoms of φ, then a (subset-)minimal set $\mathcal{E} \subseteq \mathcal{H}$ is a prime implicant if, (i) $\psi \wedge \mathcal{E} \vDash t$; and (ii) $\mathcal{E} \nvDash \bot$. As before, condition (ii) is trivially satisfied. Hence, a prime implicant of φ (given $\mathcal{H}$) is a subset-minimal set of literals $\mathcal{E} \subseteq \mathcal{H}$ such that $\psi \wedge \mathcal{E} \vDash t$.

Propositional Languages. A propositional language represents a subset of the set of propositional formulas, and several such subsets have been extensively studied [94,95,100][10]. One well-known example is negation normal form (NNF), representing a directed-acyclic graph of $\wedge$ and $\vee$ operators, where the leaves are atomic propositions or their negation. Other well-known examples are DNF and CNF formulas. By imposing additional constraints on the $\vee$ and $\wedge$ nodes of NNF formulas, one can devise classes of propositional languages that exhibit important tractability properties. A detailed analysis of propositional languages is available in [100]. Some results on formal explainability have been derived for propositional languages in recent years [25,29,97,165,320].

2.1.2 First Order Logic

This section briefly mentions one well-known extension of propositional logic, namely first order logic (FOL). FOL extends propositional logic with predicates, functions, constants and quantifiers, and such that variables are allowed to take values from arbitrary domains. In contrast with propositional logic, where an interpretation is an assignment of values to the formula's atoms, in the case of FOL, an interpretation must ascribe a meaning to predicates, functions and constants. Whereas validity in FOL is undecidable [45], one can reason in concrete theories, with a well-known example being satisfiability modulo theories.

Satisfiability Modulo Theories (SMT). By providing first order logic with concrete theories, e.g. integer arithmetic, real arithmetic or mixed integer-real arithmetic, among many other possibilities, one obtains decidable fragments, for which practically efficient reasoners have been developed over the last two

---

[10] For brevity, we will not delve into defining propositional languages and queries/transformations of interest. The interested reader is referred to the bibliography [100].

decades. (There exist undecidable theories in SMT [218], but that is beyond the goals of this document. SMT solvers generalize SAT to reason with fragments of first order logic [55,81,218]. Throughout this paper, we will use SMT reasoners solely as an alternative for mixed-integer linear programming reasoners (see below), even though SMT reasoners allow for significantly more general fragments of FOL. Similar to the case of SAT, we can solve optimization problems over SMT formulas (MaxSMT), and we can also reason about inconsistency. Previous definitions (see Sect. 2.1.1) also apply in this setting.

Mixed Integer Linear Programming (MILP). MILP can be formulated as a first-order logic theory (e.g. [67], where variables can take values from boolean, integer and real domains, and where the allowed binary functions are $+$ and $-$, with their usual meanings, and the allowed binary predicates are $=$ and $\leq$, also with their usual meanings. We will also allow a countable number of unary constant functions $b\cdot$, with $b \in \mathbb{R}$ (thus accounting for the other possible cases of $\mathbb{B}$ and $\mathbb{Z}$), and where each $b\cdot$ represents a coefficient. Starting from a set V of (variable) numbers, i.e. $V = \{1, \ldots, m\}$, we consider a partition of V into B, I and R. The general MILP formulation is thus:

$$\begin{aligned}
\min \quad & \sum_{j=1}^{n} c_j x_j \\
\text{s.t.} \quad & \sum_{j=1}^{n} a_{ij} x_j \leq b_i, i = 1, \ldots, r \\
& x_j \in \{0, 1\}, j \in B \\
& x_j \in \mathbb{Z}, j \in I \\
& x_j \in \mathbb{R}, j \in R \\
& a_{ij}, b_i \in \mathbb{R}
\end{aligned}$$

Several proprietary and publicly available MILP solvers are available[11], with significant performance gains reported over the years [57,58,212].

Additional Definitions. The definitions introduced in the propositional logic case can be generalized to the case of FOL, SMT, MILP, etc. These generalizations include entailment, prime implicants and implicates, but also the definitions associated with reasoning about inconsistency. A discussion of some of these concepts beyond propositional logic is available for example in [246].

2.1.3 Encodings and Interfacing Reasoners

Throughout the document, we will extensively refer to SAT, SMT and MILP reasoners. Consistency checking with a reasoner for theory $\mathcal{T}$ on a $\mathcal{T}$-theory formula $\varphi_{\mathcal{T}}$ is represented by $\mathbf{CO}(\varphi_{\mathcal{T}}; \mathcal{T})$, and denotes whether $\varphi_{\mathcal{T}}$ has at least one model (given $\mathcal{T}$), i.e. an interpretation that satisfies $\varphi_{\mathcal{T}}$. For simplicity, the parameterization on $\mathcal{T}$ is omitted, and so we use $\mathbf{CO}(\varphi_{\mathcal{T}})$ instead. These theory reasoners operate on formulas of a suitable logic language. Given some logic formula φ, $[\![\varphi]\!]_{\mathcal{T}}$ denotes the encoding of φ in a representation suitable for reasoning by a decision oracle for theory $\mathcal{T}$. (For simplicity, we just use $[\![\varphi]\!]$.) As

---

[11] For example, https://www.ibm.com/ae-en/analytics/cplex-optimizer, https://www.gurobi.com/, https://sourceforge.net/projects/lpsolve/.

shown below, the computation of formal explanations assumes the existence of a reasoner that decides the satisfiability (or consistency) of a statement expressed in theory $\mathcal{T}$.

For the case of propositional theories, SAT reasoners most often work with clausal representations. As noted earlier, there exist procedures for converting arbitrary (non-clausal) logic formulas into clausal form [286,336], which require the use of additional propositional atoms. There are also well-known encodings of constraints into clausal form [55, Chapters 02, 28]. Examples include cardinality constraints, e.g. AtMost$K$ (i.e. $\sum_i x_i \leq K$, with boolean x_i) or AtLeast$K$ (i.e. $\sum_i \geq k$, with boolean x_i) constraints, and pseudo-boolean constraints ($\sum i a_i x_i \leq b$, also with boolean x_i), among many others.

2.2 Classification Problems

Classification problems in ML are defined on a set of features (or attributes) $\mathcal{F} = \{1, \ldots, m\}$ and a set of classes $\mathcal{K} = \{c_1, c_2, \ldots, c_K\}$. Each feature $i \in \mathcal{F}$ takes values from a domain $\mathcal{D}_i$. In general, domains can be categorical or ordinal, with values that can be boolean or integer. (Although real-valued could be considered for some of the classifiers studied in the paper, we opt not to specifically address real-valued features.) The set of domains is represented by $\mathbb{D} = (\mathcal{D}_1, \ldots, \mathcal{D}_m)$. Feature space is defined as $\mathbb{F} = \mathcal{D}_1 \times \mathcal{D}_2 \times \ldots \times \mathcal{D}_m$; $|\mathbb{F}|$ represents the total number of points in $\mathbb{F}$. For boolean domains, $\mathcal{D}_i = \{0,1\} = \mathcal{B}$, $i = 1, \ldots, m$, and $\mathbb{F} = \mathcal{B}^m$. The notation $\mathbf{x} = (x_1, \ldots, x_m)$ denotes an arbitrary point in feature space, where each x_i is a variable taking values from $\mathcal{D}_i$. The set of variables associated with features is $X = \{x_1, \ldots, x_m\}$. Moreover, the notation $\mathbf{v} = (v_1, \ldots, v_m)$ represents a specific point in feature space, where each v_i is a constant representing one concrete value from $\mathcal{D}_i$. With respect to the set of classes $\mathcal{K}$, the size of $\mathcal{K}$ is assumed to be finite; no additional restrictions are imposed on $\mathcal{K}$. Nevertheless, with the goal of simplicity, the paper considers examples where $|\mathcal{K}| = 2$, concretely $\mathcal{K} = \{0,1\}$, or alternatively $\mathcal{K} = \{\ominus, \oplus\}$. An ML classifier $\mathcal{M}$ is characterized by a (non-constant) *classification function* κ that maps feature space $\mathbb{F}$ into the set of classes $\mathcal{K}$, i.e. $\kappa : \mathbb{F} \to \mathcal{K}$. Each classifier $\mathcal{M}$ is represented unambiguously by the tuple $(\mathcal{F}, \mathbb{D}, \mathbb{F}, \mathcal{K}, \kappa)$. (With a mild abuse of notation, we also write $\mathcal{M} = (\mathcal{F}, \mathbb{D}, \mathbb{F}, \mathcal{K}, \kappa)$.) An *instance* (or observation) denotes a pair $(\mathbf{v}, c)$, where $\mathbf{v} \in \mathbb{F}$ and $c \in \mathcal{K}$, with $c = \kappa(\mathbf{v})$.

The *classifier decision problem* (CDP) is to decide whether the logic statement $\exists(\mathbf{x} \in \mathbb{F}).(\kappa(\mathbf{x}) = c)$, for $c \in \mathcal{K}$, is true. Given some target class $c \in \mathcal{K}$, the goal of CDP is to decide whether there exists some point $\mathbf{x}$ in feature space for which the prediction is c. For example, for a neural network or a random forest, it is easy to prove that CDP is NP-complete. In contrast, for univariate decision trees, CDP is in P. This is further discussed in the next section.

2.2.1   Examples of Classifiers

This paper studies decision trees (DTs), decision sets (DSs) and decision lists (DLs) in greater detail. Nevertheless, formal explainability has been studied in the context of several other well-known families of classifiers, including naive bayes classifiers (NBCs) [239], decision diagrams and graphs [166], tree ensembles [170,172,180,191], monotonic classifiers [84,240], neural networks [178], and bayesian network classifiers [320,321]. Additional information can be found in the cited references.

Decision Trees (DTs). DTs are among the still most widely used family of classifiers, with applications in both ML and data mining (DM) [71,124,293, 294,363]. A decision tree is a directed acyclic graph, with one root node that has no incoming edges, and the remaining nodes having exactly one incoming edge. Terminal nodes have no outgoing edges, and non-terminal nodes have two or more outgoing edges. Each terminal node is associated with a class, i.e. the predicted class for the node. Each non-terminal node is associated with exactly one feature[12]. Each outgoing edge is associated with a literal defined using the values of the feature, and such that any value of the feature domain is consistent with exactly one of the literals of the outgoing edges. A tree path $\mathcal{P}$ connects the root node with one of the tree's terminal nodes. Common (implicit) assumptions of DTs are that: (i) all paths in a DT are consistent; and (ii) for each point $\mathbf{v}$ in feature space, there exists exactly one path $\mathcal{P}$ that is consistent with $\mathbf{v}$. (Observe that (ii) requires that the branches at each node capture all values in the domain of the tested feature and that the branches' conditions be mutually disjoint.) Given these assumptions of DTs, it is easy to see that CDP is in P. One simply picks the target class and a terminal node predicting the class, and reconstructs the path to the root; a procedure that runs in linear time on the size of the tree. An example of a DT is shown in Fig. 2a. (This example will be analyzed in greater detail below.)

Decision Lists (DLs) and Sets (DSs). DLs and DSs also find a wide range of applications [17,18,80,124,220]. DLs and DSs represent, respectively, ordered and unordered rule sets. There exist in-depth studies of DLs [303], but in contrast DSs are less well-understood. Each rule is of the form:

$$R_j\colon \text{IF} \quad (\tau_j) \quad \text{THEN} \quad d_j$$

where τ_j represents a boolean expression defined on the features and their domains, and $d_j \in \mathcal{K}$. We say that the rule *fires* if its literal (τ_j) is consistent (or holds true). For DLs, and with the exception of the first rule, all other rules are of the form:

$$R_l\colon \text{ELSE IF} \quad (\tau_l) \quad \text{THEN} \quad d_l$$

---

[12] Thus, this paper only considers *univariate* DTs, for which where each non-terminal node test a single feature. In contrast, for multivariable DTs [72], we assume that each non-terminal node can test arbitrary functions of the features. For ordinal features, multivariate DTs are also referred to as *oblique* [267].

For the last (default) rule, it is required that τ_l is a tautology, i.e. the rule always fires if all others do not. (This basically corresponds to solely having ELSE as the rule's condition.) The default rule is marked as R_{DEF}. An example of a DL is shown in Fig. 1a. An example of a DS would be the same DL, but without the ELSE's, i.e. there would be no order among the listed rules. (The DL example will be analyzed in greater detail below.) In contrast with DLs, the lack of order of rules in DSs raises a number of issues [181]. One issue is *overlap*, i.e. two or more rules predicting different classes may fire on the same point of feature space. A second issue is *coverage*, i.e. without a default rule, it may happen that no rule fires on some points of feature space. It is conjectured that is Σ_2^P-hard to learn DSs that ensure both no overlap and ensuring coverage of all points in feature space [181].

Neural Networks (NNs). We consider a simple architecture for an NN, concretely feed-forward NNs, which we refer to as NNs. (A comprehensive treatment of NNs can be found elsewhere [142].) An NN is composed of a number of layers of neurons. The output values of the neurons in a given layer $\mathbf{x}^l$ are computed given the output values of the neurons in the previous layer $\mathbf{x}^{l-1}$, up to a number L of layers, and such that the inputs represent layer 0. Furthermore, each neuron computes an intermediate value given the output values of the neurons in the previous layer, and the weights of the connections between layers. For each layer, the intermediate computed values are represented by $\mathbf{y}^l$. The output value of each neuron is the result of applying a non-linear activation function on the values of $\mathbf{y}^l$, thus obtaining $\mathbf{x}^l$. Assuming a ReLU [269] activation function, one obtained the following:

$$\mathbf{y}^l = \mathbf{A}^l \cdot (\mathbf{x}^{l-1})^{\mathrm{T}}$$
$$\mathbf{x}^l = \max(\mathbf{y}^l, \mathbf{0}) \tag{3}$$

where $\mathbf{x}^0$ denote the input values, $\mathbf{x}^L$ denotes the output values, and $\mathbf{A}^l$ denotes the weights matrix (that also accounts for a possible bias vector, by including a variable $x_0^{l-1} = 1$). For classification problems, there are different mechanisms to predict the actual class associated with the computed output values. One option is to have each output represent a class. Another option is to pick the class depending on the range of values taken by the output variable. This alternative is illustrated with the running example presented later in this section.

A recent alternative to NNs, namely binarized neural networks (BNNs) [169] has also been investigated from the perspective of explainability [272].

Monotonic Classifiers. Monotonic classifiers find a number of important applications, and have been studied extensively in recent years [120,231,324,364]. Let $\preccurlyeq$ denote a partial order on the set of classes $\mathcal{K}$. For example, we assume $c_1 \preccurlyeq c_2 \preccurlyeq \ldots c_K$. Furthermore, we assume that each domain D_i is ordered such that the value taken by feature i is between a lower bound $\lambda(i)$ and an upper bound $\mu(i)$. Given $\mathbf{v}_1 = (v_{11}, \ldots, v_{1i}, \ldots, v_{1m})$ and $\mathbf{v}_2 = (v_{21}, \ldots, v_{2i}, \ldots, v_{2m})$, we say that $\mathbf{v}_1 \leq \mathbf{v}_2$ if, $\forall (i \in \mathcal{F}).v_{1i} \leq v_{2i}$. Finally, a classifier is monotonic if whenever $\mathbf{v}_1 \leq \mathbf{v}_2$, then $\kappa(\mathbf{v}_1) \preccurlyeq \kappa(\mathbf{v}_2)$.

Additional Families of Classifiers. Formal explainability has been studied in the context of other families of classifiers, including random forests (RFs) [66,191], boosted trees (BTs) [170,172,180], tree ensembles (TEs, which include both RFs and BTs) [172], decision graphs (DGs) & diagrams [166], naive bayes classifiers (NBCs) [239], monotonic classifiers [240], propositional language classifiers [165], and bayesian network classifiers [320,321]. Most of these classifiers are covered in standard references on ML [124,142,316].

A random forest is represented by a set of decision trees, each tree trained from a random sample of the original dataset. In the originally proposed formulation of RFs [69], the selected class is picked by majority voting among all trees. As an example, we show that CDP for RFs is NP-complete.

Proposition 4. *For RFs, CDP is NP-complete.*

Proof. The decision problem is clearly in NP. Simply pick a point in feature space, and then compute in polynomial time the prediction of the RF, the decision problem answers **true** if the prediction is c, and it answers **false** if the prediction is other than c.

To prove NP-hardness, we reduce the decision problem for propositional formulas represented in CNF, a problem well-known to be complete for NP. Let ψ be a CNF formula with m propositional variables and n clauses, $\varsigma_1, \ldots, \varsigma_n$:

- Create n decision trees, one for each clause ς_j, and such that DT j predicts 1 if at least one literal of ς_j is satisfied, and 0 if all literals of ς_j are falsified.
- Also, create $n - 1$ decision trees, each with a single terminal node with prediction 0.

Clearly, the reduction runs in polynomial time. Moreover, it is immediate that the RF picks class 1 if and only if the formula is satisfied. Let the assignment to ψ be such that $\psi(x_1, \ldots, x_m)$ is satisfied. In this case, each DT associated with a clause will predict 1 and the other $n - 1$ DTs will predict 0; hence the prediction will be 1. Furthermore, for the prediction to be 1, it must be the case that the n DTs associated with the clauses must predict 1, since one must offset the $n - 1$ trees that guaranteedly predict 0.   □

A simpler argument could be used to prove that CDP for multivariate decision trees is also NP-complete. As an example, the CNF formula could be tested on a single tree node.

R$_1$:	IF	($x_1 = 1$)	THEN	0
R$_2$:	ELSE IF	($x_2 = 1$)	THEN	1
R$_3$:	ELSE IF	($x_4 = 1$)	THEN	0
R$_{\text{DEF}}$:	ELSE		THEN	1

(a) Decision list

Item	Definition
$\mathcal{F}_1$	$\{1, 2, 3, 4\}$
$\mathcal{D}_{1i}, i = 1, 2, 3$	$\{0, 1\}$
$\mathcal{D}_{14}$	$\{0, 1, 2\}$
$\mathcal{K}_1$	$\{0, 1\}$

(b) Classification problem

Feature #	Feature Name	Original & Mapped Domain
1	Gills	$\{\text{No}\rightarrow 0, \text{Yes}\rightarrow 1\}$
2	Teeth	$\{\text{Few}\rightarrow 0, \text{Many}\rightarrow 1\}$
3	Beak	$\{\text{No}\rightarrow 0, \text{Yes}\rightarrow 1\}$
4	Length	$\{3\rightarrow 0, 4\rightarrow 1, 5\rightarrow 2\}$
Classes		$\{\text{No}\rightarrow 0, \text{Yes}\rightarrow 1\}$

(c) Mapping of features

Fig. 1. Decision list, adapted from [124]

2.2.2 Running Examples
Throughout the paper, the following running examples will be used to illustrate some of the main results.

Example 5 (DL). The first running example is a simple DL, that is adapted from [124, Section 6.1]. (The original classification problem is to decide whether some animal is a dolphin. The features have been numbered, respectively 1 is Gills, 2 is Teeth, 3 is Beak, and 4 is Length. Moreover, the feature values have been replaced by numbers. These changes are meant to facilitate the logical analysis of the classifier, and do not affect in any way the computed explanations.) As a result, $\mathcal{F}_1 = \{1, 2, 3, 4\}$, $\mathcal{D}_{1i} = \{0, 1\}, i = 1, 2, 3$, $\mathcal{D}_{14} = \{0, 1, 2\}$, $\mathcal{K}_1 = \{0, 1\}$, and κ_1 is defined by Fig. 1a. Clearly, $\mathbb{F} = \{0, 1\} \times \{0, 1\} \times \{0, 1\} \times \{0, 1, 2\}$. Moreover, the target instance is $(\mathbf{v}, c) = ((0, 0, 1, 2), 1)$. Each of the rules R$_1$, R$_2$, and R$_3$ tests a single literal, and a final default rule R$_{\text{DEF}}$ fires on the points in feature space inconsistent with the other rules. Finally, Table 1 lists the class predicted by the DL for every point in feature space.   ◁

Example 6 (DT). The second running example is the decision tree shown in Fig. 2. (This DT is adapted from [162] by replacing the names of the features and renaming the binary domains to boolean. The original DT was produced with the tool OSDT (optimal sparse decision trees) [162].) For this DT classifier (see Fig. 2b), $\mathcal{F}_2 = \{1, 2, 3, 4, 5\}$, $\mathcal{D}_{2i} = \{0, 1\}, i = 1, \ldots, 5$, $\mathcal{K}_2 = \{0, 1\}$, and κ_2

Table 1. Truth table for Example 5, where the target instance $(\mathbf{v}, c) = ((0, 0, 1, 2), 1)$ corresponds to entry 05.

Entry	x_1	x_2	x_3	x_4	Rule	$\kappa_1(x_1, x_2, x_3, x_4)$
00	0	0	0	0	R_{DEF}	1
01	0	0	0	1	R_3	0
02	0	0	0	2	R_{DEF}	1
03	0	0	1	0	R_{DEF}	1
04	0	0	1	1	R_3	0
05	0	0	1	2	R_{DEF}	1
06	0	1	0	0	R_2	1
07	0	1	0	1	R_2	1
08	0	1	0	2	R_2	1
09	0	1	1	0	R_2	1
10	0	1	1	1	R_2	1
11	0	1	1	2	R_2	1
12	1	0	0	0	R_1	0
13	1	0	0	1	R_1	0
14	1	0	0	2	R_1	0
15	1	0	1	0	R_1	0
16	1	0	1	1	R_1	0
17	1	0	1	2	R_1	0
18	1	1	0	0	R_1	0
19	1	1	0	1	R_1	0
20	1	1	0	2	R_1	0
21	1	1	1	0	R_1	0
22	1	1	1	1	R_1	0
23	1	1	1	2	R_1	0

is captured by the DT shown in the Fig. 2a. As can be observed, the DT has 15 nodes, with the non-terminal nodes being $N = \{1, 2, 4, 5, 7, 8, 10\}$ and the terminal nodes being $T = \{3, 6, 9, 11, 12, 13, 14, 15\}$. Each non-terminal node is associated with a feature from $\mathcal{F}$ (we assume univariate DTs), and each outgoing edge tests one or more values from the feature's domain. For example, the edge $(2, 4)$ is associated with the literal $x_2 = 0$, being consistent with points in feature space where x_2 takes value 0. Each terminal node is associated with a prediction from $\mathcal{K}$. The set of paths is $\mathcal{R}$. Throughout the paper, $\mathcal{R}$ is partitioned into two sets, namely $\mathcal{P}$ associated with prediction 1, and $\mathcal{Q}$ associated with prediction 0. (The split of $\mathcal{R}$ serves to aggregate paths according to their prediction, but the naming is arbitrary, and we could consider other splits, e.g. $\mathcal{P}$ for prediction 0, and $\mathcal{Q}$ for prediction 1.) Moreover, $\mathcal{P} = \{P_1, P_2, P_3, P_4, P_5\}$, with $P_1 = \langle 1, 2, 4, 7, 10, 15 \rangle$,

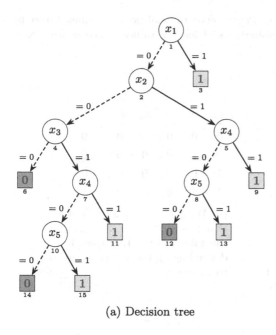

(a) Decision tree

Feature in [162]	Boolean feature
middle-middle=x	x_1
top-left=x	x_2
bottom-right=x	x_3
bottom-left=x	x_4
top-right=x	x_5

Definitions	
$\mathcal{F}_2$	$\{1,2,3,4,5\}$
$\mathcal{D}_{21},\ldots,\mathcal{D}_{25}$	$\{0,1\}$
$\mathcal{K}_2$	$\{0,1\}$

(b) Mapping of features

Fig. 2. Decision tree, adapted from [162, Figure 5b], for the tic-tac-toe dataset, and also studied in [187]

$P_2 = \langle 1,2,4,7,11 \rangle$, $P_3 = \langle 1,2,5,8,13 \rangle$, $P_4 = \langle 1,2,5,9 \rangle$, and $P_5 = \langle 1,3 \rangle$. Similarly, $\mathcal{Q} = \{Q_1, Q_2, Q_3\}$, with $Q_1 = \langle 1,2,4,6 \rangle$, $Q_2 = \langle 1,2,4,7,10,14 \rangle$, and $Q_3 = \langle 1,2,5,8,12 \rangle$. Furthermore, the target instance we will study is $(\mathbf{v}, c) = ((0,0,1,0,1),1)$, being consistent with path P_1 and so with prediction 1. Finally, Table 2 shows parts of the truth table of the example DT, that will be used later when analyzing the instance $(\mathbf{v}, c) = ((0,0,1,0,1),1)$.   ◁

Example 7 (NN). The third running example is an NN, as shown in Fig. 3. For this example, $\mathcal{F}_3 = \{1,2\}$, $\mathbb{D} = \{\mathcal{D}_{31}, \mathcal{D}_{32}\}$, with $\mathcal{D}_{31} = \mathcal{D}_{32} = \{0,1\}$, and so $\mathbb{F}_3 = \{0,1\}^2$, $\mathcal{K} = \{0,1\}$, and $\kappa_3(x_1, x_2) = (\max(x_1 + x_2 - 0.5, 0) > 0)$. We also have, from (3):

$$\mathbf{A}^1 = \begin{bmatrix} -0.5 & +1 & +1 \end{bmatrix}$$
$$\mathbf{x}^0 = \begin{bmatrix} 1 & x_1^0 & x_2^0 \end{bmatrix}$$
$$\mathbf{y}^1 = \begin{bmatrix} y_1^1 \end{bmatrix} = \mathbf{A}^1 \cdot (\mathbf{x}^0)^{\mathrm{T}}$$

It is easy to conclude that the classifier corresponds to the Boolean function $f(x_1, x_2) = x_1 \vee x_2$. This is confirmed by the truth table shown in Fig. 3b. For this example, the instance considered is $(\mathbf{v}, c) = ((1,0),1)$.   ◁

Table 2. Partial truth tables of κ_2. These serve to analyze the values taken by $\kappa_2(x_1, x_2, x_3, x_4, x_5)$ for different combinations of feature values, starting from $\mathbf{x} = (0, 0, 1, 0, 1)$.

x_3	x_5	x_1	x_2	x_4	$\kappa_2(\mathbf{x})$
1	1	0	0	0	1
1	1	0	0	1	1
1	1	0	1	0	1
1	1	0	1	1	1
1	1	1	0	0	1
1	1	1	0	1	1
1	1	1	1	0	1
1	1	1	1	1	1

(a) With $x_3 = x_5 = 1$, it is that case that $\kappa_2(x_1, x_2, x_3, x_4, x_5) = 1$, independently of the values of the other features

x_3	x_5	x_1	x_2	x_4	$\kappa_2(\mathbf{x})$
0	0	0	0	0	0
0	1	0	0	0	0
1	0	0	0	0	0
1	1	0	0	0	1

(b) With $x_1 = x_2 = x_4 = 0$, it is that case that $\kappa_2(x_1, x_2, x_3, x_4, x_5)$ can take a value other than 1, depending on the values assigned to x_3 and x_5

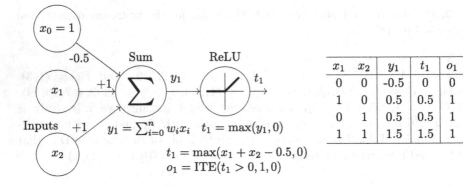

x_1	x_2	y_1	t_1	o_1
0	0	-0.5	0	0
1	0	0.5	0.5	1
0	1	0.5	0.5	1
1	1	1.5	1.5	1

$y_1 = \sum_{i=0}^{n} w_i x_i \quad t_1 = \max(y_1, 0)$

$t_1 = \max(x_1 + x_2 - 0.5, 0)$

$o_1 = \mathrm{ITE}(t_1 > 0, 1, 0)$

(a) NN computing $\kappa(x_1, x_2) = x_1 \vee x_2$ (b) Truth table

Fig. 3. Simple neural network

Example 8 (Monotonic classifier). The fourth and final running example is a monotonic classifier, adapted from [240]. The goal is to predict a student's grade given the grades on the different components of assessment. The different grading components have domain $\{0, \ldots, 10\}$. It is also the case that $F \preccurlyeq E \preccurlyeq D \preccurlyeq C \preccurlyeq B \preccurlyeq A$, where the operator $\preccurlyeq$ is used to represent the order between different grades. The details of the classifier are summarized in Fig. 4.

Feature id	Feature variable	Feature name	Domain
1	Q	Quiz	$\{0, \ldots, 10\}$
2	X	Exam	$\{0, \ldots, 10\}$
3	H	Homework	$\{0, \ldots, 10\}$
4	R	Project	$\{0, \ldots, 10\}$

(a) Features and domains

Variable	Meaning	Range
S	Final score	$\in \{0, \ldots, 10\}$
$\kappa(\cdot) \triangleq M$	Student grade	$\in \{A, B, C, D, E, F\}$

(b) Definition of κ_4

Fig. 4. Example of a monotonic classifier [240]

The classifier "predicts" a student's grade given the grades in different grading components, using the following formulas:

$$M = \mathrm{ite}(S \geq 9, A, \mathrm{ite}(S \geq 7, B, \mathrm{ite}(S \geq 5, C, \mathrm{ite}(S \geq 4, D, \mathrm{ite}(S \geq 2, E, F)))))$$
$$S = \max\left[0.3 \times Q + 0.6 \times X + 0.1 \times H, R\right]$$

Also, it is clearly the case that, $\kappa_4(\mathbf{x_1}) \preccurlyeq \kappa_4(\mathbf{x_2})$ if $\mathbf{x_1} \leq \mathbf{x_2}$, and so the classifier is monotonic.   ◁

2.3   Non-formal Explanations

As observed in Sect. 1, most of past work on XAI has studied non-formal explainability approaches. We will briefly summarize the main ideas. The interested reader is referred to the many surveys on the topic [1,149,159,160,263,299,309, 310,335]. There is a burgeoning and fast growing body of work on non-formal approaches for computing explanations. The best known approaches offer no guarantees of rigor, and include model-agnostic approaches or solutions based on saliency maps for neural networks.

Model-Agnostic Methods. The most visible approaches for explaining ML models are model-agnostic methods [235,301,302]. These can be organized into methods that learn a simpler interpretable model, e.g. a linear model or a decision tree. This is the case with LIME [301] and SHAP [235]. The difference between LIME and SHAP is the approach used to learn the model, with LIME being based on iterative sampling, and SHAP based on the *approximate* computation of Shapley values. (It should be underscored that the Shapley values in SHAP are not computed exactly, but only approximated. Indeed, the complexity of exactly computing Shapley values is unwieldy [20, 73], with one exception being a fairly restricted form of boolean circuits [20], referred to as deterministic, decomposable boolean circuits [100], and which capture binary decision trees[13]. These model agnostic methods can also be viewed as associating a measure of relative importance to each features, being often referred to as *feature attribution* methods. One alternative model-agnostic approach is to identify which features are the most relevant for the prediction. We refer to such approaches as *feature selection* methods. One concrete example is Anchor [302]. Similar to other model agnostic approaches, Anchor is based on sampling. It should be noted that model-agnostic approaches exhibit a number of important drawbacks, the most critical of which is unsoundness [170, 180, 272]. Despite critical limitations, including the risk of unsound explanations, the impact of these tools can only be viewed as impressive[14].

Neural Networks and Saliency Maps. In the concrete case of neural networks, past work proposed the use of variants of saliency maps [263, 309, 310, 322], that give a graphical interpretation of a prediction. One popular approach is based on so-called layerwise relevancy propagation [36]. However, recent work has revealed important drawbacks of these approaches [2, 209, 325, 350].

Intrinsic Interpretability. Some authors have advocated the use of so-called *interpretable* ML models, for which the explanation is the model itself [43, 77, 230, 262, 304, 305, 314, 357]. For example, it is widely accepted that decision trees are interpretable. Claims about the interpretability of decision trees go back at least until the early 2000s [70, Sec. 9, Page 206]. Motivated by their interpretability, decision trees have been applied to a wide range of domains, including the medical domain [224, 333, 340]. Unfortunately, recent results [187] demonstrate that decision trees can hardly be deemed interpretable, at least as long as interpretability correlates with the succinctness of explanations. Interpretability of decision lists and sets is at least as problematic as it is for decision trees. If that were not the case, then one would be able to just represent DTs as DLs or DSs [303]. The bottom line is that even interpretable ML models should be explained, as the comprehensive results in earlier work [187] demonstrate.

Assessment. A number of additional limitations of non-formal explanations have been reported in recent years [75, 108, 135, 189, 216, 221, 326]. Furthermore, a number of authors have raised concerns about the current uses of XAI and its technology [199, 268, 274], with examples of misuse also reported [184].

---

[13] Earlier work [234] also investigated the exact computation of Shapley values for decision trees. However, issues about the proposed algorithm have been raised by more recent work [20, 73].

[14] See for example https://bit.ly/3eXIiNU, https://bit.ly/3BJL4z7, and https://bit.ly/3djA1Do.

3   Formal Explainability

Formal explanation approaches have been studied in a growing body of research in recent years [11–13, 19, 21, 22, 24–29, 38, 40, 60–62, 65, 66, 84, 85, 96–99, 101, 122, 145, 163–168, 170–172, 174, 177–180, 185, 186, 186, 187, 189–192, 219, 232, 233, 237, 239, 240, 242, 272, 297, 298, 319–321, 354, 355, 362, 367, 368]. This section introduces formal explanations and describes some of their properties.

Explanation Problems. Given a classifier $\mathcal{M} = (\mathcal{F}, \mathbb{D}, \mathbb{F}, \mathcal{K}, \kappa)$, we consider two explanation problems. First, we mostly study a given *local* explanation problem $\mathcal{E}_L = (\mathcal{M}, \mathbf{v}, c)$, with $\mathbf{v} \in \mathbb{F}$, $c \in \mathcal{K}$ and $c = \kappa(\mathbf{v})$, which respects a concrete point in feature space, i.e. a concrete prediction. Second, we will also consider a *global* explanation problem $\mathcal{E}_G = (\mathcal{M}, c)$, with $c \in \mathcal{K}$, which respects solely a concrete prediction c, that can be predicted in many points of feature space.

As a result, a tuple $(\mathcal{M}, (\mathbf{v}, c))$ will allow us to unambiguously represent the classification problem $\mathcal{M}$ for which we want to compute the local AXp's and CXp's given the instance $(\mathbf{v}, c)$. Similarly, $(\mathcal{M}, c)$ also unambiguously represents the classification problem for which we want to compute the global AXp's given the prediction c.

3.1   Abductive Explanations

This paper uses the definition of *abductive explanation* [178] (AXp), which corresponds to a PI-explanation [320] in the case of boolean classifiers. AXp's represent prime implicants of the discrete-valued classifier function (which computes the predicted class)[15]. AXp's can also be viewed as an instantiation of logic-based abduction [74, 111, 128, 313]. Throughout this paper we will opt to use the acronym AXp to refer to abductive explanations.

Let us consider a given classifier, computing a classification function κ on feature space $\mathbb{F}$, a point $\mathbf{v} \in \mathbb{F}$, with prediction $c = \kappa(\mathbf{v})$, and let $\mathcal{X}$ denote a subset of the set of features $\mathcal{F}$, $\mathcal{X} \subseteq \mathcal{F}$. $\mathcal{X}$ is a weak AXp for the instance $(\mathbf{v}, c)$ if,

$$\mathsf{WeakAXp}(\mathcal{X}) \quad := \quad \forall (\mathbf{x} \in \mathbb{F}).\ \left[\bigwedge_{i \in \mathcal{X}} (x_i = v_i) \right] \rightarrow (\kappa(\mathbf{x}) = c) \qquad (4)$$

(We could highlight that WeakAXp is parameterized on κ, $\mathbf{v}$ and c, but opt not to clutter the notation, and so these dependencies will be left implicit.) Thus, given an instance $(\mathbf{v}, c)$, a (weak) AXp is a subset of features which, if fixed to the values dictated by $\mathbf{v}$, then the prediction is guaranteed to be c, independently of the values assigned to the other features.

Example 9 With respect to the DL of Fig. 1, it is apparent that $\mathcal{X} = \{1, 4\}$ is a (weak) abductive explanation for the instance $(\mathbf{v}, c) = ((0, 0, 1, 2), 1)$. Indeed, if

---

[15] There exist also standard references with detailed overviews of the uses of prime implicants in the context of boolean functions [87, 151]. Generalizations of prime implicants beyond boolean domains have been considered before [249]. Prime implicants have also been referred to as minimum satisfying assignments in first-order logic (FOL) [107], and have been studied in modal and description logics [54].

$(x_1 = 0) \wedge (x_4 = 2)$, then the prediction will be 1, independently of the values taken by the other features. This can easily be concluded from Table 1; if x_1 and x_4 are fixed, then the possible entries are 02, 05, 08 and 11, all with prediction 1. Hence, we can write that,

$$\forall(\mathbf{x} \in \mathbb{F}_1). \, [(x_1 = 0) \wedge (x_4 = 2)] \to (\kappa_1(\mathbf{x}) = 1)$$

Observe that any set $\mathcal{Z}$, with $\mathcal{X} \subseteq \mathcal{Z} \subseteq \mathcal{F}$, is also a weak AXp.   ◁

Moreover, $\mathcal{X} \subseteq \mathcal{F}$ is an AXp if, besides being a weak AXp, it is also subset-minimal, i.e.

$$\mathsf{AXp}(\mathcal{X}) \quad := \quad \mathsf{WeakAXp}(\mathcal{X}) \wedge \forall(\mathcal{X}' \subsetneq \mathcal{X}).\neg\mathsf{WeakAXp}(\mathcal{X}') \tag{5}$$

Example 10. From Table 1, and given the weak AXp $\{1, 4\}$ (see Example 9) it is also possible to conclude that if either x_1 or x_4 are allowed to change their value, then the prediction can be changed. Hence, $\mathcal{X} = \{1, 4\}$ is effectively an AXp.   ◁

Observe that an AXp can be viewed as a possible irreducible answer to a "**Why?**" question, i.e. why is the classifier's prediction c? It should be plain in this work, but also in earlier work, that the representation of AXp's using subsets of features aims at simplicity. The sufficient condition for the prediction is evidently the conjunction of literals associated with the features contained in the AXp.

The following example demonstrates the importance of explaining decision trees, even if these are most often deemed interpretable.

Example 11. We consider the DT from Fig. 2, and the instance $((0, 0, 1, 0, 1), 1)$. Intrinsic interpretability [262, 304] would argue that the explanation for this instance is the path consistent with the instance. Hence, we would claim that,

$$\text{IF} \quad [(x_1 = 0) \wedge (x_2 = 0) \wedge (x_3 = 1) \wedge (x_4 = 0) \wedge (x_5 = 1)] \quad \text{THEN} \quad 1$$

However, Table 2 clarifies that, as long as features 3 and 5 are assigned the same value, then the prediction remains unchanged. Hence, a far more *intuitive* explanation would be,

$$\text{IF} \quad [(x_3 = 1) \wedge (x_5 = 1)] \quad \text{THEN} \quad 1$$

Clearly, the (only) AXp for the given instance is exactly that one, i.e. $\mathcal{X} = \{3, 5\}$, and we can state,

$$\forall(\mathbf{x} \in \mathbb{F}_2). \, [(x_3 = 1) \wedge (x_5 = 1)] \to (\kappa_2(\mathbf{x}) = 1)$$

                    ◁

Example 11 illustrates important limitations of DTs in terms of interpretability, and justifies recent work on explaining DTs [186–188]. More importantly, it has been shown that the redundancy in tree paths (i.e. features unnecessary for the prediction) can be arbitrarily large on the number of features [187]. Given the recent efforts on learning optimal (and quasi-optimal) "interpretable" models [4, 5, 10, 17, 18, 32, 33, 51, 52, 78, 105, 106, 136–138, 161, 162, 173, 181, 196, 220, 228, 238, 255, 271, 275, 276, 280, 306, 312, 318, 346–349, 352, 353, 356, 358, 365, 366], that include learning optimal decision trees and sets, recent results demonstrate [174, 187] that even such optimal and interpretable models should be explained.

3.2   Contrastive Explanations

Similarly to the case of AXp's, one can define (weak) contrastive explanations (CXp's) [177, 261]. $\mathcal{Y} \subseteq \mathcal{F}$ is a weak CXp for the instance $(\mathbf{v}, c)$ if,

$$\mathsf{WeakCXp}(\mathcal{Y}) \quad := \quad \exists(\mathbf{x} \in \mathbb{F}). \left[\bigwedge_{i \notin \mathcal{Y}}(x_i = v_i)\right] \wedge (\kappa(\mathbf{x}) \neq c) \tag{6}$$

(As before, for simplicity we keep the parameterization of $\mathsf{WeakCXp}$ on κ, $\mathbf{v}$ and c implicit.) Thus, given an instance $(\mathbf{v}, c)$, a (weak) CXp is a subset of features which, if allowed to take any value from their domain, then there is an assignment to the features that changes the prediction to a class other than c, this while the features not in the explanation are kept to their values (*ceteris paribus*).

Example 12. For the DT of Fig. 2, and the instance $(\mathbf{v}, c) = ((0, 0, 1, 0, 1), 1)$, it is the case that $\mathcal{Y} = \{3\}$ is a (weak) contrastive explanation. Indeed, if we allow the value of feature 3 to change, then there exists some point in feature space, e.g. $(0, 0, 0, 0, 1)$, for which the remaining features take the values in $\mathbf{v}$, and such that the prediction changes to 0. Hence, we can write,

$$\exists(\mathbf{x} \in \mathbb{F}_2). [(x_1 = 0) \wedge (x_2 = 0) \wedge (x_4 = 0) \wedge (x_5 = 1)] \wedge (\kappa_2(\mathbf{x}) \neq 1)$$

Intuitively, we are saying that it suffices to change the value of feature 3 to get a different prediction. ◁

Furthermore, a set $\mathcal{Y} \subseteq \mathcal{F}$ is a CXp if, besides being a weak CXp, it is also subset-minimal, i.e.

$$\mathsf{CXp}(\mathcal{Y}) \quad := \quad \mathsf{WeakCXp}(\mathcal{Y}) \wedge \forall(\mathcal{Y}' \subsetneq \mathcal{Y}).\neg\mathsf{WeakCXp}(\mathcal{Y}') \tag{7}$$

Example 13. For the DL of Fig. 1, it is plain that if x_1 is allowed to change value (i.e. entry 14 of Table 1) or if x_4 is allowed to change value (i.e. entry 01 of Table 1), then the prediction will change. Hence, either $\{1\}$ or $\{4\}$ are weak contrastive explanations for the given instance. Furthermore, both weak CXp's are irreducible, and so both are effectively CXp's. ◁

A CXp can be viewed as a possible irreducible answer to a **"Why Not?"** question, i.e. why isn't the classifier's prediction a class other than c? A different perspective for a contrastive explanation is as the answer to a *How?* question, i.e. how to change the features so as to change the prediction. In recent literature this alternative view has been investigated under the name *actionable recourse* [200, 201, 339, 345]. It should be underlined that whereas AXp's correspond to prime implicants of the boolean function ($\kappa(\mathbf{x}) = c$) that are consistent with some point $\mathbf{v} \in \mathbb{F}$, CXp's are *not* prime implicates of function ($\kappa(\mathbf{x}) = c$). Nevertheless, the concept of *counterexample* studied in formal explainability [178] corresponds to prime implicates of the function ($\kappa(\mathbf{x}) = c$) (which are not restricted to be consistent with some specific point $\mathbf{v} \in \mathbb{F}$).

One important observation is that, independently of what κ represents, the WeakAXp and WeakCXp predicates (respectively defined using (4) and (6)) are *monotone*[16]. This means that the tests for minimality (i.e., respectively (5) and (7)) can be simplified to:

$$\mathsf{AXp}(\mathcal{X}) \quad := \quad \mathsf{WeakAXp}(\mathcal{X}) \wedge \forall(t \in \mathcal{X}).\neg\mathsf{WeakAXp}(\mathcal{X} \setminus \{t\}) \tag{8}$$

and,

$$\mathsf{CXp}(\mathcal{Y}) \quad := \quad \mathsf{WeakCXp}(\mathcal{Y}) \wedge \forall(t \in \mathcal{Y}).\neg\mathsf{WeakCXp}(\mathcal{Y} \setminus \{t\}) \tag{9}$$

Observe that, instead of considering all possible subsets of $\mathcal{X}$ (resp. $\mathcal{Y}$), it suffices to consider the subsets obtained by removing a single element from $\mathcal{X}$ (resp. $\mathcal{Y}$). This observation is at the core of the algorithms proposed in recent years for computing AXp's and CXp's of a growing range of families of classifiers [164, 166, 174, 178, 179, 186, 191, 237, 239, 240, 272]. As will be clarified in Sect. 4, the computation of AXp's can be related with MUS extraction, and the computation of CXp's can be related with MCS extraction.

Given a local explanation problem $\mathcal{E}$, the sets of AXp's and CXp's are defined as follows,

$$\mathbb{A}(\mathcal{E}) = \{\mathcal{X} \subseteq \mathcal{F} \mid \mathsf{AXp}(X)\} \tag{10}$$

$$\mathbb{C}(\mathcal{E}) = \{\mathcal{Y} \subseteq \mathcal{F} \mid \mathsf{CXp}(X)\} \tag{11}$$

3.3 Global Abductive Explanations and Counterexamples

The definition of AXp's considered until now is *localized*, in that it takes a concrete point $\mathbf{v}$ into account. However, abductive explanations can be defined only with respect to the class, and ignore concrete points in feature space; these are referred to as global AXp's. Following [179], let $\pi : \mathbb{F} \to \{0, 1\}$, represent a term that is a prime implicant of the predicate $[\kappa(\mathbf{x}) = c]$, i.e.,

$$\forall(\mathbf{x} \in \mathbb{F}).\pi(\mathbf{x}) \to (\kappa(\mathbf{x}) = c)$$

---

[16] Clearly, from the definition of WeakAXp (resp. WeakCXp), if WeakAXp($\mathcal{Z}$) (resp. WeakCXp($\mathcal{Z}$)) holds, then WeakAXp($\mathcal{Z}'$) (resp. WeakCXp($\mathcal{Z}'$)) also holds for any superset $\mathcal{Z}'$ of $\mathcal{Z}$. If WeakAXp($\mathcal{Z}$) (resp. WeakCXp($\mathcal{Z}$)) does not hold, then WeakAXp($\mathcal{Z}'$) (resp. WeakCXp($\mathcal{Z}'$)) also does not hold for any subset $\mathcal{Z}'$ of $\mathcal{Z}$.

Table 3. Global abductive explanations and counterexamples for the DL of Fig. 1a.

Global AXp's	$\{\{x_1 = 1\}, \{x_2 = 0, x_4 = 1\}\}$
Counterexamples	$\{x_1 = 0, x_2 = 1\}, \{x_1 = 0, x_4 = 0\}$

(Each literal will be of the form $x_i = u_i$, where u_i is taken from $\mathcal{D}_i$.) The set of literals of π is a global abductive explanation of the prediction c.

We are also interested in the prime implicates of the predicate $[\kappa(\mathbf{x}) = c]$, which will be convenient to represent by $\neg\eta$, where η is a term $\eta : \mathbb{F} \to \{0, 1\}$,

$$\forall(\mathbf{x} \in \mathbb{F}). (\kappa(\mathbf{v}) = c) \to [\neg\eta(\mathbf{x})]$$

This statement can be rewritten as follows,

$$\forall(\mathbf{x} \in \mathbb{F}).\eta(\mathbf{x}) \to (\kappa(\mathbf{v}) \neq c)$$

The set of literals in η is referred to as a *counterexample* (CEx) for the prediction c, and represents the negation of a prime implicate for the predicate $[\kappa(\mathbf{x}) = c]$. Clearly, both global AXp's and CEx's are irreducible (and so subset-minimal).

Example 14. For the DL of Fig. 1a, let $c = 0$, i.e. the predicted class is 0. It is plain that the predicted class is 0 whenever $x_1 = 1$. Thus, $\{(x_1 = 1)\}$ is a global abductive explanation for class $c = 0$. Similarly, if $x_2 = 0$ and $x_4 = 1$, then the predicted class is again guaranteed to be 0. Thus, the other global abductive explanation is $\{(x_2 = 0), (x_4 = 1)\}$. We could use minimal hitting set duality between prime implicants and implicates [307] to list the counterexamples. However, we can also directly reason in terms of the DL to uncover the CEx's, as shown in Table 3.   ◁

(Local) AXp's, CXp's and global AXp's and CEx's reveal important relationships between prime implicants and implicates, as discussed later in Sect. 3.5.

3.4   Duality Results

This section overviews duality results in formal explainability, which have been established in recent years [177,179].

Duality Between AXp's and CXp's. Given the definition of sets of AXp's and CXp's (see (10) and (11)), and by building on Reiter's seminal work [300], recent work [177] proved the following duality between minimal hitting sets:

Proposition 5 (Minimal hitting-set duality between AXp's and CXp's). *Given a local explanation problem $\mathcal{E}$, we have that,*

1. *$\mathcal{X} \subseteq \mathcal{F}$ is an AXp (and so $\mathcal{X} \in \mathbb{A}(\mathcal{E})$) iff $\mathcal{X}$ is an MHS of the CXp's in $\mathbb{C}(\mathcal{E})$.*
2. *$\mathcal{Y} \subseteq \mathcal{F}$ is a CXp (and so $\mathcal{X} \in \mathbb{C}(\mathcal{E})$) iff $\mathcal{Y}$ is an MHS of the AXp's in $\mathbb{A}(\mathcal{E})$.*

We refer to Proposition 5 as MHS duality between AXp's and CXp's. The previous result has been used in more recent papers for enabling the enumeration of explanations [166,174,240].

Example 15. For the DL of Example 5, and the instance $(\mathbf{v}, c) = ((0, 0, 1, 2), 1)$, we have argued (see Examples 9, 10 and 13) that an AXp is $\{1, 4\}$ and that $\{1\}$ and $\{4\}$ are CXp's. Clearly, the AXp is a MHS of the CXp's and vice-versa. Hence, we have listed all the AXp's and CXp's for this instance.   ◁

Furthermore, a consequence of Proposition 5 is the following result:

Proposition 6. *Given a classifier function* $\kappa : \mathbb{F} \to \mathcal{K}$, *defined on a set of features* $\mathcal{F}$, *a feature* $i \in \mathcal{F}$ *is included in some AXp iff* i *is included in some CXp.*

Duality Between Global AXp's and Counterexamples [179]. Another minimal hitting-set duality result, different from Proposition 5, was investigated in earlier work [179], and relates *global* AXp's (i.e. not restricted to be consistent with a specific point $\mathbf{v} \in \mathbb{F}$) and counterexamples (see also Page 28). Given the definition of (global) AXp's and CEx's (see Sect. 3.3), we say that two sets of literals *break* each other if these have inconsistent literals. Furthermore, [179] proves the following result,

Proposition 7. *For a global explanation problem, every CEx breaks every global AXp and vice-versa.*

Example 16. From Example 14, it is plain to conclude (see Table 3) that each global abductive explanation breaks each counterexample and vice-versa.   ◁

3.5   Additional Notes

Relationship with Non-formal Explainability. Past work has shown how formal explanations can serve to assess the quality or rigor of non-formal explanations [170,180,272]. For example, a non-formal explanation can be *corrected* and made subset-minimal, using the non-formal explanation as a starting point for the computation of some other, formal, explanations [170,180]. Moreover, some authors have recently noticed what is referred to as the *disagreement problem in XAI* [216]. From the perspective of formal explainability, differences in explanations just represent different AXp's, which can exist. More important, as discussed in Sect. 6, it is conceptually feasible, and often practically efficient, to navigate the space of explanations.

Literals Based on the Equality Operator. As can be observed, both running examples use literals of the form $(x_i = u_i)$. The same applies to the definitions of (weak) AXp's and CXp's. This need not be the case, as discussed elsewhere [187]. In the case of DTs, more general literals have been associated with explanations [187], e.g. by describing literals using set membership. Nevertheless, and for simplicity, in this document we will use literals that use solely the equality operator.

Prime Implicants and Implicates vs. MUSes and MCSes. For global abductive explanations, the duality result established in earlier work [179] essentially relates prime implicants and implicates of some boolean function $\varsigma : \mathbb{F} \rightarrow \{0, 1\}$, with $\varsigma(\mathbf{x}) = (\kappa(\mathbf{x}) = c)$. In contrast, the duality results established in more recent work [177] relate localized AXp's and CXp's, and can instead be viewed as relating MUSes and MCSes of some inconsistent formula (see Sect. 4 for additional detail). These results reveal a more fine-grained relationship between prime implicants and prime implicates, than what is proposed in earlier work [288, 307].

Formal Explainability and Model-Based Diagnosis. Although we approach formal explainability as a problem of abduction, there are other possible ways to represent the problem of explainability. One well-known example is model-based diagnosis (MBD) [300]. We consider a system description SD consisting of a set of first-order logic statements, and a set of constants Comp, representing the system's components. Each component may or may not be operating correctly, and we use a predicate Ab to indicate whether the component C_j is operating incorrectly (i.e. $\mathsf{Ab}(C_j)$ holds, denoting abnormal behavior), or correctly (i.e. $\neg\mathsf{Ab}(C_j)$ holds, denoting normal behavior). Furthermore, we also assume some observation Obs about the system's expected behavior. In a diagnosis scenario, where Obs disagrees with expected result, it is the case that,

$$\mathsf{SD} \cup \{\neg\mathsf{Ab}(C_1), \neg\mathsf{Ab}(C_2), \ldots, \neg\mathsf{Ab}(C_n)\} \cup \mathsf{Obs} \vDash \bot \tag{12}$$

A conflict set is a (subset)-minimal set CS of Comp such that,

$$\mathsf{SD} \cup \{\neg\mathsf{Ab}(C_i) \mid C_i \in \mathsf{CS}\} \cup \mathsf{Obs} \vDash \bot \tag{13}$$

A diagnosis is a subset-minimal set Δ of Comp such that,

$$\mathsf{SD} \cup \{\neg\mathsf{Ab}(C_i) \mid C_i \in \mathsf{Comp} \setminus \Delta\} \cup \mathsf{Obs} \nvDash \bot \tag{14}$$

A simple reduction of the problem of finding abductive explanations to model based diagnosis, can be organized as follows:

1. SD is given by, $[\![\wedge_{i \in \mathcal{F}} [(x_i = v_i) \vee \mathsf{Ab}(i)]]\!]$, where $[\![\cdot]\!]$ denotes a logic encoding in a suitable logic theory.
2. Obs is given by $[\![\kappa(\mathbf{x}) \neq c]\!]$.

Clearly, if all components operate correctly, then the system description is inconsistent with the stated observation, as expected. (And in this case the stated observation is *not* observing c.) Furthermore, it is easy to see that a

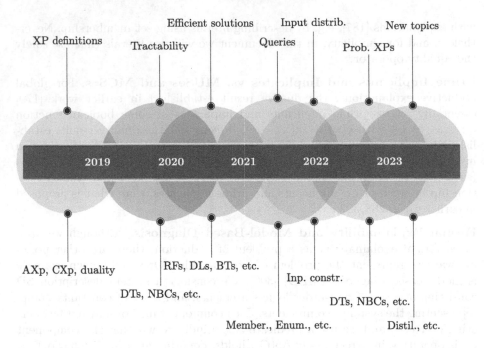

Fig. 5. A timeline of research on formal explainability

minimal conflict is an abductive explanation, and a minimal diagnosis is a contrastive explanation. It should be underlined that the proposed reduction aims at simplicity, but it can also be perceived as somewhat artificial. Clearly, the computation of κ could be deemed part of the system description, such that its operation was forced to be correct. Other variations could be envisioned. Given the progress observed in MBD in recent years [244, 258], it would be interesting to assess the scalability of MBD tools in the context of explainability.

3.6   A Timeline for Formal Explainability

Figure 5 depicts the evolution in time of the main areas of research in formal explainability. The initial focus (in 2019–2020) was on the definition of explanations, duality results, but also approaches for the computation of explanations. The next major effort (in 2020–2021) was on classifiers exhibiting tractable computation of one explanation. This was soon followed by efforts on the efficient computation of explanations even when the computation of explanations was computationally hard (in 2021–2022). More recently, there has been research on addressing different explainability queries (in 2021–2022), tackling input distributions (started in 2022), and computing probabilistic explanations in practice (also started in 2022). There are additional topics of research, which are also discussed in this document. Although there is ongoing research in most areas of research shown in Fig. 5, it is also the case that the most recent topics exhibit more open research questions. The rest of this paper, overviews the areas of research in formal explainability shown in Fig. 5.

4 Computing Explanations

This section covers the computation of explanations, both abductive and contrastive. The focus are on families of classifiers for which computing one explanation is computationally hard. The next section covers families of classifiers for which there exist polynomial-time algorithms for computing one abductive/contrastive explanation.

4.1 Progress in Computing Explanations

Since 2019, there has been steady progress in the practical efficiency of computing formal explanations. Figure 6 summarizes the observed progress. For some families of classifiers, including decision trees, graphs and diagrams, naive bayes classifiers, monotonic classifiers, restricted propositional language classifiers and others, it has been shown that computing one AXp is tractable [84, 165, 166, 186, 188, 239, 240]. For some other families of classifiers, e.g. decision lists and sets, random forests and tree ensembles, it has been established the computational hardness of computing one AXp [174, 191]. However, and also for these families of classifiers, existing logical encodings enable the efficient computation of one AXp [170, 172, 174, 180, 191] in practice. Finally, for a few other families of classifiers [178, 320], computing one AXp is not only computationally hard, but existing algorithms are not efficient in practice, at least for large scale ML models. The next sections analyze some of these results in more detail.

4.2 General Oracle-Based Approach

The main approach for computing explanations is based on exploiting automated reasoners (e.g. SAT, SMT, MILP, etc.) as oracles. We start by analyzing how to decide whether a subset $\mathcal{X}$ of features is a weak AXp. From (4), negating twice, we get:

$$\neg\exists(\mathbf{x} \in \mathbb{F}). \left[\bigwedge_{i\in\mathcal{X}}(x_i = v_i)\right] \wedge (\kappa(\mathbf{x}) \neq c)$$

This corresponds to deciding the consistency of a logic formula, as follows:

$$\neg\, \mathsf{CO}\left(\left[\!\left[\left[\bigwedge_{i\in\mathcal{X}}(x_i = v_i)\right] \wedge (\kappa(\mathbf{x}) \neq c)\right]\!\right]_{\mathcal{T}}\right)$$

The computation of a single AXp or a single CXp can be achieved by adapting existing algorithms provided a few requirements are met. First, reasoning in theory $\mathcal{T}$ is required to be monotone, i.e. *in*consistency is preserved if constraints are added to a set of constraints, and consistency is preserved if constraints are

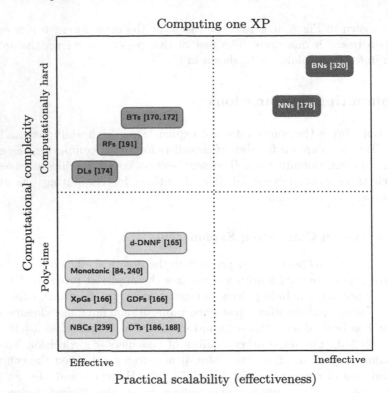

Fig. 6. Progress in formal explainability

removed from a set of constraints. Second, for computing one AXp, the predicate
to consider is:

$$\mathbb{P}_{\text{axp}}(\mathcal{S}; \mathcal{T}, \mathcal{F}, \kappa, \mathbf{v}) \triangleq \neg \mathbf{CO}\Big(\Big[\Big(\bigwedge_{i \in \mathcal{S}}(x_i = v_i)\Big) \wedge (\kappa(\mathbf{x}) \neq c)\Big]\Big) \qquad (15)$$

and for computing one CXp, the predicate to consider is:

$$\mathbb{P}_{\text{cxp}}(\mathcal{S}; \mathcal{T}, \mathcal{F}, \kappa, \mathbf{v}) \triangleq \mathbf{CO}\Big(\Big[\Big(\bigwedge_{i \in \mathcal{F} \setminus \mathcal{S}}(x_i = v_i)\Big) \wedge (\kappa(\mathbf{x}) \neq c)\Big]\Big) \qquad (16)$$

where, the starting set $\mathcal{S}$ can be any set that respects the invariant of the predicate for which it serves as an argument. For example, for computing a AXp, $\mathcal{S}$
can represent any weak AXp, and for computing a CXp, $\mathcal{S}$ can represent any
weak CXp. (Similar to the case of $\mathbf{CO}$, $\mathbb{P}_{\text{axp}}$ and $\mathbb{P}_{\text{cxp}}$ are parameterized by $\mathcal{T}$, $\mathcal{F}$,
κ, $\mathbf{v}$, and also $c = \kappa(\mathbf{v})$. For simplicity, this parameterization will be left implicit
when convenient. Also, the parameterization on $c = \kappa(\mathbf{v})$, given the ones on
κ and $\mathbf{v}$.) Observe that, since (4) and (6) are monotone, then $\mathbb{P}_{\text{axp}}$ and $\mathbb{P}_{\text{cxp}}$
are also monotone with respect to set $\mathcal{S}$.   Moreover, the monotonicity of $\mathbb{P}_{\text{axp}}$
and $\mathbb{P}_{\text{cxp}}$ enables adapting standard algorithms for computing one explanation.

Algorithm 1. Finding one AXp/CXp

Input: Seed $S \subseteq \mathcal{F}$, parameters $\mathbb{P}$, $\mathcal{T}$, $\mathcal{F}$, κ, $\mathbf{v}$
Output: One XP $\mathcal{W}$

1: **procedure** oneXP($S; \mathbb{P}, \mathcal{T}, \mathcal{F}, \kappa, \mathbf{v}$)
2:     $\mathcal{W} \leftarrow S$ ▷ Initialization: $\mathbb{P}(\mathcal{W})$ holds
3:     **for** $i \in S$ **do**   ▷ Loop invariant: $\mathbb{P}(\mathcal{W})$ holds
4:         **if** $\mathbb{P}(\mathcal{W} \setminus \{i\}; \mathcal{T}, \mathcal{F}, \kappa, \mathbf{v})$ **then**
5:             $\mathcal{W} \leftarrow \mathcal{W} \setminus \{i\}$ ▷ Update $\mathcal{W}$ only if $\mathbb{P}(\mathcal{W} \setminus \{i\})$ holds
6:     **return** $\mathcal{W}$ ▷ Returned set $\mathcal{W}$: $\mathbb{P}(\mathcal{W})$ holds

---

Algorithm 1 illustrates one possible approach[17]. For computing one AXp or one CXp, the initial seed set S of Algorithm 1 is set to $\mathcal{F}$. However, as long as the precondition $\mathbb{P}(S)$ holds, then any set $S \subseteq \mathcal{F}$ can be considered.

Example 17. We consider the DT of Fig. 2, and both the computation of one AXp and one CXp when $S = \{3, 4, 5\}$. For the AXp, it is plain that if features $\{3, 4, 5\}$ are fixed, then the prediction does not change (as shown in Table 2a). Table 4 summarizes the execution of Algorithm 1 when computing one AXp and one CXp, starting from a set of literals (i.e. the seed) $S = \{3, 4, 5\}$. (Without additional information, we would start from $S = \mathcal{F}$, and so the table would include a few more lines.) The difference between the two executions is the result of the predicate used.   ◁

In some settings, it may be relevant to compute one smallest AXp or one smallest CXp. Computing one CXp can be achieved by computing a smallest(-cost) MCS. Hence, a MaxSAT/MaxSMT reasoner can be used in this case. For AXp's, and given their relationship with MUSes, a different approach needs to be devised. For a given theory $\mathcal{T}$, let

$$\mathsf{Decide}(\mathcal{X}) \quad := \quad \mathsf{CO}\big(\llbracket \big[\bigwedge_{i \in \mathcal{X}}(x_i = v_i)\big] \wedge (\kappa(\mathbf{x}) \neq c) \rrbracket_{\mathcal{T}}\big) \qquad (17)$$

Furthermore, we assume that $\mathsf{Decide}(\mathcal{X})$ returns a pair (outc, μ), indicating whether the formula is indeed consistent and, if it is, the computed assignment. Algorithm 2 illustrates the use of dualization for computing one smallest AXp,

---

[17] This algorithm is referred to as the *deletion-based* algorithm [79], but it can be traced back to the work of Valiant [341] (and some authors [197] argue that it is implicit in works from the 19th century [259]). Although variants of Algorithm 1 are most often used in practical settings, there are several alternative algorithms that can also be used, including QuickXplain [198], Progression [243], or even insertion-based [323], among others [34, 44]. As illustrated by Algorithm 1, it is now known that most of these algorithms can be formalized in an abstract way, thus allowing them to be used to solve subset-minimal problems when these problems can be represented by monotonic predicates [245]. As argued earlier, predicates $\mathbb{P}_{\mathrm{axp}}$ (see Eq. 15) and $\mathbb{P}_{\mathrm{cxp}}$ (see Eq. 16) are both monotonic.

Table 4. Computation of 1 AXp and 1 CXp starting from seed $\mathcal{S} = \{3, 4, 5\}$. The partial truth tables in Tables 2a and 2b can be used for computing both $\mathbb{P}_{\text{axp}}$ and $\mathbb{P}_{\text{cxp}}$. Table 2a serves to validate whether the prediction remains unchanged. Table 2b serves to assess whether there are points in feature space for which the prediction changes.

$\mathcal{W}$	i	$\mathbb{P}_{\text{axp}}$	Decision
$\{3, 4, 5\}$	3	0	Keep 3
$\{3, 4, 5\}$	4	1	Drop 4
$\{3, 5\}$	5	0	Keep 5

(a) Finding 1 AXp

$\mathcal{W}$	i	$\mathbb{P}_{\text{cxp}}$	Decision
$\{3, 4, 5\}$	3	1	Drop 3
$\{4, 5\}$	4	1	Drop 4
$\{5\}$	5	0	Keep 5

(b) Finding 1 CXp

Algorithm 2. Finding one smallest AXp

Input: Algorithm parameterized by $\mathcal{T}, \mathcal{F}, \kappa, \mathbf{v}$
Output: Smallest AXp $\mathcal{M}$

```
1: procedure minXP
2:     H ← ∅
3:     while true do
4:         M ← MinimumHS(H)
5:         (outc, μ) ← Decide(M; T, F, κ, v)
6:         if not outc then
7:             return M
8:         else
9:             L ← PickFalseLits(F \ M, μ)
10:            H ← H ∪ L
```

---

and builds on earlier work on computing smallest MUSes [182]. Any minimum-size hitting set such that the picked (fixed) features represent a weak AXp must be a smallest AXp.

Relationship with MUSes and MCSes. We can relate the computation of AXp's and CXp's respectively with the extraction of MUSes and MCSes. We construct a formula $\varphi = \mathcal{B} \cup \mathcal{S}$ in some theory $\mathcal{T}$ where the background knowledge $\mathcal{B}$ corresponds to,

$$\mathcal{B} \triangleq [\![\kappa(\mathbf{x}) \neq c]\!]_{\mathcal{T}} \tag{18}$$

and the soft constraints $\mathcal{S}$ correspond to,

$$\mathcal{S} \triangleq \{[\![x_i = v_i]\!]_{\mathcal{T}} \mid i \in \mathcal{F}\} \tag{19}$$

Clearly, $\varphi = \mathcal{B} \cup \mathcal{S}$ is inconsistent, i.e. if all features are fixed, then the prediction must be c. As a result, an MUS $\mathcal{U}$ of $\mathcal{B} \cup \mathcal{S}$ (i.e. a subset of $\mathcal{U}$ of $\mathcal{S}$) is such that $\mathcal{U} \cup \mathcal{S}$ is inconsistent. Thus, $\mathcal{U}$ represents a subset-minimal set of features which, if fixed, ensure inconsistency (and so the prediction must be c); hence, $\mathcal{U}$ is an AXp. Similarly, an MCS $\mathcal{C}$ of $\mathcal{B} \cup \mathcal{S}$ (i.e. a subset of $\mathcal{C}$ of $\mathcal{S}$) is such that $\mathcal{B} \cup (\mathcal{S} \setminus \mathcal{C})$ is consistent. Thus, $\mathcal{C}$ represents a subset-minimal set of features which, if allowed to change their, ensure consistency (and so the prediction can be different from c); hence, $\mathcal{C}$ is a CXp.

4.3 Explaining Decision Lists

This section details the computation of AXp's/CXp's in the case of DLs. Furthermore, it is briefly mentioned the relationship with computing explanations for DSs and DTs.

Explaining DLs. The computation of AXp's has been shown to be computationally hard, both for DLs and DSs [174]. As a result, the solution approach is to follow the general approach detailed in Sect. 4.2. However, we will devise a propositional encoding and use SAT solvers as NP oracles.

To illustrate the computation of explanations (both AXp's and CXp's), we consider a DL with the following structure:

$$
\begin{array}{llll}
R_1: & \text{IF} & (\tau_1) & \text{THEN} \quad d_1 \\
R_2: & \text{ELSE IF} & (\tau_2) & \text{THEN} \quad d_2 \\
& \cdots & & \\
R_j: & \text{ELSE IF} & (\tau_j) & \text{THEN} \quad d_j \\
& \cdots & & \\
R_n: & \text{ELSE IF} & (\tau_n) & \text{THEN} \quad d_n \\
R_{\text{DEF}}: & \text{ELSE} & & \text{THEN} \quad d_{n+1}
\end{array}
$$

where $d_r \in \mathcal{K}, r = 1, \ldots, n+1$, and τ_j is a conjunction of literals, or in general some logic formula.

Let $[\![\phi]\!]_{\mathcal{T}}$ denote the propositional CNF encoding of ϕ. This encoding can introduce not only a number of additional clauses, but also fresh propositional variables. The resulting formula will be represented by $\mathfrak{E}_\phi(z_1, \ldots)$, where z_1 is a propositional variable taking value 1 iff ϕ takes value 1. To develop a propositional CNF encoding, we let $\mathfrak{E}_{\tau_j}(t_j, \ldots)$ represent the clauses associated with $[\![\tau_j]\!]_{\mathcal{T}}$, i.e. the propositional CNF encoding of $\tau_j, j = 1, \ldots, n$, and where t_j represents a new propositional variable that takes value 1 only in points of feature space where τ_j is true. (Additional propositional variables may be used, and these are represented by $\ldots$ at this stage.) Let the target class be c and define the propositional constant e_j to be 1 iff d_j matches c.

Moreover, since literals may require propositional encodings, let $\mathfrak{E}_{x_i = v_i}$ $(l_i, \ldots)$ represent the clauses associated $[\![x_i = v_i]\!]_{\mathcal{T}}, i = 1, \ldots, m$, and where l_i represents a new propositional variable that takes value 1 only in points of feature space where $x_i = v_i$. (Additional propositional variables may be used, and these are represented by $\ldots$ at this stage. Also, we can envision re-using and sharing common encodings; this will be discussed in Example 18 below.)

Clearly, for some point **x** in feature space, the prediction changes if it is the case that,

1. For τ_j, with $e_j = 0$ and $1 \leq j \leq n$, it is the case that τ_j is true, and for any $1 \leq k < j$, with $e_k = 1$, τ_k is false:

$$\left[f_j \leftrightarrow \left(t_j \wedge \bigwedge\nolimits_{1 \leq k < j, e_k = 1} \neg t_k \right) \right]$$

where f_j is a new propositional variable, denoting that rule j with a different prediction would fire (and so it would *flip* its previous status). (Clearly, if some other rule R_r, τ_r with $r < j$ and $e_r = 0$, fires then the prediction will also change as intended, and this is covered by some other constraint. Hence, there is no need to account for such rules.)

2. Moreover, we require that at least one f_j, with $e_j = 0$ and $1 \leq j \leq n$, to be true:

$$\left(\bigvee\nolimits_{1 \leq j \leq n, e_j = 0} f_j \right)$$

Given the above, we now organize the propositional encoding in two components, one composed of soft clauses and the other composed of hard clauses:

– The set of soft clauses is given by:

$$\mathcal{S} \triangleq \{(l_i), i = 1, \ldots, m\} \tag{20}$$

– The set of hard clauses is given by:

$$\mathcal{B} \triangleq \bigwedge\nolimits_{1 \leq i \leq m} \mathfrak{E}_{x_i = v_i}(l_i, \ldots) \wedge \bigwedge\nolimits_{1 \leq j \leq n} \mathfrak{E}_{\tau_j}(t_j, \ldots) \wedge$$

$$\bigwedge\nolimits_{1 \leq j \leq n, e_j = 0} \left(f_j \leftrightarrow \left(t_j \wedge \bigwedge\nolimits_{1 \leq k < j, e_k = 1} \neg t_k \right) \right) \wedge$$

$$\left(\bigvee\nolimits_{1 \leq j \leq n, e_j = 0} f_j \right) \tag{21}$$

It is plain that $\mathcal{B} \cup \mathcal{S}$ represents an inconsistent propositional formula. Any MUS of $\mathcal{B} \cup \mathcal{S}$ is a subset of $\mathcal{S}$, and represents one AXp. Moreover, any MCS is also a subset of $\mathcal{S}$, and represents one CXp. As argued earlier, AXp's are MHSes of CXp's and vice-versa [56,177,300]. This observation also means that we can use *any* algorithm for MUS/MCS extraction/enumeration for computing explanations of DLs [246].

Finally, the propositional encoding proposed above differs slightly from the one proposed in earlier work [174], offering a more streamlined encoding.

Example 18. Let us investigate how we can encode the computation of one AXp for the DL running example (see Fig. 1). The soft clauses are given by,

$$\mathcal{S} = \{l_1, l_2, l_3, l_4\}$$

where l_i is associated with $[\![x_i = v_i]\!]_T$, i.e. it is one of the variables used in $\mathfrak{E}_{x_i = v_i}$. For simplicity, there is no need to encode $x_i = v_i$ for $i = 1, 2, 3$, with

$\mathbf{v} = (0, 0, 1, 2)$, and so we let $l_1 \leftrightarrow \neg x_1$, $l_2 \leftrightarrow \neg x_2$, and $l_3 \leftrightarrow x_3$. However, for $x_4 = 2$, a dedicated propositional encoding is required. Hence, we use three propositional variables, $\{x_{41}, x_{42}, x_{43}\}$, and pick a one hot encoding to get $\mathfrak{E}_{\tau_3}(l_4, \ldots) \triangleq l_4 \leftrightarrow x_{43} \wedge \text{EqualsOne}(x_{41}, x_{42}, x_{43})$, where $x_{43} = 1$ iff $x_4 = 1$. There are many propositional encodings for $\text{EqualsOne}(x_{41}, x_{42}, x_{43})$ [55] constraints. One simple solution is,

$$(\neg x_{41} \vee \neg x_{42}) \wedge (\neg x_{41} \vee \neg x_{43}) \wedge (\neg x_{42} \vee \neg x_{43}) \wedge (x_{41} \vee x_{42} \vee x_{43})$$

For each rule we need to encode τ_j. It is immediate to get $t_1 \leftrightarrow x_1$ for τ_1, and $t_2 \leftrightarrow x_2$ for τ_2. With respect to τ_3, we can use the same encoding as above (for x_4), and so we get $t_3 \leftrightarrow x_{42}$. (It is clear that the constraints for encoding the possible values of x_4 would be the same as before, and so there is no need to replicate them.)

Furthermore, we must encode the change of prediction. Since the prediction for $(0, 0, 1, 2)$ is 1, then we are interested in rules R_1 and R_3, since these are the only options to change the prediction. As a result, we get,

$$f_1 \leftrightarrow t_1$$
$$f_3 \leftrightarrow (t_3 \wedge \neg t_2)$$

indicating that the prediction changes if either t_1 is true (i.e. rule R_1 fires), or t_3 is true *and* t_2 is false (i.e. rule R_3 fires and rule R_2 does not fire, and earlier rules are already covered by other constraints). Finally, we need the constraint $(f_1 \vee f_3)$, to enforce that a change of prediction will take place.

Given the above, we get that,

$$\begin{aligned} \mathcal{B} = &(l_1 \leftrightarrow \neg x_1) \wedge (l_2 \leftrightarrow \neg x_2) \wedge (l_3 \leftrightarrow x_3) \wedge (l_4 \leftrightarrow x_{43}) \wedge \\ &\text{EqualsOne}(x_{41}, x_{42}, x_{43}) \wedge \\ &(t_1 \leftrightarrow x_1) \wedge (t_2 \leftrightarrow x_2) \wedge (t_3 \leftrightarrow x_{42}) \wedge \\ &(f_1 \leftrightarrow t_1) \wedge (f_3 \leftrightarrow (t_3 \wedge \neg t_2)) \wedge (f_1 \vee f_3) \end{aligned}$$

Moreover, and by inspection, the tuple $(\mathcal{S}, \mathcal{B})$ can be simplified to,

$$\mathcal{S} = \{\neg x_1, \neg x_2, x_3, x_{43}\}$$

and,

$$\mathcal{B} = \text{EqualsOne}(x_{41}, x_{42}, x_{43}) \wedge (f_1 \leftrightarrow x_1) \wedge (f_3 \leftrightarrow (x_{42} \wedge \neg x_2)) \wedge (f_1 \vee f_3)$$

It is apparent that $\mathcal{B} \cup \mathcal{S}$ is inconsistent. Finally, we can also observe that for tuple $(\mathcal{S}', \mathcal{B})$ with,

$$\mathcal{S}' = \{\neg x_1, x_{43}\}$$
$$\mathcal{B} = \text{EqualsOne}(x_{41}, x_{42}, x_{43}) \wedge (f_1 \leftrightarrow x_1) \wedge (f_3 \leftrightarrow (x_{42} \wedge \neg x_2)) \wedge (f_1 \vee f_3)$$

$\mathcal{B} \cup \mathcal{S}'$ is still inconsistent. Thus, $\mathcal{S}' = \{\neg x_1, x_{43}\}$ is an unsatisfiable subset (which we can prove to be irreducible), and so $\mathcal{X} = \{1, 4\}$ is a weak AXp (which we can prove to be an AXp). $\triangleleft$

Existing results indicate that the computation of explanations for DLs is very efficient in practice [174].

4.4 From DLs to DTs and DSs

Explaining DTs as DLs. A conceptually straightforward approach for explaining DTs is to represent a DT as a DL. Hence, the propositional encoding proposed above for explaining DLs can also be used for explaining DTs. Nevertheless, as argued in Sect. 5.1, in the case of DTs there are polynomial time algorithms for computing one abductive explanation, and there are polynomial time algorithms for enumerating all the contrastive explanations.

The Case of DSs. The fact that DSs are unordered raises a number of technical difficulties, including the fact that, if there can be rules that predict different classes and fire on the same input, then the classifier does not compute a function. This is referred to as *overlap* [181]. If the rules predicting each class are represented as a DNF, then one call to an NP oracle suffices to decide whether overlap exists.

Let a DS be represented by a set of DNF formulas, one for each class in $\mathcal{K}$. Moreover, let z_r represent the value computed for DNF r, which predicts class $c_r \in \mathcal{K}$. There exists *no* overlap is the following condition does *not* hold:

$$\sum_{r=1}^{K} z_r > 1$$

If we also want to ensure that there is a prediction for any point in feature space, then we can instead require that the following constraint is inconsistent:

$$\sum_{r=1}^{K} z_r \neq 1 \tag{22}$$

i.e. we want the sum to be equal to 1 on each point of feature space. (Clearly, the constraint above must be inconsistent given the logic encoding of the classifier. The actual encoding of each z_r will depend on how the DNFs are represented, and there is no restriction of considering purely boolean classifiers.)

Under the standard assumption that (22) is inconsistent, then the encoding proposed for DLs can be adapted to the case of DSs. We will have to encode each term (i.e. each unordered rule), and then encode the disjunction of terms for each DNF. We will briefly outline a propositional encoding for computing abductive (and contrastive) explanations. The approach differs from the DL case since we do not have order in the rules. Hence, each class is analyzed as a DNF. As usual, we consider an instance $(\mathbf{v}, c_s)$, where $c_s \in \mathcal{K}$ is the predicted class. The constraints for the encodings are organized as follows:

1. The DNF r of class $c_r \in \mathcal{K}$, it is a disjunction of n_r terms $\tau_{rj}, r = 1, \ldots, n_r$.
2. Each term τ_{rj} is encoded into $\mathfrak{E}_{\tau_{rj}}(t_{rj}, \ldots)$, such that $t_j = 1$ iff the term τ_{rj} takes value 1.
3. The literals of the form $(x_i = v_i)$ will be encoded into the clauses $\mathfrak{E}_{x_i=v_i}(l_i, \ldots)$.

   (As mentioned earlier in this section in the case of DLs, the encoding from the original feature variables to propositional variables is assumed in all these encodings.)

4. The soft clauses will be (l_i), $i = 1, \ldots, m$.
5. A class c_r is picked iff $p_r = 1$, where p_i is a fresh propositional variable. Hence, we define p_r, for class c_r as follows: $p_r \leftrightarrow \left(\vee_{j=1}^{n_r} t_{rj} \right)$
6. The prediction changes if $p_s = 0$.

   (Observe that we could instead introduce another propositional variable s, defined as follows $s \leftrightarrow \vee_{c_r \in \mathcal{K} \backslash \{c_s\}} p_r$, such that $s = 1$ would mean that the prediction changes. However, this is unnecessary.)

Given the above, we can write down a propositional encoding for a DS classifier which respects (22). The set of soft clauses is given by:

$$\mathcal{S} \triangleq \{(l_i), i = 1, \ldots, m\} \tag{23}$$

The set of hard clauses is given by:

$$\mathcal{B} \triangleq \bigwedge_{1 \le i \le m} \mathfrak{E}_{x_i = v_i}(l_i, \ldots) \wedge \bigwedge_{1 \le r \le K} \bigwedge_{1 \le j \le n_r} \mathfrak{E}_{\tau_{rj}}(t_{rj}, \ldots) \wedge$$

$$\bigwedge_{1 \le j \le K} p_r \leftrightarrow \left(\vee_{j=1}^{n_r} t_{rj} \right) \tag{24}$$

4.5   Explaining Neural Networks

To illustrate the modeling flexibility of the approach proposed in the previous section, let us develop an MILP/SMT encoding for the problem of computing one AXp for a neural network. The encoding to be used is based on the MILP representation of NNs proposed in earlier work [123] and is illustrated with the NN running example of Fig. 3. The MILP encoding is shown in Fig. 7a.

To decide whether a set $\mathcal{X} \subseteq \mathcal{F}$ is a weak AXp, we would have to decide the *inconsistency* of (adapted from Fig. 7a):

$$\bigwedge_{i \in \mathcal{X}} (x_i = v_i) \wedge$$

$$[(x_1 + x_2 - 0.5 = t_1 - s_1) \wedge (z_1 = 1 \rightarrow t_1 \le 0) \wedge (z_1 = 0 \rightarrow s_1 \le 0) \wedge$$

$$(o_1 = (t_1 > 0)) \wedge (t_1 \ge 0) \wedge (s_1 \ge 0)] \wedge [(o_1 \ne 1)] \tag{25}$$

where $\mathcal{D}_{x_1} = \mathcal{D}_{x_2} = \mathcal{D}_{z_1} = \mathcal{D}_{z_2} = \{0, 1\}$ and $\mathcal{D}_{s_1} = \mathcal{D}_{t_1} = \mathbb{R}$. (The definition of domains introduces a mild abuse of notation, since the indices used are the names of feature variables and not the names of features. However, the meaning is clear.)

Example 19. To compute an AXp for the NN running example, we could iteratively call an MILP solver on (25), starting from $\mathcal{F}$ and iteratively removing features (see Algorithm 1). However, the very simple encoding for the example NN allows us to analyze the constraints without calling an MILP reasoner. The analysis is summarized in Fig. 7. We first consider allowing x_1 to take any value. In this case, this means allowing x_1 to take value 0 (besides the value 1 it is assigned to). As can be observed (see Fig. 7b), the prediction is allowed to change (actually, in this case it is forced to change). Hence, the feature 1 must

$$x_1 + x_2 - 0.5 = t_1 - s_1$$
$$z_1 = 1 \rightarrow t_1 \le 0$$
$$z_1 = 0 \rightarrow s_1 \le 0$$
$$o_1 = (t_1 > 0)$$
$$x_1, x_2, z_1, o_1 \in \{0, 1\}$$
$$t_1, s_1 \ge 0$$

(a) Logic representation [123]

$$1 + 0 - 0.5 = 0.5 - 0$$
$$1 \lor 0.5 \le 0$$
$$0 \lor 0 \le 0$$
$$1 = (0.5 > 0)$$
$$x_1 = 1, x_2 = 0, z_1 = 0, o_1 = 1$$
$$t_1 = 0.5, s_1 = 0$$

(b) Instance $(\mathbf{x}, c) = ((1, 0), 1)$

$$0 + 0 - 0.5 = 0 - 0.0$$
$$0 \lor 0 \le 0$$
$$1 \lor 0.5 \le 0$$
$$0 = (0 > 0)$$
$$x_1 = 0, x_2 = 0, z_1 = 1, o_1 = 0$$
$$t_1 = 0, s_1 = 0.5$$

(c) Checking $(x_1, x_2) = (0, 0)$

$$1 + 1 - 0.5 = 1.5 - 0$$
$$1 \lor 1.5 \le 0$$
$$0 \lor 0 \le 0$$
$$1 = (1.5 > 0)$$
$$x_1 = 1, x_2 = 1, z_1 = 0, o_1 = 1$$
$$t_1 = 1.5, s_1 = 0$$

(d) Checking $(x_1, x_2) = (1, 1)$

Fig. 7. Computing one AXp with an NN

be included in the AXp. In contrast, by changing x_2 from 0 to 1, the prediction cannot change (see Fig. 7d). This means that, if the other features remain unchanged, the prediction is 1, no matter the value taken by x_2. Hence, the feature 2 is dropped from the working set of features. As a result, the AXp in this case is $\mathcal{X} = \{1\}$.   ◁

The computation of AXp's in the case of NNs was investigated in earlier work on computing formal explanations [178]. However, and in contrast with the families of classifiers studied earlier in this section, the computation of AXp's/CXp's in the case of NNs scales up to a few tens of neurons. It is plain that the ability to efficiently compute AXp's/CXp's for NNs will track the ability to reason efficiently about NNs. Although there have been steady improvements on reasoners for NNs [202, 203, 229], it is also the case that scalability continues to be a challenge.

4.6   Other Families of Classifiers

Tree Ensembles (TEs). Based on the general approach detailed in Sect. 4.2, there have been proposals for computing explanations for boosted trees (BTs) [170, 172, 180], and random forests (RFs) [66, 191]. For RFs, it has been shown that the decision problem of computing one AXp is complete for D^P [191]. Nevertheless, the proposed encodings [191], which are purely propositional, enable computing AXp's/CXp's for RFs with thousands of nodes. At present, such RF sizes are representative of what is commonly deployed in practical applications. It should be noted that the existing propositional encodings consider the organization of RFs as proposed originally [70], i.e. the class is picked by majority voting. For other ways of selecting the chosen class, the encoding is not purely propositional. For BTs, the most recent results also confirm the scalability to classifiers deployed in practical settings.

Bayesian Network Classifiers. The explanations of Bayesian network classifiers (BNCs) have been studied since 2018 [320,321]. Whereas in the case of NNs, SMT and MILP solvers were used, and followed the approach outlined in Sect. 4.2, in the case of BNCs, explanations are computed using compilation into a canonical representation (see Sect. 4.7 below). However, and similarly to NNs, scalability is currently a challenge.

4.7   An Alternative – Compilation-Based Approaches

One alternative to the computation of AXp's and CXp's as proposed in the previous sections is to compile the explanations into some canonical representation, from which the explanations can then be queried for. Such compilation-based approaches have been studied in a number of works [96–99,319–321].

Past work has focused on binary classification with binary features. The extension to non-binary classification and non-binary features raises a number of challenges. Another limitation is that canonical representations are worst-case exponential, and the worst-case behavior is commonly observed. For example, the performance gap between the two approaches in solving related problems is often significant [99,187].

5   Tractable Explanations

Since 2020, several tractability results have been established in formal explainability [84,165,166,186,187,239,240]. Most of these tractability results concern the computation of one explanation, and apply both to computing one AXp or one CXp [84]. However, there are examples of families of classifiers for which there exist polynomial delay algorithms for enumeration of explanations [239], or even for computing all (contrastive) explanations [166,187].

5.1   Decision Trees

Given a classification problem for a DT, and an instance $(\mathbf{v}, c)$, a set of literals is consistent with c as long there is at least one inconsistent literal for any path that predicts a class other than c.

Abductive Explanations. Given the observation above, a simple algorithm for computing one AXp is organized as follows:

1. For each path Q_k with prediction other than c, let I_k denote the features which take values inconsistent with the path.
2. Pick a subset-minimal hitting set H of all the sets I_k.

3. Clearly, as long as the features in H are fixed, then at least one literal in each path Q_k will be inconsistent, and so the prediction is guaranteed to be c.

It is well-known that there exists simple polynomial time algorithms for computing one subset-minimal hitting set [112]. Hence, the proposed algorithm runs in polynomial time.

Example 20. For the DT of the second running example (see Fig. 2a), and instance $(\mathbf{v}, c) = ((0, 0, 1, 0, 1), 1)$, we have the following sets:

- $Q_1 = \langle 1, 2, 4, 6 \rangle$, with set $I_1 = \{3\}$.
- $Q_2 = \langle 1, 2, 4, 7, 10, 14 \rangle$, with set $I_2 = \{5\}$.
- $Q_3 = \langle 1, 2, 5, 8, 12 \rangle$, with set $I_3 = \{2, 5\}$.

Clearly, an MHS of $\{I_1, I_2, I_3\}$ is $\{3, 5\}$, which represents a weak AXp for the given instance. It is simple to conclude that it is irreducible, and so it effectively represents an AXp. In addition, it is also plain to establish that there are no other AXp's. Finally, it should be noted that the abductive explanation computed above concurs with what was presented in Example 11, where a truth-table was used to justify the abductive explanations. (Of course, construction of the truth table would not in general be realistic, whereas the algorithm proposed above runs in linear time on the size of the DT.)   ◁

The simple algorithm described above was first proposed in earlier work [186]. Nevertheless, one can envision other algorithms, which offer more flexibility [187]. (For example, the algorithm described below allows for constraints on the inputs, in cases for which not all points in feature space are possible.)

Abductive Explanations by Propositional Horn Encoding. A more flexible approach (see Sect. 8) is the representation of the problem of computing one AXp as the problem of computing one MUS (or one MCS) of an inconsistent Horn formula[18]. There are simple encodings that are worst-case quadratic on the size of the DT [187]. We describe one encoding that is linear on the size of the DT [187].

Let us consider a path P_k, with prediction $c \in \mathcal{K}$. Moreover, let $\mathcal{Q}$ denote the paths yielding a prediction other than c. Since the prediction is c, then any path in $\mathcal{Q}$ has some feature for which the allowed values are inconsistent with $\mathbf{v}$. We say that the paths in $\mathcal{Q}$ are *blocked*. (To be clear, a path is blocked as long as some of its literals are inconsistent.)

For each feature i associated with some node of path P_k, introduce a variable u_i. u_i denotes whether feature i is deemed *universal*, i.e. feature i is not included in the AXp that we will be computing. (Our goal is to find a subset maximal set of features that can be deemed universal, such that all the paths resulting in a prediction other than c remain blocked. Alternatively, we seek to find a subset-minimal set of features to declare non-universal or fixed, such that paths

---

[18] Since we have tractability, the formulation can be geared towards computing one MUS or instead computing one MCS.

with a prediction other than c remain blocked.) Furthermore, for each DT node r, introduce variable b_r, denoting that all sub-paths from node r to any terminal node labeled $d \in \mathcal{K} \setminus \{c\}$ must be blocked, i.e. some literal in the sub-path must remain inconsistent. (Our goal is to guarantee that all paths to terminal nodes labeled $d \in \mathcal{K} \setminus \{c\}$ remain blocked even when some variables are allowed to become universal.)

The soft clauses $\mathcal{S}$ are given by $\{(u_i) \mid i \in \mathcal{F}\}$, i.e. one would ideally want to declare universal as many features as possible, thus minimizing the size of the explanation. (As noted above, we will settle for finding subset-maximal solutions.) We describe next the hard constraints $\mathcal{H}$ for representing consistent assignments to the u_i variables.

We proceed to describe the proposed Horn encoding. Here, we opt to describe first the Horn encoding for computing one AXp[19]. The hard constraints are created as follows:

B1. For the root node r, add the constraint $\top \rightarrow b_r$.
(The root node must be blocked.)

B2. For each terminal node r with prediction c, add the constraint $\top \rightarrow b_r$.
(Each terminal node with prediction c is also blocked. Also, observe that this condition is on the node, not on the path.)

B3. For each terminal node r with prediction $d \in \mathcal{K} \setminus \{c\}$, add the constraint $b_r \rightarrow \bot$.
(Terminal nodes predicting $d \neq c$ cannot be blocked. Also, and as above, observe that this condition is on the node, not on the path.)

B4. For a node r associated with feature i, and connected to the child node s, such that the edge value(s) is(are) *consistent* with the value of feature i in $\mathbf{v}$, add the constraint $b_r \rightarrow b_s$.
(If all sub-paths from node r must be blocked, then all sub-paths from node s must all be blocked, independently of the value taken by feature i.)

B5. For a node r associated with feature i, and connected to the child node s, such that the edge value(s) is(are) *inconsistent* with the value of feature i in $\mathbf{v}$, add the constraint $b_r \wedge u_i \rightarrow b_s$.
(In this case, the blocking condition along an edge inconsistent with the value of feature i in $\mathbf{v}$ is only relevant if the feature is deemed universal.)

Example 21. For the running example of Fig. 2a, let $(\mathbf{v}, c) = ((0, 0, 1, 0, 1), 1)$. As dictated by the proposed Horn encoding, two sets of variables are introduced. The first set represents the variables denoting whether a feature is universal, corresponding to 5 variables: $\{u_1, u_2, u_3, u_4, u_5\}$. The second set represents the variables denoting whether a node is blocked, corresponding to 15 variables: $\{b_1, b_2, b_3, b_4, b_5, b_6, b_7, b_8, b_9, b_{10}, b_{11}, b_{12}, b_{13}, b_{14}, b_{15}\}$. The resulting propositional Horn encoding contains hard ($\mathcal{H}$) and soft ($\mathcal{B}$) constraints, and it is organized as shown in Table 5.

---

[19] As discussed in recent work [187], different types of AXp's can be computed in the case of DTs; we specifically consider the so-called path-unrestricted AXp's.

Table 5. Horn clauses for the DT of Fig. 2a for computing one AXp with $(\mathbf{v}, c) = ((0, 0, 1, 0, 1), 1)$

Hard constraint type	Horn clauses
B1	$\{(b_1)\}$
B2	$\{(b_3), (b_9), (b_{11}), (b_{13}), (b_{15})\}$
B3	$\{(\neg b_6), (\neg b_{12}), (\neg b_{14})\}$
B4	$\{(b_1 \rightarrow b_2), (b_2 \rightarrow b_4), (b_4 \rightarrow b_7), (b_5 \rightarrow b_8),$ $(b_7 \rightarrow b_{10}), (b_8 \rightarrow b_{13}), (b_{10} \rightarrow b_{15})\}$
B5	$\{(b_1 \wedge u_1 \rightarrow b_3), (b_2 \wedge u_2 \rightarrow b_5), (b_4 \wedge u_3 \rightarrow b_6),$ $(b_5 \wedge u_4 \rightarrow b_9), (b_7 \wedge u_4 \rightarrow b_{11}), (b_8 \wedge u_5 \rightarrow b_{12}),$ $(b_{10} \wedge u_5 \rightarrow b_{14})\}$
Soft constraints, $\mathcal{S}$	$\{(u_1), (u_2), (u_3), (u_4), (u_5)\}$

It is easy to see that, if $u_1 = u_2 = u_3 = u_4 = u_5 = 1$, then $\mathcal{B}$ is falsified. Concretely, $(b_1) \wedge (b_1 \rightarrow b_2) \wedge (b_2 \rightarrow b_4) \wedge (u_3) \wedge (b_4 \wedge u_3 \rightarrow b_6) \wedge (\neg b_6) \nvDash \bot$. The goal is then to find a maximal subset $\mathcal{M}$ of $\mathcal{S}$ such that $\mathcal{M} \cup \mathcal{B}$ is consistent. (Alternatively, the algorithm finds a minimal set $\mathcal{C} \subseteq \mathcal{S}$, such that $\mathcal{S} \setminus \mathcal{C} \cup \mathcal{H}$ is consistent.) For this concrete example, one such minimal set is obtained by picking $u_1 = u_2 = u_4 = 1$ and $u_3 = u_5 = 0$, and by setting $b_1 = b_2 = b_3 = b_4 = b_5 = b_7 = b_8 = b_9 = b_{10} = b_{11} = b_{13} = b_{15} = 1$ and $b_6 = b_{12} = b_{14} = 0$. Hence, all clauses are satisfied, and so $\{3, 5\}$ is a weak AXp. An MCS extractor [241, 256, 257] would confirm that $\{3, 5\}$ is subset-minimal, and so it is an AXp.   ◁

Contrastive Explanations. In the case of DTs, recent work devised efficient polynomial-time algorithms for computing (in fact listing all) contrastive explanations [166]. The main ideas can be summarized as follows:

- For each path Q_k with prediction other than c, list the features with literals inconsistent with the instance as set I_k.
- Remove any set I_l that is a superset of some other set I_k.
- Each of the remaining sets I_k is a CXp.

Since the number of paths is polynomial (in fact linear) on the number of tree nodes, then we have a polynomial time algorithm for listing all contrastive explanations.

Example 22. Using the sets I_k computed in Example 20, we observe that I_3 is a superset of I_2, and so it has to be dropped. As a result, I_1 and I_2 each represent an CXp. Furthermore, we can confirm again Proposition 5, since the only AXp for this instance, i.e. $\{3, 5\}$ is an MHS of the two CXp's, i.e. $\{3\}$ and $\{5\}$, and vice-versa.   ◁

As noted in recent work, the fact that there exists a polynomial time algorithm to enumerate all CXp's, implies that are quasi-polynomial algorithms for the enumeration of AXp's [166,187]. This is discussed in further detail in Sect. 6.1.

Moreover, and although the Horn encoding proposed earlier for computing one AXp could also be used for computing one CXp, there is no real need for that, given the simplicity of the algorithm for enumerating all CXp's of a DT.

5.2   Monotonic Classifiers

This section illustrates how one AXp (or CXp) can be computed in the case of monotonic classifiers. In the case of classifiers for which computing the prediction runs in polynomial time on the size of the classifier, recent work proved that there exist polynomial time algorithms both for computing one AXp and one CXp [240]. The algorithms are dual of each other; as a result, we will just detail the computation of one AXp. Nevertheless, we present the pseudo-code for both algorithms. For computing one AXp, we maintain two vectors, one yielding a lower bound on the computed class, i.e. $\mathbf{v}_L$, and another yielding an upper bound on the computed class, i.e. $\mathbf{v}_U$. In the case of one AXp, the algorithm requires that $\kappa(\mathbf{v}_L) = \kappa(\mathbf{v}_U) = \kappa(\mathbf{v})$. The goal is to allow features to take any possible value in their domain, i.e. to make them *universal* and so we will use an auxiliary function FreeAttr:

$$\mathbf{v}_L \leftarrow (v_{L_1}, \ldots, \lambda(i), \ldots, v_{L_N})$$
$$\mathbf{v}_U \leftarrow (v_{U_1}, \ldots, \mu(i), \ldots, v_{U_N})$$
$$(\mathcal{A}, \mathcal{B}) \leftarrow (\mathcal{A} \setminus \{i\}, \mathcal{B} \cup \{i\})$$
return $(\mathbf{v}_L, \mathbf{v}_U, \mathcal{A}, \mathcal{B})$

If making a feature universal allows the prediction to change, then the feature must be *fixed* again (to the value dictated by $\mathbf{v}$), and for that we use the auxiliary function FixAttr:

$$\mathbf{v}_L \leftarrow (v_{L_1}, \ldots, v_i, \ldots, v_{L_N})$$
$$\mathbf{v}_U \leftarrow (v_{U_1}, \ldots, v_i, \ldots, v_{U_N})$$
$$(\mathcal{A}, \mathcal{B}) \leftarrow (\mathcal{A} \setminus \{i\}, \mathcal{B} \cup \{i\})$$
return $(\mathbf{v}_L, \mathbf{v}_U, \mathcal{A}, \mathcal{B})$

Given these auxiliary functions, the computation of one AXp is shown in Algorithm 3 (and the computation of one CXp is shown in Algorithm 4).

The algorithm starts from some set $\mathcal{S} \subseteq \mathcal{F}$ (which can be the empty set) of universal features, which is required to ensure that $\kappa(\mathbf{v}_L) = \kappa(\mathbf{v}_U) = \kappa(\mathbf{v})$, and iteratively attempts to add features to set $\mathcal{S}$, i.e. to make them universal. Monotonicity of entailment (and the discussion in previous sections) ensures soundness of the algorithm.

Example 23. For the monotonic classifier of Fig. 4, and instance $((Q, X, H, R), M) = ((10, 10, 5, 0), A)$, we show how one AXp can be computed. For each feature i, $1 \leq i \leq 4$, $\lambda(i) = 0$ and $\mu(i) = 10$. Moreover, features are analyzed in order: $\langle 1, 2, 3, 4 \rangle$; the order is arbitrary. The algorithm's execution is summarized in Table 6.

Algorithm 3. Computing one AXp for a monotonic classifier

Input: Features $\mathcal{F}$, Seed $\mathcal{S} \subseteq \mathcal{F}$, Point in $\mathbb{F}$ $\mathbf{v}$
Output: One AXp $\mathcal{P}$

1: **procedure** oneAXp($\mathcal{F}; \mathcal{S}, \mathbf{v}$)
2: 　　$\mathbf{v}_L \leftarrow (v_1, \ldots, v_N)$
3: 　　$\mathbf{v}_U \leftarrow (v_1, \ldots, v_N)$　　　　　　　　　$\triangleright$ Ensures: $\kappa(\mathbf{v}_L) = \kappa(\mathbf{v}_U)$
4: 　　$(\mathcal{C}, \mathcal{D}, \mathcal{P}) \leftarrow (\mathcal{F}, \emptyset, \emptyset)$
5: 　　**for all** $i \in \mathcal{S}$ **do**　　　　　$\triangleright$ Require: $\kappa(\mathbf{v}_L) = \kappa(\mathbf{v}_U)$, given $\mathcal{S}$
6: 　　　　$(\mathbf{v}_L, \mathbf{v}_U, \mathcal{C}, \mathcal{D}) \leftarrow$ FreeAttr($i, \mathbf{v}, \mathbf{v}_L, \mathbf{v}_U, \mathcal{C}, \mathcal{D}$)
7: 　　**for all** $i \in \mathcal{F} \setminus \mathcal{S}$ **do**　　　　　$\triangleright$ Loop inv.: $\kappa(\mathbf{v}_L) = \kappa(\mathbf{v}_U)$
8: 　　　　$(\mathbf{v}_L, \mathbf{v}_U, \mathcal{C}, \mathcal{D}) \leftarrow$ FreeAttr($i, \mathbf{v}, \mathbf{v}_L, \mathbf{v}_U, \mathcal{C}, \mathcal{D}$)
9: 　　　　**if** $\kappa(\mathbf{v}_L) \neq \kappa(\mathbf{v}_U)$ **then**　　　$\triangleright$ If invariant broken, fix it
10: 　　　　　　$(\mathbf{v}_L, \mathbf{v}_U, \mathcal{D}, \mathcal{P}) \leftarrow$ FixAttr($i, \mathbf{v}, \mathbf{v}_L, \mathbf{v}_U, \mathcal{D}, \mathcal{P}$)
11: 　　**return** $\mathcal{P}$

Algorithm 4. Computing one CXp for a monotonic classifier

Input: Features $\mathcal{F}$, Seed $\mathcal{S} \subseteq \mathcal{F}$, Point in $\mathbb{F}$ $\mathbf{v}$
Output: One CXp $\mathcal{P}$

1: **procedure** oneCXp($\mathcal{F}; \mathcal{S}, \mathbf{v}$)
2: 　　$\mathbf{v}_L \leftarrow (\lambda(1), \ldots, \lambda(N))$
3: 　　$\mathbf{v}_U \leftarrow (\mu(1), \ldots, \mu(N))$　　　　　　　$\triangleright$ Ensures: $\kappa(\mathbf{v}_L) \neq \kappa(\mathbf{v}_U)$
4: 　　$(\mathcal{C}, \mathcal{D}, \mathcal{P}) \leftarrow (\mathcal{F}, \emptyset, \emptyset)$
5: 　　**for all** $i \in \mathcal{S}$ **do**　　　　　$\triangleright$ Require: $\kappa(\mathbf{v}_L) \neq \kappa(\mathbf{v}_U)$, given $\mathcal{S}$
6: 　　　　$(\mathbf{v}_L, \mathbf{v}_U, \mathcal{C}, \mathcal{D}) \leftarrow$ FixAttr($i, \mathbf{v}, \mathbf{v}_L, \mathbf{v}_U, \mathcal{C}, \mathcal{D}$)
7: 　　**for all** $i \in \mathcal{F} \setminus \mathcal{S}$ **do**　　　　　$\triangleright$ Loop inv.: $\kappa(\mathbf{v}_L) \neq \kappa(\mathbf{v}_U)$
8: 　　　　$(\mathbf{v}_L, \mathbf{v}_U, \mathcal{C}, \mathcal{D}) \leftarrow$ FixAttr($i, \mathbf{v}, \mathbf{v}_L, \mathbf{v}_U, \mathcal{C}, \mathcal{D}$)
9: 　　　　**if** $\kappa(\mathbf{v}_L) = \kappa(\mathbf{v}_U)$ **then**　　　$\triangleright$ If invariant broken, fix it
10: 　　　　　　$(\mathbf{v}_L, \mathbf{v}_U, \mathcal{D}, \mathcal{P}) \leftarrow$ FreeAttr($i, \mathbf{v}, \mathbf{v}_L, \mathbf{v}_U, \mathcal{D}, \mathcal{P}$)
11: 　　**return** $\mathcal{P}$

As can be observed, features 1 and 2 are kept as part of the AXp, and features 3 and 4 are dropped from the AXp. Thus, the AXp for the given instance is $\{1, 2\}$, representing the literals $\{Q = 10, X = 10\}$.　　　　　　　　　　　　$\triangleleft$

Besides monotonic classifiers, recent work that similar ideas have been shown to apply in the case of other (related) families of classifiers [84].

5.3　Other Families of Classifiers

A number of additional tractability results have been uncovered. Recent work [166] showed that the computation of explanations for decision graphs [279], decision diagrams and trees could be unified, and explanations computed in

Table 6. Execution of algorithm for finding one AXp

Feat.	Initial values		Changed values		Predictions		Dec.	Resulting values	
	v_L	v_U	v_L	v_U	$\kappa(v_L)$	$\kappa(v_U)$		v_L	v_U
1	(10,10,5,0)	(10,10,5,0)	(0,10,5,0)	(10,10,5,0)	C	A	✓	(10,10,5,0)	(10,10,5,0)
2	(10,10,5,0)	(10,10,5,0)	(10,0,5,0)	(10,10,5,0)	E	A	✓	(10,10,5,0)	(10,10,5,0)
3	(10,10,5,0)	(10,10,5,0)	(10,10,0,0)	(10,10,5,0)	A	A	✗	(10,10,0,0)	(10,10,10,0)
4	(10,10,0,0)	(10,10,10,0)	(10,10,0,0)	(10,10,10,10)	A	A	✗	(10,10,0,0)	(10,10,10,10)

polynomial time. For NBCs, it is now known that a smallest explanation can be computed in polynomial time [239], that there exists a polynomial delay algorithm for enumeration of abductive explanations (but it is straightforward to apply the same ideas to the case of CXp's). In the case of classifiers represented as propositional languages, including the broad class d-DNNF, it has been shown that there exist polynomial time algorithms for computing one AXp/CXp [165].

6 Explainability Queries

Besides the computation of explanations, recent research considered a number of explainability queries [25, 29, 163, 166, 167, 177, 239]. This section considers two concrete queries: enumeration of explanations and feature membership. Additional queries have been investigated in the listed references.

Enumeration addresses a crucial problem in explainability. If a human decision maker does not accept the (abductive or contrastive) explanation provided by an explanation tool, how can one compute some other explanation, assuming one exists? Most non-formal explainability approaches do not propose a solution to this problem. The problem of feature membership is to decide whether some (possibly sensitive) feature is included in some explanation of an instance, among all possible explanations. Feature membership is relevant when assessing whether a classifier can exhibit bias.

6.1 Enumeration of Explanations

Given an explanation problem, and some set of already computed explanations (AXp's and/or CXp's), the query of enumeration of explainability is to find one explanation (AXp or CXp) among those that are not included in the set of explanations.

For NBCs, it has been shown that there is a polynomial-delay algorithm for the enumeration AXp's [239]. A similar approach yields a solution for the enumeration of CXp's.

For most other families of classifiers, it is conceptually simple to devise algorithms that enumerate CXp's, without the need of computing or enumerating AXp's. In contrast, the enumeration of AXp's is obtained through duality

---

Algorithm 5. Finding all AXp/CXp

   Input: Parameters $\mathbb{P}_{\text{axp}}$, $\mathbb{P}_{\text{cxp}}$, $\mathcal{T}$, $\mathcal{F}$, κ, $\mathbf{v}$

1: $\mathcal{H} \leftarrow \emptyset$ ▷ $\mathcal{H}$ defined on set $U = \{u_1, \ldots, u_m\}$
2: **repeat**
3:     $(\text{outc}, \mathbf{u}) \leftarrow \mathsf{SAT}(\mathcal{H})$
4:     **if** outc $=$ **true then**
5:        $\mathcal{S} \leftarrow \{i \in \mathcal{F} \mid u_i = 0\}$ ▷ $\mathcal{S}$: *fixed* features
6:        $\mathcal{U} \leftarrow \{i \in \mathcal{F} \mid u_i = 1\}$ ▷ $\mathcal{U}$: *universal* features; $\mathcal{F} = \mathcal{S} \cup \mathcal{U}$
7:        **if** $\mathbb{P}_{\text{cxp}}(\mathcal{U}; \mathcal{T}, \mathcal{F}, \kappa, \mathbf{v})$ **then**   ▷ $\mathcal{U} \supseteq$ some CXp
8:            $\mathcal{P} \leftarrow \mathsf{oneXP}(\mathcal{U}; \mathbb{P}_{\text{cxp}}, \mathcal{T}, \mathcal{F}, \kappa, \mathbf{v})$
9:            $\mathsf{reportCXp}(\mathcal{P})$
10:          $\mathcal{H} \leftarrow \mathcal{H} \cup \{(\vee_{i \in \mathcal{P}} \neg u_i)\}$
11:        **else**   ▷ $\mathcal{S} \supseteq$ some AXp
12:            $\mathcal{P} \leftarrow \mathsf{oneXP}(\mathcal{S}; \mathbb{P}_{\text{axp}}, \mathcal{T}, \mathcal{F}, \kappa, \mathbf{v})$
13:            $\mathsf{reportAXp}(\mathcal{P})$
14:          $\mathcal{H} \leftarrow \mathcal{H} \cup \{(\vee_{i \in \mathcal{P}} u_i)\}$
15: **until** outc $=$ **false**

---

between AXp's and CXp's (see Sect. 3.4 and additional detail in [177]). One solution for enumerating AXp's is to compute all CXp's, and then use hitting set dualization for computing the AXp's. Unfortunately, the number of CXp's is often exponential, and this may prevent the enumeration of any AXp. Thus, and building on fairly recent work on the enumeration of MUSes [226], the solution is to iteratively compute AXp's/CXp's by exploiting hitting set duality, using a SAT solver for iteratively picking a set of features to serve as a seed for either computing one AXp or one CXp. A number of recent works have reported results on the enumeration of explanations [165,172,174,240]. The query of explanation enumeration has also been studied in terms of its complexity [25,29]. One important observation is that, for families of classifiers for which computing one explanation is poly-time, then the enumeration of the next explanation (either AXp or CXp) requires a single call to an NP oracle [240].

    A general-purpose approach for the enumeration of explanations is shown in Algorithm 5[20]. Variants of this algorithm have been studied in recent work [165,166,172,174,177,240].

---

[20] The algorithm mimics the on-demand MUS enumeration algorithm proposed elsewhere [225,226,289], which enumerates both MUSes and MCSes. There are several other alternative MUS enumeration algorithms, which could also be considered [34,35,37,46–48,64,86,127,148,204–207,225,236,270,300]. For some of these algorithms, a first required step is the complete enumeration of MCSes, for which a wealth of algorithms also exists [121,146,147,227,241,256,257,265,290,291]. Furthermore, there is a tight relationship between MUS/MCS enumeration and several other computational problems [245,246], which allows devising generic algorithms for solving families of related problems.

Table 7. Example execution of enumeration algorithm

Iter.	u	$\mathcal{S}$	$\mathbb{P}_{cxp}(\cdot)$	AXp	CXp	Clause
1	$(1,1,1,1,1)$	$\emptyset$	1	–	$\{3\}$	$(\neg u_3)$
2	$(1,1,0,1,1)$	$\{3\}$	1	–	$\{5\}$	$(\neg u_5)$
3	$(1,1,0,1,0)$	$\{3,5\}$	0	$\{3,5\}$	–	$(u_3 \vee u_5)$
5	[outc = **false**]	–	–	–	–	–

Table 8. Another possible execution of enumeration algorithm

Iter.	u	$\mathcal{S}$	$\mathbb{P}_{cxp}(\cdot)$	AXp	CXp	Clause
1	$(0,0,0,0,0)$	$\{1,2,3,4,5\}$	0	$\{3,5\}$	–	$(u_3 \vee u_5)$
2	$(0,0,1,0,0)$	$\{1,2,4,5\}$	1	–	$\{3\}$	$(\neg u_3)$
3	$(0,0,1,0,1)$	$\{1,2,4\}$	1	–	$\{5\}$	$(\neg u_5)$
5	[outc = **false**]	–	–	–	–	–

Example 24. For the DT of Fig. 2, Tables 7 and 8 show possible executions of the explanation enumeration algorithm. The difference between the two tables is the assignments picked by the SAT solver. (Tables 2a and 2b are used to decide the values of the predicates tested in the algorithm's execution.) Depending on that assignment **u**, either there is a pick of features that changes the prediction or there is none. If the prediction can be changed, then one CXp is computed. Otherwise, one AXp is computed. In both cases, Algorithm 1 is used, but a different predicate is considered in each case. The clause added after each AXp/CXp is computed prevents the repetition of explanations. The algorithm terminates when all AXp's/CXp's have been enumerated.   ◁

As noted in recent work [166,187], and in the case of DTs, the fact that all CXp's are computed in poly-time enables using more efficient quasi-polynomial algorithms for the enumeration of AXp's (e.g. using well-known results in monotone dualization [127]).

6.2 Explanation Membership

The problem of deciding whether a given (possibly sensitive) feature is included in some explanation is referred to as the *feature membership problem* (FMP) [166].

Definition 3 (FMP). *Given an explanation problem* $\mathcal{E}_L = (\mathcal{M}, \mathbf{v}, c)$*, with* $\mathcal{M} = (\mathcal{F}, \mathbb{D}, \mathbb{F}, \mathcal{K}, \kappa)$*, and some target feature* $t \in \mathcal{F}$*, the feature membership problem is to decide whether there exists an AXp (resp. CXp)* $\mathcal{X} \subseteq \mathcal{F}$ $(\mathcal{Y} \subseteq \mathcal{F})$ *such that* $t \in \mathcal{X}$ *(resp.* $t \in \mathcal{Y}$*)*

It should be observed that FMP is tightly related with queries in logic-based abduction, namely *relevancy/irrelevancy* [111,128,313].

Example 25. For the DL of Fig. 1a, and the instance $(\mathbf{v}, c) = ((0, 0, 1, 2), 1)$, from the list of explanations, $\mathbb{A} = \{\{1, 4\}\}$ (for the AXp's), and $\mathbb{C} = \{\{1\}, \{4\}\}$ (for the CXp's), it is plain that features 2 and 3 and not included in any explanation, and 1 and 4 are included in some explanation.   ◁

The MHS duality between AXp's and CXp's yields the following result:

Proposition 8. *Given an explanation problem $\mathcal{E}_L = (\mathcal{M}, \mathbf{v}, c)$, with $\mathcal{M} = (\mathcal{F}, \mathbb{D}, \mathbb{F}, \mathcal{K}, \kappa)$, and some target feature $t \in \mathcal{F}$, t is included in some AXp of $\mathcal{E}_L$ iff t is included in some CXp of $\mathcal{E}_L$.*

Hence, when devising algorithms for FMP, one can either study the membership in some AXp or the membership in some CXp.

FMP has a simple QBF formulation:

$$\exists(\mathcal{X} \subseteq \mathcal{F}). [(t \in \mathcal{X}) \wedge \mathsf{AXp}(\mathcal{X}) \wedge (\forall(\mathcal{X}' \subsetneq \mathcal{X}). \neg\mathsf{AXp}(\mathcal{X}'))]$$

There are several optimizations that can be introduced to this basic QBF formulation, but that is beyond the scope of this document. More importantly, there are some known results about the complexity of FMP. These can be briefly summarized as follows,

Proposition 9 ([166]). *FMP for a DNF classifier is Σ_2^p-hard.*

Since a DNF classifier can be reduced to more expressive classifiers, like RFs and other tree ensembles like BTs, but also NNs, then we have the following result,

Proposition 10. *FMP is Σ_2^p-hard for RFs, BTs and NNs.*

One important recent result has been the proof of membership in Σ_2^p. As a result, one solution approach for FMP is the use of QBF/2QBF solvers [55][21].

Despite the complexity of FMP in general settings, there are families of classifiers for which deciding FMP is in P [166]. An immediate consequence of the fact that CXp's can be enumerated in polynomial time for DTs is:

Proposition 11 ([166]). *FMP for a DT is in P.*

More recently, additional results on FMP have been proved,

Proposition 12 ([168]). *For a classifier for which it is in P to decide whether a set of features is a WAXp, then deciding FMP is in NP.*

---

[21] There have been observable improvements in the performance of QBF solvers in recent years, which can largely be attributed to the use of abstraction refinement methods [193–195,295,296].

Proof. [Sketch] To prove that FMP is in NP in this case, one proceeds are follows. First, one guesses (non-deterministically) a set $\mathcal{X}$ containing the target feature t. By hypothesis, this set is decided to be a weak AXp in poly-time, Next, we show that removing any feature causes the resulting set to no longer represent a weak AXp. Once again, by hypothesis there exists a polynomial time algorithm for deciding whether such a reduced set is a WAXp. Thus, deciding FMP is in P. □

6.3   Additional Explainability Queries

A wealth of additional explainability queries have been studied in recent years [25, 29, 101]. Examples include finding mandatory and/or forbidden features, counting and/or enumerating instances, among others. Queries can be broadly categorized as class queries or explanation queries [25, 29]. Examples of class queries include mandatory/forbidden features for a class and necessary features for a class. Examples of explanation queries include finding smallest AXp's, finding one AXp and finding one CXp. Some of these queries have been studied earlier in this document as well. Complexity-wise, [25] proves the NP-hardness of these queries for the families of classifiers DLs, RFs, BTs, boolean NNs, and binarized NNs (BNNs). In contrast, and also as shown in this paper, for DTs, most queries can be answered in polynomial time. It should be noted that some of the queries studied in recent work can also be related with queries in logic-based abduction [111, 128, 313], concretely relevancy/irrelevancy but also necessity. More recent work on feature relevancy in explanations includes dedicated algorithms for arbitrary classifiers [167], and NP-hardness proofs for some families of classifiers [163].

Validation of ML Models. Recent work [59] illustrates the use of formal explanations for identifying apparent flaws in ML models. For example, the DT shown in Fig. 8 has been proposed in the field of medical diagnosis [224], aiming at providing a solution for non-invasive diagnosis of Meningococcal Disease (MD) meningitis. (The actual feature names, and their domains, are shown in Table 9.) Unfortunately, the DT has a number of issues, in that it allows MD meningitis to be diagnosed for patients that exhibit no symptoms whatsoever. The use of formal explanations, namely AXp's, allows demonstrating these issues.

As one concrete example, the computation of AXp's allows concluding that MD meningitis will be predicted whenever a patient has more than 5 years of age and lives in a rural area, i.e. without exhibiting any symptoms of the disease, at least among those tested for. To prove that this is the case, one considers the path $\langle 1, 3, 6, 8, 10, 14 \rangle$, and confirms that there is an explanation that does not include any of the symptoms (i.e. Petechiae, Stiff neck, and Vomiting). Here, the query is to assess the existence of explanations for which the symptoms need not be tested for. The conclusion is that one can diagnose MD meningitis without testing any of the symptoms of meningitis.

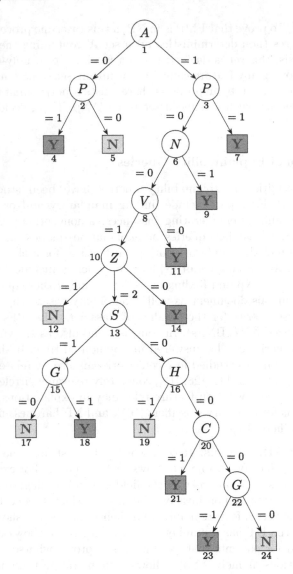

Fig. 8. Decision tree adapted from [224, Fig. 9]

As the previous example illustrates, reasoning about formal explanations, including different kinds of queries, can serve to to help decision makers in assessing whether an ML model offers sufficient guarantees of quality to be deployed. The previous example also illustrates the fundamental importance of formal verification of ML models [242,315] in reduce the likelihood of accidents [53].

Table 9. Features and domains from [224]

Feat. #	Name	Meaning	Definition	Domain	Trait/Symp.
1	A	Age	Age > 5?	$\{0,1\}$	T
2	P	Petechiae	Petechiae?	$\{0,1\}$	S
3	N	Stiff Neck	Stiff Neck?	$\{0,1\}$	S
4	V	Vomiting	Vomiting?	$\{0,1\}$	S
5	Z	Zone	Zone=?	$\{0,1,2\}$	T
6	S	Seizures	Seizures?	$\{0,1\}$	S
7	G	Gender	Gender?	$\{0\,(F),1\,(M)\}$	T
8	H	Headache	Headache?	$\{0,1\}$	S
9	C	Coma	Coma?	$\{0,1\}$	S

7 Probabilistic Explanations

The cognitive limits of human beings are well-known [260]. Unfortunately, it is also the case that formal explanations are often larger than such cognitive limits. One possible solution is to compute explanations that are not as rigorous as AXp's, but which offer strong probabilistic guarantees of rigor. We refer to these explanations as *probabilistic explanations*. There is recent initial work on the complexity of computing probabilistic explanations [354,355], where the name *probabilistic prime implicants* is used. Following more recent work [185,189,190,192], we will use the term(s) (weak) *probabilistic abductive explanations* ((W)PAXp's). To simplify the section contents, features are assumed to be categorical or ordinal, in which case the values are restricted to being boolean or integer.

7.1 Problem Formulation

A probabilistic (weak) AXp generalizes the definition of weak AXp, by allowing the prediction to change in some points of feature space, where a weak AXp would require the prediction not to change, but such that those changes have small probability. One is thus interested in sets $\mathcal{X} \subseteq \mathcal{F}$ such that,

$$\mathrm{Pr}_{\mathbf{x}}(\kappa(\mathbf{x}) = c \,|\, \mathbf{x}_{\mathcal{X}} = \mathbf{v}_{\mathcal{X}}) \geq \delta \tag{26}$$

where $0 < \delta \leq 1$ is some given threshold, and $\mathbf{x}_{\mathcal{X}} = \mathbf{v}_{\mathcal{X}}$ holds for any point in feature space for which $\wedge_{i \in \mathcal{X}}(x_i = v_i)$. Clearly, for $\delta = 1$, (26) corresponds to stating that,

$$\forall(\mathbf{x} \in \mathbb{F}). \left[\bigwedge_{i \in \mathcal{X}}(x_i = v_i)\right] \rightarrow (\kappa(\mathbf{x}) = c) \tag{27}$$

Recent work [354,355] established that, for binary classifiers represented by boolean circuits, it is $\mathrm{NP}^{\mathrm{PP}}$-complete to decide the existence of a set $\mathcal{X} \subseteq \mathcal{F}$, with $|\mathcal{X}| \leq k$, such that (26) holds. Despite this unwieldy complexity, it has been shown that for specific families of classifiers [185, 190, 192], it is computationally easier and practically efficient to compute (approximate) subset-minimal sets such that (26) holds. Concretely, instead of (4), we will instead consider:

$$\mathsf{WeakPAXp}(\mathcal{X}; \mathbb{F}, \kappa, \mathbf{v}, c, \delta) \quad := \quad \mathrm{Pr}_{\mathbf{x}}(\kappa(\mathbf{x}) = c \,|\, \mathbf{x}_{\mathcal{X}} = \mathbf{v}_{\mathcal{X}}) \geq \delta \qquad (28)$$

where $\mathsf{WeakPAXp}$ denotes a weak probabilistic AXp (PAXp). Similarly to the deterministic case, a PAXp is a subset-minimal weak AXp. A set $\mathcal{X} \subseteq \mathcal{F}$ such that (28) holds is also referred to as *relevant set*. In the next section, we will illustrate how PAXp's are computed in the case of DTs.

7.2   Probabilistic Explanations for Decision Trees

Path Probabilities for DTs. Next, we investigate how to compute, in the case of DTs, the conditional probability,

$$\mathrm{Pr}_{\mathbf{x}}(\kappa(\mathbf{x}) = c \,|\, \mathbf{x}_{\mathcal{X}} = \mathbf{v}_{\mathcal{X}}) \qquad (29)$$

where $\mathcal{X}$ is a set of *fixed* features (whereas the other features are not fixed, being deemed *universal*), and P_t is a path in the DT consistent with the instance $(\mathbf{v}, c)$. (Also, note that (29) is the left-hand side of the definition of $\mathsf{WeakPAXp}$ in (28) above.) To motivate the proposed approach, let us first analyze how we can compute $\mathrm{Pr}_{\mathbf{x}}(\kappa(\mathbf{x}) = c)$, where $\mathcal{P} \subseteq \mathcal{R}$ is the set of paths in the DT with prediction c. Let $\Lambda(R_k)$ denote the set of literals (each of the form $x_i \in \mathbb{E}_i$) in some path $R_k \in \mathcal{R}$. If a feature i is tested multiple times along path R_k, then $\mathbb{E}_i$ is the intersection of the sets in each of the literals of R_k on i. The number of values of $\mathbb{D}_i$ consistent with literal $x_i \in \mathbb{E}_i$ is $|\mathbb{E}_i|$. Finally, the features *not* tested along R_k are denoted by $\Psi(R_k)$. For path R_k, the probability that a randomly chosen point in feature space is consistent with R_k (i.e. the *path probability* of R_k) is given by,

$$\mathrm{Pr}(R_k) = \left[\Pi_{(x_i \in \mathbb{E}_i) \in \Lambda(R_k)} |\mathbb{E}_i| \times \Pi_{i \in \Psi(R_k)} |\mathbb{D}_i|\right]/|\mathbb{F}| \qquad (30)$$

As a result, we get that,

$$\mathrm{Pr}_{\mathbf{x}}(\kappa(\mathbf{x}) = c) = \sum_{R_k \in \mathcal{P}} \mathrm{Pr}(R_k) \qquad (31)$$

Given an instance $(\mathbf{v}, c)$ and a set of fixed features $\mathcal{X}$ (and so a set of universal features $\mathcal{F} \setminus \mathcal{X}$), we now detail how to compute (29). Since some features will now be declared universal, multiple paths with possibly different conditions can become consistent. Although universal variables might seem to complicate the computation of the conditional probability, this is not the case.

A key observation is that the feature values that make a path consistent are disjoint from the values that make other paths consistent. This observation allows us to compute the models consistent with each path and, as a result, to compute (28). Let $R_k \in \mathcal{R}$ represent some path in the decision tree. (Recall that $P_t \in \mathcal{P}$ is the target path, which is consistent with $\mathbf{v}$.) Let n_{ik} represent the (integer) number of assignments to feature i that are consistent with path $R_k \in \mathcal{R}$, given $\mathbf{v} \in \mathbb{F}$ and $\mathcal{X} \subseteq \mathcal{F}$. For a feature i, let $\mathbb{E}_i$ denote the set of domain values of feature i that is consistent with path R_k. Hence, for path R_k, we consider a literal $(x_i \in \mathbb{E}_i)$. Given the above, the value of n_{ik} is defined as follows:

1. If i is fixed:
   (a) If i is tested along R_k and the value of x_i is inconsistent with $\mathbf{v}$, i.e. there exists a literal $(x_i \in \mathbb{E}_i) \in \Lambda(R_k)$ and $\{v_i\} \cap \mathbb{E}_i = \emptyset$, then $n_{ik} = 0$;
   (b) If i is tested along R_k and the value of x_i is consistent with R_k, i.e. there exists a literal $(x_i \in \mathbb{E}_i) \in \Lambda(R_k)$ and $\{v_i\} \cap \mathbb{E}_i \neq \emptyset$, then $n_{ik} = 1$;
   (c) If i is not tested along R_k, then $n_{ik} = 1$.
2. Otherwise, i is universal:
   (a) If i is tested along R_k, with some literal $x_i \in \mathbb{E}_i$, then $n_{ik} = |\mathbb{E}_i|$;
   (b) If i is not tested along R_k, then $n_{ik} = |\mathbb{D}_i|$.

Using the definition of n_{ik}, we can then compute the number of assignments consistent with R_k as follows:

$$\#(R_k; \mathbf{v}, \mathcal{X}) = \prod_{i \in \mathcal{F}} n_{ik} \tag{32}$$

Finally, (29) is given by,

$$\mathrm{Pr}_{\mathbf{x}}(\kappa(\mathbf{x}) = c \,|\, \mathbf{x}_{\mathcal{X}} = \mathbf{v}_{\mathcal{X}}) = \sum_{P_k \in \mathcal{P}} \#(P_k; \mathbf{v}, \mathcal{X}) \Big/ \sum_{R_k \in \mathcal{R}} \#(R_k; \mathbf{v}, \mathcal{X}) \tag{33}$$

As can be concluded, and in the case of a decision tree, both $\mathrm{Pr}_{\mathbf{x}}(\kappa(\mathbf{x}) = c \,|\, \mathbf{x}_{\mathcal{X}} = \mathbf{v}_{\mathcal{X}})$ and $\mathsf{WeakPAXp}(\mathcal{X}; \mathbb{F}, \kappa, \mathbf{v}, c, \delta)$ are computed in polynomial time on the size of the DT.

Example 26. For the DT of Fig. 2a, with instance $(\mathbf{v}, c) = ((0, 0, 1, 0, 1), 1)$, we know that an AXp is $\{3, 5\}$. Let $\delta = 0.85$, and let us assess whether $\{5\}$ represents a weak probabilistic explanation. Table 10 shows the path counts given $\mathcal{X} = \{5\}$ and $\mathbf{v} = (0, 0, 1, 0, 1)$. From the table, we get that,

$$\mathrm{Pr}_{\mathbf{x}}(\kappa(\mathbf{x}) = c \,|\, \mathbf{x}_{\mathcal{X}} = \mathbf{v}_{\mathcal{X}}) = \sum_{P_k \in \mathcal{P}} \#(P_k; \mathbf{v}, \mathcal{X}) \Big/ \sum_{R_k \in \mathcal{R}} \#(R_k; \mathbf{v}, \mathcal{X}) = {}^{14}\!/_{16} = 0.875$$

And so, $\{5\}$ is a weak PAXp.   ◁

7.3   Additional Results

For classifiers represented as boolean circuits, the computation of probabilistic abductive explanations is $\mathrm{NP}^{\mathrm{PP}}$-hard [354, 355]. Motivated by this complexity, expected to be beyond the reach of modern reasoners, recent efforts studied specific families of classifiers. In the case of DTs, the approach summarized in the previous section was proposed elsewhere [185, 189, 190], and shown to be effective in practice. Also in the case of DTs, computational hardness results have been proved in more recent work [21, 22]. Furthermore, an approach based on dynamic programming was used for computing probabilistic explanations in the case of NBCs [185, 192].

Table 10. Path probabilities for DT of Fig. 2a

Path (R_k)	Nodes of R_k	$\#(R_k; \mathbf{v}, \mathcal{X})$	Obs
P_1	$\langle 1, 2, 4, 7, 10, 15 \rangle$	1	
P_2	$\langle 1, 2, 4, 7, 11 \rangle$	1	
P_3	$\langle 1, 2, 5, 8, 13 \rangle$	2	
P_4	$\langle 1, 2, 5, 9 \rangle$	2	
P_5	$\langle 1, 3 \rangle$	8	
		14	Total for $\mathcal{P}$
Q_1	$\langle 1, 2, 4, 6 \rangle$	2	
Q_2	$\langle 1, 2, 4, 7, 10, 14 \rangle$	0	
Q_3	$\langle 1, 2, 5, 8, 12 \rangle$	0	
		2	Total for $\mathcal{Q}$

8   Input Constraints and Distributions

A critical assumption implicit on most work on formal explainability is that all inputs are possible (and equally likely). Unfortunately, this is often not the case. For example, consider a classification problem with features 'order', denoting the animal order, and 'winged', denoting whether the animal has wings. It might be expected that points in feature space having 'order=Proboscidea' (i.e. that includes elephants) and 'winged=true' would be disallowed. In contrast, 'order=Chiroptera' (i.e. that includes bats) and 'winged=true' would be allowed. If such constraints on the features are known a priori, then one can take them into account when computing explanations. However, in most cases, such constraints are unknown. This section summarizes recent work on the general topic of handling of input constraints.

Constraints on the Features. Let us assume that a given classifier $\mathbb{C}$ is characterized by a constraint set $\mathcal{I}_{\mathbb{C}}$ capturing the allowed points in feature space. (In general, we view $\mathcal{I}_{\mathbb{C}}$ as a predicate, mapping points in feature space into $\{0, 1\}$.) The definition of weak AXp can be adapted to account for such constraint set as follows,

$$\forall (\mathbf{x} \in \mathbb{F}). \left[\bigwedge_{i \in \mathcal{X}} (x_i = v_i) \right] \rightarrow [\mathcal{I}_{\mathbb{C}}(\mathbf{x}) \rightarrow (\kappa(\mathbf{x}) = c)] \tag{34}$$

Similarly, the definition of weak CXp can be adapted to account for $\mathcal{I}_{\mathbb{C}}$,

$$\exists (\mathbf{x} \in \mathbb{F}). \left[\bigwedge_{i \notin \mathcal{Y}} (x_i = v_i) \right] \wedge [\mathcal{I}_{\mathbb{C}}(\mathbf{x}) \wedge (\kappa(\mathbf{x}) \neq c)] \tag{35}$$

A number of observations can be made:

1. The definitions of AXp and CXp, given the definitions of input constraint aware weak AXp/CXp's, remain unchanged.
2. Duality between AXp's and CXp's (see Sect. 3.4) still holds.

3. Depending on the family of classifiers and the representation of the constraints, the complexity of computing one explanation need not change. For example, if the constraints are represented as propositional Horn clauses (and this is the case with propositional rules), then the propositional encoding for computing explanations of DTs will still enable computing explanations in polynomial time.
4. Finally, the same approach can also be used with probabilistic explanations.

Given the above, and as long as the allowed points in feature space are represented by a constraint set, then we can take those constraints into account when computing AXp's and CXp's. The original ideas on accounting for input constraints were presented in recent work [145], and extended more recently for contrastive explanations [367]. However, a major difficulty with the handling input constraints is how to infer those input constraints in the first place. A possible solution to this challenge has been proposed in recent work [367].

Inferring Constraints. When given a dataset and an ML classifier, one can exploit standard ML learning approaches for inferring constraints that are consistent with training data. Recent work studied the learning of rules on the features given the training data [367]. The experimental results substantiate the importance of inferring constraints on the features, that also lead to smaller abductive explanations and *larger* contrastive explanations.

Research Directions. Inferring *good* constraints from training data is a promising direction of research. The goal will be to find the best possible rules, that improve the accuracy of explanations, but that do not impact significantly the performance of formal explainers. Another line of research is to account input distributions when these are either known or can be inferred.

9 Formal Explanations with Surrogate Models

As briefly discussed in Sect. 2.3, the most visible (non-formal) explainability approaches consist of approximating a complex classifier with a much simpler classifier (e.g. a linear classifier or a decision tree) which, due to its simplicity, is interpretable and so represents an explanation for the complex classifier [235, 301].

Despite the numerous shortcomings of such line of research (see Sect. 2.3), it is also the case that approximating complex ML models *locally* with much simpler (or surrogate) ML models, has been studied in several other works [41, 42, 129]. Furthermore, there has been work on finding surrogate models, that locally approximate a complex ML model, such that computing formal explanations for the surrogate model is efficient in practice [66].

Let $\mathbb{C}$ represent a complex ML model, e.g. a neural network, and let $(\mathbf{v}, c)$ represent a target instance. Moreover, let $\mathbb{A}$ represent an approximating (surrogate) ML model, e.g. a random forest, which *approximates* $\mathbb{C}$ in points of feature space that are sufficiently close to $\mathbf{v}$, i.e. for point $\mathbf{x} \in \mathbb{F}$, with $||\mathbf{x} - \mathbf{v}|| \leq \epsilon$, for some small $\epsilon > 0$, it is the case that $\kappa_{\mathbb{C}}(\mathbf{x})$ and $\kappa_{\mathbb{A}}(\mathbf{x})$ coincide with high probability.

The conjecture out forward in recent work [66] is that a (rigorous) explanation (either AXp or CXp) of the instance $(\mathbf{v}, c)$ computed for $\mathbb{A}$ is also a sufficiently accurate explanation for $\mathbb{C}$ on the same instance. At present, this novel line of research requires further validation. For example, past work has not shown in practice that formal explanations computed for the surrogate model are sufficiently accurate for the complex model. Although past work considered random forests as the surrogate model, it is plain to conclude that other surrogate models can be considered, e.g. decision trees or NBCs. The reason for considering simpler ML models is that probabilistic explanations can be computed efficiently, and this is not the case with random forests.

10   Additional Topics and Extensions

Links with Fairness, Robustness, etc. Formal explainability has been related with robustness and fairness. For global explanation problems, it is now known that the minimal hitting sets of abductive explanations (which have been referred to as counterexamples) contain one or more adversarial examples [179]. Moreover, initial links with fairness were investigated in more recent work [171]. Finally, the relationship between model learning and explainability is a topic of future research.

Explanation Literals. By definition, the definition of AXp and CXp assumes literals based on equality. This is justified by the fact that AXp's and CXp's are computed with respect to a concrete point in feature space. In some settings, it has been shown that literals based on equality can be generalized to the literals that occur in the model itself. This is the case with decision trees [187], where literals can be defined using the set membership operator, and so explanations can be related with such literals. Similar ideas are yet to be investigated in the case of other ML models.

Localized Explanations. Non-formal explainability methods emphasize the *local* nature of their explanations. In situations where such locality if of interest, one may wonder whether formal explainability can be adapted to further emphasize locality. Given the diverse nature of features, we opt to define the Hamming distance between two points in feature space,

$$\mathfrak{D}_h(\mathbf{x}_1, \mathbf{x}_2) = \sum_{i=1}^{m} \text{ITE}(x_{1i} = x_{2i}, 1, 0) \tag{36}$$

Given the definition of Hamming distance, we can now propose a definition of *localized* weak abductive and contrastive explanations.

$\mathsf{WeakLAXp}(\mathcal{X}) := \forall(\mathbf{x} \in \mathbb{F}).$

$$\left[\mathfrak{D}_h(\mathbf{x}, \mathbf{v}) \le \epsilon \wedge \bigwedge_{i \in \mathcal{X}}(x_i = v_i)\right] \rightarrow (\kappa(\mathbf{x}) = c) \tag{37}$$

$\mathsf{WeakLCXp}(\mathcal{Y}) := \exists(\mathbf{x} \in \mathbb{F}).$

$$\left[\mathfrak{D}_h(\mathbf{x}, \mathbf{v}) \le \epsilon \wedge \bigwedge_{i \notin \mathcal{Y}}(x_i = v_i)\right] \wedge (\kappa(\mathbf{x}) \ne c) \tag{38}$$

for some target $\epsilon > 0$. The definitions of subset-minimal sets remain unchanged, i.e. localized AXp's and CXp's can be computed using (8) and (9), by replacing WeakAXp and WeakAXp, respectively by WeakLAXp and WeakLCXp. Finally, although we opted to use Hamming distance, (37) and (38) could consider other measures of distance.

Explanations Beyond ML. Although at present ML model explainability of ML models is the most studied theme in the general field of explainability, it is also the case that explainability has been studied in AI for decades [14–16, 111, 118, 119, 128, 283, 313, 317, 331, 332], with a renewed interest in recent years. For example, explanations have recently been studied in AI planning [76, 109, 110, 126, 158, 215, 327, 328, 330, 344], constraint satisfaction and problem solving [63, 114, 130, 150, 328], among other examples [329]. Furthermore, there is some agreement that regulations like EU's General Data Protection Regulation (GDPR) [115] effectively impose the obligation of explanations for any sort of algorithmic decision making [144, 208]. Despite representing fairly distinct areas of research, it is the case that most explainability approaches focus on computing explanations by computing MUSes or variants thereof. This is the case in planning [109], in constraint solving [63], besides explanations in ML as detailed in earlier sections of this paper (see Sect. 4).

11   Future Research and Conclusions

This section concludes the paper. As the previous sections illustrate, formal explainability has blossomed into a number of important areas of research. Thus, we start by overviewing a number of research directions. Afterwards, we summarize the paper's contributions.

11.1   Research Directions

As the second part of the paper reveals (see Sects. 6 to 10), there exist a vast number of ongoing research topics in the field of formal explainability.

Definitions of Explanations. Although the existing definitions of (formal) explanations offer important theoretical advantages, e.g. duality of explanations, researchers have looked at alternative definitions, with the purpose of improving the efficiency of algorithms for computing explanations, or improving the expressiveness of explanations [26, 28].

Computation of Explanations. The ability to devise more efficient tools to reason about NNs represents a critical topic of research. Significant improvements in the tools used to reason about NNs would allow explaining more complex classifiers, and so extend the rage of applicability of formal explainability. The grand challenges in the computation of explanations is to devise novel methods for efficiently computing explanations of neural networks and bayesian network classifiers. Recent progress in the analysis of NNs [202, 203, 229] suggests initial directions. A related line of research is the computation of approximate explanations with formal guarantees [40].

Explainability Queries. Besides enumeration of explanations, a related question is the enumeration of explanations that are preferred or that take user suggestions into account. This is the subject of future research. Regarding the feature membership, several research problems can be envisioned. One is to efficiently decide membership in the case of arbitrary classifiers, e.g. random forests and other tree ensembles. Another direction of research is to chart the complexity of FMP for the many families of classifiers that can be used in practical settings. For example, given the result that FMP is in NP for families of classifiers for which computing one explanation is in P, then proving/disproving hardness results would allow selecting the most adequate tools to use when solving FMP in practice.

Probabilistic Explanations. One key difficulty of computing probabilistic explanations is the computational complexity of the problem [355]. Although researchers have made progress in devising efficient algorithms for efficiently computing probabilistic explanations for specific families of classifiers [190,192], but also in understanding the computational hardness of computing probabilistic explanations in such cases [22], a number of topics of research can be envisioned. Concretely, one topic is to devise a more complete chart of the computational complexity of the problem, and a second topic is to devise practically efficient algorithms for families of classifiers that have not yet been investigated, e.g. decision lists and sets and tree ensembles, among others.

Explanation Certification. It is well-known that algorithms proved correct can be implemented incorrectly. In areas where the rigor of results is paramount, there have been efforts to devise mechanisms for ascertaining the correctness of either implemented algorithms or their computed results [8,9,88,89,92,113,139–141,154,155,250,359]. A natural topic of research is to apply similar solutions in the case of the computation of explanations, but also in the case of explainability queries. For example, existing algorithms for computing one explanation can be formalized in a proof assistant (e.g. [50]), from which a certified executable can then be extracted. Explanation of certification is expected to be relevant in settings that are deemed high-risk or safety-critical.

Additional Topics. The accounting for input constraints can play a key role in formal explainability. As a result, the inference of *good* constraints from training data is a promising direction of research. The goal will be to find the best possible rules, that improve the accuracy of explanations, but that do not impact significantly the performance of formal explainers. Another line of research is to account input distributions when these are either known or can be inferred. As noted in Sect. 9, the use of surrogate models to compute explanations of complex models holds great promise, but it also requires further assessment. It is open such assessment is to be made. In classification problems with a large number of features, it is often important to be able to aggregate features. In formal explainability, this issue has not yet been addressed, and it is a topic of future research. The previous sections also mentioned in passing several topics of research, that could contribute to raising the impact of formal explainability.

11.2 Concluding Remarks

This paper summarizes the recent developments in the emerging field of formal explainability. The paper overviews the definition of explanations, and covers the computation of explanations, addressing specific families of classifiers, both families for which computing one explanation is computationally hard, and families for which computing one explanation is tractable. The paper also covers a wide range of ongoing topics of active research including explainability queries, probabilistic explanations, accounting for input constraints, and formal explainability using surrogate models. In most cases, the paper also highlights existing topics of research.

As shown throughout the paper, formal explainability borrows extensively from a number of areas of research in AI, including automated reasoning and model-based diagnosis. Different reasoners, including SAT, MILP, and SMT, among others, have been and continue to be exploited in devising ways of computing explanations, both exact and probabilistic, but also answering explainability queries.

Acknowledgements. This document was motivated by the opportunity to give a short course on formal XAI at the 18th Reasoning Web Summer School (https://2022. declarativeai.net/events/reasoning-web), organized by Leopoldo Bertossi and Guohui Xiao. The work summarized in this document results in part from collaborations and discussions with several colleagues, including F. Arenas, N. Asher, R. Béjar, M. Cooper, B. German, T. Gerspacher, E. Hebrard, X. Huang, A. Hurault, A. Ignatiev, Y. Izza, O. Létoffé, X. Liu, E. Lorini, C. Mencía, A. Morgado, N. Narodytska, J. Planes, R. Passos, M. Siala, M. Tavassoli, J. Veron, among others. Some colleagues offered detailed comments on earlier drafts of this document, namely Y. Izza, C. Mencía, A. Morgado, and J. Planes. This work was supported by the AI Interdisciplinary Institute ANITI, funded by the French program "Investing for the Future – PIA3" under Grant agreement no. ANR-19-PI3A-0004, and by the H2020-ICT38 project COALA "Cognitive Assisted agile manufacturing for a Labor force supported by trustworthy Artificial intelligence". Finally, I acknowledge the incentive provided by the ERC who, by not funding this research nor a handful of other grant applications between 2012 and 2022, has had a lasting impact in framing the research presented in this paper.

References

1. Adadi, A., Berrada, M.: Peeking inside the black-box: a survey on explainable artificial intelligence (XAI). IEEE Access **6**, 52138–52160 (2018). https://doi.org/10.1109/ACCESS.2018.2870052
2. Adebayo, J., Gilmer, J., Muelly, M., Goodfellow, I.J., Hardt, M., Kim, B.: Sanity checks for saliency maps. In: NeurIPS, pp. 9525–9536 (2018)
3. Adee, S.: Bad bugs: the worst disasters caused by software fails (2013). https://www.newscientist.com/gallery/software-bugs/
4. Aglin, G., Nijssen, S., Schaus, P.: Learning optimal decision trees using caching branch-and-bound search. In: AAAI, pp. 3146–3153 (2020)
5. Aglin, G., Nijssen, S., Schaus, P.: PyDL8.5: a library for learning optimal decision trees, pp. 5222–5224 (2020)

6. AI Incident Database (2023). https://incidentdatabase.ai/
7. Algorithm Watch: AI ethics guidelines global inventory (2020). https://inventory.algorithmwatch.org/
8. Alkassar, E., Böhme, S., Mehlhorn, K., Rizkallah, C.: Verification of certifying computations. In: Gopalakrishnan, G., Qadeer, S. (eds.) CAV 2011. LNCS, vol. 6806, pp. 67–82. Springer, Heidelberg (2011). https://doi.org/10.1007/978-3-642-22110-1_7
9. Alkassar, E., Böhme, S., Mehlhorn, K., Rizkallah, C.: A framework for the verification of certifying computations. J. Autom. Reason. **52**(3), 241–273 (2014). https://doi.org/10.1007/s10817-013-9289-2
10. Alos, J., Ansotegui, C., Torres, E.: Learning optimal decision trees using MaxSAT. CoRR abs/2110.13854 (2021). https://arxiv.org/abs/2110.13854
11. Amgoud, L.: Non-monotonic explanation functions. In: Vejnarová, J., Wilson, N. (eds.) ECSQARU 2021. LNCS (LNAI), vol. 12897, pp. 19–31. Springer, Cham (2021). https://doi.org/10.1007/978-3-030-86772-0_2
12. Amgoud, L.: Int. J. Approx. Reason. (2023, in Press)
13. Amgoud, L., Ben-Naim, J.: Axiomatic foundations of explainability. In: IJCAI, pp. 636–642 (2022)
14. Amgoud, L., Prade, H.: Explaining qualitative decision under uncertainty by argumentation. In: AAAI, pp. 219–224 (2006)
15. Amgoud, L., Prade, H.: Using arguments for making and explaining decisions. Artif. Intell. **173**(3–4), 413–436 (2009)
16. Amgoud, L., Serrurier, M.: Agents that argue and explain classifications. Auton. Agents Multi Agent Syst. **16**(2), 187–209 (2008)
17. Angelino, E., Larus-Stone, N., Alabi, D., Seltzer, M., Rudin, C.: Learning certifiably optimal rule lists for categorical data. J. Mach. Learn. Res. **18**, 234:1–234:78 (2017)
18. Angelino, E., Larus-Stone, N., Alabi, D., Seltzer, M.I., Rudin, C.: Learning certifiably optimal rule lists. In: KDD, pp. 35–44 (2017)
19. Arenas, M., Baez, D., Barceló, P., Pérez, J., Subercaseaux, B.: Foundations of symbolic languages for model interpretability. In: NeurIPS, pp. 11690–11701 (2021)
20. Arenas, M., Barceló, P., Bertossi, L.E., Monet, M.: The tractability of SHAP-score-based explanations for classification over deterministic and decomposable Boolean circuits. In: AAAI, pp. 6670–6678 (2021)
21. Arenas, M., Barceló, P., Romero, M., Subercaseaux, B.: On computing probabilistic explanations for decision trees. In: NeurIPS (2022)
22. Arenas, M., Barceló, P., Romero, M., Subercaseaux, B.: On computing probabilistic explanations for decision trees. CoRR abs/2207.12213 (2022). https://doi.org/10.48550/arXiv.2207.12213
23. Arora, S., Barak, B.: Computational Complexity - A Modern Approach. Cambridge University Press (2009). https://www.cambridge.org/catalogue/catalogue.asp?isbn=9780521424264
24. Asher, N., Paul, S., Russell, C.: Fair and adequate explanations. In: Holzinger, A., Kieseberg, P., Tjoa, A.M., Weippl, E. (eds.) CD-MAKE 2021. LNCS, vol. 12844, pp. 79–97. Springer, Cham (2021). https://doi.org/10.1007/978-3-030-84060-0_6
25. Audemard, G., Bellart, S., Bounia, L., Koriche, F., Lagniez, J., Marquis, P.: On the computational intelligibility of Boolean classifiers. In: KR, pp. 74–86 (2021)
26. Audemard, G., Bellart, S., Bounia, L., Koriche, F., Lagniez, J., Marquis, P.: On preferred abductive explanations for decision trees and random forests. In: IJCAI, pp. 643–650 (2022)

27. Audemard, G., Bellart, S., Bounia, L., Koriche, F., Lagniez, J., Marquis, P.: On the explanatory power of Boolean decision trees. Data Knowl. Eng. **142**, 102088 (2022)
28. Audemard, G., Bellart, S., Bounia, L., Koriche, F., Lagniez, J., Marquis, P.: Trading complexity for sparsity in random forest explanations. In: AAAI, pp. 5461–5469 (2022)
29. Audemard, G., Koriche, F., Marquis, P.: On tractable XAI queries based on compiled representations. In: KR, pp. 838–849 (2020)
30. Australian Gov.: Australia's artificial intelligence ethics framework (2021). https://tiny.cc/ey8juz. Accessed 01 Dec 2021
31. Australian Gov.: Australia's AU action plan. tiny.cc/hy8juz (2021). Accessed 01 Dec 2021
32. Avellaneda, F.: Learning optimal decision trees from large datasets. CoRR abs/1904.06314 (2019). https://arxiv.org/abs/1904.06314
33. Avellaneda, F.: Efficient inference of optimal decision trees. In: AAAI, pp. 3195–3202 (2020)
34. Bacchus, F., Katsirelos, G.: Using minimal correction sets to more efficiently compute minimal unsatisfiable sets. In: Kroening, D., Păsăreanu, C.S. (eds.) CAV 2015. LNCS, vol. 9207, pp. 70–86. Springer, Cham (2015). https://doi.org/10.1007/978-3-319-21668-3_5
35. Bacchus, F., Katsirelos, G.: Finding a collection of MUSes incrementally. In: Quimper, C.-G. (ed.) CPAIOR 2016. LNCS, vol. 9676, pp. 35–44. Springer, Cham (2016). https://doi.org/10.1007/978-3-319-33954-2_3
36. Bach, S., Binder, A., Montavon, G., Klauschen, F., Müller, K.R., Samek, W.: On pixel-wise explanations for non-linear classifier decisions by layer-wise relevance propagation. PLoS ONE **10**(7), e0130140 (2015)
37. Bailey, J., Stuckey, P.J.: Discovery of minimal unsatisfiable subsets of constraints using hitting set dualization. In: Hermenegildo, M.V., Cabeza, D. (eds.) PADL 2005. LNCS, vol. 3350, pp. 174–186. Springer, Heidelberg (2005). https://doi.org/10.1007/978-3-540-30557-6_14
38. Barceló, P., Monet, M., Pérez, J., Subercaseaux, B.: Model interpretability through the lens of computational complexity. In: NeurIPS (2020)
39. Barker, C.: The top 10 IT disasters of all time (2007). https://www.zdnet.com/article/the-top-10-it-disasters-of-all-time/
40. Bassan, S., Katz, G.: Towards formal approximated minimal explanations of neural networks. In: TACAS (2023)
41. Bastani, O., Kim, C., Bastani, H.: Interpretability via model extraction. CoRR abs/1706.09773 (2017)
42. Bastani, O., Kim, C., Bastani, H.: Interpreting blackbox models via model extraction. CoRR abs/1705.08504 (2017)
43. Behrouz, A., Lécuyer, M., Rudin, C., Seltzer, M.I.: Fast optimization of weighted sparse decision trees for use in optimal treatment regimes and optimal policy design. In: CIKM Workshops (2022)
44. Belov, A., Lynce, I., Marques-Silva, J.: Towards efficient MUS extraction. AI Commun. **25**(2), 97–116 (2012). https://doi.org/10.3233/AIC-2012-0523
45. Ben-Ari, M.: Mathematical Logic for Computer Science. Springer, Cham (2012). https://doi.org/10.1007/978-1-4471-4129-7
46. Bendík, J., Černá, I.: MUST: minimal unsatisfiable subsets enumeration tool. In: TACAS 2020. LNCS, vol. 12078, pp. 135–152. Springer, Cham (2020). https://doi.org/10.1007/978-3-030-45190-5_8

47. Bendík, J., Cerna, I.: Rotation based MSS/MCS enumeration. In: LPAR, pp. 120–137 (2020)
48. Bendík, J., Černá, I., Beneš, N.: Recursive online enumeration of all minimal unsatisfiable subsets. In: Lahiri, S.K., Wang, C. (eds.) ATVA 2018. LNCS, vol. 11138, pp. 143–159. Springer, Cham (2018). https://doi.org/10.1007/978-3-030-01090-4_9
49. Bengio, Y., LeCun, Y., Hinton, G.E.: Deep learning for AI. Commun. ACM **64**(7), 58–65 (2021). https://doi.org/10.1145/3448250
50. Bertot, Y., Castéran, P.: Interactive Theorem Proving and Program Development - Coq'Art: The Calculus of Inductive Constructions. Texts in Theoretical Computer Science. An EATCS Series, Springer, Cham (2004). https://doi.org/10.1007/978-3-662-07964-5
51. Bertsimas, D., Dunn, J.: Optimal classification trees. Mach. Learn. **106**(7), 1039–1082 (2017). https://doi.org/10.1007/s10994-017-5633-9
52. Bessiere, C., Hebrard, E., O'Sullivan, B.: Minimising decision tree size as combinatorial optimisation. In: Gent, I.P. (ed.) CP 2009. LNCS, vol. 5732, pp. 173–187. Springer, Heidelberg (2009). https://doi.org/10.1007/978-3-642-04244-7_16
53. Bianchi, F., Curry, A.C., Hovy, D.: Viewpoint: artificial intelligence accidents waiting to happen? J. Artif. Intell. Res. **76**, 193–199 (2023). https://doi.org/10.1613/jair.1.14263
54. Bienvenu, M.: Prime implicates and prime implicants: from propositional to modal logic. J. Artif. Intell. Res. **36**, 71–128 (2009). https://doi.org/10.1613/jair.2754
55. Biere, A., Heule, M., van Maaren, H., Walsh, T. (eds.): Handbook of Satisfiability. IOS Press (2021)
56. Birnbaum, E., Lozinskii, E.L.: Consistent subsets of inconsistent systems: structure and behaviour. J. Exp. Theor. Artif. Intell. **15**(1), 25–46 (2003). https://doi.org/10.1080/0952813021000026795
57. Bixby, R.E.: Solving real-world linear programs: a decade and more of progress. Oper. Res. **50**(1), 3–15 (2002). https://doi.org/10.1287/opre.50.1.3.17780
58. Bixby, R.E., Rothberg, E.: Progress in computational mixed integer programming - a look back from the other side of the tipping point. Ann. Oper. Res. **149**(1), 37–41 (2007). https://doi.org/10.1007/s10479-006-0091-y
59. Béjar, R., Morgado, A., Planes, J., Marques-Silva, J.: Logic-based explainability with missing data (2023, working paper)
60. Blanc, G., Koch, C., Lange, J., Tan, L.: The query complexity of certification. In: STOC, pp. 623–636 (2022)
61. Blanc, G., Koch, C., Lange, J., Tan, L.: A query-optimal algorithm for finding counterfactuals. In: ICML, pp. 2075–2090 (2022)
62. Blanc, G., Lange, J., Tan, L.: Provably efficient, succinct, and precise explanations. In: NeurIPS (2021)
63. Bogaerts, B., Gamba, E., Guns, T.: A framework for step-wise explaining how to solve constraint satisfaction problems. Artif. Intell. **300**, 103550 (2021). https://doi.org/10.1016/j.artint.2021.103550
64. Boros, E., Elbassioni, K., Gurvich, V., Khachiyan, L.: An efficient implementation of a quasi-polynomial algorithm for generating hypergraph transversals. In: Di Battista, G., Zwick, U. (eds.) ESA 2003. LNCS, vol. 2832, pp. 556–567. Springer, Heidelberg (2003). https://doi.org/10.1007/978-3-540-39658-1_51
65. Boumazouza, R., Cheikh-Alili, F., Mazure, B., Tabia, K.: A symbolic approach for counterfactual explanations. In: Davis, J., Tabia, K. (eds.) SUM 2020. LNCS (LNAI), vol. 12322, pp. 270–277. Springer, Cham (2020). https://doi.org/10.1007/978-3-030-58449-8_21

66. Boumazouza, R., Alili, F.C., Mazure, B., Tabia, K.: ASTERYX: a model-agnostic sat-based approach for symbolic and score-based explanations. In: CIKM, pp. 120–129 (2021)
67. Bradley, A.R., Manna, Z.: The Calculus of Computation: Decision Procedures with Applications to Verification. Springer, Cham (2007)
68. Bradley, A.R., Manna, Z.: Checking safety by inductive generalization of counterexamples to induction. In: FMCAD, pp. 173–180 (2007)
69. Breiman, L.: Random forests. Mach. Learn. 45(1), 5–32 (2001). https://doi.org/10.1023/A:1010933404324
70. Breiman, L.: Statistical modeling: the two cultures. Stat. Sci. 16(3), 199–231 (2001)
71. Breiman, L., Friedman, J.H., Olshen, R.A., Stone, C.J.: Classification and Regression Trees. Wadsworth (1984)
72. Brodley, C.E., Utgoff, P.E.: Multivariate decision trees. Mach. Learn. 19(1), 45–77 (1995)
73. den Broeck, G.V., Lykov, A., Schleich, M., Suciu, D.: On the tractability of SHAP explanations. In: AAAI, pp. 6505–6513 (2021)
74. Bylander, T., Allemang, D., Tanner, M.C., Josephson, J.R.: The computational complexity of abduction. Artif. Intell. 49(1–3), 25–60 (1991). https://doi.org/10.1016/0004-3702(91)90005-5
75. Camburu, O., Giunchiglia, E., Foerster, J., Lukasiewicz, T., Blunsom, P.: Can I trust the explainer? Verifying post-hoc explanatory methods. CoRR abs/1910.02065 (2019). https://arxiv.org/abs/1910.02065
76. Chakraborti, T., Sreedharan, S., Kambhampati, S.: The emerging landscape of explainable automated planning & decision making. In: IJCAI, pp. 4803–4811 (2020)
77. Chen, C., Lin, K., Rudin, C., Shaposhnik, Y., Wang, S., Wang, T.: A holistic approach to interpretability in financial lending: Models, visualizations, and summary-explanations. Decis. Support Syst. 152, 113647 (2022). https://doi.org/10.1016/j.dss.2021.113647
78. Chen, C., Rudin, C.: An optimization approach to learning falling rule lists. In: AISTATS, pp. 604–612 (2018)
79. Chinneck, J.W., Dravnieks, E.W.: Locating minimal infeasible constraint sets in linear programs. INFORMS J. Comput. 3(2), 157–168 (1991)
80. Clark, P., Niblett, T.: The CN2 induction algorithm. Mach. Learn. 3, 261–283 (1989). https://doi.org/10.1007/BF00116835
81. Clarke, E.M., Henzinger, T.A., Veith, H., Bloem, R. (eds.): Springer, Cham (2018). https://doi.org/10.1007/978-3-319-10575-8
82. CNN: Tesla is under investigation because its cars keep hitting emergency vehicles (2021). https://cnn.it/3z6NXGF
83. Cook, S.A.: The complexity of theorem-proving procedures. In: Harrison, M.A., Banerji, R.B., Ullman, J.D. (eds.) STOC, pp. 151–158 (1971)
84. Cooper, M.C., Marques-Silva, J.: On the tractability of explaining decisions of classifiers. In: Michel, L.D. (ed.) CP, pp. 21:1–21:18 (2021)
85. Cooper, M.C., Marques-Silva, J.: Tractability of explaining classifier decisions. Artif. Intell. (2023). https://www.sciencedirect.com/science/article/pii/S0004370222001813
86. Cosmadakis, S.S., Kavvadias, D.J., Panagopoulou, L.: Resolution based algorithms for the transversal hypergraph generation problem. Theor. Comput. Sci. 815, 1–10 (2020). https://doi.org/10.1016/j.tcs.2020.02.033

87. Crama, Y., Hammer, P.L.: Boolean Functions - Theory, Algorithms, and Applications. Cambridge University Press (2011). https://www.cambridge.org/gb/knowledge/isbn/item6222210/?site_locale=en_GB

88. Cruz-Filipe, L., Marques-Silva, J., Schneider-Kamp, P.: Efficient certified resolution proof checking. In: Legay, A., Margaria, T. (eds.) TACAS 2017. LNCS, vol. 10205, pp. 118–135. Springer, Heidelberg (2017). https://doi.org/10.1007/978-3-662-54577-5_7

89. Cruz-Filipe, L., Marques-Silva, J., Schneider-Kamp, P.: Formally verifying the solution to the Boolean pythagorean triples problem. J. Autom. Reason. **63**(3), 695–722 (2019). https://doi.org/10.1007/s10817-018-9490-4

90. Cygan, M., et al.: Parameterized Algorithms. Springer, Cham (2015). https://doi.org/10.1007/978-3-319-21275-3

91. Daily, M., Medasani, S., Behringer, R., Trivedi, M.M.: Self-driving cars. Computer **50**(12), 18–23 (2017). https://doi.org/10.1109/MC.2017.4451204

92. Darbari, A., Fischer, B., Marques-Silva, J.: Industrial-strength certified SAT solving through verified SAT proof checking. In: Cavalcanti, A., Deharbe, D., Gaudel, M.-C., Woodcock, J. (eds.) ICTAC 2010. LNCS, vol. 6255, pp. 260–274. Springer, Heidelberg (2010). https://doi.org/10.1007/978-3-642-14808-8_18

93. DARPA: DARPA explainable Artificial Intelligence (XAI) program (2016). https://www.darpa.mil/program/explainable-artificial-intelligence. Accessed 01 Dec 2021

94. Darwiche, A.: Decomposable negation normal form. J. ACM **48**(4), 608–647 (2001). https://doi.org/10.1145/502090.502091

95. Darwiche, A.: On the tractable counting of theory models and its application to truth maintenance and belief revision. J. Appl. Non Class. Logics **11**(1–2), 11–34 (2001). https://doi.org/10.3166/jancl.11.11-34

96. Darwiche, A.: Three modern roles for logic in AI. In: PODS, pp. 229–243 (2020)

97. Darwiche, A., Hirth, A.: On the reasons behind decisions. In: ECAI, pp. 712–720 (2020)

98. Darwiche, A., Hirth, A.: On the (complete) reasons behind decisions. J. Logic Lang. Inf. 1–26 (2022, in press)

99. Darwiche, A., Ji, C.: On the computation of necessary and sufficient explanations. In: AAAI, pp. 5582–5591 (2022)

100. Darwiche, A., Marquis, P.: A knowledge compilation map. J. Artif. Intell. Res. **17**, 229–264 (2002). https://doi.org/10.1613/jair.989

101. Darwiche, A., Marquis, P.: On quantifying literals in Boolean logic and its applications to explainable AI. J. Artif. Intell. Res. (2021)

102. Davis, M., Logemann, G., Loveland, D.W.: A machine program for theorem-proving. Commun. ACM **5**(7), 394–397 (1962). https://doi.org/10.1145/368273.368557

103. Davis, M., Putnam, H.: A computing procedure for quantification theory. J. ACM **7**(3), 201–215 (1960). https://doi.org/10.1145/321033.321034

104. DeArman, A.: The wild, wild west: a case study of self-driving vehicle testing in Arizona. Ariz. L. Rev. **61**, 983 (2019)

105. Demirovic, E., et al.: Murtree: optimal decision trees via dynamic programming and search. J. Mach. Learn. Res. **23**, 26:1–26:47 (2022). https://jmlr.org/papers/v23/20-520.html

106. Demirovic, E., Stuckey, P.J.: Optimal decision trees for nonlinear metrics. In: AAAI, pp. 3733–3741 (2021)

107. Dillig, I., Dillig, T., McMillan, K.L., Aiken, A.: Minimum satisfying assignments for SMT. In: Madhusudan, P., Seshia, S.A. (eds.) CAV 2012. LNCS, vol. 7358, pp. 394–409. Springer, Heidelberg (2012). https://doi.org/10.1007/978-3-642-31424-7_30

108. Dimanov, B., Bhatt, U., Jamnik, M., Weller, A.: You shouldn't trust me: learning models which conceal unfairness from multiple explanation methods. In: ECAI, pp. 2473–2480 (2020)

109. Eifler, R., Cashmore, M., Hoffmann, J., Magazzeni, D., Steinmetz, M.: A new approach to plan-space explanation: analyzing plan-property dependencies in over-subscription planning. In: AAAI, pp. 9818–9826 (2020)

110. Eifler, R., Frank, J., Hoffmann, J.: Explaining soft-goal conflicts through constraint relaxations. In: IJCAI, pp. 4621–4627 (2022). https://doi.org/10.24963/ijcai.2022/641

111. Eiter, T., Gottlob, G.: The complexity of logic-based abduction. J. ACM **42**(1), 3–42 (1995). https://doi.org/10.1145/200836.200838

112. Eiter, T., Gottlob, G.: Identifying the minimal transversals of a hypergraph and related problems. SIAM J. Comput. **24**(6), 1278–1304 (1995)

113. Elffers, J., Gocht, S., McCreesh, C., Nordström, J.: Justifying all differences using pseudo-boolean reasoning. In: AAAI, pp. 1486–1494 (2020)

114. Espasa, J., Gent, I.P., Hoffmann, R., Jefferson, C., Lynch, A.M.: Using small MUSes to explain how to solve pen and paper puzzles. CoRR abs/2104.15040 (2021). https://arxiv.org/abs/2104.15040

115. EU: General Data Protection Regulation (2016). https://eur-lex.europa.eu/eli/reg/2016/679/oj. Accessed 01 Dec 2021

116. EU: Artificial Intelligence Act (2021). https://tiny.cc/wy8juz. Accessed 01 Dec 2021

117. EU: Coordinated plan on artificial intelligence - 2021 review (2021). https://bit.ly/3hJG2HF. Accessed 01 Dec 2021

118. Falappa, M.A., Kern-Isberner, G., Simari, G.R.: Explanations, belief revision and defeasible reasoning. Artif. Intell. **141**(1/2), 1–28 (2002)

119. Fan, X., Toni, F.: On computing explanations in abstract argumentation. In: ECAI, pp. 1005–1006 (2014)

120. Fard, M.M., Canini, K.R., Cotter, A., Pfeifer, J., Gupta, M.R.: Fast and flexible monotonic functions with ensembles of lattices. In: NeurIPS, pp. 2919–2927 (2016)

121. Felfernig, A., Schubert, M., Zehentner, C.: An efficient diagnosis algorithm for inconsistent constraint sets. AI EDAM **26**(1), 53–62 (2012). https://doi.org/10.1017/S0890060411000011

122. Ferreira, J., de Sousa Ribeiro, M., Gonçalves, R., Leite, J.: Looking inside the black-box: logic-based explanations for neural networks. In: KR, pp. 432–442 (2022)

123. Fischetti, M., Jo, J.: Deep neural networks and mixed integer linear optimization. Constraints Int. J. **23**(3), 296–309 (2018). https://doi.org/10.1007/s10601-018-9285-6

124. Flach, P.A.: Machine Learning - The Art and Science of Algorithms that Make Sense of Data. CUP (2012)

125. Fomin, F.V., Kratsch, D.: Exact Exponential Algorithms. Texts in Theoretical Computer Science. An EATCS Series, Springer, Cham (2010). https://doi.org/10.1007/978-3-642-16533-7

126. Fox, M., Long, D., Magazzeni, D.: Explainable planning. CoRR abs/1709.10256 (2017). https://arxiv.org/abs/1709.10256

127. Fredman, M.L., Khachiyan, L.: On the complexity of dualization of monotone disjunctive normal forms. J. Algorithms **21**(3), 618–628 (1996)
128. Friedrich, G., Gottlob, G., Nejdl, W.: Hypothesis classification, abductive diagnosis and therapy. In: Gottlob, G., Nejdl, W. (eds.) Expert Systems in Engineering Principles and Applications. LNCS, vol. 462, pp. 69–78. Springer, Heidelberg (1990). https://doi.org/10.1007/3-540-53104-1_32
129. Frosst, N., Hinton, G.E.: Distilling a neural network into a soft decision tree. In: CExAIIA (2017)
130. Gamba, E., Bogaerts, B., Guns, T.: Efficiently explaining CSPs with unsatisfiable subset optimization. In: IJCAI, pp. 1381–1388 (2021)
131. Ganesh, V., Vardi, M.Y.: On the unreasonable effectiveness of SAT solvers. In: Roughgarden, T. (ed.) Beyond the Worst-Case Analysis of Algorithms, pp. 547–566. Cambridge University Press (2020). https://doi.org/10.1017/9781108637435. 032
132. Ganzinger, H., Korovin, K.: New directions in instantiation-based theorem proving. In: LICS, pp. 55–64 (2003)
133. Garfinkel, S.: History's worst software bugs (2005). https://www.wired.com/2005/11/historys-worst-software-bugs/
134. Gebser, M., Kaminski, R., Kaufmann, B., Schaub, T.: Answer Set Solving in Practice. Synthesis Lectures on Artificial Intelligence and Machine Learning. Morgan & Claypool Publishers (2012)
135. Ghassemi, M., Oakden-Rayner, L., Beam, A.L.: The false hope of current approaches to explainable artificial intelligence in health care. Lancet Digit. Health **3**(11), e745–e750 (2021)
136. Ghosh, B., Malioutov, D., Meel, K.S.: Classification rules in relaxed logical form. In: ECAI, pp. 2489–2496 (2020)
137. Ghosh, B., Malioutov, D., Meel, K.S.: Efficient learning of interpretable classification rules. J. Artif. Intell. Res. **74**, 1823–1863 (2022). https://doi.org/10.1613/jair.1.13482
138. Ghosh, B., Meel, K.S.: IMLI: an incremental framework for MaxSAT-based learning of interpretable classification rules. In: AIES, pp. 203–210 (2019)
139. Gocht, S., McBride, R., McCreesh, C., Nordström, J., Prosser, P., Trimble, J.: Certifying solvers for clique and maximum common (connected) subgraph problems. In: Simonis, H. (ed.) CP 2020. LNCS, vol. 12333, pp. 338–357. Springer, Cham (2020). https://doi.org/10.1007/978-3-030-58475-7_20
140. Gocht, S., McCreesh, C., Nordström, J.: Subgraph isomorphism meets cutting planes: solving with certified solutions. In: IJCAI, pp. 1134–1140 (2020)
141. Gocht, S., Nordström, J.: Certifying parity reasoning efficiently using pseudo-boolean proofs. In: AAAI, pp. 3768–3777 (2021)
142. Goodfellow, I.J., Bengio, Y., Courville, A.C.: Deep Learning. Adaptive Computation and Machine Learning. MIT Press (2016). https://www.deeplearningbook.org/
143. Goodfellow, I.J., et al.: Generative adversarial networks. Commun. ACM **63**(11), 139–144 (2020). https://doi.org/10.1145/3422622
144. Goodman, B., Flaxman, S.R.: European union regulations on algorithmic decision-making and a "right to explanation". AI Mag. **38**(3), 50–57 (2017). https://doi.org/10.1609/aimag.v38i3.2741
145. Gorji, N., Rubin, S.: Sufficient reasons for classifier decisions in the presence of domain constraints. In: AAAI (2022)
146. Grégoire, É., Izza, Y., Lagniez, J.: Boosting MCSes enumeration. In: IJCAI, pp. 1309–1315 (2018)

147. Grégoire, É., Lagniez, J., Mazure, B.: An experimentally efficient method for (MSS, CoMSS) partitioning. In: AAAI, pp. 2666–2673 (2014)
148. Greiner, R., Smith, B.A., Wilkerson, R.W.: A correction to the algorithm in Reiter's theory of diagnosis. Artif. Intell. **41**(1), 79–88 (1989). https://doi.org/10.1016/0004-3702(89)90079-9
149. Guidotti, R., Monreale, A., Ruggieri, S., Turini, F., Giannotti, F., Pedreschi, D.: A survey of methods for explaining black box models. ACM Comput. Surv. **51**(5), 93:1–93:42 (2019)
150. Gupta, S.D., Genc, B., O'Sullivan, B.: Explanation in constraint satisfaction: a survey. In: ICJAI, pp. 4400–4407 (2021)
151. Hachtel, G.D., Somenzi, F.: Logic Synthesis and Verification Algorithms. Springer, Cham (2006). https://doi.org/10.1007/0-387-31005-3
152. Hartshorne, C., Weiss, P. (eds.): Collected Papers of Charles Sanders Peirce. Harvard University Press (1931)
153. Hempel, C.G., Oppenheim, P.: Studies in the logic of explanation. Philos. Sci. **15**(2), 135–175 (1948)
154. Heule, M.J.H.: Schur number five. In: AAAI, pp. 6598–6606 (2018)
155. Heule, M.J.H., Kullmann, O.: The science of brute force. Commun. ACM **60**(8), 70–79 (2017). https://doi.org/10.1145/3107239
156. HLEG AI: Ethics guidelines for trustworthy AI (2019). https://digital-strategy.ec.europa.eu/en/library/ethics-guidelines-trustworthy-ai. Accessed 01 Dec 2021
157. HLEG AI: Assessment list for trustworthy artificial intelligence (ALTAI) for self-assessment (2020). https://bit.ly/3jAeHds. Accessed 01 Dec 2021
158. Hoffmann, J., Magazzeni, D.: Explainable AI planning (XAIP): overview and the case of contrastive explanation (extended abstract). In: Krötzsch, M., Stepanova, D. (eds.) RW, pp. 277–282 (2019)
159. Holzinger, A., Goebel, R., Fong, R., Moon, T., Müller, K., Samek, W. (eds.): LNAI, vol. 13200. Springer, Cham (2022). https://doi.org/10.1007/978-3-031-04083-2
160. Holzinger, A., Saranti, A., Molnar, C., Biecek, P., Samek, W.: Explainable AI methods - a brief overview. In: Holzinger, A., Goebel, R., Fong, R., Moon, T., Müller, K.R., Samek, W. (eds.) xxAI 2020. LNCS, vol. 13200, pp. 13–38. Springer, Cham (2022). https://doi.org/10.1007/978-3-031-04083-2_2
161. Hu, H., Siala, M., Hebrard, E., Huguet, M.: Learning optimal decision trees with MaxSAT and its integration in AdaBoost. In: IJCAI, pp. 1170–1176 (2020)
162. Hu, X., Rudin, C., Seltzer, M.I.: Optimal sparse decision trees. In: NeurIPS, pp. 7265–7273 (2019)
163. Huang, X., Cooper, M.C., Morgado, A., Planes, J., Marques-Silva, J.: Feature necessity & relevancy in ML classifier explanations. In: TACAS (2023)
164. Huang, X., Izza, Y., Ignatiev, A., Cooper, M.C., Asher, N., Marques-Silva, J.: Efficient explanations for knowledge compilation languages. CoRR abs/2107.01654 (2021). https://arxiv.org/abs/2107.01654
165. Huang, X., Izza, Y., Ignatiev, A., Cooper, M.C., Asher, N., Marques-Silva, J.: Tractable explanations for d-DNNF classifiers. In: AAAI, pp. 5719–5728 (2022)
166. Huang, X., Izza, Y., Ignatiev, A., Marques-Silva, J.: On efficiently explaining graph-based classifiers. In: KR, pp. 356–367 (2021)
167. Huang, X., Izza, Y., Marques-Silva, J.: Solving explainability queries with quantification: the case of feature membership. In: AAAI (2023)
168. Huang, X., Marques-Silva, J.: On deciding feature membership in explanations of SDD & related classifiers. CoRR abs/2202.07553 (2022). https://arxiv.org/abs/2202.07553

169. Hubara, I., Courbariaux, M., Soudry, D., El-Yaniv, R., Bengio, Y.: Binarized neural networks. In: NeurIPS, pp. 4107–4115 (2016)

170. Ignatiev, A.: Towards trustable explainable AI. In: IJCAI, pp. 5154–5158 (2020)

171. Ignatiev, A., Cooper, M.C., Siala, M., Hebrard, E., Marques-Silva, J.: Towards formal fairness in machine learning. In: Simonis, H. (ed.) CP 2020. LNCS, vol. 12333, pp. 846–867. Springer, Cham (2020). https://doi.org/10.1007/978-3-030-58475-7_49

172. Ignatiev, A., Izza, Y., Stuckey, P.J., Marques-Silva, J.: Using MaxSAT for efficient explanations of tree ensembles. In: AAAI, pp. 3776–3785 (2022)

173. Ignatiev, A., Lam, E., Stuckey, P.J., Marques-Silva, J.: A scalable two stage approach to computing optimal decision sets. In: AAAI, pp. 3806–3814 (2021)

174. Ignatiev, A., Marques-Silva, J.: SAT-based rigorous explanations for decision lists. In: Li, C.-M., Manyà, F. (eds.) SAT 2021. LNCS, vol. 12831, pp. 251–269. Springer, Cham (2021). https://doi.org/10.1007/978-3-030-80223-3_18

175. Ignatiev, A., Morgado, A., Marques-Silva, J.: Propositional abduction with implicit hitting sets, pp. 1327–1335 (2016)

176. Ignatiev, A., Morgado, A., Marques-Silva, J.: PySAT: a python toolkit for prototyping with SAT oracles. In: Beyersdorff, O., Wintersteiger, C.M. (eds.) SAT 2018. LNCS, vol. 10929, pp. 428–437. Springer, Cham (2018). https://doi.org/10.1007/978-3-319-94144-8_26

177. Ignatiev, A., Narodytska, N., Asher, N., Marques-Silva, J.: From contrastive to abductive explanations and back again. In: Baldoni, M., Bandini, S. (eds.) AIxIA 2020. LNCS (LNAI), vol. 12414, pp. 335–355. Springer, Cham (2021). https://doi.org/10.1007/978-3-030-77091-4_21

178. Ignatiev, A., Narodytska, N., Marques-Silva, J.: Abduction-based explanations for machine learning models. In: AAAI, pp. 1511–1519 (2019)

179. Ignatiev, A., Narodytska, N., Marques-Silva, J.: On relating explanations and adversarial examples. In: NeurIPS, pp. 15857–15867 (2019)

180. Ignatiev, A., Narodytska, N., Marques-Silva, J.: On validating, repairing and refining heuristic ML explanations. CoRR abs/1907.02509 (2019). https://arxiv.org/abs/1907.02509

181. Ignatiev, A., Pereira, F., Narodytska, N., Marques-Silva, J.: A SAT-based approach to learn explainable decision sets. In: IJCAR, pp. 627–645 (2018)

182. Ignatiev, A., Previti, A., Liffiton, M., Marques-Silva, J.: Smallest MUS extraction with minimal hitting set dualization. In: Pesant, G. (ed.) CP 2015. LNCS, vol. 9255, pp. 173–182. Springer, Cham (2015). https://doi.org/10.1007/978-3-319-23219-5_13

183. Irish Times: 'It happened so fast': Inside a fatal Tesla Autopilot crash. https://bit.ly/3mnvzFJ

184. Israni, E.: Algorithmic due process: mistaken accountability and attribution in State v. Loomis. Harvard J. Law Technol. (2017). https://bit.ly/389PYcq

185. Izza, Y., Huang, X., Ignatiev, A., Narodytska, N., Cooper, M.C., Marques-Silva, J.: On computing probabilistic abductive explanations. CoRR abs/2212.05990 (2022). https://doi.org/10.48550/arXiv.2212.05990

186. Izza, Y., Ignatiev, A., Marques-Silva, J.: On explaining decision trees. CoRR abs/2010.11034 (2020). https://arxiv.org/abs/2010.11034

187. Izza, Y., Ignatiev, A., Marques-Silva, J.: On tackling explanation redundancy in decision trees. J. Artif. Intell. Res. **75**, 261–321 (2022). https://jair.org/index.php/jair/article/view/13575/

188. Izza, Y., Ignatiev, A., Marques-Silva, J.: On tackling explanation redundancy in decision trees. CoRR abs/2205.09971 (2022). https://doi.org/10.48550/arXiv. 2205.09971

189. Izza, Y., Ignatiev, A., Narodytska, N., Cooper, M.C., Marques-Silva, J.: Efficient explanations with relevant sets. CoRR abs/2106.00546 (2021). https://arxiv.org/ abs/2106.00546

190. Izza, Y., Ignatiev, A., Narodytska, N., Cooper, M.C., Marques-Silva, J.: Provably precise, succinct and efficient explanations for decision trees. CoRR abs/2205.09569 (2022). https://doi.org/10.48550/arXiv.2205.09569

191. Izza, Y., Marques-Silva, J.: On explaining random forests with SAT. In: IJCAI, pp. 2584–2591 (2021)

192. Izza, Y., Marques-Silva, J.: On computing relevant features for explaining NBCs. CoRR abs/2207.04748 (2022). https://doi.org/10.48550/arXiv.2207.04748

193. Janota, M., Klieber, W., Marques-Silva, J., Clarke, E.M.: Solving QBF with counterexample guided refinement. Artif. Intell. **234**, 1–25 (2016). https://doi.org/10. 1016/j.artint.2016.01.004

194. Janota, M., Marques-Silva, J.: Abstraction-based algorithm for 2QBF. In: Sakallah, K.A., Simon, L. (eds.) SAT 2011. LNCS, vol. 6695, pp. 230–244. Springer, Heidelberg (2011). https://doi.org/10.1007/978-3-642-21581-0_19

195. Janota, M., Marques-Silva, J.: Solving QBF by clause selection. In: IJCAI, pp. 325–331 (2015)

196. Janota, M., Morgado, A.: SAT-based encodings for optimal decision trees with explicit paths. In: Pulina, L., Seidl, M. (eds.) SAT 2020. LNCS, vol. 12178, pp. 501–518. Springer, Cham (2020). https://doi.org/10.1007/978-3-030-51825-7_35

197. Juba, B.: Learning abductive reasoning using random examples. In: AAAI, pp. 999–1007 (2016)

198. Junker, U.: QUICKXPLAIN: preferred explanations and relaxations for overconstrained problems. In: AAAI, pp. 167–172 (2004)

199. Kahn, J.: What's wrong with "explainable A.I." (2016). https://bit.ly/3rLENgZ

200. Karimi, A., Barthe, G., Schölkopf, B., Valera, I.: A survey of algorithmic recourse: definitions, formulations, solutions, and prospects. CoRR abs/2010.04050 (2020). https://arxiv.org/abs/2010.04050. Accepted for publication at ACM Computing Surveys

201. Karimi, A., Schölkopf, B., Valera, I.: Algorithmic recourse: from counterfactual explanations to interventions. In: FAccT, pp. 353–362 (2021)

202. Katz, G., Barrett, C., Dill, D.L., Julian, K., Kochenderfer, M.J.: Reluplex: an efficient SMT solver for verifying deep neural networks. In: Majumdar, R., Kunčak, V. (eds.) CAV 2017. LNCS, vol. 10426, pp. 97–117. Springer, Cham (2017). https://doi.org/10.1007/978-3-319-63387-9_5

203. Katz, G., et al.: The marabou framework for verification and analysis of deep neural networks. In: Dillig, I., Tasiran, S. (eds.) CAV 2019. LNCS, vol. 11561, pp. 443–452. Springer, Cham (2019). https://doi.org/10.1007/978-3-030-25540-4_26

204. Kavvadias, D.J., Stavropoulos, E.C.: Evaluation of an algorithm for the transversal hypergraph problem. In: Vitter, J.S., Zaroliagis, C.D. (eds.) WAE 1999. LNCS, vol. 1668, pp. 72–84. Springer, Heidelberg (1999). https://doi.org/10.1007/3-540-48318-7_8

205. Kavvadias, D.J., Stavropoulos, E.C.: An efficient algorithm for the transversal hypergraph generation. J. Graph Algorithms Appl. **9**(2), 239–264 (2005). https:// doi.org/10.7155/jgaa.00107

206. Khachiyan, L., Boros, E., Elbassioni, K., Gurvich, V.: A new algorithm for the hypergraph transversal problem. In: Wang, L. (ed.) COCOON 2005. LNCS, vol. 3595, pp. 767–776. Springer, Heidelberg (2005). https://doi.org/10.1007/11533719_78

207. Khachiyan, L., Boros, E., Elbassioni, K.M., Gurvich, V.: An efficient implementation of a quasi-polynomial algorithm for generating hypergraph transversals and its application in joint generation. Discret. Appl. Math. 154(16), 2350–2372 (2006). https://doi.org/10.1016/j.dam.2006.04.012

208. Kim, T.W., Routledge, B.R.: Why a right to an explanation of algorithmic decision-making should exist: a trust-based approach. Bus. Ethics Q. 32(1), 75–102 (2022)

209. Kindermans, P.-J., et al.: The (un)reliability of saliency methods. In: Samek, W., Montavon, G., Vedaldi, A., Hansen, L.K., Müller, K.-R. (eds.) Explainable AI: Interpreting, Explaining and Visualizing Deep Learning. LNCS (LNAI), vol. 11700, pp. 267–280. Springer, Cham (2019). https://doi.org/10.1007/978-3-030-28954-6_14

210. Kleine Büning, H., Lettmann, T.: Propositional Logic - Deduction and Algorithms, Cambridge Tracts in Theoretical Computer Science, vol. 48. Cambridge University Press (1999)

211. Knight, J.C.: Safety critical systems: challenges and directions. In: ICSE, pp. 547–550 (2002)

212. Koch, T., Berthold, T., Pedersen, J., Vanaret, C.: Progress in mathematical programming solvers from 2001 to 2020. EURO J. Comput. Optim. 100031 (2022)

213. Korovin, K.: iProver - an instantiation-based theorem prover for first-order logic (system description). In: IJCAR, pp. 292–298 (2008)

214. Kovács, L., Voronkov, A.: First-order theorem proving and VAMPIRE. In: Sharygina, N., Veith, H. (eds.) CAV 2013. LNCS, vol. 8044, pp. 1–35. Springer, Heidelberg (2013). https://doi.org/10.1007/978-3-642-39799-8_1

215. Krarup, B., Krivic, S., Magazzeni, D., Long, D., Cashmore, M., Smith, D.E.: Contrastive explanations of plans through model restrictions. J. Artif. Intell. Res. 72, 533–612 (2021). https://doi.org/10.1613/jair.1.12813

216. Krishna, S., et al.: The disagreement problem in explainable machine learning: a practitioner's perspective. CoRR abs/2202.01602 (2022). https://arxiv.org/abs/2202.01602

217. Krizhevsky, A., Sutskever, I., Hinton, G.E.: ImageNet classification with deep convolutional neural networks. Commun. ACM 60(6), 84–90 (2017). https://doi.org/10.1145/3065386

218. Kroening, D., Strichman, O.: Decision Procedures - An Algorithmic Point of View. Texts in Theoretical Computer Science. An EATCS Series, 2nd edn. Springer, Cham (2016). https://doi.org/10.1007/978-3-662-50497-0

219. Labreuche, C.: Explanation of pseudo-boolean functions using cooperative game theory and prime implicants. In: Dupin de Saint-Cyr, F., Öztürk-Escoffier, M., Potyka, N. (eds.) SUM 2022. LNAI, vol. 13562, pp. 295–308. Springer, Cham (2022). https://doi.org/10.1007/978-3-031-18843-5_20

220. Lakkaraju, H., Bach, S.H., Leskovec, J.: Interpretable decision sets: a joint framework for description and prediction. In: KDD, pp. 1675–1684 (2016)

221. Lakkaraju, H., Bastani, O.: "How do I fool you?": manipulating user trust via misleading black box explanations. In: AIES, pp. 79–85 (2020)

222. LeCun, Y., Bengio, Y., Hinton, G.: Deep learning. Nature 521(7553), 436–444 (2015)

223. Lee, T.B.: Report: software bug led to death in Uber's self-driving crash (2018). https://arstechnica.com/tech-policy/2018/05/report-software-bug-led-to-death-in-ubers-self-driving-crash/
224. Lelis, V.M., Guzmán, E., Belmonte, M.: Non-invasive meningitis diagnosis using decision trees. IEEE Access **8**, 18394–18407 (2020)
225. Liffiton, M.H., Malik, A.: Enumerating infeasibility: finding multiple MUSes quickly. In: Gomes, C., Sellmann, M. (eds.) CPAIOR 2013. LNCS, vol. 7874, pp. 160–175. Springer, Heidelberg (2013). https://doi.org/10.1007/978-3-642-38171-3_11
226. Liffiton, M.H., Previti, A., Malik, A., Marques-Silva, J.: Fast, flexible MUS enumeration. Constraints Int. J. **21**(2), 223–250 (2016). https://doi.org/10.1007/s10601-015-9183-0
227. Liffiton, M.H., Sakallah, K.A.: Algorithms for computing minimal unsatisfiable subsets of constraints. J. Autom. Reason. **40**(1), 1–33 (2008). https://doi.org/10.1007/s10817-007-9084-z
228. Lin, J., Zhong, C., Hu, D., Rudin, C., Seltzer, M.I.: Generalized and scalable optimal sparse decision trees. In: ICML, pp. 6150–6160 (2020)
229. Liu, C., Arnon, T., Lazarus, C., Strong, C.A., Barrett, C.W., Kochenderfer, M.J.: Algorithms for verifying deep neural networks. Found. Trends Optim. **4**(3–4), 244–404 (2021). https://doi.org/10.1561/2400000035
230. Liu, J., Zhong, C., Li, B., Seltzer, M., Rudin, C.: FasterRisk: fast and accurate interpretable risk scores. In: NeurIPS (2022)
231. Liu, X., Han, X., Zhang, N., Liu, Q.: Certified monotonic neural networks. In: NeurIPS (2020)
232. Liu, X., Lorini, E.: A logic for binary classifiers and their explanation. In: Baroni, P., Benzmüller, C., Wáng, Y.N. (eds.) CLAR 2021. LNCS (LNAI), vol. 13040, pp. 302–321. Springer, Cham (2021). https://doi.org/10.1007/978-3-030-89391-0_17
233. Liu, X., Lorini, E.: A logic of "Black Box" classifier systems. In: Ciabattoni, A., Pimentel, E., de Queiroz, R.J.G.B. (eds.) WoLLIC 2022. LNCS, vol. 13468, pp. 158–174. Springer, Cham (2022). https://doi.org/10.1007/978-3-031-15298-6_10
234. Lundberg, S.M., et al.: From local explanations to global understanding with explainable AI for trees. Nat. Mach. Intell. **2**(1), 56–67 (2020)
235. Lundberg, S.M., Lee, S.: A unified approach to interpreting model predictions. In: NeurIPS, pp. 4765–4774 (2017)
236. Luo, J., Liu, S.: Accelerating MUS enumeration by inconsistency graph partitioning. Sci. China Inf. Sci. **62**(11), 212104:1–212104:11 (2019)
237. Malfa, E.L., Michelmore, R., Zbrzezny, A.M., Paoletti, N., Kwiatkowska, M.: On guaranteed optimal robust explanations for NLP models. In: IJCAI, pp. 2658–2665 (2021)
238. Maliotov, D., Meel, K.S.: MLIC: a MaxSAT-based framework for learning interpretable classification rules. In: Hooker, J. (ed.) CP 2018. LNCS, vol. 11008, pp. 312–327. Springer, Cham (2018). https://doi.org/10.1007/978-3-319-98334-9_21
239. Marques-Silva, J., Gerspacher, T., Cooper, M.C., Ignatiev, A., Narodytska, N.: Explaining Naive Bayes and other linear classifiers with polynomial time and delay. In: NeurIPS (2020)
240. Marques-Silva, J., Gerspacher, T., Cooper, M.C., Ignatiev, A., Narodytska, N.: Explanations for monotonic classifiers. In: ICML, pp. 7469–7479 (2021)
241. Marques-Silva, J., Heras, F., Janota, M., Previti, A., Belov, A.: On computing minimal correction subsets. In: IJCAI, pp. 615–622 (2013)

242. Marques-Silva, J., Ignatiev, A.: Delivering trustworthy AI through formal XAI. In: AAAI, pp. 12342–12350 (2022)
243. Marques-Silva, J., Janota, M., Belov, A.: Minimal sets over monotone predicates in Boolean formulae. In: Sharygina, N., Veith, H. (eds.) CAV 2013. LNCS, vol. 8044, pp. 592–607. Springer, Heidelberg (2013). https://doi.org/10.1007/978-3-642-39799-8_39
244. Marques-Silva, J., Janota, M., Ignatiev, A., Morgado, A.: Efficient model based diagnosis with maximum satisfiability. In: IJCAI, pp. 1966–1972 (2015)
245. Marques-Silva, J., Janota, M., Mencía, C.: Minimal sets on propositional formulae. Problems and reductions. Artif. Intell. **252**, 22–50 (2017). https://doi.org/10.1016/j.artint.2017.07.005
246. Marques-Silva, J., Mencía, C.: Reasoning about inconsistent formulas. In: IJCAI, pp. 4899–4906 (2020)
247. Marques-Silva, J., Sakallah, K.A.: GRASP - a new search algorithm for satisfiability. In: Rutenbar, R.A., Otten, R.H.J.M. (eds.) ICCAD, pp. 220–227 (1996)
248. Marques-Silva, J., Sakallah, K.A.: GRASP: a search algorithm for propositional satisfiability. IEEE Trans. Comput. **48**(5), 506–521 (1999). https://doi.org/10.1109/12.769433
249. Marquis, P.: Extending abduction from propositional to first-order logic. In: Jorrand, P., Kelemen, J. (eds.) FAIR 1991. LNCS, vol. 535, pp. 141–155. Springer, Heidelberg (1991). https://doi.org/10.1007/3-540-54507-7_12
250. McConnell, R.M., Mehlhorn, K., Näher, S., Schweitzer, P.: Certifying algorithms. Comput. Sci. Rev. **5**(2), 119–161 (2011). https://doi.org/10.1016/j.cosrev.2010.09.009
251. McGregor, S.: Preventing repeated real world AI failures by cataloging incidents: the AI incident database. CoRR abs/2011.08512 (2020). https://arxiv.org/abs/2011.08512
252. McGregor, S.: Preventing repeated real world AI failures by cataloging incidents: the AI incident database. In: AAAI, pp. 15458–15463 (2021)
253. McGregor, S., Paeth, K., Lam, K.: Indexing AI risks with incidents, issues, and variants. CoRR abs/2211.10384 (2022). https://doi.org/10.48550/arXiv.2211.10384
254. McQuaid, P.A.: Software disasters - understanding the past, to improve the future. J. Softw. Evol. Process. **24**(5), 459–470 (2012). https://doi.org/10.1002/smr.500
255. McTavish, H., et al.: How smart guessing strategies can yield massive scalability improvements for sparse decision tree optimization. In: AAAI (2022)
256. Mencía, C., Ignatiev, A., Previti, A., Marques-Silva, J.: MCS extraction with sublinear oracle queries. In: Creignou, N., Le Berre, D. (eds.) SAT 2016. LNCS, vol. 9710, pp. 342–360. Springer, Cham (2016). https://doi.org/10.1007/978-3-319-40970-2_21
257. Mencía, C., Previti, A., Marques-Silva, J.: Literal-based MCS extraction. In: IJCAI, pp. 1973–1979 (2015)
258. Metodi, A., Stern, R., Kalech, M., Codish, M.: A novel SAT-based approach to model based diagnosis. J. Artif. Intell. Res. **51**, 377–411 (2014). https://doi.org/10.1613/jair.4503
259. Mill, J.S.: A System of Logic, Ratiocinative and Inductive, vol. 1. John W. Parker (1843)
260. Miller, G.A.: The magical number seven, plus or minus two: some limits on our capacity for processing information. Psychol. Rev. **63**(2), 81–97 (1956)
261. Miller, T.: Explanation in artificial intelligence: insights from the social sciences. Artif. Intell. **267**, 1–38 (2019)

262. Molnar, C.: Interpretable Machine Learning. Leanpub (2020). https://tiny.cc/6c76tz

263. Montavon, G., Samek, W., Müller, K.: Methods for interpreting and understanding deep neural networks. Digit. Signal Process. **73**, 1–15 (2018)

264. Morgado, A., Heras, F., Liffiton, M.H., Planes, J., Marques-Silva, J.: Iterative and core-guided MaxSAT solving: a survey and assessment. Constraints Int. J. **18**(4), 478–534 (2013)

265. Morgado, A., Liffiton, M., Marques-Silva, J.: MaxSAT-based MCS enumeration. In: Biere, A., Nahir, A., Vos, T. (eds.) HVC 2012. LNCS, vol. 7857, pp. 86–101. Springer, Heidelberg (2013). https://doi.org/10.1007/978-3-642-39611-3_13

266. Morgan, C.G.: Hypothesis generation by machine. Artif. Intell. **2**(2), 179–187 (1971)

267. Murthy, S.K., Kasif, S., Salzberg, S.: A system for induction of oblique decision trees. J. Artif. Intell. Res. **2**, 1–32 (1994)

268. Nagendran, M., et al.: Artificial intelligence versus clinicians: systematic review of design, reporting standards, and claims of deep learning studies. Bmj **368** (2020)

269. Nair, V., Hinton, G.E.: Rectified linear units improve restricted Boltzmann machines. In: ICML, pp. 807–814 (2010)

270. Narodytska, N., Bjørner, N.S., Marinescu, M.V., Sagiv, M.: Core-guided minimal correction set and core enumeration. In: IJCAI, pp. 1353–1361 (2018)

271. Narodytska, N., Ignatiev, A., Pereira, F., Marques-Silva, J.: Learning optimal decision trees with SAT. In: IJCAI, pp. 1362–1368 (2018)

272. Narodytska, N., Shrotri, A., Meel, K.S., Ignatiev, A., Marques-Silva, J.: Assessing heuristic machine learning explanations with model counting. In: Janota, M., Lynce, I. (eds.) SAT 2019. LNCS, vol. 11628, pp. 267–278. Springer, Cham (2019). https://doi.org/10.1007/978-3-030-24258-9_19

273. National Science and Technology Council (US). Select Committee on Artificial Intelligence: The national artificial intelligence research and development strategic plan: 2019 update (2019). https://www.nitrd.gov/pubs/National-AI-RD-Strategy-2019.pdf

274. Newman, J.: Explainability won't save AI. (2021)

275. Nijssen, S., Fromont, É.: Mining optimal decision trees from itemset lattices. In: KDD, pp. 530–539 (2007)

276. Nijssen, S., Fromont, É.: Optimal constraint-based decision tree induction from itemset lattices. Data Min. Knowl. Discov. **21**(1), 9–51 (2010). https://doi.org/10.1007/s10618-010-0174-x

277. OECD: Recommendation of the council on artificial intelligence (2021). https://legalinstruments.oecd.org/en/instruments/OECD-LEGAL-0449. Accessed 01 Dec 2021

278. Ohrimenko, O., Stuckey, P.J., Codish, M.: Propagation via lazy clause generation. Constraints **14**(3), 357–391 (2009)

279. Oliver, J.J.: Decision graphs - an extension of decision trees. Technical report. 92/173, Monash University (1992)

280. Ordyniak, S., Szeider, S.: Parameterized complexity of small decision tree learning. In: AAAI, pp. 6454–6462 (2021)

281. Papadimitriou, C.H.: Computational Complexity. Addison Wesley (1994)

282. Papadimitriou, C.H., Wolfe, D.: The complexity of facets resolved. J. Comput. Syst. Sci. **37**(1), 2–13 (1988). https://doi.org/10.1016/0022-0000(88)90042-6

283. Pérez, R.P., Uzcátegui, C.: Preferences and explanations. Artif. Intell. **149**(1), 1–30 (2003)

284. Perrow, C.: Normal Accidents: Living with High Risk Technologies. Basic Books (1984)
285. Pittaras, N., McGregor, S.: A taxonomic system for failure cause analysis of open source AI incidents. CoRR abs/2211.07280 (2022). https://doi.org/10.48550/arXiv.2211.07280
286. Plaisted, D.A., Greenbaum, S.: A structure-preserving clause form translation. J. Symb. Comput. **2**(3), 293–304 (1986). https://doi.org/10.1016/S0747-7171(86)80028-1
287. Pople, H.E.: On the mechanization of abductive logic. In: IJCAI, pp. 147–152 (1973)
288. Previti, A., Ignatiev, A., Morgado, A., Marques-Silva, J.: Prime compilation of non-clausal formulae. In: IJCAI, pp. 1980–1988 (2015)
289. Previti, A., Marques-Silva, J.: Partial MUS enumeration. In: AAAI (2013)
290. Previti, A., Mencía, C., Järvisalo, M., Marques-Silva, J.: Improving MCS enumeration via caching. In: Gaspers, S., Walsh, T. (eds.) SAT 2017. LNCS, vol. 10491, pp. 184–194. Springer, Cham (2017). https://doi.org/10.1007/978-3-319-66263-3_12
291. Previti, A., Mencía, C., Järvisalo, M., Marques-Silva, J.: Premise set caching for enumerating minimal correction subsets. In: AAAI, pp. 6633–6640 (2018)
292. ProPublica: Machine bias (2016). https://bit.ly/3zaHb2F
293. Quinlan, J.R.: Induction of decision trees. Mach. Learn. **1**(1), 81–106 (1986)
294. Quinlan, J.R.: C4.5: Programs for Machine Learning. Morgan-Kaufmann (1993)
295. Rabe, M.N., Seshia, S.A.: Incremental determinization. In: Creignou, N., Le Berre, D. (eds.) SAT 2016. LNCS, vol. 9710, pp. 375–392. Springer, Cham (2016). https://doi.org/10.1007/978-3-319-40970-2_23
296. Rabe, M.N., Tentrup, L.: CAQE: a certifying QBF solver. In: FMCAD, pp. 136–143 (2015)
297. Rago, A., Cocarascu, O., Bechlivanidis, C., Lagnado, D.A., Toni, F.: Argumentative explanations for interactive recommendations. Artif. Intell. **296**, 103506 (2021)
298. Rago, A., Cocarascu, O., Bechlivanidis, C., Toni, F.: Argumentation as a framework for interactive explanations for recommendations. In: KR, pp. 805–815 (2020)
299. Ras, G., Xie, N., van Gerven, M., Doran, D.: Explainable deep learning: a field guide for the uninitiated. J. Artif. Intell. Res. **73**, 329–396 (2022). https://doi.org/10.1613/jair.1.13200
300. Reiter, R.: A theory of diagnosis from first principles. Artif. Intell. **32**(1), 57–95 (1987). https://doi.org/10.1016/0004-3702(87)90062-2
301. Ribeiro, M.T., Singh, S., Guestrin, C.: "Why should I trust you?": explaining the predictions of any classifier. In: KDD, pp. 1135–1144 (2016)
302. Ribeiro, M.T., Singh, S., Guestrin, C.: Anchors: high-precision model-agnostic explanations. In: AAAI, pp. 1527–1535 (2018)
303. Rivest, R.L.: Learning decision lists. Mach. Learn. **2**(3), 229–246 (1987)
304. Rudin, C.: Stop explaining black box machine learning models for high stakes decisions and use interpretable models instead. Nat. Mach. Intell. **1**(5), 206–215 (2019)
305. Rudin, C., Chen, C., Chen, Z., Huang, H., Semenova, L., Zhong, C.: Interpretable machine learning: fundamental principles and 10 grand challenges. Stat. Surv. **16**, 1–85 (2022)

306. Rudin, C., Ertekin, S.: Learning customized and optimized lists of rules with mathematical programming. Math. Program. Comput. **10**(4), 659–702 (2018). https://doi.org/10.1007/s12532-018-0143-8
307. Rymon, R.: An SE-tree-based prime implicant generation algorithm. Ann. Math. Artif. Intell. **11**(1–4), 351–366 (1994). https://doi.org/10.1007/BF01530750
308. Saikko, P., Wallner, J.P., Järvisalo, M.: Implicit hitting set algorithms for reasoning beyond NP. In: KR, pp. 104–113 (2016)
309. Samek, W., Montavon, G., Lapuschkin, S., Anders, C.J., Müller, K.: Explaining deep neural networks and beyond: a review of methods and applications. Proc. IEEE **109**(3), 247–278 (2021). https://doi.org/10.1109/JPROC.2021.3060483
310. Samek, W., Montavon, G., Vedaldi, A., Hansen, L.K., Müller, K. (eds.): Springer, Cham (2019)
311. Savoca, K.: When software kills (2019). https://medium.com/swlh/when-software-kills-ab6f48a15825
312. Schidler, A., Szeider, S.: SAT-based decision tree learning for large data sets. In: AAAI, pp. 3904–3912 (2021)
313. Selman, B., Levesque, H.J.: Abductive and default reasoning: a computational core. In: AAAI, pp. 343–348 (1990)
314. Semenova, L., Rudin, C., Parr, R.: On the existence of simpler machine learning models. In: FAccT, pp. 1827–1858 (2022)
315. Seshia, S.A., Sadigh, D., Sastry, S.S.: Toward verified artificial intelligence. Commun. ACM **65**(7), 46–55 (2022). https://doi.org/10.1145/3503914
316. Shalev-Shwartz, S., Ben-David, S.: Understanding Machine Learning - From Theory to Algorithms. Cambridge University Press (2014). https://bit.ly/3LBlznb
317. Shanahan, M.: Prediction is deduction but explanation is abduction. In: IJCAI, pp. 1055–1060 (1989)
318. Shati, P., Cohen, E., McIlraith, S.A.: SAT-based approach for learning optimal decision trees with non-binary features. In: CP, pp. 50:1–50:16 (2021)
319. Shi, W., Shih, A., Darwiche, A., Choi, A.: On tractable representations of binary neural networks. In: KR, pp. 882–892 (2020)
320. Shih, A., Choi, A., Darwiche, A.: A symbolic approach to explaining Bayesian network classifiers. In: IJCAI, pp. 5103–5111 (2018)
321. Shih, A., Choi, A., Darwiche, A.: Compiling Bayesian network classifiers into decision graphs. In: AAAI, pp. 7966–7974 (2019)
322. Simonyan, K., Vedaldi, A., Zisserman, A.: Deep inside convolutional networks: visualising image classification models and saliency maps. In: ICLR (2014)
323. de Siqueira N., J.L., Puget, J.: Explanation-based generalisation of failures. In: ECAI, pp. 339–344 (1988)
324. Sivaraman, A., Farnadi, G., Millstein, T.D., den Broeck, G.V.: Counterexample-guided learning of monotonic neural networks. In: NeurIPS (2020)
325. Sixt, L., Granz, M., Landgraf, T.: When explanations lie: why many modified BP attributions fail. In: ICML, pp. 9046–9057 (2020)
326. Slack, D., Hilgard, S., Jia, E., Singh, S., Lakkaraju, H.: Fooling LIME and SHAP: adversarial attacks on post hoc explanation methods. In: AIES, pp. 180–186 (2020)
327. Sreedharan, S., Chakraborti, T., Kambhampati, S.: Foundations of explanations as model reconciliation. Artif. Intell. **301**, 103558 (2021). https://doi.org/10.1016/j.artint.2021.103558
328. Sreedharan, S., Soni, U., Verma, M., Srivastava, S., Kambhampati, S.: Bridging the gap: providing post-hoc symbolic explanations for sequential decision-making problems with inscrutable representations. In: ICLR (2022)

329. Sreedharan, S., Srivastava, S., Kambhampati, S.: Using state abstractions to compute personalized contrastive explanations for AI agent behavior. Artif. Intell. **301**, 103570 (2021). https://doi.org/10.1016/j.artint.2021.103570

330. Sreedharan, S., Srivastava, S., Smith, D.E., Kambhampati, S.: Why can't you do that HAL? Explaining unsolvability of planning tasks. In: IJCAI, pp. 1422–1430 (2019)

331. Swartout, W.R.: A digitalis therapy advisor with explanations. In: IJCAI, pp. 819–825 (1977)

332. Swartout, W.R.: XPLAIN: a system for creating and explaining expert consulting programs. Artif. Intell. **21**(3), 285–325 (1983)

333. Tanner, L., et al.: Decision tree algorithms predict the diagnosis and outcome of dengue fever in the early phase of illness. PLoS Neglected Trop. Dis. **2**(3), e196 (2008)

334. The Verge: UK ditches exam results generated by biased algorithm after student protests (2020). https://bit.ly/3kevIsB

335. Tjoa, E., Guan, C.: A survey on explainable artificial intelligence (XAI): toward medical XAI. IEEE Trans. Neural Netw. Learn. Syst. **32**(11), 4793–4813 (2021). https://doi.org/10.1109/TNNLS.2020.3027314

336. Tseitin, G.: On the complexity of derivation in propositional calculus. In: Studies in Constructive Mathematics and Mathematical Logic, pp. 115–125 (1968)

337. Umans, C., Villa, T., Sangiovanni-Vincentelli, A.L.: Complexity of two-level logic minimization. IEEE Trans. Comput. Aided Des. Integr. Circuits Syst. **25**(7), 1230–1246 (2006). https://doi.org/10.1109/TCAD.2005.855944

338. UNESCO: Draft recommendation on the ethics of artificial intelligence (2021). https://unesdoc.unesco.org/ark:/48223/pf0000374266. Accessed 01 Dec 2021

339. Ustun, B., Spangher, A., Liu, Y.: Actionable recourse in linear classification. In: FAT, pp. 10–19 (2019)

340. Valdes, G., Luna, J.M., Eaton, E., Simone, C.B., Ungar, L.H., Solberg, T.D.: MediBoost: a patient stratification tool for interpretable decision making in the era of precision medicine. Sci. Rep. **6**(1), 1–8 (2016)

341. Valiant, L.G.: A theory of the learnable. Commun. ACM **27**(11), 1134–1142 (1984). https://doi.org/10.1145/1968.1972

342. Vardi, M.Y.: On P, NP, and computational complexity. Commun. ACM **53**(11), 5 (2010). https://doi.org/10.1145/1839676.1839677

343. Vardi, M.Y.: Boolean satisfiability: theory and engineering. Commun. ACM **57**(3), 5 (2014). https://doi.org/10.1145/2578043

344. Vasileiou, S.L., Yeoh, W., Son, T.C., Kumar, A., Cashmore, M., Magazzeni, D.: A logic-based explanation generation framework for classical and hybrid planning problems. J. Artif. Intell. Res. **73**, 1473–1534 (2022). https://doi.org/10.1613/jair.1.13431

345. Venkatasubramanian, S., Alfano, M.: The philosophical basis of algorithmic recourse. In: FAT, pp. 284–293 (2020)

346. Verhaeghe, H., Nijssen, S., Pesant, G., Quimper, C., Schaus, P.: Learning optimal decision trees using constraint programming. Constraints Int. J. **25**(3–4), 226–250 (2020). https://doi.org/10.1007/s10601-020-09312-3

347. Verhaeghe, H., Nijssen, S., Pesant, G., Quimper, C., Schaus, P.: Learning optimal decision trees using constraint programming (extended abstract). In: IJCAI, pp. 4765–4769 (2020)

348. Verwer, S., Zhang, Y.: Learning decision trees with flexible constraints and objectives using integer optimization. In: Salvagnin, D., Lombardi, M. (eds.) CPAIOR

2017. LNCS, vol. 10335, pp. 94–103. Springer, Cham (2017). https://doi.org/10.1007/978-3-319-59776-8_8

349. Verwer, S., Zhang, Y.: Learning optimal classification trees using a binary linear program formulation. In: AAAI, pp. 1625–1632 (2019)

350. Viering, T.J., Wang, Z., Loog, M., Eisemann, E.: How to manipulate CNNs to make them lie: the GradCAM case. CoRR abs/1907.10901 (2019). https://arxiv.org/abs/1907.10901

351. Voronkov, A.: AVATAR: the architecture for first-order theorem provers. In: Biere, A., Bloem, R. (eds.) CAV 2014. LNCS, vol. 8559, pp. 696–710. Springer, Cham (2014). https://doi.org/10.1007/978-3-319-08867-9_46

352. Vos, D., Verwer, S.: Efficient training of robust decision trees against adversarial examples. In: ICML, pp. 10586–10595 (2021)

353. Vos, D., Verwer, S.: Robust optimal classification trees against adversarial examples. In: AAAI, pp. 8520–8528 (2022)

354. Wäldchen, S.: Towards explainable artificial intelligence - interpreting neural network classifiers with probabilistic prime implicants. Ph.D. thesis, Technischen Universität Berlin (2022)

355. Wäldchen, S., MacDonald, J., Hauch, S., Kutyniok, G.: The computational complexity of understanding binary classifier decisions. J. Artif. Intell. Res. 70, 351–387 (2021). https://doi.org/10.1613/jair.1.12359

356. Wang, F., Rudin, C.: Falling rule lists. In: AISTATS (2015)

357. Wang, H., Shakerin, F., Gupta, G.: FOLD-RM: a scalable, efficient, and explainable inductive learning algorithm for multi-category classification of mixed data. Theory Pract. Log. Program. 22(5), 658–677 (2022). https://doi.org/10.1017/S1471068422000205

358. Wang, T., Rudin, C., Doshi-Velez, F., Liu, Y., Klampfl, E., MacNeille, P.: A Bayesian framework for learning rule sets for interpretable classification. J. Mach. Learn. Res. 18, 70:1–70:37 (2017)

359. Weber, T., Amjad, H.: Efficiently checking propositional refutations in HOL theorem provers. J. Appl. Logic 7(1), 26–40 (2009). https://doi.org/10.1016/j.jal.2007.07.003

360. Wei, M., Zhou, Z.: AI ethics issues in real world: evidence from AI incident database. CoRR abs/2206.07635 (2022). https://doi.org/10.48550/arXiv.2206.07635

361. Williams, R.M., Yampolskiy, R.V.: Understanding and avoiding AI failures: a practical guide. CoRR abs/2104.12582 (2021). https://arxiv.org/abs/2104.12582

362. Wolf, L., Galanti, T., Hazan, T.: A formal approach to explainability. In: AIES, pp. 255–261 (2019)

363. Wu, X., Kumar, V. (eds.): The Top Ten Algorithms in Data Mining. CRC Press (2009)

364. You, S., Ding, D., Canini, K.R., Pfeifer, J., Gupta, M.R.: Deep lattice networks and partial monotonic functions. In: NeurIPS, pp. 2981–2989 (2017)

365. Yu, J., Ignatiev, A., Stuckey, P.J., Le Bodic, P.: Computing optimal decision sets with SAT. In: Simonis, H. (ed.) CP 2020. LNCS, vol. 12333, pp. 952–970. Springer, Cham (2020). https://doi.org/10.1007/978-3-030-58475-7_55

366. Yu, J., Ignatiev, A., Stuckey, P.J., Bodic, P.L.: Learning optimal decision sets and lists with SAT. J. Artif. Intell. Res. 72, 1251–1279 (2021). https://doi.org/10.1613/jair.1.12719

367. Yu, J., Ignatiev, A., Stuckey, P.J., Narodytska, N., Marques-Silva, J.: Eliminating the impossible, whatever remains must be true. CoRR abs/2206.09551 (2022). https://doi.org/10.48550/arXiv.2206.09551

368. Yu, J., Ignatiev, A., Stuckey, P.J., Narodytska, N., Marques-Silva, J.: Eliminating the impossible, whatever remains must be true: on extracting and applying background knowledge in the context of formal explanations. In: AAAI (2023)

Causal Inference in Data Analysis with Applications to Fairness and Explanations

Sudeepa Roy[1(✉)] and Babak Salimi[2]

[1] Duke University, Durham, NC, USA
sudeepa@cs.duke.edu
[2] University of California, San Diego, CA, USA
bsalimi@ucsd.edu

Abstract. Causal inference is a fundamental concept that goes beyond simple correlation and model-based prediction analysis, and is highly relevant in domains such as health, medicine, and the social sciences. Causal inference enables the estimation of the impact of an intervention or treatment on the world, making it critical for sound and robust policy making. However, randomized controlled experiments, which are typically considered as the gold standard for inferring causal conclusions, are often not feasible due to ethical, cost, or other constraints. Fortunately, there is a rich literature in Artificial Intelligence (AI), Machine Learning (ML), and Statistics on observational studies, which are methods for causal inference on observed or collected data under certain assumptions. In this paper, we provide an overview of popular formal and rigorous techniques for causal inference on observed data from the AI and Statistics literature. Furthermore, we discuss how concepts from causal inference can be used to infer fairness and enable explainability in machine learning models, which are critical in responsible data science when ML is used in making high-stake decisions in various contexts. Our discussion highlights the importance of using causal inference in ML models and provides insights on how to develop more transparent and responsible AI systems.

1 Introduction

The problem of *causal inference* goes beyond simple correlation, association, or model-based prediction analysis, and is practically indispensable in domains such as health, medicine, and the social sciences. For example, a medical researcher may want to determine whether a new drug is effective in curing a specific type of cancer. An economist may be interested in understanding whether a job-training program improves employment prospects, or whether an economic depression affects people's spending habits. A sociologist might study the effect of domestic violence on children's education or the effect of a special curricular activity on their class performance. A public health researcher may want to find out if providing incentives, such as reduced insurance premiums, for not smoking helps people quit.

Causal inference is crucial for sound and robust policy making, as it provides a means to estimate the impact of an intervention on the world. For instance, it has been observed that an increase in crime is strongly correlated with increased ice cream sales. However, having more ice cream does not causally relate to committing a crime. In this case, the common cause or confounding factor is the summer season, which increases both ice cream sales and the crime rate (e.g., see [1]). While this is an extreme example, it illustrates the potential pitfalls and waste of resources that can occur when wrong decisions are made based on correlations or predictions without proper causal analysis. In this paper, we will survey techniques for formal and rigorous causal analysis, and explore their applications in inferring fairness and explainability in data analysis.

The formal study of causality was initiated in statistical science in the 1920s and 1930s by Neyman [51] and Fisher [15], and later investigated by Rubin [68, 69] and Holland [29], among others. The gold standard in causal analysis is performing *controlled experiments* or *randomized trials*, which have the following basic idea: given a *population* consisting of individual *units* or subjects (such as patients, students, people, or plots of land), randomly divide them into *treatment* (or *active treatment*) and *control* (or *control treatment*) groups. The units in the treatment group receive the treatment whose effect we want to measure (such as a drug, special training program, or discount on insurance premiums), while the units in the control group do not. At the end of the experiment, the difference in the *outcome* (such as the status of a disease, grades in a class, smoking status, or crop production) is measured as the *causal effect* of the treatment. Of course, additional assumptions and considerations are needed in experiment design to ensure that the results reflect the true causal effect of the treatment.

On the other hand, it is often difficult or even infeasible to answer causal questions, including some of the examples mentioned earlier, through controlled experiments due to ethical reasons (e.g., understanding the causal effect of smoking on lung diseases) or logistic constraints such as time, cost, or the lack of instruments to enforce treatment. Some extreme examples from sociology, psychology, and the health sciences that have been studied in the past include the effects of laws limiting access to handguns on criminal violence [63], the effects on children of parental occupational exposures to lead, and the long-term psychological effects of the death of a close relative. These types of questions cannot be analyzed through controlled experiments.

However, in many cases, we have observational datasets that record units, their treatment assignment, and their outcomes, potentially collected by research agencies, hospitals, businesses, or governments through surveys. Inferring causal relationships between a treatment and an outcome variable using such observed data is known as causal analysis using observational studies [64]. In this paper, we will provide a brief overview of two prevalent formal models for observational studies: Pearl's graphical causal model [55], which is popular in artificial intelligence (AI) research, and Rubin's (also known as Neyman-Rubin's) potential outcome framework [68,69], which is popular in statistical research.

In observational studies, when units are not assigned treatment at random, or when their *environment* determines their treatment (e.g., people in wealthy neighborhoods receive a special training program as treatment, while those in poorer neighborhoods form the control group), differences in their outcomes may be due to these initial *selection biases*, rather than the treatment itself. Some sources of these biases may be measured (called *observed covariates* or *overt biases* [63], e.g., age, gender, neighborhood, etc.), while others may remain unmeasured in the observed data (called *unobserved covariates* or *hidden biases*, e.g., some unrecorded health conditions). Observed covariates can be accounted for in observational studies, e.g., by *matching* treated and control units with the same or similar values of these covariates (discussed in Sect. 3), under certain assumptions.

The variables or covariates chosen for adjustment can significantly affect the results of data analysis. Consider a dataset with several *variables* (also called *attributes* in data management and *features* in machine learning). If we want to understand the effect of one variable X on another numeric variable Y, we might plot bar charts. However, the way we plot these bars can significantly change our observations and conclusions. For example, we could plot the bars directly for different values of X measuring Y. Alternatively, we could choose another variable Z (or a set of variables $Z, W, \cdots$) and plot the bars for X vs. Y for different values of Z (or $Z, W, \cdots$). Depending on which approach we take, our conclusions may be significantly different, or even opposite of each other. This phenomenon, in which a trend is present when data is combined but reverses or disappears when the data is grouped, is known as *Simpson's Paradox* [56]. An example is provided below.

Example 1. An apparent gender-based discrimination was observed in graduate school admissions at UC Berkeley in 1973, when it was found that 34.6% of females were admitted, compared to 44.3% of males. However, when the admission rates were broken down by department, a slight bias toward female applicants was observed, a result that did not constitute evidence for gender-based discrimination. Statisticians examined this issue more closely [6], and found that females tended to apply to departments with lower overall acceptance rates. Below is a hypothetical dataset (not from the actual study) illustrating this situation in two departments:

Department A		
Male	27	100	27%
Female	60	200	30%

Department B		
Male	150	200	75%
Female	78	100	78%

Total		
Male	177	300	59%
Female	138	300	46%

As the above example illustrates, a dataset can tell very contradictory stories depending on how it is analyzed. It is therefore crucial to understand the appropriate way to analyze a given dataset, specifically, which variables to consider before making any conclusions, particularly causal conclusions. We will see how graphical models can be used to infer the relevant set of variables when we have a graph showing the causal dependencies of different variables of interest. In addition, we will discuss popular statistical methods like *propensity score* and *matching* that can be used in observational studies to control for biased conclusions.

In addition to providing an overview of causal analysis techniques in AI and statistics, we will also examine recent applications of causal analysis to *fairness* and *Explainable Artificial Intelligence* (XAI). The increasing concerns about the complexity and lack of transparency in data-driven decision making systems, which are often used to make consequential decisions in areas such as healthcare, criminal justice, and finance, has led to a surge of interest in research on these topics:

- *Algorithmic Fairness:* The goal of research on algorithmic fairness is to make machine learning algorithms fair and unbiased. It has been shown that there are many different ways to formally define algorithmic fairness, and it may be impossible to achieve fairness according to all of these definitions simultaneously (see [78] for an overview of fairness definitions). However, most of the literature on algorithmic fairness captures fairness in terms of the lack of *statistical association* between sensitive attributes such as race, gender, etc. and the outcome of a decision-making algorithm. It has been argued, however, that fairness definitions based on statistical associations lack universality and are unable to capture subtle fairness situations such as the Berkeley admissions example in Example 1. In contrast, causal notions of fairness, which capture discrimination in terms of various causal effects of sensitive attributes and the outcome of an ML algorithm, provide a richer and more consistent formal language for capturing fairness situations that are otherwise impossible to capture through associational notions of fairness. In Sect. 4, we briefly overview various associational and causal notions of algorithmic fairness.
- *Causality and XAI:* The aim of research in XAI (Explainable Artificial Intelligence) is to provide human-understandable explanations of the outcomes of algorithmic decision-making systems (see [46] for a recent survey). Previous work in this field has focused on attributing responsibility for an algorithm's decisions to its inputs (e.g., see [3,14,16,22,23,30,61,62]). However, these methods can produce incorrect and misleading explanations because they focus on the *correlation* between the input and output of algorithms rather than their *causal* relationship (e.g., see [2,17,25,31,39,46]). Furthermore, several recent works have argued for the use of *contrastive explanations* (also known as counterfactual explanations or recourse) which are typically obtained by considering the smallest perturbation in an algorithm's input that can lead to the desired outcome [42,44,49,77,79]. However, due to the causal dependency between variables, these perturbations are not translatable into real-world interventions and therefore fail to generate insights that are actionable in the real world [36]. It has been argued that a principled way to address the aforementioned limitations of existing XAI tools is to incorporate causal reasoning in the process of generating explanations. We will briefly overview these attempts in Sect. 5.

Outline. We will first discuss two popular models for (observational) causal inference and related techniques, Pearl's graphical causal model (Sect. 2) and

Rubin's potential outcome framework (Sect. 3). Section 4 discusses causal fairness, and Sect. 5 discusses causal explanations for ML/AI algorithms. We conclude in Sect. 6. We refer the reader to standard textbooks for causal inference [27,33,55,58] for more details on the concepts reviewed in this paper.

2 Pearl's Graphical Causal Model

Notations. We denote variables by uppercase letters (e.g., X, Y, Z, V), their values with lowercase letters (e.g., x, y, z, v), and sets of variables or values using boldface (e.g., $\mathbf{X}$ or $\mathbf{x}$). $Dom(X)$ denotes the domain of a variable X. $\mathbb{P}(X = x)$ denotes the probability that the variable X takes value x; when the variable X is clear from the context, we simply use $\mathbb{P}(x)$. For a set of variables $\mathbf{X}$, we use $\mathbb{P}(\mathbf{X} = \mathbf{x})$, or simply $\mathbb{P}(\mathbf{x})$ when it is clear from the context, to represent the joint probability distribution of variables in $\mathbf{X}$. As standard, an *event* denotes the assignment of a (set of) value(s) to a (set of) variable(s). Events are denoted by uppercase letters A, B, C or X, Y, Z. The *conditional probability* $\mathbb{P}(A \mid B)$ denotes the probability of an event A conditioned on the fact that event B has already occurred, e.g., $\mathbb{P}(X = x \mid Y = y)$ denotes the probability that variable X takes value x conditioned on Y has taken value y. Two events A and B are *independent* if $\mathbb{P}(A \mid B) = \mathbb{P}(A)$. Two events A and B are *conditionally independent given another event C* if $\mathbb{P}(A \mid B, C) = \mathbb{P}(A \mid C)$. One important formula involving conditional independence is given by the *Bayes' rule:* $\mathbb{P}(A \mid B) = \frac{\mathbb{P}(B \mid A)\mathbb{P}(A)}{\mathbb{P}(B)}$. We will assume the reader is familiar with other standard notions and rules in probability theory.

2.1 Graphical Models

A graph consists of a set of *nodes* $\mathbf{V}$, and a set of *edges* $\mathbf{E}$ of the form (u, v), where $u, v \in \mathbf{V}$. If the edges (u, v) are *directed* from u to v (equivalently, written as $u \to v$ or $v \leftarrow u$), then the graph is a *directed graph*, otherwise the graph is *undirected*. A *path* of length p between nodes u, v is a sequence of edges $(u = u_0, u_1), (u_1, u_2), \ldots, (u_{p-1}, u_p = v)$. The path is directed if all the edges between u, v are directed, and can be specified as $u_0(u) \to u_1 \to \cdots \to u_{p-1} \to u_p(v)$. If there is a directed path from a node to itself, then the graph is called *cyclic*, otherwise, it is a *directed acyclic graph (DAG)*. In this article, we will use directed graphical models, specifically acyclic directed graphical models, to capture conditional independences and causal dependencies among variables. Therefore, all references to a graph in this article refer to a DAG unless mentioned otherwise explicitly. However, we may consider an undirected path between two nodes in a directed graph by ignoring the directions of edges along the path. In the literature on graphical models, conditional independence has also been studied using undirected graphical models [54], which we do not discuss in this paper.

Next, we discuss how directed graphs can represent a set of conditional independences. A path p is **blocked** by a set of nodes $\mathbf{Z}$ if:

1. p contains a *chain* of the form $A \rightarrow B \rightarrow C$, or a *fork* of the form $A \leftarrow B \rightarrow C$ such that $B \in \mathbf{Z}$, or,
2. p contains a *collider node* B of the form $A \rightarrow B \leftarrow C$ such that neither B nor any descendants of B are in $\mathbf{Z}$.

If a set of nodes $\mathbf{Z}$ blocks every path between two nodes X and Y, then X and Y are **d-separated** [57,58] conditioned on $\mathbf{Z}$. A probability distribution $\mathbb{P}$ and DAG G are Markov compatible if d-separation in G implies conditional independence in $\mathbb{P}$, i.e., if X and Y are d-separated conditioned on $\mathbf{Z}$, then X and Y are also conditionally independent given $\mathbf{Z}$ in $\mathbb{P}$.

Intuitively, to block a path p that creates a spurious correlation between X and Y, one must condition on at least one non-collider node, and avoid conditioning on any collider node or its descendants. The latter requirement corresponds to a general pattern in which observing a common effect of two independent causes tends to make those causes dependent (this phenomenon is known as Berkson's paradox or the "explain away" effect [55]).

2.2   Structural, Graphical, and Probabilistic Causal Model

A **Structural Causal Model** $\mathcal{M} = \langle \mathbf{U}, \mathbf{V}, \mathbf{F} \rangle$ consists of a set of *observable or endogenous* variables $\mathbf{V}$ that are inside the model, a set of *background or exogenous* variables $\mathbf{U}$ that are outside of the model, and a set of *structural equations* $\mathbf{F}$. The structural equations assign every endogenous variable a value based on other endogenous and exogenous variables. Formally, $\mathbf{F} = (F_X)_{X \in \mathbf{V}}$, where F_X denotes the structural equation for the variable $X \in V$ and is of the form

$$F_X : Dom(\mathbf{Pa_V}(X)) \times Dom(\mathbf{Pa_U}(X)) \rightarrow Dom(X),$$

where $\mathbf{Pa_U}(X) \subseteq \mathbf{U}$ and $\mathbf{Pa_V}(X) \subseteq \mathbf{V} - X$ are called *exogenous parents* and *endogenous parents* of X, respectively. Intuitively, these equations represent how the values of each endogenous variable is assigned based on the other endogenous and exogenous variables. Typically, it is assumed that each endogenous variable has at least one exogenous parent denoting *noise* or all unknown factors affecting the variable. Since exogenous variables are outside the model, they are not explained with a structural equation.

A **Graphical Causal Model** (or **causal diagram**) for a structural causal model $\mathcal{M} = \langle \mathbf{U}, \mathbf{V}, \mathbf{F} \rangle$ is a graph $G(\mathbf{U} \cup \mathbf{V}, E)$ where there is a node for each exogenous and endogenous variable in $\mathcal{M}$. The edges E in the causal diagram correspond to the structural equations $\mathbf{F}$ of the structural causal model. For each structural equation $F_X \in \mathbf{F}$ for $X \in \mathbf{V}$, there is a directed edge from each node in $\mathbf{Pa_V}(X) \cup \mathbf{Pa_U}(X)$ to X. We say a variable X is a *direct cause* of another variable Z if there is an edge from X to Z. We say a variable Z is a *descendant* of another variable X (equivalently, X is an ancestor of Z) if Z is *caused* (either *directly* or *indirectly*) by X, i.e., if there is a directed edge or a directed path from X to Z in G; otherwise, we say that Z is a *non-descendant* of X. We will denote the set of parents, ancestors, and descendants of a node X

by $\mathbf{Pa}(X), \mathbf{Anc}(X)$, and $\mathbf{Desc}(X)$ respectively. In this article, we will assume that all graphical causal models are acyclic, i.e., the graph G is a DAG. Note that exogenous variables do not have any structural equations and therefore no parents in the corresponding graphical model.

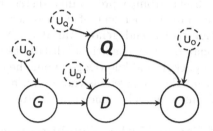

Fig. 1. Example of a causal graph.

Example 21. *Figure 1 shows a small fragment of the causal DAG of the admission process in a college. Admissions decisions are made independently by each department and are based on a rich collection of information about the candidates', such as test scores, grades, etc. These characteristics affect not only the admission decisions, but also which department the candidate chooses to apply to. We show only a tiny fragment of the causal graph, where O = admission outcome, D = department, G = candidate's gender, and Q = candidates qualifications. Since different genders may apply to departments at different rates, there is an edge G → D. Some departments may tend to attract applicants with certain attributes (e.g., the math department may attract applicants who play chess), so we also include an edge Q → D. Here {Q, G, D, O} form the set of endogenous variables V in the causal model M = ⟨U, V, F⟩. Each endogenous variable also has an exogenous parent denoting hidden/unknown factors or noise. Here {U_Q, U_G, U_D, U_O} form the set of exogenous variables U. The structural equations are given as follows, which correspond to edges in the causal diagram:*

$$G = f_G(U_G)$$
$$\mathbf{Q} = f_{\mathbf{Q}}(U_{\mathbf{Q}})$$
$$D = f_D(U_D, G, \mathbf{Q})$$
$$O = f_O(U_O, D, \mathbf{Q})$$

Note: A graphical causal model contains less information than the corresponding structural causal model. However, graphical models are still useful as they provide useful and convenient qualitative information about how a variable depends on other variables, particularly transitively through a path from other variables. Obtaining an accurate quantitative structural equation is practically infeasible.

If we know the values of all exogenous variables $\mathbf{U}$ and the structural equations $\mathbf{F}$ in a structural causal model $\mathcal{M}$, and the corresponding graphical model is acyclic, we can determine the values of all endogenous variables in the model. However, in practice, the structural equations and exogenous variables are typically unobserved. As a result, we typically assume that the values of exogenous variables $\mathbf{U}$ are drawn from a probability distribution $\mathbb{P}(\mathbf{u})$, and often it is assumed that they are independent of each other. This in turn induces a probability distribution on the endogenous variables. As a result, the endogenous variables are associated with a conditional distributions given their parents. Without any additional background knowledge about the exogenous variables, it is common to assume that these exogenous (noise) variables are mutually independent. This type of causal model is known as a Probabilistic Causal Model (PCM) $\langle \mathcal{M}, \mathbb{P} \rangle$.

The assumption of **Causal Markov Condition** relates causal and dependency structure of a system and plays a key role in causal inference using causal diagram. A PCM $\langle \mathcal{M}, \mathbb{P} \rangle$ with the corresponding graphical model $G(V, E)$, satisfies the *Causal Markov Condition* if for every node $X \in V$, the following holds:

$$X \perp\!\!\!\perp (V \setminus (\mathbf{Desc}(X) \cup \mathbf{Pa}(X))) \mid \mathbf{Pa}(X) \tag{1}$$

i.e., each node is independent of its non-descendants given its parents, or equivalently, each node is d-separated from its non-descendants given its parents. As in a Bayesian network, under the causal Markov condition, the probability distribution Pr for the PCM $\mathbf{M}$ for a set of nodes $X_1, \cdots, X_c$ can be factorized as:

$$\mathbb{P}(X_1, \ldots, X_c) = \prod_i \mathbb{P}(X_i \mid Pa(X_i)) \tag{2}$$

2.3 Interventions, Do-Operators, and Counterfactuals

A model for *interventions* is needed to capture the effects on all variables in a model when the reality or world is changed. Formally, an *intervention* or an *action* on a set of (endogenous) variables $\mathbf{X} \subseteq \mathbf{V}$, denoted $\mathbf{X} \leftarrow \mathbf{x}$, is an operation that *modifies* the underlying causal model by replacing the structural equations associated with $\mathbf{X}$ with a constant $\mathbf{x} \in Dom(\mathbf{X})$. Equivalently, in the corresponding graphical causal model, all incoming edges to all variables in $\mathbf{X}$ are removed. Pearl and others [55,58] model intervention using two mechanisms: (i) do-operator, and (ii) potential outcomes and counterfactuals.

The Do-Operator. In standard probability theory, $\Pr(X = x \mid Y = y)$ denotes the probability of variable X taking value x if it has been *observed* that variable Y has taken value y. This does not change the underlying causal model or world, only the perception of the observer about the world changes having observed $Y = y$. This probability can be computed using standard rules of probabilities.

In causal inference, as discussed above, we use *intervention* to change the world and the underlying causal model by forcefully setting $X = x$. In Pearl's model [55] this is denoted by

$$\mathsf{do}(X = x)$$

or, $\mathsf{do}(\mathbf{X} = \mathbf{x})$ when a set of variables is changed. When X is forcefully set to x in the process of intervention, the value of another variable (outcome) Y is denoted by

$$Y(X = x), Y_{X \leftarrow x}, \ or, \ Y(x)$$

when X is clear from the context. For the intervention when X is set to x for all *units* in the population, the probability that Y takes the value of y is denoted by

$$\mathbb{P}(Y(x) = y), \mathbb{P}(Y = y \mid \mathsf{do}(X = x)), \ or, \mathbb{P}(y \mid \mathsf{do}(x)).$$

One of the key goals in probabilistic causal model is to compute this probability under intervention using the standard observed conditional probabilities that can be estimated from the observed data that we discuss in Sect. 2.4. Then we can assess the effect of treatment by comparing the distributions at different interventions, e.g.,

$$\mathbb{P}(Y = y \mid \mathsf{do}(X = 1)) - \mathbb{P}(Y = y \mid \mathsf{do}(X = 0)). \tag{3}$$

Counterfactuals. The *potential outcome* of a variable Y after the intervention $\mathbf{X} \leftarrow \mathbf{x}$ in a context $\mathbf{u} \in Dom(\mathbf{U})$, denoted $Y_{\mathbf{X} \leftarrow \mathbf{x}}(\mathbf{u})$, is the *solution* to Y in the modified set of structural equations. Potential outcomes satisfy the following *consistency rule*:

$$\mathbf{X}(\mathbf{u}) = \mathbf{x} \implies Y_{\mathbf{X} \leftarrow \mathbf{x}}(\mathbf{u}) = y \tag{4}$$

This rule states that in exogenous contexts where $\mathbf{X} = \mathbf{x}$, the outcome is invariant to the intervention $\mathbf{X} \leftarrow \mathbf{x}$. For example, hypothetically changing the gender of applicants to female does not change the admission decisions for those who were already female before the intervention.

The distribution $\mathbb{P}(\mathbf{u})$ induces a probability distribution over endogenous variables and potential outcomes. Using PCMs, one can express *counterfactual queries* of the form

$$\mathbb{P}(Y_{\mathbf{X} \leftarrow \mathbf{x}} = y \mid \mathbf{k}), \ or, \ \mathbb{P}(y_{\mathbf{X} \leftarrow \mathbf{x}} \mid \mathbf{k}),$$

where $\mathbf{K} \subseteq V$; this reads as "For a subpopulation with $\mathbf{K} = \mathbf{k}$, what is the probability that we would observe $Y = y$ had $\mathbf{X}$ been $\mathbf{x}$?" and is given by the following expression by considering all possible values of the exogenous variables $\mathbf{U} = \mathbf{u}$:

$$\mathbb{P}(y_{\mathbf{X} \leftarrow \mathbf{x}} \mid \mathbf{k}) = \sum_{\mathbf{u}} \mathbb{P}(y_{\mathbf{X} \leftarrow \mathbf{x}}(\mathbf{u})) \, \mathbb{P}(\mathbf{u} \mid \mathbf{k}) \tag{5}$$

Equation (5) readily suggests Pearl's three-step procedure for answering counterfactual queries [58]: (1) update $\mathbb{P}(\mathbf{u})$ to obtain $\mathbb{P}(\mathbf{u} \mid \mathbf{k})$ (*abduction*), (2) modify the causal model to reflect the intervention $\mathbf{X} \leftarrow \mathbf{x}$ (*action*), and (3) evaluate the RHS of (5) using the function $\mathbb{P}(Y_{\mathbf{X} \leftarrow \mathbf{x}}(\mathbf{u}) = y)$ (*prediction*). However, performing this procedure requires the underlying PCM to be fully observed, i.e., the distribution $\mathbb{P}(\mathbf{u})$ and the underlying structural equations $\mathbf{F}$ must be known, which is an impractical requirement. As discussed in [58] with examples, while estimating effects of intervention using do-operators typically only need to use the underlying causal diagrams and not the explicit structural equations, computation of counterfactuals using the three step process mentioned above may need to assume that the structural equations are known.

Counterfactuals vs. Interventional Queries. The do-operator is a population-level operator, meaning it can only express queries about the effect of an intervention at population level; in contrast, counterfactuals can express queries about the effect of an intervention on a sub-population or an individual. Therefore, every interventional query can be expressed in terms of counterfactuals, but not vice versa (see [58, Chapter 4] for more details). For instance, $\mathbb{P}(y \mid \mathrm{do}(\mathbf{x})) = \mathbb{P}(y_{\mathbf{X} \leftarrow \mathbf{x}})$; however, the counterfactual query $\mathbb{P}(y_{\mathbf{X} \leftarrow \mathbf{x}} \mid \mathbf{x}', y')$, which asks about the effect of the intervention $\mathbf{X} \leftarrow \mathbf{x}$ on a sub-population with attributes $\mathbf{x}'$ and y', cannot be expressed in terms of the do-operator. Note that the expression $\mathbb{P}(y \mid \mathrm{do}(\mathbf{x}), \mathbf{k})$, where $X \notin \mathbf{K}$, treats the condition $\mathbf{K} = \mathbf{k}$ as a post intervention condition and captures the probability of observing $Y = y$ after the intervention $\mathbf{X} \leftarrow \mathbf{x}$ on a subset of population with attribute $\mathbf{K} = \mathbf{k}$ *after* the intervention. This is in contrast with the expression $\mathbb{P}(y_{\mathbf{X} \leftarrow \mathbf{x}} \mid \mathbf{K} = \mathbf{k})$ that captures the probability of observing $Y = y$ after the intervention $\mathbf{X} \leftarrow \mathbf{x}$ on a subset of population with attribute $\mathbf{K} = \mathbf{k}$ *before* the intervention. Since intervening on X may change attributes $\mathbf{K}$, $\mathbb{P}(y \mid \mathrm{do}(\mathbf{x}), \mathbf{k}) \neq \mathbb{P}(y_{\mathbf{X} \leftarrow \mathbf{x}} \mid \mathbf{K} = \mathbf{k})$. The expression $\mathbb{P}(y \mid \mathrm{do}(\mathbf{x}), \mathbf{k})$ is in correspondence with the counterfactual statement $\mathbb{P}(y_{\mathbf{X} \leftarrow \mathbf{x}} \mid \mathbf{K}_{\mathbf{X} \leftarrow \mathbf{x}} = \mathbf{k})$.

2.4   Identification and Estimation

Suppose we want to estimate the causal effect of a *treatment variable* X ($\mathrm{do}(X) = x$) on an *outcome variable* Y, i.e., want to estimate a probability $\mathbb{P}(Y = y \mid \mathrm{do}(X) = x)$, which can be used in turn to compute other quantities of interest (e.g., (3), or (10), (11) showed later). The goal is to express this probability distribution involving do-operators as standard conditional probabilities. For $\mathbb{P}(Y = y \mid \mathrm{do}(X) = x)$, an *adjustment estimand* is an expression of the from

$$E_{\mathbf{z}}(y \mid x, \mathbf{z}) = \sum_{\mathbf{z}} \mathbb{P}(y \mid x, \mathbf{z}) \mathbb{P}(\mathbf{z}), \tag{6}$$

where the set $\mathbf{Z}$ is chosen to include variables judged to be "confounders" or "covariates". By adjusting for these variables, one hopes to create conditions that eliminate spurious dependence and thus obtain an unbiased estimate of the causal effect of X and Y. The set $\mathbf{Z}$ is called "admissible (for adjustment) covariates" for estimating the causal effect of X on Y if

$$\sum_{\mathbf{z}} \mathbb{P}(y \mid x, \mathbf{z})\mathbb{P}(\mathbf{z}) = \mathbb{P}(\mathbf{y} \mid \mathbf{do}(\mathbf{x})). \tag{7}$$

Given a graphical causal model G for a PCM, one of the approaches to find a set of admissible covariates is through the use of the *back-door criteria*, which we will discuss next.

Back-Door Criterion. Given a graphical causal model $G(\mathbf{V}, \mathbf{E})$, a treatment variable X, and an outcome variable Y, a sufficient condition for a set $\mathbf{Z}$ to be admissible for estimating the causal effect of X on Y is that it satisfies the following two conditions known as the back-door criterion [55]:

- No element of $\mathbf{Z}$ is a descendant of X,
- In the modified graph where all outgoing edges from the nodes in X are removed, then $\mathbf{Z}$ blocks all *back-door paths* from X to Y, namely all paths that end with an arrow pointing to X.[1]

For example, in the causal DAG in Fig. 1, to compute the effect of D on O, $\mathbf{Q}$ satisfies the back-door criterion.

Estimating Causal Effect. Because $\mathbb{P}(y \mid \mathbf{do}(x))$ is a probability distribution, one can ask about $\mathbb{E}[Y \mid \mathbf{do}(x)]$, when it makes sense for Y to have an expectation value. This is called the *average effect* of $\mathbf{do}(x)$ and is given by the following:

$$\mathbb{E}[Y \mid \mathbf{do}(x)] = \sum_y y\mathbb{P}(y \mid \mathbf{do}(x)), \tag{8}$$

If we identify the effect of X on Y through an admissible covariate $\mathbf{Z}$ (ref. (7)), then:

$$\begin{aligned}
\mathbb{E}[Y \mid \mathbf{do}(x)] &= \sum_y y\mathbb{P}(y \mid \mathbf{do}(x)) \\
&= \sum_y \sum_{\mathbf{z}} y\mathbb{P}(y \mid x, \mathbf{z})\mathbb{P}(\mathbf{z}) \\
&= \sum_{\mathbf{z}} \sum_y y\mathbb{P}(y \mid x, \mathbf{z})\mathbb{P}(\mathbf{z}) \\
&= \sum_{\mathbf{z}} \mathbb{P}(\mathbf{z})\mathbb{E}[Y \mid x, \mathbf{z}]. \tag{9}
\end{aligned}$$

We are typically interested in comparing the effect of interventions on different levels (or types, states) of X on Y. In addition to the ACE (Eq. (3)), other common measures for this purpose are

$$\text{Average Difference: } \mathbb{E}(Y \mid \mathbf{do}(x')) - \mathbb{E}(Y \mid \mathbf{do}(x)) \tag{10}$$

$$\text{Risk Ratio: } \frac{\mathbb{E}(Y \mid \mathbf{do}(x'))}{\mathbb{E}(Y \mid \mathbf{do}(x))}, \tag{11}$$

---

[1] For proof and intuition behind the back-door criteria, along with other sufficient conditions, see [55].

where x and x' are two levels (or types, states) of X selected for comparison [57]. Note that in order to compute these measures using Eq. (7), we also need the *overlap* assumption which states that for each $t \in \{x, x'\}$ and $\mathbf{z} \in \mathbf{Z}$, $0 < \mathbb{P}(t \mid \mathbf{z}) < 1$. In practice, the overlap assumption is enforced by pruning a subset of observations (units) for which the overlap assumption fails. This preprocessing and adjustment using Eq. (7) is called *subclassification* or *matching* [32] (discussed further as the *strong ignorability* condition [66] in Sect. 3).

3   Rubin's Potential Outcome Framework

The commonly used model for causal analysis in statistics is known as the Rubin's (or, Neyman-Rubin's) *potential outcome framework (POF)*, which was first proposed in Neyman's work [51], and was later popularized by Rubin [68,69]. The basic notions are similar to the ones presented in Sect. 2, but here no graphs are involved. Suppose the goal is to estimate the causal effect of a *treatment* X (*e.g.*, a drug to treat fever) on an *outcome* Y (*e.g.*, the body temperature). The treatment variable X assumes binary values (which can be generalized to multi-level treatment), where $X = 1$ means that the *treatment (or, active treatment)* has been applied, and $X = 0$ means that the *control treatment (or control)* has been applied to a *unit* (e.g., a person). Several units form the *population*. For unit i, we denote its outcome and treatment by Y_i and X_i.

The potential outcome model defines two random variables denoting the *potential outcomes* $Y(1), Y(0)$ for binary treatments X, which can be generalized to > 2 treatments. For unit i, the value of the *potential outcome* is $Y_i(0)$ when $X_i = 0$ and is $Y_i(1)$ when $X_i = 1$. The potential outcome model on n units can be represented in a tabular form as shown in Table 1. We will explain the set of *covariates* $\mathbf{Z}$ in Sect. 3.1.

Table 1. Neyman-Rubin's potential outcome framework [69]

Unit	Covariates $\mathbf{Z}$	Treatment X	$Y(1)$	$Y(0)$	$Y(1) - Y(0)$
1	$\mathbf{Z}_1$	X_1	$Y_1(1)$	$Y_1(0)$	$Y_1(1) - Y_1(0)$
2	$\mathbf{Z}_2$	X_2	$Y_2(1)$	$Y_2(0)$	$Y_2(1) - Y_2(0)$
...	...	...	...	...	...
n	$\mathbf{Z}_n$	X_n	$Y_n(1)$	$Y_n(0)$	$Y_n(1) - Y_n(0)$

A standard goal is to estimate the *Average Treatment Effect (ATE)* by taking the average of causal effects $Y_i(1) - Y_i(0)$ over the entire population (similar to (10)):

$$ATE = E[Y(1) - Y(0)] \tag{12}$$

In the above equation, we want to estimate the difference in effects of administering both $X_i = 1$ and $X_i = 0$ to the same unit i, *i.e.*, ideally, we want to compute both $Y_i(1), Y_i(0)$. But the *fundamental problem of causal inference* is that for each unit we only know either $Y_i(1)$ or $Y_i(0)$ but not both. If $X_i = 1$, then the observed outcome is $Y_i = Y_i(1)$, and if $X_i = 0$, then the observed outcome is $Y_i = Y_i(0)$, i.e., $Y_i = X_i Y_i(1) + (1 - X_i) Y_i(0)$. This reduces the causal inference problem to a missing data problem [29,65].

In randomized controlled experiments, randomly assigning treatments to units (each patient is randomly given either the drug for fever or a placebo) gives an unbiased estimate of ATE. In this case, *the treatment assignment X is independent of the potential outcomes $Y(1), Y(0)$, i.e.,*

$$X \perp\!\!\!\perp Y(1), Y(0). \tag{13}$$

Therefore, $E[Y(1)] = E[Y(1) \mid X = 1]$ and $E[Y(0)] = E[Y(0) \mid X = 0]$, and from (12) we get,

$$ATE = E[Y(1)] - E[Y(0)]$$
$$= E[Y(1) \mid X = 1] - E[Y(0) \mid X = 0]. \tag{14}$$

Now the ATE can be estimated by taking the difference of average *observed outcomes* Y of the treated and control units under the two following assumptions, known as the **Stable Unit Treatment Value Assumption (SUTVA)** [10,69]: (i) There is no *interference* among units, i.e., both $Y_i(1), Y_i(0)$ of a unit i are unaffected by what action X_j any other unit $j \neq i$ receives, and (ii) There are no hidden versions or levels of treatments, i.e., no matter *how* unit i received treatment $X_i = 1$ (resp. 0), the same outcome $Y_i(1)$ (resp. $Y_i(0)$) will be observed. Relaxations of these assumptions have been studied in the literature, e.g., for studying causal inference when units are connected in a network and have interference with each other (Sect. 3.3).

3.1 Observational Studies with Potential Outcome Framework and Ignorability

In a randomized controlled experiment, biases due to observed and unobserved covariates are controlled through randomization, as described in Eq. (14). However, as we discussed in the introduction, randomized controlled experiments cannot be performed for many causal questions (e.g., the effect of smoking on health) due to ethical, cost, or other constraints. The alternative to randomized controlled experiments is performing causal inference on observed or collected data. However, when we attempt to perform causal analysis on observational data, Eq. (13), i.e., $X \perp\!\!\!\perp Y(1), Y(0)$) may no longer hold. For instance, in an observational study examining the impact of a special program on students' grades, it is possible that students with stronger academic backgrounds or higher socioeconomic status are more likely to enroll in the program. In turn, the unbiased estimates of ATE as shown in Eq. (14) may not be true.

Fortunately, for observational studies, one can still adjust for selection biases due to observed covariates with the following **unconfoundedness assumption**, also known as the **strong ignorability assumption**, which was proposed by Rosenbaum and Rubin in a seminal paper [65]. It assumes that (i) for all combination of covariate values $\mathbf{Z} = \mathbf{z}$, $0 < \Pr(\mathbf{z}) < 1$, and (ii) the potential outcomes $(Y(0), Y(1))$ and treatment X are conditionally independent given relevant covariates $\mathbf{Z}$:

$$X \perp\!\!\!\perp Y(0), Y(1) \mid \mathbf{Z} \tag{15}$$

Using (15), we can express ATE (12) as follows by conditioning on covariates $\mathbf{Z}$ and then taking an expectation on $\mathbf{Z}$:

$$ATE = E_{\mathbf{Z}}\left[E[Y(1) \mid X = 1, \mathbf{Z}]\right] - E_{\mathbf{Z}}[E[Y(0) \mid X = 0, \mathbf{Z}]] \tag{16}$$

Since $Y(1) = Y$ (observed outcome) for treatment $X = 1$ and $Y(0) = Y$ for treatment $X = 0$, the expression in Eq. (16) can again be estimated using observational data by computing the difference of average observed outcome values of treated and controlled units for each combination of values of covariates $\mathbf{Z} = \mathbf{z}$ as a subgroup, and then taking an weighted average over all such subgroup to have an estimate of ATE. This approach to observational studies is known as **subclassification** [65] or **exact matching**. Both benefits of limitations of subclassification or exact matching had been identified in the causal inference literature early [65]. On one hand, it is considered an **interpretable** method for observational studies since one can see exactly which units have been matched together and how the final ATE value was computed, which is helpful for understanding why a group of units have been matched together and for troubleshooting, especially for users with limited background in statistics. On the other hand, It requires that all combinations of covariate values $\mathbf{Z} = \mathbf{z}$ have non-zero probability, and there have to be at least one treated and at least one control unit in each subgroup to compute the expression in (16), which may not be feasible when the number of covariates is large. Even when the number of covariates is small, it may not be possible to *match* every treated and controlled unit exactly on all covariate values. In statistical observational studies, several other techniques for estimating ATE have been studied over the years, which we briefly discuss in the next subsection.

3.2   Methods for Observational Causal Inference in Statistics

In general, **matching** refers to the generic technique of estimating ATE by putting treated and controlled units into subgroups, taking the difference of their average observed outcomes, and then taking a weighted average over different subgroups. A number of matching techniques have been discussed in the survey by Stuart [76] based on (i) how *"closeness* or the distance measure is defined to determine whether an individual is a good match for another, (ii) implementation of the matching method given a measure of closeness, (iii) assessing the quality of the resulting matched samples, and repeating steps (i) and (ii) until well-matched samples are produced, and finally, (iv) analysis of the outcome and estimation of treatment effects from the matching.

Rosenbaum and Rubin [65] proposed the *propensity score matching*, where units with the same or similar values of the *propensity score* defined as $\mathbb{P}(X = 1 \mid \mathbf{Z} = \mathbf{z})$, which measures the *propensity* of units to get the treatment assignment, are matched together. They showed that matching units based on their propensity score values gives an unbiased estimate of the ATE. However, there are limitations of this approach: propensity score methods require selecting a good model for treatment assignment $X = 1$ given the covariates $\mathbf{Z}$, which is typically unknown and can be prone to errors. Moreover, propensity score matching is *not* an interpretable method since units with completely different values of covariates $\mathbf{Z}$ may have the same propensity scores $\mathbb{P}(X = 1 \mid \mathbf{Z} = \mathbf{z})$ and may be matched together.

Exact matching, where units having the same values of a set of covariates $\mathbf{Z}$ are matched together is an interpretable method for observational studies as mentioned earlier, since an analyst can see which tuples contributed to a matched group and the ATE. In addition to ATE, i.e., the average treatment effect over all units, it can also be used to estimate the *conditional ATE (CATE)* for every unit or for a subgroup of units. This allows the analyst to decide whether to trust the returned CATE or overall ATE, or whether to exclude/include covariates.

A good matching depends on a good *covariate selection*, which chooses a subset of variables from available variables so that units can be grouped based on the same or similar values of such covariates. Covariate selection is a challenging problem: to maintain strong ignorability, we need to ensure that (i) each valid matched group has to have at least one treated and one control unit, which is tough for high-dimensional data, favoring selection of as few variables as possible, as well as (ii) the treatment and potential outcomes should be independent given the selected covariates, which may require choosing many covariates. To ensure that most of the units are matched in the presence of a large number of covariates, approximate matching methods have been proposed that match units on *similar* values of covariates rather than the same values of covariates, like *k-nearest neighbors matching* [67] or *coarsened exact matching* [32]. Under the standard assumptions in observational studies, several other methods have been proposed in the causal inference literature, including doubly robust ML methods [18] and causal BART [26]. A simple approach to observational studies is using *regressions*, where a model for the outcome given the treatment and covariates is learned from the observed units. Although this technique is very efficient, its performance is largely dependent on not having a model wrongly specified, e.g., if the true model is non-linear but a linear model is learned from the data, regression techniques do not perform well [81].

Given a high-dimensional dataset, two practical challenges in exact matching are scalability and matching a large number of units since each matched group needs to have at least one treated and one control unit. To address this issue, a new framework called *Almost Matching Exactly (AME)* [12,48,81] has been developed, which operates on the principle that units should be matched together if they are close in their covariates according to an appropriate metric. Because high dimensional settings make it unlikely that units are similar in *all* their covariates, matches must be made on a *subset* of all possible covariates. Humans are not naturally adept at the task of deciding which high dimensional covariates one should match on, so this framework uses machine learning on a holdout dataset to learn measures of covariate importance and thereby identify high quality subsets.

One interesting observation from [81] is that matching is closely related to the *"group-by"* operator in database queries in SQL, which is declarative (the user needs to specify 'what' is needed and not 'how'), robust, and supported in standard relational database systems that are optimized over decades, and hence SQL queries can be used to implement efficient matching algorithms on large datasets [71,81]. In fact, it has been observed that the database implementation of the FLAME (Fast Large Scale Almost Matching Exactly) [81] algorithm performs efficient matching for causal inference on big datasets that do not fit in memory, whereas all other state-of-the-art methods fail in terms of scalability.

3.3 Causal Inference on Networked and Relational Data

Both graphical causal model and the potential outcome framework typically assume *homogeneous units* with no interference, i.e., all the units have the same set of covariates, treatment, and outcome variables, and the units do not interfere with each other. In other words, the units can be represented in a single table as shown in Table 1. On the other hand, there may be causal questions when units interact with each other in a network, e.g., whether isolation in college dorms where students interact with their friends helps stop spread of flu. In a network, SUTVA does not hold and there may be interference – the treatment assigned to one unit may affect the treatment or outcome of another unit. Causal analysis approaches for network data are recently being developed [5,52,53]. A more general problem is causal inference on *relational data*, where data is heterogeneous and stored in multiple related tables for different entities and relationships (e.g., hospitals, doctors, patients, treatment, hospital-stay information etc. all are related but need to be stored in different tables), and such relational observed data is abundant in practice. Our initial work called *causal relational learning* [73] develops causal inference methods for relational datasets by adapting graphical causal model for relational data, proposing a declarative language for causal queries, and reducing the problem of causal analysis on relational data to standard causal analysis with homogeneous data by properly defining units, treatment, outcome, and confounding variables.

4   Causal Algorithmic Fairness

Algorithmic fairness considers a set of variables $\mathbf{V}$, which includes a set of *protected attributes* $\mathbf{S}$ and a binary *response* or *outcome variable* O. The classification algorithm $\mathcal{A} : \mathrm{Dom}(\mathbf{X}) \to \mathrm{Dom}(O)$ takes an input $\mathbf{X} \subseteq \mathbf{V}$ and maps it to an outcome O. We assume that there is a protected attribute $S \in \mathbf{S}$ that divides the population into two categories: disadvantaged ($S = 0$) and privileged ($S = 1$) For example, minority and non-minority groups for race or gender (see [83] for a survey).

The first task is to formally define when an algorithm $\mathcal{A}$ is *fair* with respect to the protected attribute S. As we shall see, this is not an easy task. Fairness definitions can be classified as associational or causal, which we will briefly review next. Throughout this section, we will use the college admission example from Example 1 as a running example assuming binary gender values $S = 0$ for female and $S = 1$ for male, although other values of the gender attribute may form the minority group as well. We also assume that $O = 1$ denotes the positive outcome (student is admitted in our example) and $O = 0$ denotes the negative outcome (student is not admitted).

4.1 Associational Fairness

One simple and appealing approach to defining fairness is to measure the correlation between the protected attribute S and the outcome O. Different fairness definitions vary in how they measure this correlation. Below we describe some popular notions of associational fairness:

Demographic Parity (DP) [13] requires an algorithm to classify both the disadvantaged and the privileged groups with the same probability. That is, $\mathbb{P}(O = 1 \mid S = 1) = \mathbb{P}(O = 1 \mid S = 0)$. In our college admission example, it requires an equal probability of admission for male and female applicants.

Conditional Statistical Parity (CSP) [9] controls for a set of admissible factors $\mathbf{A}$. That is, $\mathbb{P}(O = 1 \mid S = 1, \mathbf{A} = a) = \mathbb{P}(O = 1 \mid S = 0, \mathbf{A} = a)$. The definition is satisfied if subjects in both the disadvantaged and privileged groups have an equal probability of being assigned to the positive class, controlling for a set of admissible variables. In our running example, assuming that the choice of department is an admissible factor, this definition requires equal probability of male and female applicants being admitted to each department.

Equalized Odds (EO) is another popular measure used for predictive classification algorithms. It requires that both disadvantaged and privileged groups have the same false positive (FP) rate, $\mathbb{P}(O = 1 \mid S = 1, Y = 0) = \mathbb{P}(O = 1 \mid S = 0, Y = 0)$, and the same false negative (FN) rate, $\mathbb{P}(O = 0 \mid S = 1, Y = 1) = \mathbb{P}(O = 0 \mid S = 0, Y = 1)$, or equivalently, $(O \perp\!\!\!\perp S \mid Y)$. In our example, let Y be a binary variable that indicates degree attainment, which is considered to be the desired outcome for admitted students. Then, EO requires that among those applicants who (do not) graduate, the rate of admitted students should be independent of applicants' gender.

Predictive Parity (PP) requires that both disadvantaged and privileged groups have the same predicted positive value (PPV), $\mathbb{P}(Y = 1 \mid O = i, S = 0) = \mathbb{P}(Y = 1 \mid O = i, S = 1)$ for $i = 1, 0$, or equivalently, $Y \perp\!\!\!\perp S \mid O$. In our example, this implies that the probability of an applicant who attains a college degree after being admitted and the probability of an applicant who does not attain a college degree after being (incorrectly) admitted should be the same for male and female applicants.

Limitations of Associational Fairness. Much of the literature on algorithmic fairness has been motivated by controversies surrounding a widely used commercial risk assessment system for recidivism called COMPAS by Northpointe [41].

In 2016, a team of journalists from ProPublica constructed a dataset of more than 7,000 individuals arrested in Broward County, Florida, between 2013 and 2014, in order to analyze the efficacy of COMPAS. In addition, they collected data on future arrests for these defendants through the end of March 2016. Their assessment suggested that COMPAS scores were biased against African Americans. The false positive rate for African Americans (44.9%) was twice as high as the false positive rate for white people (23.5%), while the false negative rate for whites (47.7%) was twice as high as the false negative rate for African Americans (28.0%). In other words, COMPAS scores were shown to violate Equalized Odds (EO). In response to ProPublica, Northpointe showed that COMPAS scores satisfy Predictive Parity (PP), meaning that the likelihood of recidivism among high-risk offenders is the same regardless of race.

This story, along with the fact that associational notions of fairness are subject to statistical anomalies such as Simpson's paradox (see Example 1), shows that associational definitions are not expressive enough to capture the intuition behind fairness. Indeed, it has been shown that EO and PP are incompatible. In particular, Chouldechova [8] proves the following impossibility result. Suppose that the *base rate* of the two populations differs, i.e.,

$$\mathbb{P}(Y = 1 \mid S = 0) \neq \mathbb{P}(Y = 1 \mid S = 1) \tag{17}$$

Then, Equalized Odds and Predictive Parity cannot both hold simultaneously for any non-trivial classifier unless it is perfect (i.e., the false positive and false negative rates are 0). EO implies that $FP_i/(1 - FN_i)$ is the same for both populations $S = i$, $i = 0, 1$, while PP implies that $(1 - PPV_i)/PPV_i$ must be the same. Hence the following identity holds.

$$\frac{FP_i}{1 - FN_i} = \frac{\mathbb{P}(O = 1 \mid S = i, Y = 0)}{\mathbb{P}(O = 1 \mid S = i, Y = 1)} = \frac{\mathbb{P}(Y = 1 \mid S = i)}{\mathbb{P}(Y = 0 \mid S = i)} \frac{\mathbb{P}(Y = 0 \mid O = 1, S = i)}{\mathbb{P}(Y = 1 \mid O = 1, S = i)}$$
$$= \frac{\mathbb{P}(Y = 1 \mid S = i)}{\mathbb{P}(Y = 0 \mid S = i)} \frac{1 - PPV_i}{PPV_i}. \tag{18}$$

For $i = 0, 1$, (18) implies that $\mathbb{P}(Y = 1 \mid S = 0) = \mathbb{P}(Y = 1 \mid S = 1)$, which violates the assumption in (17).

4.2   Causal Fairness

The lack of universality and the impossibility result for fairness definitions based on associational fairness have motivated the search for definitions based on causality [19,38,40,50,70,72]. Intuitively, causal notions of fairness capture fairness in terms of the lack of a causal relationship between protected attributes and the outcome of an ML model. The difference between different causal notions of fairness lies in whether they capture fairness using interventional or counterfactual distributions to measure the causal relationship between the protected attribute and the outcome of an ML model. Next, we review some of the most widely used notions of causal fairness in the literature. For a comprehensive review, we refer readers to surveys [34,45].

Total Causal Effect Fairness. This notion can be seen as a causal counterpart of demographic parity and requires that the total causal effect of the protected attribute S on the outcome O be zero, i.e.,

$$P(O = 1 \mid do(\mathbf{S} = \mathbf{0})) = P(O = 1 \mid do(\mathbf{S} = \mathbf{1})) \tag{19}$$

Total causal effect is often decomposed into indirect (causal influence mediated by other attributes) and direct (influence that is not mediated) effects, or path-specific effects (influence through particular causal pathways) that are needed in many real-world situations [7]. However, identifying and estimating more fine-grained causal quantities is challenging in general [4]

$$P(O = 1 \mid do(\mathbf{S} = \mathbf{0})) = P(O = 1 \mid do(\mathbf{S} = \mathbf{1})) \tag{20}$$

Proxy Fairness. Proxy fairness was proposed by Kilbertus et al. [38] as the lack of a causal effect between the proxy of protected attributes and the outcome. The proxy is defined as a descendant of the protected attributes S and can be included in the set of proxies $\mathbf{P}$ along with other proxies. Intuitively, a proxy refers to a variable that is not the protected attribute itself but is highly correlated with it and used by the algorithm to make decisions. For example, in the context of college admission decisions, an applicant's hobby might be considered as a proxy for race since it is highly correlated with race. A fair algorithm should not be biased against or in favor of any group based on the proxies used.

The definition of proxy fairness can be expressed as the equation:

$$P(O = 1 \mid do(\mathbf{P} = \mathbf{p})) = P(O = 1 \mid do(\mathbf{P} = \mathbf{p}')) \tag{21}$$

for any $\mathbf{p}, \mathbf{p}' \in Dom(\mathbf{P})$. Intuitively, a classifier satisfies proxy fairness in (21) if the distribution of O under two interventional regimes in which $\mathbf{P}$ is set to $\mathbf{p}$ and $\mathbf{p}'$ is the same.

Counterfactual Fairness. Counterfactual fairness was introduced by Kusner et al. [40] as a definition of fairness that ensures that a protected attribute S is not a cause of the outcome variable O at an individual level. It is defined as follows: given a set of features $\mathbf{X}$, a protected attribute S, and a set of unobserved exogenous background variables $\mathbf{U}$, a predictor O is considered *counterfactually fair* if for any $\mathbf{x} \in Dom(\mathbf{X})$, $s, s' \in Dom(\mathbf{S})$ and $o \in Dom(\mathbf{O})$:

$$P(O_{S \leftarrow s}(\mathbf{u}) = o \mid \mathbf{X} = \mathbf{x}, S = s) = P(O_{S \leftarrow s'}(\mathbf{u}) = o \mid \mathbf{X} = \mathbf{x}, S = s) \tag{22}$$

The goal of counterfactual fairness is to prevent unfair treatment of individuals based on their protected attributes, such as race or gender, by ensuring that the outcome of an ML model is not influenced by such attributes. By comparing the outcome of two individuals who are identical except for their protected attribute, counterfactual fairness seeks to eliminate any causal relationship between the attribute and the outcome.

Individual Equalized Counterfactual Odds. Pfohl et al. [59] proposed the notion of individual equalized counterfactual odds as a counterfactual counterpart to the equality of odds. A predictor is considered individually equalized counterfactual odds fair if it satisfies the following condition for any $\mathbf{x} \in \text{Dom}(\mathbf{X})$, $s, s' \in \text{Dom}(\mathbf{S})$, $\mathbf{o} \in \text{Dom}(\mathbf{O})$, and $Y \in \text{Dom}(\mathbf{Y})$, where Y is the actual outcome:

$$P(O_{S \leftarrow s}(\mathbf{u}) = o \mid \mathbf{X} = \mathbf{x}, Y_{S \leftarrow s} = y, S = s) = P(O_{S \leftarrow s'}(\mathbf{u}) = o \mid \mathbf{X} = \mathbf{x}, Y_{S \leftarrow s'} = y, S = s) \tag{23}$$

This definition implies that the predictor is fair if it is counterfactually fair in a context where the actual outcome matches the counterfactual outcome. In the context of our running example, this definition implies that the rate of admitted applicants from the privileged group with features $\mathbf{x}$ who do not attain a college degree matches the counterfactual rate of admitted applicants with features $\mathbf{x}$ who would not attain a college degree if they belonged to the minority group. As before, Y is a binary variable that indicates degree attainment.

Interventional Fairness. Salimi et al. [74] proposed a definition of fairness that avoids issues with the aforementioned causal definitions. They define interventional fairness as follows: an algorithm $\mathcal{A} : Dom(\mathbf{X}) \to Dom(O)$ is $\mathbf{K}$-fair, for a set of attributes $\mathbf{K} \subseteq \mathbf{V} - S, O$, with respect to a protected attribute S if, for any context $\mathbf{K} = \mathbf{k}$ and every predicted outcome $O = o$, the following holds:

$$\mathbb{P}(O = o \mid do(S = 0), do(\mathbf{K} = \mathbf{k})) = \mathbb{P}(O = o \mid do(S = 1), do(\mathbf{K} = \mathbf{k})) \tag{24}$$

An algorithm is called *interventionally fair* if it is $\mathbf{K}$-fair for every set $\mathbf{K}$. Unlike proxy fairness, this notion correctly captures group-level fairness, because it ensures that S does not affect O in any configuration of the system obtained by fixing other variables at some arbitrary values. Unlike counterfactual fairness, it does not attempt to capture fairness at the individual level and therefore it uses the standard definition of intervention (the do-operator).

In practice, interventional fairness is often too restrictive. For example, in the UC Berkeley case, admission decisions were not interventional fair since gender affected the admission result via an applicant's choice of department. To make it practical, Salimi et al. [74] proposed a notion of fairness that relies on partitioning variables into *admissible* and *inadmissible*. The former are variables through which it is permissible for the protected attribute to influence the outcome, and this partitioning expresses fairness social norms and values that come from the users. In the admissions example, the user can label the department as admissible since it is considered a fair use in admissions decisions, and (implicitly) labels all other variables as inadmissible, such as hobby.

Then, an algorithm is called *justifiability fair* if it is $\mathbf{K}$-fair with respect to all supersets $\mathbf{K} \supseteq \mathbf{A}$, where $\mathbf{A}$ are admissible attributes. This notion of fairness uses admissible variables to calculate intervention and quantify the influence of the protected attribute, but only requires fairness to hold for a certain subset of variables.

5   Causal Explanations for ML Models

A natural and principled approach to quantifying the responsibility of input features for output of an algorithm is to measure their causal effect on the output, e.g., by measuring total effect, direct and indirect effect or more nuanced quantities such as path-specific effects. Furthermore, there have been recent attempts to incorporate causality into existing XAI frameworks. For instance, [75] proposed a method that incorporates causal relationships in the process of learning surrogates. There have also been some efforts to integrate causality with the concept of Shapley values. Asymmetric Shapley values [17] incorporate causality by discarding coalitions that do not follow a causal ordering, sacrificing the symmetry axiom of vanilla Shapley values in the process. Causal Shapley values [28] use causal interventions and allow for explanations that are able to decompose a feature's influence into direct and indirect effects without violating any of the original Shapley value axioms. Shapley flow [80] interprets models by assigning credit to the edges in a graph, extending the set-based view of Shapley values to a graph-based approach. There have also been attempts to integrate causality with generating actionable counterfactual explanations and recourse [35,37,44,60].

Recently, Galhotra et al. [20] proposed a new causality-based framework for XAI that unifies many existing methods and addresses their limitations. The explanations generated by this framework provide insights into the causes of an algorithm's decisions at the global, local, and contextual (sub-population) levels, and recommend actionable recourse that can be applied in the real world. The framework is based on probabilistic contrastive counterfactuals, which take the following form:

"For individual(s) with attribute(s) <actual-value> for whom an algorithm made the decision <actual-outcome>, the decision would have been <foil-outcome> with *probability* <score> had the attribute been <counterfactual-value>." $\qquad(25)$

Contrastive counterfactuals are at the core of the philosophical, cognitive, and social foundations of theories that address how humans generate and select explanations [11,21,24,43,47,55,57,82]. Based on them, Galhotra et al. [20] proposed three counterfactual measures for quantifying the influence of an attribute on decisions made by an algorithm, which we briefly review next.

We are given a decision-making algorithm $f : \text{Dom}(\mathbf{I}) \rightarrow \text{Dom}(O)$, where $\mathbf{I}$ is the set of input features and O is a binary outcome, where $O = o$ denotes the positive decision and $O = o'$ denotes the negative decision. Consider an attribute $X \in \mathbf{V}$ and a pair of attribute values $x, x' \in \text{Dom}(X)$. Galhotra et al. [20] proposed the following counterfactuals to quantify the influence of the attribute value x relative to a baseline x' on decisions made by an algorithm, using the following scores (implicitly assuming an ordering $x > x'$):

Definition 51 (Explanation Scores). *Given a PCM $\langle \mathcal{M}, \mathbb{P} \rangle$ and an algorithm $f : Dom(\mathbf{X}) \rightarrow Dom(O)$, a variable $X \in \mathbf{V}$, and a pair of attribute values $x, x' \in Dom(X)$, the influence of x relative to x' on the algorithm's decisions* in the context $\mathbf{k} \in Dom(\mathbf{K})$, where $\mathbf{K} \subseteq \mathbf{V} - \{X, O\}$, is quantified using the following measures:

- The necessity score:

$$\text{Nec}(\mathbf{k}) \overset{def}{=} \mathbb{P}(o'_{X \leftarrow x'} \mid x, o, \mathbf{k}) \tag{26}$$

- The sufficiency score:

$$\text{Suf}(\mathbf{k}) \overset{def}{=} \mathbb{P}(o_{X \leftarrow x} \mid x', o', \mathbf{k}) \tag{27}$$

- The necessity and sufficiency score:

$$\text{NeSuf}(\mathbf{k}) \overset{def}{=} \mathbb{P}(o_{X \leftarrow x}, o'_{X \leftarrow x'} \mid \mathbf{k}), \tag{28}$$

where the distribution $\mathbb{P}(o_{X \leftarrow x})$ is well-defined and can be computed from the algorithm $f(\mathbf{I})$. Specifically, for deterministic $f(\mathbf{I})$, $\mathbb{P}(o_{X \leftarrow x}) = \sum_{i \in Dom(\mathbf{I})} \mathbb{1}_{\{f(i)=o\}} \mathbb{P}(\mathbf{I}_{X \leftarrow x} = i)$, where $\mathbb{1}_{\{f(i)=o\}}$ is an indicator function.

The sufficiency score in equation (27) can be interpreted as follows: given a set of input features $\mathbf{k}$, it measures the probability that the algorithm's decision would have been positive instead of negative if the value of attribute X were changed from x' to x. In other words, the sufficiency score asks the question: "What would be the probability of a positive decision, for individuals with attributes $\mathbf{k}$, if X were x instead of x'?"

On the other hand, the necessity score is the dual of the sufficiency score. It measures the probability that the algorithm's decision would have been negative instead of positive if X were x instead of x', given input features $\mathbf{k}$. The necessity score establishes a balance between sufficiency and necessity, capturing the probability that the algorithm responds in both ways.

As mentioned in Sect. 2.3, if the structural equation model and exogenous variables are observed, then explanation scores and counterfactual recourse can be computed using Eq. (5). However, in practice, the causal model may not be fully observed, and in such cases, it becomes necessary to estimate explanation scores from data. Galhotra et al. [20] have established sufficient conditions for estimating explanations from data under partial specification of the underlying causal model.

Counterfactual Recourse. In cases where an algorithm's decision is negative for a particular individual, it is possible to generate an explanation by identifying a minimal intervention on a user-specified set of actionable variables with a high *sufficiency score*. This intervention can then be made in order to produce a positive decision with high probability. The explanations can be used either as a justification in case the decision is challenged, or as a recommendation for recourse in terms of a feasible action that the individual can perform to improve the outcome in the future.

Given an individual with attributes $\mathbf{v}$, a set of actionable variables $\mathbf{A} \subseteq \mathbf{V}$, and a cost function $\text{Cost}(\mathbf{a}, \hat{\mathbf{a}})$ that determines the cost of an intervention that changes **A** from its current value **a** to **â**, the problem of computing *counterfactual recourse* is introduced in [20] as the following optimization problem:

$$\operatorname*{argmin}_{\mathbf{a}} \operatorname{Cost}(\mathbf{a}, \hat{\mathbf{a}}) \quad \text{s.t. } \mathbf{a} \in Dom(\mathbf{A}) \text{ and } \operatorname{SUF}_{\hat{\mathbf{a}}}(\mathbf{v}) \geq \alpha \qquad (29)$$

This optimization problem treats the decision-making algorithm as a black box. The solutions to this problem provide end-users with informative, feasible, and actionable recourse by answering questions such as "What are the best courses of action that, if performed in the real world, would change the outcome for this individual with high probability?". [20] uses integer programming for efficiently solving this optimization problem.

6 Conclusions

Causal analysis is a crucial topic in the current era of big data and data science. It is necessary when users or analysts want to identify the *cause* of an observation, rather than just predicting or correlating variables, to make well-informed decisions and take appropriate actions. In this survey, we discussed two common notions of causal analysis for observed or collected data: Pearl's graphical causal model and Rubin's potential outcome framework, along with common methods for causal inference.

Despite significant progress, several future research directions remain open. The scalability of interpretable matching algorithms should be further improved to make them suitable for interactive data analysis, particularly for large high-dimensional data. It would be interesting to explore how dimensionality reduction techniques and parallel algorithms (if multiple machines are available) can help in this regard. Although some recent work on network and relational causal analysis has emerged, these methods typically rely on several assumptions, so developing better algorithms for complex data models will be useful.

Responsible data science requires understanding different aspects of fairness, bias, and explainability. Exploring data biases and algorithmic fairness and understanding their causal aspects will require a deeper study. In particular, the application of causal reasoning is crucial in understanding various types of data biases and data quality issues, such as selection bias, confounding bias, and missing data. It would be interesting to study the interaction between different types of biases and data quality issues and explore developing causal approaches to mitigate these problems. For instance, causal approaches could be used to identify and quantify the impact of specific variables on fairness and bias in machine learning models. Advancing research in these directions will lead to improved causal inference methods that can effectively support responsible data science in various high-stakes decision-making contexts, including healthcare, criminal justice, and finance. Ultimately, this will help ensure that decision-making processes are transparent, accountable, and equitable.

References

1. New York times article on crime and summer (2009). https://www.nytimes.com/2009/06/19/nyregion/19murder.html?smid=url-share
2. Alvarez-Melis, D., Jaakkola, T.S.: On the robustness of interpretability methods. arXiv preprint arXiv:1806.08049 (2018)
3. Apley, D.W., Zhu, J.: Visualizing the effects of predictor variables in black box supervised learning models. arXiv preprint arXiv:1612.08468 (2016)
4. Avin, C., Shpitser, I., Pearl, J.: Identifiability of path-specific effects (2005)
5. Awan, M.U., Morucci, M., Orlandi, V., Roy, S., Rudin, C., Volfovsky, A.: Almost-matching-exactly for treatment effect estimation under network interference. In: Chiappa, S., Calandra, R. (eds.) The 23rd International Conference on Artificial Intelligence and Statistics, AISTATS 2020, 26–28 August 2020, Online, Palermo, Sicily, Italy. Proceedings of Machine Learning Research, vol. 108, pp. 3252–3262. PMLR (2020)
6. Bickel, P.J., Hammel, E.A., O'Connell, J., et al.: Sex bias in graduate admissions: data from Berkeley. Science **187**(4175), 398–404 (1975)
7. Chiappa, S.: Path-specific counterfactual fairness. In: Proceedings of the AAAI Conference on Artificial Intelligence, vol. 33, pp. 7801–7808 (2019)
8. Chouldechova, A.: Fair prediction with disparate impact: a study of bias in recidivism prediction instruments. Big data **5**(2), 153–163 (2017)
9. Corbett-Davies, S., Pierson, E., Feller, A., Goel, S., Huq, A.: Algorithmic decision making and the cost of fairness. In: Proceedings of the 23rd ACM SIGKDD International Conference on Knowledge Discovery and Data Mining, pp. 797–806. ACM (2017)
10. Cox, D.R.: The regression analysis of binary sequences (with discussion). J. Roy. Stat. Soc. B **20**, 215–242 (1958)
11. De Graaf, M.M.A., Malle, B.F.: How people explain action (and autonomous intelligent systems should too). In: 2017 AAAI Fall Symposium Series (2017)
12. Dieng, A., Liu, Y., Roy, S., Rudin, C., Volfovsky, A.: Interpretable almost-exact matching for causal inference. In: Chaudhuri, K., Sugiyama, M. (eds.) The 22nd International Conference on Artificial Intelligence and Statistics, AISTATS 2019, 16–18 April 2019, Naha, Okinawa, Japan. Proceedings of Machine Learning Research, vol. 89, pp. 2445–2453. PMLR (2019)
13. Dwork, C., Hardt, M., Pitassi, T., Reingold, O., Zemel, R.S.: Fairness through awareness. In: ITCS, pp. 214–226. ACM (2012)
14. Fisher, A., Rudin, C., Dominici, F.: Model class reliance: variable importance measures for any machine learning model class, from the "rashomon" perspective. arXiv preprint arXiv:1801.01489, p. 68 (2018)
15. Ronald Aylmer Fisher: The Design of Experiments. Oliver and Boyd, Oxford (1935)
16. Friedman, J.H.: Greedy function approximation: a gradient boosting machine. Ann. Stat. 1189–1232 (2001)
17. Frye, C., Feige, I., Rowat, C.: Asymmetric shapley values: incorporating causal knowledge into model-agnostic explainability. arXiv preprint arXiv:1910.06358 (2019)
18. Funk, M.J., Westreich, D., Wiesen, C., Stürmer, T., Brookhart, M.A., Davidian, M.: Doubly robust estimation of causal effects. Am. J. Epidemiol. **173**, 761–767 (2011)
19. Galhotra, S., Brun, Y., Meliou, A.: Fairness testing: testing software for discrimination. In: Proceedings of the 2017 11th Joint Meeting on Foundations of Software Engineering, pp. 498–510. ACM (2017)

20. Galhotra, S., Pradhan, R., Salimi, B.: Explaining black-box algorithms using probabilistic contrastive counterfactuals. In: Proceedings of the International Conference on Management of Data, pp. 577–590 (2021)
21. Gerstenberg, T., Goodman, N.D., Lagnado, D.A., Tenenbaum, J.B.: How, whether, why: causal judgments as counterfactual contrasts. In: CogSci (2015)
22. Goldstein, A., Kapelner, A., Bleich, J., Pitkin, E.: Peeking inside the black box: visualizing statistical learning with plots of individual conditional expectation. J. Comput. Graph. Stat. **24**(1), 44–65 (2015)
23. Greenwell, B.M., Boehmke, B.C., McCarthy, A.J.: A simple and effective model-based variable importance measure. arXiv preprint arXiv:1805.04755 (2018)
24. Grynaviski, E.: Contrasts, counterfactuals, and causes. Eur. J. Int. Rel. **19**(4), 823–846 (2013)
25. Guidotti, R., Monreale, A., Ruggieri, S., Turini, F., Giannotti, F., Pedreschi, D.: A survey of methods for explaining black box models. ACM Comput. Surv. (CSUR) **51**(5), 1–42 (2018)
26. Hahn, P.R., Murray, J.S., Carvalho, C.: Bayesian regression tree models for causal inference: regularization, confounding, and heterogeneous effects (2017)
27. Hernán, M.A., Robins, J.M.: Causal inference (2010)
28. Heskes, T., Sijben, E., Bucur, I.G., Claassen, T.: Causal shapley values: exploiting causal knowledge to explain individual predictions of complex models. arXiv preprint arXiv:2011.01625 (2020)
29. Holland, P.W.: Statistics and causal inference. J. Am. Stat. Assoc. **81**(396), 945–960 (1986)
30. Hooker, G.: Discovering additive structure in black box functions. In: Proceedings of the Tenth ACM SIGKDD International Conference on Knowledge Discovery and Data Mining, pp. 575–580 (2004)
31. Hooker, G., Mentch, L.: Please stop permuting features: an explanation and alternatives. arXiv preprint arXiv:1905.03151 (2019)
32. Iacus, S.M., King, G., Porro, G., Katz, J.N.: Causal inference without balance checking: coarsened exact matching. Polit. Anal. 1–24 (2012)
33. Imbens, G.W., Rubin, D.B.: Causal Inference in Statistics, Social, and Biomedical Sciences. Cambridge University Press, Cambridge (2015)
34. Islam, M.T., Fariha, A., Meliou, A., Salimi, B.: Through the data management lens: experimental analysis and evaluation of fair classification. In: Proceedings of the 2022 International Conference on Management of Data, pp. 232–246 (2022)
35. Karimi, A.-H., Barthe, G., Belle, B., Valera, I.: Model-agnostic counterfactual explanations for consequential decisions. arXiv preprint arXiv:1905.11190 (2019)
36. Karimi, A.-H., Barthe, G., Schölkopf, B., Valera, I.: A survey of algorithmic recourse: contrastive explanations and consequential recommendations. ACM Comput. Surv. **55**(5), 1–29 (2022)
37. Karimi, A.-H., von Kügelgen, J., Schölkopf, B., Valera, I.: Algorithmic recourse under imperfect causal knowledge: a probabilistic approach. arXiv preprint arXiv:2006.06831 (2020)
38. Kilbertus, N., Carulla, M.R., Parascandolo, G., Hardt, M., Janzing, D., Schölkopf, B.: Avoiding discrimination through causal reasoning. In: Advances in Neural Information Processing Systems, pp. 656–666 (2017)
39. Kumar, I.E., Venkatasubramanian, S., Scheidegger, C., Friedler, S.: Problems with shapley-value-based explanations as feature importance measures. In: International Conference on Machine Learning, pp. 5491–5500. PMLR (2020)
40. Kusner, M.J., Loftus, J., Russell, C., Silva, R.: Counterfactual fairness. In: Advances in Neural Information Processing Systems, pp. 4069–4079 (2017)

41. Larson, J., Mattu, S., Kirchner, L., Angwin, J.: How we analyzed the compas recidivism algorithm. ProPublica **9** (2016)
42. Laugel, T., Lesot, M.-J., Marsala, C., Renard, X., Detyniecki, M.: Inverse classification for comparison-based interpretability in machine learning. arXiv preprint arXiv:1712.08443 (2017)
43. Lipton, P.: Contrastive explanation. R. Inst. Philos. Suppl. **27**, 247–266 (1990)
44. Mahajan, D., Tan, C., Sharma, A.: Preserving causal constraints in counterfactual explanations for machine learning classifiers. arXiv preprint arXiv:1912.03277 (2019)
45. Makhlouf, K., Zhioua, S., Palamidessi, C.: Survey on causal-based machine learning fairness notions. arXiv preprint arXiv:2010.09553 (2020)
46. Molnar, C.: Interpretable Machine Learning (2020). Lulu.com
47. Morton, A.: Contrastive knowledge. Contrastivism Philos. 101–115 (2013)
48. Morucci, M., Orlandi, V., Roy, S., Rudin, C., Volfovsky, A.: Adaptive hyper-box matching for interpretable individualized treatment effect estimation. In: Adams, R.P., Gogate, V. (eds.) Proceedings of the Thirty-Sixth Conference on Uncertainty in Artificial Intelligence, UAI 2020, Virtual Online, 3–6 August 2020. Proceedings of Machine Learning Research, vol. 124, pp. 1089–1098. AUAI Press (2020)
49. Mothilal, R.K., Sharma, A., Tan, C.: Explaining machine learning classifiers through diverse counterfactual explanations. In: Proceedings of the 2020 Conference on Fairness, Accountability, and Transparency, pp. 607–617 (2020)
50. Nabi, R., Shpitser, I.: Fair inference on outcomes. In: Proceedings of the AAAI Conference on Artificial Intelligence. AAAI Conference on Artificial Intelligence, vol. 2018, p. 1931. NIH Public Access (2018)
51. Neyman, J.: On the application of probability theory to agricultural experiments. Essay on Principles. Section 9. PhD thesis, Roczniki Nauk Rolniczych Tom X [in Polish] (1923). Translated in Statistical Science, vol. 5, pp. 465–480
52. Ogburn, E.L., Shpitser, I., Lee, Y.: Causal inference, social networks, and chain graphs (2018)
53. Ogburn, E.L., Sofrygin, O., Diaz, I., van der Laan, M.J.: Causal inference for social network data (2017)
54. Pearl, J.: Probabilistic Reasoning in Intelligent Systems: Networks of Plausible Inference. Morgan Kaufmann (1988)
55. Pearl, J.: Causality: Models, Reasoning, and Inference, 2nd edn. Cambridge University Press, Cambridge (2009)
56. Pearl, J.: Comment: understanding Simpson's paradox. In: Probabilistic and Causal Inference: The Works of Judea Pearl, pp. 399–412 (2022)
57. Pearl, J., et al.: Causal inference in statistics: an overview. Stat. Surv. **3**, 96–146 (2009)
58. Pearl, J., Glymour, M., Jewell, N.P.: Causal Inference in Statistics: A Primer. Wiley, Hoboken (2016)
59. Pfohl, S.R., Duan, T., Ding, D.Y., Shah, N.H.: Counterfactual reasoning for fair clinical risk prediction. In: Machine Learning for Healthcare Conference, pp. 325–358. PMLR (2019)
60. Pradhan, R., Zhu, J., Glavic, B., Salimi, B.: Interpretable data-based explanations for fairness debugging. In: SIGMOD (2022)
61. Ribeiro, M.T., Singh, S., Guestrin, C.: "Why should I trust you?" Explaining the predictions of any classifier. In: Proceedings of the 22nd ACM SIGKDD International Conference on Knowledge Discovery and Data Mining, pp. 1135–1144 (2016)
62. Ribeiro, M.T., Singh, S., Guestrin, C.: Anchors: high-precision model-agnostic explanations. In: AAAI, vol. 18, pp. 1527–1535 (2018)

63. Rosenbaum, P.R.: Observational Study. Wiley, Hoboken (2005)
64. Rosenbaum, P.R.: Design of Observational Studies, vol. 10. Springer, Heidelberg (2010)
65. Rosenbaum, P.R., Rubin, D.B.: The central role of the propensity score in observational studies for causal effects. Biometrika $70(1)$, 41–55 (1983)
66. Rosenbaum, P.R., Rubin, D.B.: Reducing bias in observational studies using subclassification on the propensity score. J. Am. Stat. Assoc. $79(387)$, 516–524 (1984)
67. Rubin, D.B.: Matching to remove bias in observational studies. Biometrics 159–183 (1973)
68. Rubin, D.B.: Estimating causal effects of treatments in randomized and nonrandomized studies. J. Educ. Psychol. $66(5)$, 688 (1974)
69. Rubin, D.B.: Causal inference using potential outcomes. J. Am. Stat. Assoc. $100(469)$, 322–331 (2005)
70. Russell, C., Kusner, M.J., Loftus, J., Silva, R.: When worlds collide: integrating different counterfactual assumptions in fairness. In: Advances in Neural Information Processing Systems, pp. 6414–6423 (2017)
71. Salimi, B., Cole, C., Ports, D.R.K., Suciu, D.: ZaliQL: causal inference from observational data at scale. Proc. VLDB Endow. $10(12)$, 1957–1960 (2017)
72. Salimi, B., Howe, B., Suciu, D.: Data management for causal algorithmic fairness. Data Eng. 24 (2019)
73. Salimi, B., Parikh, H., Kayali, M., Getoor, L., Roy, S., Suciu, D.: Causal relational learning. In: Proceedings of the 2020 ACM SIGMOD International Conference on Management of Data, pp. 241–256 (2020)
74. Salimi, B., Rodriguez, L., Howe, B., Suciu, D.: Interventional fairness: causal database repair for algorithmic fairness. In: Proceedings of the 2019 International Conference on Management of Data, pp. 793–810. ACM (2019)
75. Schwab, P., Karlen, W.: CXPlain: causal explanations for model interpretation under uncertainty. arXiv preprint arXiv:1910.12336 (2019)
76. Stuart, E.A.: Matching methods for causal inference: a review and a look forward. Statistical science: a review. J. Inst. Math. Stat. 1–21 (2010)
77. Ustun, B., Spangher, A., Liu, Y.: Actionable recourse in linear classification. In: Proceedings of the Conference on Fairness, Accountability, and Transparency, pp. 10–19 (2019)
78. Verma, S., Rubin, J.: Fairness definitions explained. In: 2018 IEEE/ACM International Workshop on Software Fairness (FairWare), pp. 1–7. IEEE (2018)
79. Wachter, S., Mittelstadt, B., Russell, C.: Counterfactual explanations without opening the black box: automated decisions and the GDPR. Harv. JL Tech. 31, 841 (2017)
80. Wang, J., Wiens, J., Lundberg, S.: Shapley flow: a graph-based approach to interpreting model predictions. In: International Conference on Artificial Intelligence and Statistics, pp. 721–729. PMLR (2021)
81. Wang, T., et al.: FLAME: a fast large-scale almost matching exactly approach to causal inference. J. Mach. Learn. Res. 22, 31:1–31:41 (2021)
82. Woodward, J.: Making Things Happen: A Theory of Causal Explanation. Oxford University Press, Oxford (2005)
83. Zliobaite, I.: A survey on measuring indirect discrimination in machine learning. arXiv preprint arXiv:1511.00148 (2015)

Statistical Relational Extension of Answer Set Programming

Joohyung Lee[✉][ID] and Zhun Yang[ID]

Arizona State University, Tempe, AZ 85287, USA
{joolee,zyang90}@asu.edu

Abstract. This tutorial presents a statistical relational extension of the answer set programming language called LP^{MLN}, which incorporates the concept of weighted rules into the stable model semantics following the log-linear models of Markov Logic. An LP^{MLN} program defines a probability distribution over "soft" stable models, which may not satisfy all rules, but the more rules with larger weights they satisfy, the higher their probabilities, thus allowing for an intuitive and elaboration tolerant representation of problems that require both logical and probabilistic reasoning. The extension provides a natural way to overcome the deterministic nature of the stable model semantics, such as resolving inconsistencies in answer set programs, associating probability to stable models, and applying statistical inference and learning with probabilistic stable models. We also present formal relations between LP^{MLN} and other related formalisms, which produce ways of performing inference and learning in LP^{MLN}.

Keywords: Answer Set Programming · Statistical Relational Learning

1 Introduction

Answer Set Programming (ASP) [23], based on the stable model semantics [12], is a widely used knowledge representation framework that facilitates elegant and efficient representations for many problem domains that require complex reasoning. However, ASP has no built-in mechanism to represent probabilistic uncertainty and to statistically induce knowledge from the data.

This tutorial presents an extension of ASP called LP^{MLN} that incorporates the concept of weighted rules following the log-linear models of Markov Logic [27]. Instead of the classical logic adopted in Markov Logic, language LP^{MLN} adopts stable models as the logical component. The relationship between LP^{MLN} and Markov Logic is analogous to the known relationship between ASP and SAT.

For example, consider the simple ASP knowledge base KB_1:

$$Bird(x) \leftarrow ResidentBird(x)$$
$$Bird(x) \leftarrow MigratoryBird(x)$$
$$\leftarrow ResidentBird(x), MigratoryBird(x).$$

© The Author(s), under exclusive license to Springer Nature Switzerland AG 2023
L. Bertossi and G. Xiao (Eds.): Reasoning Web, LNCS 13759, pp. 132–160, 2023.
https://doi.org/10.1007/978-3-031-31414-8_4

One data source KB_2 (possibly acquired by some information extraction module) says that *Jo* is a *ResidentBird*:

$$ResidentBird(Jo)$$

while another data source KB_3 states that *Jo* is a *MigratoryBird*:

$$MigratoryBird(Jo).$$

The data about *Jo* is actually inconsistent w.r.t. KB_1, so under the (deterministic) stable model semantics, the combined knowledge base $KB = KB_1 \cup KB_2 \cup KB_3$ is not so meaningful. On the other hand, it is still intuitive to conclude that *Jo* is likely a *Bird*, and may be a *ResidentBird* or a *MigratoryBird*. Such reasoning is supported in LP^{MLN}.

This paper is organized as follows. After reviewing the stable model semantics in Sect. 2, we introduce the syntax and semantics of the language LP^{MLN} in Sect. 3. Section 4 relates LP^{MLN} to other formalisms. Section 5 explains how to learn weights of LP^{MLN} programs from data, and Sect. 6 presents an implementation based on these ideas. Section 7 presents a fragment of LP^{MLN} that is simpler and has been used in defining a probabilistic action language [20] and a neural ASP extension [33].

The tutorial is based on previous publications about LP^{MLN} [18,19,21,22,33].

2   Review: Stable Model Semantics

The stable model semantics was defined for rules of a simple form [12] to arbitrary first-order formulas [9].

We assume a first-order signature σ that contains no function constants of positive arity, which yields finitely many Hedrbrand interpretations.[1] The syntax of formulas is defined the same as in the standard first-order logic. We say that a formula is *negative* if every occurrence of every atom in this formula is in the scope of negation.

In this tutorial, for simplicity, we mainly consider a *rule* of the form

$$A \leftarrow B \wedge N \tag{1}$$

where A is a disjunction of atoms, B is a conjunction of atoms, and N is a negative formula constructed from atoms using conjunction, disjunction, and negation. We identify rule (1) with formula $B \wedge N \rightarrow A$. We often use a comma for conjunction, a semi-colon for disjunction, *not* for negation, as widely used in the literature on logic programming. For example, N could be

$$\neg B_{m+1} \wedge \ldots \wedge \neg B_n \wedge \neg\neg B_{n+1} \wedge \ldots \wedge \neg\neg B_p,$$

---

[1] It is straightforward to extend LP^{MLN} to allow function constants of positive arity as long as the program is finitely groundable.

which can be also written as

$$not\ B_{m+1}, \ldots, not\ B_n, not\ not\ B_{n+1}, \ldots, not\ not\ B_p,$$

where each B_i is an atom.

We write $\{A_1\}^{\text{ch}} \leftarrow Body$, where A_1 is an atom, to denote the rule $A_1 \leftarrow Body \wedge \neg\neg A_1$. This expression is called a *choice rule* in ASP. If the head of a rule (A in (1)) is $\bot$, we often omit it and call such a rule *constraint*.

A logic program under the stable model semantics (a.k.a. *answer set program*) is a finite conjunction of rules. A logic program is called *ground* if it contains no variables.

We say that an Herbrand interpretation I is a *model* of a ground program Π if I satisfies all implications (1) in Π (as in classical logic). Such models can be divided into two groups: "stable" and "non-stable" models, which are distinguished as follows. The *reduct* of Π relative to I, denoted Π^I, consists of "$A \leftarrow B$" for all rules (1) in Π such that $I \models N$. The Herbrand interpretation I is called a *(deterministic) stable model* of Π if I is a minimal Herbrand model of Π^I. (Minimality is understood in terms of set inclusion. We identify an Herbrand interpretation with the set of atoms that are true in it.)

The definition is extended to any non-ground program Π by identifying it with $gr_\sigma[\Pi]$, the ground program obtained from Π by replacing every variable with every ground term of σ.

A *weak constraint* [5,6] has the form

$$:\sim F \quad [Weight @ Level]$$

where F is a conjunction of literals, *Weight* is a real number, and *Level* is a nonnegative integer.

Let Π be a program $\Pi_1 \cup \Pi_2$, where Π_1 is an answer set program that does not contain weak constraints, and Π_2 is a set of ground weak constraints. We call I a *stable model* of Π if it is a stable model of the standard program Π_1. For every stable model I of Π and any nonnegative integer l, the *penalty* of I at level l, denoted by $Penalty_\Pi(I, l)$, is defined as

$$\sum_{\substack{:\sim F[w@l] \in \Pi_2, \\ I \models F}} w.$$

For any two stable models I and I' of Π, we say I is *dominated* by I' if

- there is some nonnegative integer l such that $Penalty_\Pi(I', l) < Penalty_\Pi(I, l)$ and
- for all integers $k > l$, $Penalty_\Pi(I', k) = Penalty_\Pi(I, k)$.

A stable model of Π is called *optimal* if it is not dominated by another stable model of Π.

3   Language LP^{MLN}

LP^{MLN} is a probabilistic logic programming language that extends answer set programs with the concept of weighted rules, whose weight scheme is adopted from that of Markov Logic. In this section, we introduce the syntax and semantics of LP^{MLN}, and show how LP^{MLN} can be used to resolve certain inconsistencies in ASP programs or express different certainty levels with the weighting scheme.

3.1   Syntax of LP^{MLN}

The syntax of LP^{MLN} defines a set of weighted rules. More precisely, an LP^{MLN} program Π is a finite set of weighted rules $w : R$, where R is a rule of the form (1) and w is either a real number or the symbol α denoting the "infinite weight." We call rule $w : R$ *soft* rule if w is a real number, and *hard* rule if w is α.

Similar to answer set programs, we say that an LP^{MLN} program is *ground* if its rules contain no variables. We identify any LP^{MLN} program Π of signature σ with a ground LP^{MLN} program $gr_\sigma[\Pi]$, whose rules are obtained from the rules of Π by replacing every variable with every ground term of σ. The weight of a ground rule in $gr_\sigma[\Pi]$ is the same as the weight of the rule in Π from which the ground rule is obtained. By $\overline{\Pi}$ we denote the unweighted logic program obtained from Π, i.e., $\overline{\Pi} = \{R \mid w : R \in \Pi\}$.

3.2   Semantics of LP^{MLN} (Reward-Based)

A stable model of an LP^{MLN} program does not have to be obtained from the whole program. Instead, each stable model is obtained from some subset of the program, and the weights of the rules in that subset determine the probability of the stable model. It may not seem obvious if there is a *unique* maximal subset that derives such a stable model. The following proposition tells us that this is indeed the case, and furthermore that the subset is exactly the set of all rules that are satisfied by I.

Proposition 1 ([19]). *For any (unweighted) logic program Π and any subset Π' of Π, if I is a stable model of Π' and I satisfies Π, then I is a stable model of Π as well.*

The proposition tells us that if I is a stable model of a program, adding more rules to this program does not affect that I is a stable model of the resulting program as long as I satisfies the rules added. On the other hand, it is clear that I is no longer a stable model if I does not satisfy at least one of the rules added.

For any LP^{MLN} program Π, by Π_I we denote the set of rules $w : R$ in Π such that $I \models R$, and by SM$[\Pi]$ we denote the set $\{I \mid I$ is a stable model of $\overline{\Pi_I}\}$. We define the *unnormalized weight* of an interpretation I under Π, denoted $W_\Pi(I)$, as

$$W_\Pi(I) = \begin{cases} exp\left(\displaystyle\sum_{w:R \,\in\, \Pi_I} w\right) & \text{if } I \in \text{SM}[\Pi]; \\ 0 & \text{otherwise.} \end{cases}$$

Notice that SM[Π] is never empty because it always contains $\emptyset$. It is easy to check that $\emptyset$ always satisfies $\overline{\Pi_\emptyset}$, and it is the smallest set that satisfies the reduct $(\overline{\Pi_\emptyset})^\emptyset$.

The *probability* of an interpretation I under Π, denoted $P_\Pi(I)$, is defined as

$$P_\Pi(I) = \lim_{\alpha \to \infty} \frac{W_\Pi(I)}{\sum_{J \in \text{SM}[\Pi]} W_\Pi(J)}.$$

We omit the subscript Π if the context is clear. We say that I is a *(probabilistic) stable model* of Π if $P_\Pi(I) \neq 0$. Intuitively, $P_\Pi(I)$ indicates how likely it is to draw I as a stable model of some maximal subset of $\overline{\Pi}$.

For any proposition A, probability $P_\Pi(A)$ is defined as

$$P_\Pi(A) = \sum_{I:\, I \models A} P_\Pi(I).$$

Conditional probability under Π is defined as usual. For propositions A and B,

$$P_\Pi(A \mid B) = \frac{P_\Pi(A \wedge B)}{P_\Pi(B)}.$$

Often we are only interested in stable models that satisfy all hard rules (because hard rules represent definite knowledge), in which case the probabilities of stable models can be computed from the weights of the soft rules only, as described below.

For any LP^{MLN} program Π, by Π^{soft} we denote the set of all soft rules in Π, and by Π^{hard} the set of all hard rules in Π. Let SM$'$[Π] be the set

$$\{I \mid I \text{ is a stable model of } \overline{\Pi_I} \text{ that satisfy } \overline{\Pi^{\text{hard}}}\},$$

and let

$$W'_\Pi(I) = \begin{cases} exp\left(\sum_{w:R \,\in\, (\Pi^{\text{soft}})_I} w \right) & \text{if } I \in \text{SM}'[\Pi]; \\ 0 & \text{otherwise,} \end{cases}$$

$$P'_\Pi(I) = \frac{W'_\Pi(I)}{\sum_{J \in \text{SM}'[\Pi]} W'_\Pi(J)}.$$

Notice the absence of $\lim_{\alpha \to \infty}$ in the definition of $P'_\Pi[I]$. Also, unlike $P_\Pi(I)$, SM$'$[Π] may be empty, in which case $P'_\Pi(I)$ is undefined. Otherwise, the following proposition tells us that the probability of an interpretation can be computed by considering the weights of the soft rules only.

Proposition 2 ([19]). *If SM$'$[Π] is not empty, for every interpretation I, $P'_\Pi(I)$ coincides with $P_\Pi(I)$.*

It follows that if SM$'$[Π] is not empty, then every stable model of Π (with non-zero probability) should satisfy all hard rules in Π.

3.3   Examples

The weighting scheme of LP^{MLN} provides a simple and effective way to resolve certain inconsistencies in ASP programs.

Example 1. The example in the introduction can be represented in LP^{MLN} as

$$
\begin{array}{lll}
KB_1 & \alpha : Bird(x) \leftarrow ResidentBird(x) & (r_1) \\
& \alpha : Bird(x) \leftarrow MigratoryBird(x) & (r_2) \\
& \alpha : \leftarrow ResidentBird(x), MigratoryBird(x) & (r_3) \\
KB_2 & \alpha : ResidentBird(Jo) & (r_4) \\
KB_3 & \alpha : MigratoryBird(Jo) & (r_5)
\end{array}
$$

Assuming that the Herbrand universe is $\{Jo\}$, the following table shows the weight and the probability of each interpretation.

I	Π_I	$W_\Pi(I)$	$P_\Pi(I)$
$\emptyset$	$\{r_1, r_2, r_3\}$	$e^{3\alpha}$	0
$\{R(Jo)\}$	$\{r_2, r_3, r_4\}$	$e^{3\alpha}$	0
$\{M(Jo)\}$	$\{r_1, r_3, r_5\}$	$e^{3\alpha}$	0
$\{B(Jo)\}$	$\{r_1, r_2, r_3\}$	0	0
$\{R(Jo), B(Jo)\}$	$\{r_1, r_2, r_3, r_4\}$	$e^{4\alpha}$	1/3
$\{M(Jo), B(Jo)\}$	$\{r_1, r_2, r_3, r_5\}$	$e^{4\alpha}$	1/3
$\{R(Jo), M(Jo)\}$	$\{r_4, r_5\}$	$e^{2\alpha}$	0
$\{R(Jo), M(Jo), B(Jo)\}$	$\{r_1, r_2, r_4, r_5\}$	$e^{4\alpha}$	1/3

(The weight of $I = \{Bird(Jo)\}$ is 0 because I is not a stable model of $\overline{\Pi_I}$.) Thus we can check that

- $P(Bird(Jo)) = 1/3 + 1/3 + 1/3 = 1$.
- $P(Bird(Jo) \mid ResidentBird(Jo)) = 1$.
- $P(ResidentBird(Jo) \mid Bird(Jo)) = 2/3$.

Instead of α, one can assign different certainty levels to the additional knowledge bases, such as

$$
\begin{array}{lll}
KB_2' & 2 : ResidentBird(Jo) & (r_4') \\
KB_3' & 1 : MigratoryBird(Jo) & (r_5')
\end{array}
$$

Then the table for $KB_1 \cup KB_2' \cup KB_3'$ is as follows.

I	Π_I	$W_\Pi(I)$	$P_\Pi(I)$
$\emptyset$	$\{r_1, r_2, r_3\}$	$e^{3\alpha}$	$\frac{e^0}{e^2+e^1+e^0}$
$\{R(Jo)\}$	$\{r_2, r_3, r_4'\}$	$e^{2\alpha+2}$	0
$\{M(Jo)\}$	$\{r_1, r_3, r_5'\}$	$e^{2\alpha+1}$	0
$\{B(Jo)\}$	$\{r_1, r_2, r_3\}$	0	0
$\{R(Jo), B(Jo)\}$	$\{r_1, r_2, r_3, r_4'\}$	$e^{3\alpha+2}$	$\frac{e^2}{e^2+e^1+e^0}$
$\{M(Jo), B(Jo)\}$	$\{r_1, r_2, r_3, r_5'\}$	$e^{3\alpha+1}$	$\frac{e^1}{e^2+e^1+e^0}$
$\{R(Jo), M(Jo)\}$	$\{r_4', r_5'\}$	e^3	0
$\{R(Jo), M(Jo), B(Jo)\}$	$\{r_1, r_2, r_4', r_5'\}$	$e^{2\alpha+3}$	0

$P(Bird(Jo)) = (e^2 + e^1)/(e^2 + e^1 + e^0) = 0.67 + 0.24$, so it becomes less certain, though it is still a high chance that we can conclude that Jo is a Bird.

Notice that the weight changes not only affect the probability, but also the stable models (having non-zero probabilities) themselves: Instead of $\{R(Jo), M(Jo), B(Jo)\}$, the empty set is a stable model of the new program.

Assigning a different certainty level to each rule affects the probability associated with each stable model, representing how certain we can derive the stable model from the knowledge base. This could be useful as more incoming data reinforces the certainty levels of the information.

Example 2. "Markov Logic has the drawback that it cannot express (non-ground) inductive definitions" [10] because it relies on classical models. This is not the case with LP^{MLN}. For instance, consider that x may influence y if x is a friend to y, and the influence relation is a minimal relation that is closed under transitivity.

$$\alpha : Friend(A, B)$$
$$\alpha : Friend(B, C)$$
$$1 : Influence(x, y) \leftarrow Friend(x, y)$$
$$\alpha : Influence(x, y) \leftarrow Influence(x, z), Influence(z, y).$$

Note that the third rule is soft: a person does not necessarily influence his/her friend. The fourth rule says if x influences z, and z influences y, we can say x influences y. On the other hand, we do not want this relation to be vacuously true.

Assuming that there are only three people A, B, C in the domain (thus, there are $1+1+9+27$ ground rules), there are four stable models with non-zero probabilities. Let $Z = e^9 + 2e^8 + e^7$. (*Fr* abbreviates for *Friend* and *Inf* for *Influence*)

- $I_1 = \{Fr(A, B), Fr(B, C), Inf(A, B), Inf(B, C), Inf(A, C)\}$ with probability e^9/Z.
- $I_2 = \{Fr(A, B), Fr(B, C), Inf(A, B)\}$ with probability e^8/Z.
- $I_3 = \{Fr(A, B), Fr(B, C), Inf(B, C)\}$ with probability e^8/Z.
- $I_4 = \{Fr(A, B), Fr(B, C)\}$ with probability e^7/Z.

Thus we get

- $P(Inf(A, B)) = P(Inf(B, C)) = (e^9 + e^8)/Z = 0.7311$.
- $P(Inf(A, C)) = e^9/Z = 0.5344$.

Increasing the weight of the third rule yields higher probabilities for deriving $Influence(A, B)$, $Influence(B, C)$, and $Influence(A, C)$. Still, the first two have the same probability, and the third has a lower probability than the first two.

3.4   Alternative Formulation (Penalty-Based)

In the definition of the LP^{MLN} semantics in Sect. 3.2, the weight of a stable model I is computed from all ground rules $w : R$ such that $I \vDash R$. Alternatively, the semantics can be reformulated in a "penalty" based way. More precisely, we define the penalty-based weight of an interpretation I as the exponentiated negative sum of the weights of the rules that are not satisfied by I (when I is a stable model of $\overline{\Pi_I}$). Let

$$W_\Pi^{\text{pnt}}(I) = \begin{cases} exp\left(- \sum_{w:R \,\in\, \Pi \text{ and } I \nvDash R} w \right) & \text{if } I \in \text{SM}[\Pi]; \\ 0 & \text{otherwise} \end{cases}$$

and

$$P_\Pi^{\text{pnt}}(I) = \lim_{\alpha \to \infty} \frac{W_\Pi^{\text{pnt}}(I)}{\sum_{J \in \text{SM}[\Pi]} W_\Pi^{\text{pnt}}(J)}.$$

The following theorem tells us that the LP^{MLN} semantics can be equivalently reformulated using the concept of penalty-based weights.

Theorem 1 ([18]). *For any LP^{MLN} program Π and any interpretation I,*

$$W_\Pi(I) \propto W_\Pi^{\text{pnt}}(I) \quad and \quad P_\Pi(I) = P_\Pi^{\text{pnt}}(I).$$

Although the penalty-based reformulation appears to be slightly more complicated, it has a few desirable features. One of them is that adding a rule that is trivially true does not affect the penalty-based weight of an interpretation, which is not the case with the reward-based weight.

More importantly, this reformulation leads to a better translation of LP^{MLN} programs into answer set programs as will be shown in Sect. 4.1.

Example 3. Consider the LP^{MLN} program Π in Example 1.

$$\begin{array}{ll} \alpha : Bird(Jo) \leftarrow ResidentBird(Jo) & (r_1) \\ \alpha : Bird(Jo) \leftarrow MigratoryBird(Jo) & (r_2) \\ \alpha : \bot \leftarrow ResidentBird(Jo), MigratoryBird(Jo) & (r_3) \\ 2 : ResidentBird(Jo) & (r_4') \\ 1 : MigratoryBird(Jo) & (r_5') \end{array}$$

Assuming that the Herbrand universe is $\{Jo\}$, the following table shows the penalty-based weight and the probability of each interpretation.

I	Π_I	$W_\Pi^{\mathrm{pnt}}(I)$	$P_\Pi^{\mathrm{pnt}}(I)$
$\emptyset$	$\{r_1, r_2, r_3\}$	e^{-3}	$\frac{e^{-3}}{e^{-1}+e^{-2}+e^{-3}}$
$\{R(Jo)\}$	$\{r_2, r_3, r_4'\}$	$e^{-\alpha-1}$	0
$\{M(Jo)\}$	$\{r_1, r_3, r_5'\}$	$e^{-\alpha-2}$	0
$\{B(Jo)\}$	$\{r_1, r_2, r_3\}$	0	0
$\{R(Jo), B(Jo)\}$	$\{r_1, r_2, r_3, r_4'\}$	e^{-1}	$\frac{e^{-1}}{e^{-1}+e^{-2}+e^{-3}}$
$\{M(Jo), B(Jo)\}$	$\{r_1, r_2, r_3, r_5'\}$	e^{-2}	$\frac{e^{-2}}{e^{-1}+e^{-2}+e^{-3}}$
$\{R(Jo), M(Jo)\}$	$\{r_4', r_5'\}$	$e^{-3\alpha}$	0
$\{R(Jo), M(Jo), B(Jo)\}$	$\{r_1, r_2, r_4', r_5'\}$	$e^{-\alpha}$	0

Note that for each interpretation, its probability computed with penalty-based weights is exactly the same as the one computed with reward-based weights.

4   Relation to Other Languages

This section relates $\mathrm{LP}^{\mathrm{MLN}}$ to ASP, MLN, and ProbLog. The translation helps us to compute $\mathrm{LP}^{\mathrm{MLN}}$ using the tools of the related formalisms.

4.1   Relating $\mathrm{LP}^{\mathrm{MLN}}$ to ASP

An answer set program can be turned into an $\mathrm{LP}^{\mathrm{MLN}}$ program by assigning the infinite weight to every rule. That is, for any answer set program $\mathcal{P} = \{R_1, \ldots, R_n\}$, the corresponding $\mathrm{LP}^{\mathrm{MLN}}$ program $\Pi_{\mathcal{P}}$ is $\{\alpha : R_1, \ldots, \alpha : R_n\}$.

The following theorem establishes how ASP can be viewed as a fragment of $\mathrm{LP}^{\mathrm{MLN}}$.

Theorem 2 ([19]). *For any answer set program $\mathcal{P}$, the (deterministic) stable models of $\mathcal{P}$ are exactly the (probabilistic) stable models of $\Pi_{\mathcal{P}}$ whose weight is $e^{k\alpha}$, where k is the number of all (ground) rules in $\mathcal{P}$. If $\mathcal{P}$ has at least one stable model, then all stable models of $\Pi_{\mathcal{P}}$ have the same probability and are thus the stable models of $\mathcal{P}$ as well.*

The other direction, turning an $\mathrm{LP}^{\mathrm{MLN}}$ program into an answer set program, is possible with the help of weak constraints.

For any ground $\mathrm{LP}^{\mathrm{MLN}}$ program Π, the translation lpmln2asp(Π) is obtained from Π by turning each weighted rule

$$w_i : Head_i \leftarrow Body_i$$

into

$$unsat(i) \leftarrow Body_i, not\ Head_i$$
$$Head_i \leftarrow Body_i, not\ unsat(i)$$
$$:\sim unsat(i) \quad [w_i@l]$$

where $unsat(i)$ is a new atom, and $w_i@l$ is $1@1$ (denoting penalty 1 at a higher priority) if w_i is α and is $w_i@0$ (denoting penalty w_i at a lower priority) otherwise.

In the case when $Head_i$ is $\bot$, the translation can be further simplified: we simply turn $w_i : \bot \leftarrow Body_i$ into $\quad :\sim Body_i \quad [w_i@l]$.

The following theorem allows for computing LP^{MLN} using ASP solvers.

Theorem 3 ([22]). *For any* LP^{MLN} *program* Π, *there is a 1-1 correspondence* ϕ *between the most probable stable models of* Π *and the optimal stable models of* lpmln2asp(Π), *where* $\phi(I) = I \cup \{unsat(i) \mid w_i : F_i \in \Pi, I \not\models F_i\}$.

Example 4. For the LP^{MLN} program Π with 4 soft rules:

$$10 : q \leftarrow p$$
$$1 : r \leftarrow p$$
$$5 : p$$
$$-20 : \bot \leftarrow \neg r$$

SM[Π] has 5 elements: $\emptyset$, $\{p\}$, $\{p,q\}$, $\{p,r\}$, $\{p,q,r\}$. Among them, $\{p,q\}$ is the most probable stable model, whose penalty-based weight is e^{19}, while $\{p,q,r\}$ is a probabilistic stable model whose penalty-based weight is e^0. The translation lpmln2asp(Π) yields

$unsat(1) \leftarrow p, not\ q$	$q \leftarrow p, not\ unsat(1)$	$:\sim unsat(1) \quad [10@0]$
$unsat(2) \leftarrow p, not\ r$	$r \leftarrow p, not\ unsat(2)$	$:\sim unsat(2) \quad [1@0]$
$unsat(3) \leftarrow not\ p$	$p \leftarrow not\ unsat(3)$	$:\sim unsat(3) \quad [5@0]$
$unsat(4) \leftarrow not\ r$	$\bot \leftarrow not\ r, not\ unsat(4)$	$:\sim unsat(4) \ [-20@0]$

whose optimal stable model is $\{p,q,unsat(2),unsat(4)\}$ with the penalty at level 0 being $1 - 20 = -19$, while $\{p,q,r\}$ is a stable model whose penalty at level 0 is 0. Equivalently, the fourth rule in Π can be simply translated to

$$:\sim not\ r \quad [-20@0].$$

The following example illustrates how the translation accounts for the difference between hard rules and soft rules by assigning different penalty levels.

Example 5. Consider the LP^{MLN} program Π in Example 1.

$$\alpha : Bird(Jo) \leftarrow ResidentBird(Jo) \qquad\qquad (r_1)$$
$$\alpha : Bird(Jo) \leftarrow MigratoryBird(Jo) \qquad\qquad (r_2)$$
$$\alpha : \bot \leftarrow ResidentBird(Jo), MigratoryBird(Jo)\ (r_3)$$
$$2 : ResidentBird(Jo) \qquad\qquad\qquad\qquad\qquad (r_4)$$
$$1 : MigratoryBird(Jo) \qquad\qquad\qquad\qquad\qquad (r_5)$$

Π has three probabilistic stable models: $\emptyset$, $\{Bird(Jo), ResidentBird(Jo)\}$, and $\{Bird(Jo), MigratoryBird(Jo)\}$, all of which satisfy all the hard rules r_1, r_2, and r_3. Among these three probabilistic stable models, $\{Bird(Jo), ResidentBird(Jo)\}$ is the most probable stable model. The translation lpmln2asp(Π) yields

$unsat(1) \leftarrow ResidentBird(Jo), not\ Bird(Jo)$	$Bird(Jo) \leftarrow ResidentBird(Jo), not\ unsat(1)$
$unsat(2) \leftarrow MigratoryBird(Jo), not\ Bird(Jo)$	$Bird(Jo) \leftarrow MigratoryBird(Jo), not\ unsat(2)$
$unsat(4) \leftarrow not\ ResidentBird(Jo)$	$ResidentBird(Jo) \leftarrow not\ unsat(4)$
$unsat(5) \leftarrow not\ MigratoryBird(Jo)$	$MigratoryBird(Jo) \leftarrow not\ unsat(5)$

$$:\sim unsat(1) \qquad\qquad\qquad\qquad\qquad [1@1]$$
$$:\sim unsat(2) \qquad\qquad\qquad\qquad\qquad [1@1]$$
$$:\sim ResidentBird(Jo), MigratoryBird(Jo)\ [1@1]$$
$$:\sim unsat(4) \qquad\qquad\qquad\qquad\qquad [2@0]$$
$$:\sim unsat(5) \qquad\qquad\qquad\qquad\qquad [1@0]$$

whose stable models with penalty 0 at level 1 are 1-1 correspondent to 3 probabilistic stable models of Π. Among these 3 stable models, $\{Bird(Jo), ResidentBird(Jo), unsat(5)\}$ has the least penalty (i.e., 1) at level 0, thus is the optimal stable model of lpmln2asp(Π).

In some applications, one may not want any hard rules to be violated, assuming that hard rules encode definite knowledge. For that, lpmln2asp(Π) can be modified by simply turning hard rules into the usual ASP rules. Then the stable models of lpmln2asp(Π) satisfy all hard rules. For example, the LP^{MLN} program in Example 5 can be translated into the following ASP program.

$$Bird(Jo) \leftarrow ResidentBird(Jo)$$
$$Bird(Jo) \leftarrow MigratoryBird(Jo)$$
$$\bot \leftarrow ResidentBird(Jo), MigratoryBird(Jo)$$

$$unsat(4) \leftarrow not\ ResidentBird(Jo)$$
$$ResidentBird(Jo) \leftarrow not\ unsat(4)$$
$$:\sim unsat(4) \qquad\qquad\qquad\qquad\qquad [2@0]$$

$$unsat(5) \leftarrow not\ MigratoryBird(Jo)$$
$$MigratoryBird(Jo) \leftarrow not\ unsat(5)$$
$$:\sim unsat(5) \qquad\qquad\qquad\qquad\qquad [1@0]$$

4.2   Relating LP^{MLN} to MLNs

This section relates LP^{MLN} to Markov Logic Networks (MLNs).

Embedding MLNs in LP^{MLN}. Similar to the way that SAT can be embedded in ASP, Markov Logic can be easily embedded in LP^{MLN}. More precisely, any MLN $\mathbb{L}$ of signature σ can be turned into an LP^{MLN} program $\Pi_{\mathbb{L}}$ so that the models of $\mathbb{L}$ coincide with the stable models of $\Pi_{\mathbb{L}}$ while retaining the same probability distribution.

LP^{MLN} program $\Pi_{\mathbb{L}}$ is obtained from $\mathbb{L}$ by turning each weighted formula $w : F$ into weighted rule $w : \quad \bot \leftarrow \neg F$ and adding

$$w : \quad \{A\}^{\text{ch}}$$

for every ground atom A of σ and any weight w. The effect of adding the choice rules is to exempt A from minimization under the stable model semantics.

Theorem 4 ([19]). *Any MLN $\mathbb{L}$ and its LP^{MLN} representation $\Pi_{\mathbb{L}}$ have the same probability distribution over all interpretations.*

The embedding tells us that the exact inference in LP^{MLN} is at least as hard as the one in MLNs, which is #P-hard. In fact, it is easy to see that when all rules in LP^{MLN} are non-disjunctive, counting the stable models of LP^{MLN} is in #P, which yields that the exact inference for non-disjunctive LP^{MLN} programs is #P-complete. Therefore, approximation algorithms, such as Gibbs sampling, may be desirable for computing large LP^{MLN} programs.

It follows from Theorem 3 and Theorem 4 that Maximum A Posteriori (MAP) inference in MLN can also be reduced to the optimal stable model finding of an ASP program. For any ground MLN program $\mathbb{L}$, the translation mln2asp($\mathbb{L}$) is obtained from $\mathbb{L}$ by turning each weighted formula $w : F$ into the weak constraint $:\sim \neg F \ [w@0]$ and adding a choice rule $\{A\}^{\text{ch}}$ for every ground atom A of σ.[2]

Theorem 5 ([22]). *For any Markov Logic Network Π, the most probable models of Π are precisely the optimal stable models of the ASP program with weak constraints mln2asp(Π).*

Similarly, MAP inference in ProbLog and Pearl's Causal Models can be reduced to finding an optimal stable model of a program with weak constraints in view of the reduction of ProbLog to LP^{MLN} (Theorem 4 from [19]) and the reduction of Causal Models to LP^{MLN} (Theorem 4 from [15]) thereby allowing us to apply combinatorial optimization methods in standard ASP solvers to these languages.

Completion: Turning LP^{MLN} to MLN. We say that LP^{MLN} program Π is *tight* if the unweighted program $\overline{\Pi}$ is tight according to [16], i.e., the positive dependency graph of $\overline{\Pi}$ is acyclic. It is known that the stable models of a tight logic program coincide with the models of the program's completion [8]. This yielded a way to compute stable models using SAT solvers. The method can be extended to tight LP^{MLN} programs so that queries involving probabilistic stable models can be computed using existing implementations of MLNs, such as Alchemy.[3]

We define the *completion* of Π, denoted *Comp*(Π), to be the MLN which is the union of Π and the hard formula

---

[2] F in the weak constraint here is an arbitrary formula, that is more general than the form reviewed in Sect. 2. We can use a tool like F2LP [17] to turn formulas into the input language of CLINGO.

[3] http://alchemy.cs.washington.edu.

$$\alpha: \; A \rightarrow \bigvee_{\substack{w:A_1 \vee \cdots \vee A_k \leftarrow Body \in \; \Pi \\ A \in \{A_1,\ldots,A_k\}}} \left(Body \wedge \bigwedge_{A' \in \{A_1,\ldots,A_k\}\setminus\{A\}} \neg A' \right)$$

for each ground atom A. This is a straightforward extension of the completion from [16] by simply assigning the infinite weight α to the completion formulas.

Theorem 6 ([19]). *For any tight* $\mathrm{LP}^{\mathrm{MLN}}$ *program* Π *such that* $SM'[\Pi]$ *is not empty,* Π *(under the* $\mathrm{LP}^{\mathrm{MLN}}$ *semantics) and* $Comp(\Pi)$ *(under the MLN semantics) have the same probability distribution over all interpretations.*

The theorem can be generalized to non-tight programs by considering loop formulas [24], which we skip here for brevity.

4.3   Relating $\mathrm{LP}^{\mathrm{MLN}}$ to ProbLog

It turns out that $\mathrm{LP}^{\mathrm{MLN}}$ is a proper generalization of ProbLog, a well-developed probabilistic logic programming language that is based on the distribution semantics by [28].

Review of ProbLog. The review follows [10]. As before, we identify a non-ground ProbLog program with its ground instance. So for simplicity, we restrict attention to ground ProbLog programs only.

In ProbLog, ground atoms over σ are divided into two groups: *probabilistic* atoms and *derived* atoms. A *(ground) ProbLog program* $\mathcal{P}$ is a tuple $\langle PF, \Pi \rangle$, where

- PF is a set of ground probabilistic facts of the form $pr :: a$ where pr is a real number in $[0, 1]$ and a is a probabilistic atom,
- Π is a set of ground rules of the following form

$$A \leftarrow B_1, \ldots, B_m, not\; B_{m+1}, \ldots, not\; B_n$$

where A, $B_1, \ldots B_n$ are atoms from σ $(0 \leq m \leq n)$, and A is not a probabilistic atom.

Probabilistic atoms act as random variables and are assumed to be independent from each other. A *total choice* TC is any subset of the probabilistic atoms. Given a total choice $TC = \{a_1, \ldots, a_m\}$, the *probability* of a total choice TC, denoted $Pr_{\mathcal{P}}(TC)$, is defined as

$$pr(a_1) \times \ldots \times pr(a_m) \times (1 - pr(b_1)) \times \ldots \times (1 - pr(b_n))$$

where $b_1, \ldots, b_n$ are probabilistic atoms not belonging to TC, and each of $pr(a_i)$ and $pr(b_j)$ is the probability assigned to a_i and b_j according to the set PF of ground probabilistic atoms.

The ProbLog semantics is only well-defined for programs $\mathcal{P} = \langle PF, \Pi \rangle$ such that $\Pi \cup TC$ has a "total" (two-valued) well-founded model for each total choice TC. Given such $\mathcal{P}$, the probability of an interpretation I, denoted $P_{\mathcal{P}}(I)$, is defined as $Pr_{\mathcal{P}}(TC)$ if there exists a total choice TC such that I is the total well-founded model of $\Pi \cup TC$, and 0 otherwise.

ProbLog as a Special Case of LP^{MLN}. Given a ProbLog program $\mathcal{P} = \langle PF, \Pi \rangle$, we construct the corresponding LP^{MLN} program $\mathcal{P}'$ as follows:

- For each probabilistic fact $pr{::}a$ in $\mathcal{P}$, LP^{MLN} program $\mathcal{P}'$ contains
  - $ln(pr) : a$ and $ln(1-pr) :\ \leftarrow a$ if $0 < pr < 1$;
  - $\alpha : a$ if $pr = 1$;
  - $\alpha :\ \leftarrow a$ if $pr = 0$.
- For each rule $R \in \Pi$, $\mathcal{P}'$ contains $\alpha : R$. In other words, R is identified with a hard rule in $\mathcal{P}'$.

Theorem 7 ([19]). *Any well-defined ProbLog program $\mathcal{P}$ and its LP^{MLN} representation $\mathcal{P}'$ have the same probability distribution over all interpretations.*

Example 6. Consider the ProbLog program

$$0.6 :: p \qquad\qquad r \leftarrow p$$
$$0.3 :: q \qquad\qquad r \leftarrow q$$

which can be identified with the LP^{MLN} program

$$
\begin{array}{lll}
ln(0.6) :\ \ p & ln(0.3) :\ \ q & \alpha :\ \ r \leftarrow p \\
ln(0.4) :\ \leftarrow p & ln(0.7) :\ \leftarrow q & \alpha :\ \ r \leftarrow q
\end{array}
$$

Syntactically, LP^{MLN} allows more general rules than ProbLog, such as disjunctions in the head, as well as the empty head and double negations in the body. Further, LP^{MLN} allows rules to be weighted as well as facts and does not distinguish between probabilistic facts and derived atoms. Semantically, while the ProbLog semantics is based on well-founded models, LP^{MLN} handles stable model reasoning for more general classes of programs. Unlike ProbLog, which is only well-defined when each total choice leads to a unique well-founded model, LP^{MLN} can handle multiple stable models in a flexible way similar to the way MLN handles multiple models.

5   Weight Learning

In this section, we present the concept of weight learning in LP^{MLN} and learning algorithms for LP^{MLN}.

A parameterized LP^{MLN} program $\hat{\Pi}$ is defined similarly to an LP^{MLN} program Π except for that non-α weights (i.e., "soft" weights) are replaced with distinct parameters to be learned. By $\hat{\Pi}(\mathbf{w})$, where $\mathbf{w}$ is a list of real numbers whose length is the same as the number of soft rules, we denote the LP^{MLN} program obtained from $\hat{\Pi}$ by replacing the parameters with $\mathbf{w}$. The weight learning task for a parameterized LP^{MLN} program is to find the MLE (Maximum Likelihood Estimation) of the parameters as in Markov Logic. Formally, given a parameterized LP^{MLN} program $\hat{\Pi}$ and a ground formula O (often in the form of conjunctions of literals) called *observation* or *training data*, the LP^{MLN} parameter learning task is to find the values $\mathbf{w}$ of parameters such that the probability of O under the LP^{MLN} program Π is maximized. In other words, the learning task is to find

$$\operatorname*{argmax}_{\mathbf{w}} P_{\hat{\Pi}(\mathbf{w})}(O). \tag{2}$$

5.1 Gradient Method for Learning Weights from a Complete Stable Model

Same as in Markov Logic, there is no closed-form solution for (2), but the gradient ascent method can be applied to find the optimal weights in an iterative manner.

We first compute the gradient. Given a (non-ground) LP^{MLN} program Π whose SM[Π] is non-empty and given a stable model I of Π, the base-e logarithm of $P_\Pi(I)$, $lnP_\Pi(I)$, is

$$- \sum_{w_i:R_i \in \Pi^{\text{soft}}} w_i n_i(I) - ln \sum_{J \in \text{SM}[\Pi]} exp\Big(- \sum_{w_i:R_i \in \Pi^{\text{soft}}} w_i n_i(J) \Big).$$

The partial derivative of $lnP_\Pi(I)$ w.r.t. $w_i(\neq \alpha)$ is

$$\frac{\partial lnP_\Pi(I)}{\partial w_i} = -n_i(I) + \frac{\sum\limits_{J \in \text{SM}[\Pi]} exp(- \sum\limits_{w_i:R_i \in \Pi^{\text{soft}}} w_i n_i(J)) n_i(J)}{\sum\limits_{K \in \text{SM}[\Pi]} exp(- \sum\limits_{w_i:R_i \in \Pi^{\text{soft}}} w_i n_i(K))}$$

$$= -n_i(I) + \sum_{J \in \text{SM}[\Pi]} \left(\frac{exp(- \sum\limits_{w_i:R_i \in \Pi^{\text{soft}}} w_i n_i(J))}{\sum\limits_{K \in \text{SM}[\Pi]} exp(- \sum\limits_{w_i:R_i \in \Pi^{\text{soft}}} w_i n_i(K))} \right) n_i(J)$$

$$= -n_i(I) + \sum_{J \in \text{SM}[\Pi]} P_\Pi(J) n_i(J) = -n_i(I) + \mathop{E}_{J \in \text{SM}[\Pi]}[n_i(J)]$$

where $\mathop{E}\limits_{J \in \text{SM}[\Pi]}[n_i(J)] = \sum\limits_{J \in \text{SM}[\Pi]} P_\Pi(J) n_i(J)$ is the expected number of false ground rules obtained from R_i.

Since the log-likelihood above is a concave function of the weights, any local maximum is a global maximum, and maximizing $P_\Pi(I)$ can be done by the standard gradient ascent method by updating each weight w_i by $w_i + \lambda \cdot (-n_i(I) + \mathop{E}\limits_{J \in \text{SM}[\Pi]}[n_i(J)])$ until it converges.[4]

However, similar to Markov Logic, computing $\mathop{E}\limits_{J \in \text{SM}[\Pi]}[n_i(J)]$ is intractable [27]. In the next section, we turn to an MCMC sampling method to find its approximate value.

---

[4] Note that although any local maximum is a global maximum for the log-likelihood function, there can be multiple combinations of weights that achieve the maximum probability of the training data.

5.2   Sampling Method: MC-ASP

The following is an MCMC algorithm for LP^{MLN}, which adapts the algorithm MC-SAT for Markov Logic [26] by considering the penalty-based reformulation and by using an ASP solver instead of a SAT solver for sampling.

Algorithm 1. MC-ASP

Input: An LP^{MLN} program Π whose soft rules' weights are non-positive and a positive integer N.
Output: Samples $I^1, \ldots, I^N$

1. Choose a (probabilistic) stable model I^0 of Π.
2. Repeat the following for $j = 1, \ldots, N$
   (a) $M \leftarrow \emptyset$;
   (b) For each ground instance of each rule $w_i : R_i \in \Pi^{\text{soft}}$ that is false in I^{j-1}, add the ground instance to M with probability $1 - e^{w_i}$;
   (c) Randomly choose a (probabilistic) stable model I^j of Π that satisfies no rules in M.

When all the weights w_i of soft rules are nonpositive, $1 - e^{w_i}$ (in step (b)) is in the range $[0, 1)$, and thus it validly represents a probability. At each iteration, the sample is chosen from stable models of Π, and, consequently, it must satisfy all hard rules. For soft rules, the higher its weight, the less likely it is to be included in M, and thus less likely to be not satisfied by the sample generated from M.

The following theorem states that MC-ASP satisfies the MCMC criteria of ergodicity and detailed balance, which justifies the soundness of the algorithm.

Theorem 8 ([21]). *The Markov chain generated by MC-ASP satisfies ergodicity and detailed balance.*[5]

Steps 1 and 2(c) of the algorithm require finding a (probabilistic) stable model of LP^{MLN}, which can be computed by an ASP solver CLINGO using the translation lpmln2asp(Π) in Sect. 4.1. Step 2(c) also requires a uniform sampler for answer sets, which can be computed by a system like XORRO [11].

Algorithm 2 is a weight learning algorithm for LP^{MLN} based on gradient ascent using MC-ASP (Algorithm 1) for collecting samples. Step 2(b) of MC-ASP requires that w_i be non-positive in order for $1 - e^{w_i}$ to represent a probability. Unlike in the Markov Logic setting, converting positive weights into non-positive weights cannot be done in LP^{MLN} simply by replacing $w : F$ with $-w : \neg F$, due

---

[5] A Markov chain is *ergodic* if there is a number m such that any state can be reached from any other state in any number of steps greater than or equal to m.

Detailed balance means $P_\Pi(X)Q(X \rightarrow Y) = P_\Pi(Y)Q(Y \rightarrow X)$ for any samples X and Y, where $Q(X \rightarrow Y)$ denotes the probability that the next sample is Y given that the current sample is X.

Algorithm 2. Algorithm for learning weights using LPMLN2ASP

Input: Π: A parameterized LP^{MLN} program in the input language of LPMLN2ASP; O: A stable model represented as a set of constraints (that is, $\leftarrow not\ A$ is in O if a ground atom A is true; $\leftarrow A$ is in O if A is not true); δ: a fixed real number to be used for the terminating condition.

Output: Π with learned weights.

Process:

1. Initialize the weights of soft rules $R_1, \ldots, R_m$ with some initial weights $\mathbf{w}^0$.
2. Repeat the following for $j = 1, \ldots$ until $max\{|w_i^j - w_i^{j-1}| : i = 1, \ldots, m\} < \delta$:
   (a) Compute the stable model of $\Pi \cup O$ using LPMLN2ASP (see below); for each soft rule R_i, compute $n_i(O)$ by counting **unsat** atoms whose first argument is i (i is a rule index).
   (b) Create Π^{neg} by replacing each soft rule R_i of the form $w : H(\mathbf{x}) \leftarrow B(\mathbf{x})$ in Π where $w > 0$ with

   $$0 : H(\mathbf{x}) \leftarrow B(\mathbf{x}),$$
   $$\alpha : \mathbf{neg}(i, \mathbf{x}) \leftarrow B(\mathbf{x}), not\ H(\mathbf{x}),$$
   $$-w : \leftarrow not\ \mathbf{neg}(i, \mathbf{x}).$$

   (c) Run MC-ASP on Π^{neg} to collect a set S of sample stable models.
   (d) For each soft rule R_i, approximate $\sum_{J \in SM[\Pi]} P_\Pi(J) n_i(J)$ with $\sum_{J \in S} n_i(J)/|S|$, where n_i is obtained from counting the number of **unsat** atoms whose first argument is i.
   (e) For each $i \in \{1, \ldots, m\}$,
   $$w_i^{j+1} \leftarrow w_i^j + \lambda \cdot (-n_i(O) + \sum_{J \in S} n_i(J)/|S|).$$

---

to the difference in the FOL and the stable model semantics. Algorithm 2 converts Π into an equivalent program Π^{neg} whose rules' weights are non-positive, before calling MC-ASP. The following theorem justifies the soundness of this method.[6]

Theorem 9 ([21]). *When $SM[\Pi]$ is not empty, the program Π^{neg} specifies the same probability distribution as the program Π.*

Non-emptiness of $SM[\Pi]$ implies that every probabilistic stable model of Π satisfies all hard rules in Π. Thus when $SM[\Pi]$ is not empty, the probability of a stable model is proportional to its weight accumulated from the soft rules only – the translation from Π to Π^{neg} guarantees that the proportion is preserved for every stable model.

---

[6] Note that Π^{neg} is only used in MC-ASP. The output of Algorithm 2 may have positive weights.

5.3 Extensions

The base case learning in the previous section assumes that the training data is a single stable model and is a complete interpretation. This section extends the framework in a few ways.

Learning from Multiple Stable Models. The method described in the previous section allows only one stable model to be used as the training data. Now, suppose we have multiple stable models $I_1, \ldots, I_m$ as the training data. For example, consider the parameterized program $\hat{\Pi}_{coin}$ that describes a coin, which may or may not land in the head when it is flipped,

$$\alpha \ : \ \{flip\}$$
$$w \ : \ head \leftarrow flip$$

(the first rule is a choice rule) and three stable models as the training data: $I_1 = \{flip\}$, $I_2 = \{flip\}$, $I_3 = \{flip, head\}$ (the absence of $head$ in the answer set is understood as landing in tail), indicating that $\{flip, head\}$ has a frequency of $\frac{1}{3}$, and $\{flip\}$ has a frequency of $\frac{2}{3}$. Intuitively, the more we observe the $head$, the larger the weight of the second rule. Clearly, learning w from only one of I_1, I_2, I_3 won't result in a weight that captures all the three stable models: learning from each of I_1 or I_2 results in the value of w too small for $\{flip, head\}$ to have a frequency of $\frac{1}{3}$ while learning from I_3 results in the value of w too large for $\{flip\}$ to have a frequency of $\frac{2}{3}$.

To utilize the information from multiple stable models, one natural idea is to maximize the joint probability of all the stable models in the training data, which is the product of their probabilities, i.e.,

$$P(I_1, \ldots, I_m) = \prod_{j \in \{1, \ldots, m\}} P_\Pi(I_j).$$

The partial derivative of $lnP(I_1, \ldots, I_m)$ w.r.t. $w_i (\neq \alpha)$ is

$$\frac{\partial lnP(I_1, \ldots, I_m)}{\partial w_i} = \sum_{j \in \{1, \ldots, m\}} \left(-n_i(I_j) + \underset{J \in \mathrm{SM}[\Pi]}{E}[n_i(J)] \right).$$

In other words, the gradient of the log probability is simply the sum of the gradients of the probability of each stable model in the training data. To update Algorithm 2 to reflect this, we simply repeat step 2(a) to compute $n_i(I_k)$ for each $k \in \{1, \ldots, m\}$, and at step 2(e) update w_i as follows:

$$w_i^{j+1} \leftarrow w_i^j + \lambda \cdot \left(-\sum_{k \in \{1, \ldots, m\}} n_i(I_k) + m \cdot \sum_{J \in \mathrm{SM}[\Pi]} P_\Pi(J) n_i(J) \right).$$

Alternatively, learning from multiple stable models can be reduced to learning from a single stable model by introducing one more argument k to every predicate, which represents the index of a stable model in the training data, and rewriting the data to include the index.

Formally, given an LP^{MLN} program Π and a set of its stable models $I_1, \ldots, I_m$, let Π^m be an LP^{MLN} program obtained from Π by appending one more argument k to the list of arguments of every predicate that occurs in Π, where k is a schematic variable that ranges over $\{1, \ldots, m\}$. Let

$$I = \bigcup_{i \in \{1, \ldots, m\}} \{p(\mathbf{t}, i) \mid p(\mathbf{t}) \in I_i\}. \tag{3}$$

The following theorem asserts that the weights of the rules in Π that are learned from the multiple stable models $I_1, \ldots, I_m$ are identical to the weights of the rules in Π^m that are learned from the single stable model I that conjoins $\{I_1, \ldots, I_m\}$ as in (3).

Theorem 10 ([21]). *For any parameterized* LP^{MLN} *program* $\hat{\Pi}$, *its stable models* $I_1, \ldots, I_m$ *and* I *as defined as in* (3), *we have*

$$\operatorname*{argmax}_{\mathbf{w}} P_{\hat{\Pi}^m(\mathbf{w})}(I) = \operatorname*{argmax}_{\mathbf{w}} \prod_{i \in \{1, \ldots, m\}} P_{\hat{\Pi}(\mathbf{w})}(I_i).$$

Example 7. For the program $\hat{\Pi}_{coin}$, to learn from the three stable models I_1, I_2, and I_3 defined before, we consider the program $\hat{\Pi}^3_{coin}$

$$\alpha \;\; : \;\; \{flip(k)\}.$$
$$w \;\; : \;\; head(k) \leftarrow flip(k).$$

($k \in \{1, 2, 3\}$) and combine I_1, I_2, I_3 into one stable model $I = \{flip(1), flip(2), flip(3), head(3)\}$. The weight w in $\hat{\Pi}^3_{coin}$ learned from the single data I is identical to the weight w in $\hat{\Pi}_{coin}$ learned from the three stable models I_1, I_2, I_3.

5.4   Learning in the Presence of Noisy Data

So far, we assumed that the data $I_1, \ldots, I_m$ are (probabilistic) stable models of the parameterized LP^{MLN} program. Otherwise, the joint probability would be zero regardless of any weights assigned to the soft rules, and the partial derivative of $lnP(I_1, \ldots, I_m)$ is undefined. However, data gathered from the real world could be noisy, so some data I_i may not necessarily be a stable model. Even then, we still want to learn from the other "correct" instances. We may try to drop noisy data before starting training but enumerating all noisy data could be computationally expensive. Alternatively, we may mitigate the influence of the noisy data by introducing so-called "noise atoms" as follows.

Example 8. Consider again the program $\hat{\Pi}^m_{coin}$. Suppose one of the interpretations I_i in the training data is $\{head(i)\}$. The interpretation is not a stable model of $\hat{\Pi}^m_{coin}$. We obtain $\hat{\Pi}^m_{noisecoin}$ by modifying $\hat{\Pi}^m_{coin}$ to allow for the noisy atom $n(k)$ as follows.

$$
\begin{aligned}
\alpha &: \{flip(k)\}. \\
w &: head(k) \leftarrow flip(k). \\
\alpha &: head(k) \leftarrow n(k). \\
-u &: n(k).
\end{aligned}
$$

Here, u is a positive number that is "sufficiently" larger than w. $\{head(i), n(i)\}$ is a stable model of $\hat{\Pi}^m_{noisecoin}$, so that the combined training data I is still a stable model, and thus a meaningful weight w for $\hat{\Pi}^m_{noisecoin}$ can still be learned, given that other "correct" instances I_j ($j \neq i$) dominate in the learning process (as for the noisy example, the corresponding stable model gets a low weight due to the weight assigned to $n(i)$ but not 0).

Furthermore, with the same value of w, the larger u becomes, the closer the probability distribution defined by $\hat{\Pi}^m_{noisecoin}$ approximates the one defined by $\hat{\Pi}^m_{coin}$, so the value of w learned under $\hat{\Pi}^m_{noisecoin}$ approximates the value of w learned under $\hat{\Pi}^m_{coin}$ where the noisy data is dropped.

5.5   Learning from Incomplete Interpretations

In the previous sections, we assume that the training data is given as a (complete) interpretation, i.e., for each atom, it specifies whether it is true or false. In this section, we discuss the general case when the training data is given as a partial interpretation, which omits to specify some atoms to be true or false, or more generally when the training data is in the form of a formula that more than one stable model may satisfy.

Given a non-ground $\mathrm{LP}^{\mathrm{MLN}}$ program Π such that $\mathrm{SM}[\Pi]$ is not empty and given a ground formula O as the training data, we have

$$
P_\Pi(O) = \frac{\sum_{I \models O, I \in \mathrm{SM}[\Pi]} W_\Pi(I)}{\sum_{J \in \mathrm{SM}[\Pi]} W_\Pi(J)}.
$$

The partial derivative of $ln P_\Pi(O)$ w.r.t. w_i ($\neq \alpha$) turns out to be

$$
\frac{\partial ln P_\Pi(O)}{\partial w_i} = - \mathop{E}_{I \models O, I \in \mathrm{SM}[\Pi]}[n_i(I)] + \mathop{E}_{J \in \mathrm{SM}[\Pi]}[n_i(J)].
$$

It is straightforward to extend Algorithm 2 to reflect the extension. Computing the approximate value of the first term $- \mathop{E}_{I \models O, I \in \mathrm{SM}[\Pi]}[n_i(I)]$ can be done by sampling on $\Pi^{neg} \cup O$.

6   LP^{MLN} System

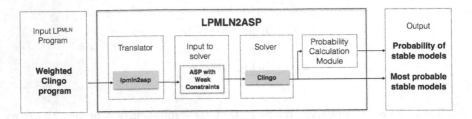

Fig. 1. Architecture of System LPMLN2ASP

System LPMLN2ASP[7] is an implementation of LP^{MLN} based on the result in Sect. 3.4 using CLINGO. It can be used for computing the probabilities of stable models, the marginal/conditional probability of a query, as well as the most probable stable models (Fig. 1).

In the input language of LPMLN2ASP, a soft rule is written in the form

$$w_i \quad Head_i \leftarrow Body_i \tag{4}$$

where w_i is a real number in decimal notation, and $Head_i \leftarrow Body_i$ is a CLINGO rule. A hard rule is written without weights and is identical to a CLINGO rule. For instance, the "Bird" example from [19] can be represented in the input language of LPMLN2ASP as follows. The first three rules represent definite knowledge, while the last two rules represent uncertain knowledge with different confidence.

```
% bird.lpmln
bird(X) :- residentbird(X).
bird(X) :- migratorybird(X).
:- residentbird(X), migratorybird(X).
2 residentbird(jo).
1 migratorybird(jo).
```

The basic command line syntax for executing LPMLN2ASP is

```
lpmln2asp -i <input file> [-r <output file>] [-e <evidence file>]
[-q <query predicates>] [-hr] [-all] [-clingo "<clingo options>"]
```

which follows the syntax of the ALCHEMY command line.

The mode of computation is determined by the options provided to LPMLN2ASP. By default, the system finds a most probable stable model of lpmln2asp$^{\mathrm{pnt}}(\Pi)$ (MAP estimate) by leveraging CLINGO's a built-in optimization method for weak constraints.

For computing marginal probability, LPMLN2ASP utilizes CLINGO's interface with Python. When CLINGO enumerates each stable model of lpmln2asp$^{\mathrm{pnt}}(\Pi)$, the computation is interrupted by the *probability computation module*—a Python

---

[7] https://github.com/azreasoners/lpmln.

program which records the stable model and its penalty specified in the unsat atoms true in the stable model. Once all the stable models are generated, the control returns to the module, which sums up the recorded penalties to compute the normalization constant and the probability of each stable model. The probabilities of the query atoms (specified by option -q) are also calculated by adding the probabilities of the stable models that contain the query atoms. For example, the probability of a query atom residentbird(jo) is $\Sigma_{I \models \text{residentbird(jo)}} P(I)$. The option -all instructs the system to display all stable models and their probabilities.

For conditional probability, the evidence file <evidence file> is specified by the option -e. The file may contain any CLINGO rules, but usually they are constraints, i.e., rules with the empty head. The main difference from the marginal probability computation is that CLINGO computes $\text{lpmln2asp}^{\text{pnt}}(\Pi) \cup$ <evidence file> instead of $\text{lpmln2asp}^{\text{pnt}}(\Pi)$.

Below we illustrate how to use the system for various inferences.

MAP (Maximum A Posteriori) Inference: The command line to use is

```
lpmln2asp -i <input file>
```

By default, LPMLN2ASP computes MAP inference. For example, lpmln2asp -i bird.lpmln returns

```
residentbird(jo) bird(jo) unsat(5,"1.000000")
Optimization: 1000
OPTIMUM FOUND
```

Marginal Probability of All Stable Models: The command line to use is

```
lpmln2asp -i <input file> -all
```

This mode finds all stable models and calculates their probabilities. For example, lpmln2asp -i bird.lpmln -all outputs

```
Answer: 1
residentbird(jo) bird(jo)
unsat(5,"1.000000")
Optimization: 1000
Answer: 2
unsat(4,"2.000000") unsat(5,"1.000000")
Optimization: 3000
Answer: 3
unsat(4,"2.000000") bird(jo)
migratorybird(jo)
Optimization: 2000

Probability of Answer 1 : 0.665240955775
Probability of Answer 2 : 0.0900305731704
Probability of Answer 3 : 0.244728471055
```

Marginal Probability of Query Atoms: The command line to use is

```
lpmln2asp -i <input file> -q <query predicates>
```

This mode calculates the marginal probability of the atoms whose predicates are specified by `-q` option. For example, `lpmln2asp -i birds.lp -q residentbird` outputs

```
residentbird(jo)  0.665240955775
```

Conditional Probability of Query Given Evidence: The command line to use is

```
lpmln2asp -i <input file> -q <query predicates> -e <evidence file>
```

This mode computes the conditional probability of a query given the evidence specified in the `<evidence file>`. For example,

```
lpmln2asp -i birds.lp -q residentbird -e evid.db
```

where `evid.db` contains

```
:- not bird(jo).
```

outputs the conditional probability $P(residentbird(X) \mid bird(jo))$:

```
residentbird(jo)  0.73105857863
```

Debugging ASP Programs: The command line to use is

```
lpmln2asp -i <input file> -hr -all
```

By default, LPMLN2ASP does not translate hard rules and passes them to CLINGO as is. The option `-hr` instructs the system to translate hard rules as well. According to Proposition 2 from [19], as long as the LP^{MLN} program has a probabilistic stable model that satisfies all the hard rules, the simpler translation that does not translate hard rules gives the same result as the full translation and is more computationally efficient. Since in many cases hard rules represent definite knowledge that should not be violated, this is desirable.

On the other hand, translating hard rules could be relevant in some other cases, such as debugging an answer set program by finding which rules cause inconsistency. For example, consider a CLINGO input program `bird.lp`, which is similar to `bird.lpmln` but drops the weights in the last two rules. CLINGO finds no stable models for this program. However, if we invoke LPMLN2ASP on the same program as

```
lpmln2asp -i bird.lp -hr
```

the output of LPMLN2ASP shows three probabilistic stable models, each of which shows a way to resolve the inconsistency by ignoring the minimal number of the rules. For instance, one of them is {`bird(jo)`, `residentbird(jo)`}, which disregards the last rule. The other two are similar.

Note that probability computation involves enumerating all stable models, so it can be much more computationally expensive than the default MAP inference. On the other hand, the computation is exact, so compared to an approximate inference, the "gold standard" result is easy to understand. Furthermore, the conditional probability is computed more effectively than the marginal probability because CLINGO effectively prunes many answer sets that do not satisfy the constraints specified in the evidence file.

Computing MLN with LPMLN2ASP. A typical example in the MLN literature is a social network domain that describes how smokers influence other people, which can be represented in LP^{MLN} as follows. We assume three people *alice*, *bob*, and *carol*, and assume that *alice* is a smoker, *alice* influences *bob*, *bob* influences *carol*, and nothing else is known.

$$w: \quad smoke(x) \land influence(x, y) \to smoke(y)$$
$$\alpha : smoke(alice) \qquad \alpha : influence(alice, bob) \qquad \alpha : influence(bob, carol).$$
$$(5)$$

(*w* is a positive number.) One may expect that *bob* is less likely to be a smoker than *alice*, and *carol* is less likely a smoker than *bob*.

Indeed, the program above defines the following distribution (we omit the *influence* relation, which has a fixed interpretation.)

Possible World	Weight
$\{smoke(alice), \neg smoke(bob), \neg smoke(carol)\}$	$k \cdot e^{8w}$
$\{smoke(alice), smoke(bob), \neg smoke(carol)\}$	$k \cdot e^{8w}$
$\{smoke(bob), \neg smoke(alice), smoke(carol)\}$	0
$\{smoke(alice), smoke(bob), smoke(carol)\}$	$k \cdot e^{9w}$

where $k = e^{3\alpha}$. The normalization constant is the sum of all weights: $k \cdot e^{9w} + 2k \cdot e^{8w}$. This means $P(smoke(alice)) = 1$ and

$$P(smoke(bob)) = \lim_{\alpha \to \infty} \frac{k \cdot e^{8w} + k \cdot e^{9w}}{k \cdot e^{9w} + 2k \cdot e^{8w}} > P(smoke(carol)) = \lim_{\alpha \to \infty} \frac{k \cdot e^{9w}}{k \cdot e^{9w} + 2k \cdot e^{8w}}.$$

The result can be verified by LPMLN2ASP. For $w = 1$, the input program smoke.lpmln is

```
        1 smoke(Y) :- smoke(X), influence(X, Y).
        smoke(alice).      influence(alice, bob).
influence(bob, carol).
```

Executing lpmln2asp -i smoke.lpmln -q smoke outputs

```
        smoke(alice) 1.00000000000000
        smoke(bob) 0.788058442382915
        smoke(carol) 0.576116884765829
```

as expected.

On the other hand, if (5) is understood under the MLN semantics (assuming `influence` relation is fixed as before), similar to the above, one can compute

$$P(smoke(bob)) = \frac{e^{8w} + e^{9w}}{3e^{8w} + e^{9w}} = P(smoke(carol)).$$

In other words, the degraded probability along the transitive relation does not hold under the MLN semantics. This is related to the fact that Markov logic cannot express the concept of transitive closure correctly as it inherits the FOL semantics.

According to Theorem 2 in [19], MLN can be easily embedded in LP^{MLN} by adding a choice rule for each atom with an arbitrary weight, similar to the way propositional logic can be embedded in ASP using choice rules. Consequently, it is possible to use system LPMLN2ASP to compute MLN, which is essentially using an ASP solver to compute MLN.

Let `smoke.mln` be the resulting program. Executing `lpmln2asp -i smoke.mln -q smoke` outputs

```
smoke(alice)  1.0
smoke(bob)    0.650244590946
smoke(carol)  0.650244590946
```

which agrees with the computation above.

7   Multi-valued Probabilistic Programs

In this section, we define a simple fragment of LP^{MLN} that represents probability in a more direct way and can be computed more efficiently. For simplicity of the presentation, we will assume a propositional signature. An extension to first-order signatures is straightforward.

We assume that the propositional signature σ is constructed from "constants" and their "values." A *constant* c is a symbol that is associated with a finite set $Dom(c)$, called the *domain*. The signature σ is constructed from a finite set of constants, consisting of atoms $c = v$[8] for every constant c and every element v in $Dom(c)$. If the domain of c is $\{\mathbf{f}, \mathbf{t}\}$ then we say that c is *Boolean*, and abbreviate $c{=}\mathbf{t}$ as c and $c{=}\mathbf{f}$ as $\sim c$.

We assume that constants are divided into *probabilistic* constants and *regular* constants. A multi-valued probabilistic program Π is a tuple $\langle PF, \Pi \rangle$, where

- *PF* contains *probabilistic constant declarations* of the following form:

$$p_1 : c{=}v_1 \mid \cdots \mid p_n : c{=}v_n \tag{6}$$

one for each probabilistic constant c, where $\{v_1, \ldots, v_n\} = Dom(c)$, $v_i \neq v_j$, $0 \leq p_1, \ldots, p_n \leq 1$ and $\sum_{i=1}^{n} p_i = 1$. We use $M_\Pi(c = v_i)$ to denote p_i. In other words, *PF* describes the probability distribution over each "random variable" c.

---

[8] Note that here "=" is just a part of the symbol for propositional atoms, and is not equality in first-order logic.

- Π is a set of rules of the form (1) such that A contains no probabilistic constants.

The semantics of such a program Π is defined as a shorthand for LP^{MLN} program $T(\Pi)$ of the same signature as follows.

- For each probabilistic constant declaration (6), $T(\Pi)$ contains, for each $i = 1, \ldots, n,$
  - $ln(p_i) : c=v_i$ if $0 < p_i < 1$;
  - $\alpha : c=v_i$ if $p_i = 1$;
  - $\alpha : \leftarrow c=v_i$ if $p_i = 0$.
- For each rule in Π of form (1), $T(\Pi)$ contains

$$\alpha : \quad A \leftarrow B, N.$$

- For each constant c, $T(\Pi)$ contains the uniqueness of value constraints

$$\alpha : \perp \leftarrow c=v_1 \wedge c = v_2 \tag{7}$$

for all $v_1, v_2 \in Dom(c)$ such that $v_1 \neq v_2$. For each probabilistic constant c, $T(\Pi)$ also contains the existence of value constraint

$$\alpha : \perp \leftarrow \neg \bigvee_{v \in Dom(c)} c=v . \tag{8}$$

This means that a regular constant may be undefined (i.e., have no values associated with it), while a probabilistic constant is always associated with some value.

Example 9. The multi-valued probabilistic program

$$0.25 : Outcome=6 \mid 0.15 : Outcome=5$$
$$\mid 0.15 : Outcome=4 \mid 0.15 : Outcome=3$$
$$\mid 0.15 : Outcome=2 \mid 0.15 : Outcome=1$$
$$Win \leftarrow Outcome=6.$$

is understood as shorthand for the LP^{MLN} program

$$ln(0.25) : Outcome=6$$
$$ln(0.15) : Outcome=i \qquad\qquad (i = 1, \ldots, 5)$$
$$\alpha : Win \leftarrow Outcome=6$$
$$\alpha : \perp \leftarrow Outcome=i \wedge Outcome=j \;\; (i \neq j)$$
$$\alpha : \perp \leftarrow \neg \bigvee_{i=1,\ldots 6} Outcome=i.$$

We say an interpretation of Π is *consistent* if it satisfies the hard rules (7) for every constant and (7) for every probabilistic constant. For any consistent interpretation I, we define the set $TC(I)$ ("Total Choice") to be $\{c = v \mid c$ is a probabilistic constant such that $c = v \in I\}$ and define

$$SM''[\Pi] = \{I \mid I \text{ is consistent}$$
$$\text{and is a stable model of } \Pi \cup TC(I)\}.$$

For any interpretation I, we define

$$W''_\Pi(I) = \begin{cases} \prod_{c=v \in TC(I)} M_\Pi(c = v) & \text{if } I \in SM''[\Pi] \\ 0 & \text{otherwise} \end{cases}$$

and

$$P''_\Pi(I) = \frac{W''_\Pi(I)}{\sum_{J \in SM''[\Pi]} W''_\Pi(J)}.$$

The following proposition tells us that the probability of an interpretation can be computed from the probabilities assigned to probabilistic atoms, similar to the way ProbLog is defined.

Proposition 3 ([19]). *For any multi-valued probabilistic program Π such that each p_i in (6) is positive for every probabilistic constant c, if $SM''[\Pi]$ is not empty, then for any interpretation I, $P''_\Pi(I)$ coincides with $P_{T(\Pi)}(I)$.*

MVPP has been used in extending action language $\mathcal{BC}+$ [2,3] to a probabilistic manner [20,30,31], and as a basis of NeurASP to extend probabilistic answer set programs to embrace neural networks [33].

8   Conclusion

There are more works on LP^{MLN} that we do not discuss here. Strong equivalence between LP^{MLN} programs was studied in [25]. Parallel LP^{MLN} solver appeared in [32]. Splitting theorem for LP^{MLN} program is studied in [29]. PCM can be embedded in LP^{MLN} [15]. The relationship between LP^{MLN} and P-Log was shown in [4].

LP^{MLN} has served as the basis of or link between other formalisms. A decision-theoretic extension of LP^{MLN} (DT-LP^{MLN}) was presented in [30] where a utility measure is associated to each (probabilistic) stable model in addition to its probability. Based on this, a translation from $p\mathcal{BC}+$ to Partially Observable Markov Decision Processes (POMDPs) was designed [31] where LP^{MLN} is used to generate components of POMDP, including states, actions, transitions, and their probabilities. [14] extended event calculus with probabilistic reasoning empowered by LP^{MLN}. Recently, a new system PLINGO [13] was presented as a probabilistic extension of CLINGO where LP^{MLN} serves as a middle-ground formalism connecting available input languages of PLINGO, including LP^{MLN}, P-log, ProbLog, and ASP.

LP^{MLN} has been applied in many domains to model probabilistic inference. [7] showed that the classification of objects in an image could be improved by considering their semantic context, where LP^{MLN} is used to model both constraints and probabilistic information provided by the classifier. [1] designed an automated and interpretable fact-checking system where uncertain rules and facts extracted from knowledge graphs and web documents are modeled by LP^{MLN}.

We conclude this tutorial by inviting the readers to explore further along this line of research. One particular promising direction is with the notion of probability, one can link soft models of logic programs with neural networks [33], which helps avoid some issues with a pure deep learning approach.

Acknowledgements. This work was partially supported by the National Science Foundation under Grants IIS-1815337 and IIS-2006747.

References

1. Ahmadi, N., Lee, J., Papotti, P., Saeed, M.: Explainable fact checking with probabilistic answer set programming. In: Conference for Truth and Trust Online (2019)
2. Babb, J., Lee, J.: Action language $\mathcal{BC}+$: preliminary report. In: Proceedings of the AAAI Conference on Artificial Intelligence (AAAI) (2015)
3. Babb, J., Lee, J.: Action language $\mathcal{BC}+$. J. Logic Comput. **30**(4), 899–922 (2020)
4. Balai, E., Gelfond, M.: On the relationship between P-log and LPMLN. In: IJCAI (2016)
5. Buccafurri, F., Leone, N., Rullo, P.: Enhancing disjunctive datalog by constraints. IEEE Trans. Knowl. Data Eng. **12**(5), 845–860 (2000)
6. Calimeri, F., et al.: ASP-Core-2: Input language format. ASP Standardization Working Group, Technical report (2012)
7. Eiter, T., Kaminski, T.: Exploiting contextual knowledge for hybrid classification of visual objects. In: Michael, L., Kakas, A. (eds.) JELIA 2016. LNCS (LNAI), vol. 10021, pp. 223–239. Springer, Cham (2016). https://doi.org/10.1007/978-3-319-48758-8_15
8. Erdem, E., Lifschitz, V.: Tight logic programs. Theory Pract. Logic Program. **3**, 499–518 (2003)
9. Ferraris, P., Lee, J., Lifschitz, V.: Stable models and circumscription. Artif. Intell. **175**, 236–263 (2011)
10. Fierens, D., et al.: Inference and learning in probabilistic logic programs using weighted Boolean formulas. Theory Pract. Logic Program. **15**(03), 358–401 (2015)
11. Gebser, M., Schaub, T., Marius, S., Thiele, S.: xorro: near uniform sampling of answer sets by means of XOR (2016). https://potassco.org/labs/2016/09/20/xorro.html
12. Gelfond, M., Lifschitz, V.: The stable model semantics for logic programming. In: Kowalski, R., Bowen, K. (eds.) Proceedings of International Logic Programming Conference and Symposium, pp. 1070–1080. MIT Press (1988)
13. Hahn, S., Janhunen, T., Kaminski, R., Romero, J., Rühling, N., Schaub, T.: *Plingo*: a system for probabilistic reasoning in clingo based on LP^{MLN}. In: Governatori, G., Turhan, A.Y. (eds.) RuleML+RR 2022. LNCS, vol. 13752, pp. 54–62. Springer, Cham (2022). https://doi.org/10.1007/978-3-031-21541-4_4
14. Katzouris, N., Artikis, A.: WOLED: a tool for online learning weighted answer set rules for temporal reasoning under uncertainty. In: Proceedings of the International Conference on Principles of Knowledge Representation and Reasoning, vol. 17, pp. 790–799 (2020)
15. Lee, J., Meng, Y., Wang, Y.: Markov logic style weighted rules under the stable model semantics. In: CEUR Workshop Proceedings, vol. 1433 (2015)
16. Lee, J., Lifschitz, V.: Loop formulas for disjunctive logic programs. In: Palamidessi, C. (ed.) ICLP 2003. LNCS, vol. 2916, pp. 451–465. Springer, Heidelberg (2003). https://doi.org/10.1007/978-3-540-24599-5_31

17. Lee, J., Palla, R.: System F2LP – computing answer sets of first-order formulas. In: Erdem, E., Lin, F., Schaub, T. (eds.) LPNMR 2009. LNCS (LNAI), vol. 5753, pp. 515–521. Springer, Heidelberg (2009). https://doi.org/10.1007/978-3-642-04238-6_51

18. Lee, J., Talsania, S., Wang, Y.: Computing LPMLN using ASP and MLN solvers. Theory Pract. Logic Program. (2017). https://doi.org/10.1017/S1471068417000400

19. Lee, J., Wang, Y.: Weighted rules under the stable model semantics. In: Proceedings of International Conference on Principles of Knowledge Representation and Reasoning (KR), pp. 145–154 (2016)

20. Lee, J., Wang, Y.: A probabilistic extension of action language $\mathcal{BC}+$. Theory Pract. Logic Program. **18**(3–4), 607–622 (2018)

21. Lee, J., Wang, Y.: Weight learning in a probabilistic extension of answer set programs. In: Proceedings of International Conference on Principles of Knowledge Representation and Reasoning (KR), pp. 22–31 (2018)

22. Lee, J., Yang, Z.: LPMLN, weak constraints, and P-log. In: Proceedings of the AAAI Conference on Artificial Intelligence (AAAI), pp. 1170–1177 (2017)

23. Lifschitz, V., Pearce, D., Valverde, A.: Strongly equivalent logic programs. ACM Trans. Comput. Log. **2**, 526–541 (2001)

24. Lin, F., Zhao, Y.: ASSAT: computing answer sets of a logic program by SAT solvers. Artif. Intell. **157**, 115–137 (2004)

25. Luo, M., Lee, J.: Strong equivalence for LPMLN programs. In: ICLP (Technical Communications) (2019)

26. Poon, H., Domingos, P.: Sound and efficient inference with probabilistic and deterministic dependencies. In: AAAI, vol. 6, pp. 458–463 (2006)

27. Richardson, M., Domingos, P.: Markov logic networks. Mach. Learn. **62**(1–2), 107–136 (2006)

28. Sato, T.: A statistical learning method for logic programs with distribution semantics. In: Proceedings of the 12th International Conference on Logic Programming (ICLP), pp. 715–729 (1995)

29. Wang, B., Zhang, Z., Xu, H., Shen, J.: Splitting an LPMLN program. In: Proceedings of the AAAI Conference on Artificial Intelligence, vol. 32, no. 1 (2018)

30. Wang, Y., Lee, J.: Elaboration tolerant representation of Markov decision process via decision-theoretic extension of probabilistic action language $p\mathcal{BC}+$. In: Balduccini, M., Lierler, Y., Woltran, S. (eds.) LPNMR 2019. LNAI, vol. 11481, pp. 224–238. Springer, Cham (2019). https://doi.org/10.1007/978-3-030-20528-7_17

31. Wang, Y., Zhang, S., Lee, J.: Bridging commonsense reasoning and probabilistic planning via a probabilistic action language. Theory Pract. Logic Program. **19**(5–6), 1090–1106 (2019)

32. Wu, W., et al.: LPMLNModels: a parallel solver for LPMLN. In: 2018 IEEE 30th International Conference on Tools with Artificial Intelligence (ICTAI), pp. 794–799. IEEE (2018)

33. Yang, Z., Ishay, A., Lee, J.: NeurASP: embracing neural networks into answer set programming. In: Proceedings of International Joint Conference on Artificial Intelligence (IJCAI), pp. 1755–1762 (2020). https://doi.org/10.24963/ijcai.2020/243

Vadalog: Overview, Extensions and Business Applications

Teodoro Baldazzi[7], Luigi Bellomarini[1], Markus Gerschberger[2], Aditya Jami[3],
Davide Magnanimi[1,4], Markus Nissl[5], Aleksandar Pavlović[5],
and Emanuel Sallinger[5,6(✉)]

[1] Bank of Italy, Rome, Italy
[2] Josef Ressel Centre for Real-Time Value Network Visibility, Logistikum,
University of Applied Sciences Upper Austria, Wels, Austria
[3] Meltwater, San Francisco, USA
[4] Politecnico di Milano, Milan, Italy
[5] TU Wien, Vienna, Austria
[6] University of Oxford, Oxford, UK
sallinger@dbai.tuwien.ac.at
[7] Università Roma Tre, Rome, Italy

Abstract. Knowledge graphs (KGs) have in recent years gained a large
momentum both in academic research and in business applications. They
have become a bridge between databases, artificial intelligence (AI), data
science, the (semantic) web, linked data, and many other areas. In particular, in declarative AI, they have become a bridge between logic-based
reasoning, and machine learning-based reasoning. Languages for KGs on
the one hand, and systems for KGs – i.e., Knowledge Graph Managa-
ment System (KGMS) – on the other hand, have garnered increasing
attention. Of particular importance are language and system extensions
– such as probabilistic reasoning, numeric reasoning, etc. – supporting
various real-world applications, and the business applications that can
be built using such extensions.

In this work, we give an overview of the Vadalog language and system, a KGMS. We focus on three areas: (1) a basic overview, including
an introduction to dependencies, the Datalog and Vadalog languages,
(2) the extensions of the system, including arithmetic and aggregation,
real-world data interfaces, temporal reasoning, and machine learning,
and (3) the business applications, including: corporate governance, media
intelligence, supply chains, collateral eligibility, hostile takeovers, smart
anonymization, and anti-money laundering.

1 Introduction

In this work, we give an overview of the Vadalog language and system, a Knowledge Graph Management System (KGMS). Instead of starting with a long introduction to what Knowledge Graphs are, and how Knowledge Graph Management
Systems that power them are built (there are other works which do that, which

L. Bertossi and G. Xiao (Eds.): Reasoning Web, LNCS 13759, pp. 161–198, 2023.
https://doi.org/10.1007/978-3-031-31414-8_5

we discuss in Sect. 2), in this work we focus on two main facets: the **extensions** of the Vadalog language and system, and the **business applications** that they power. Of course before that, we introduce the **base** of Vadalog, namely the language Datalog.

This work is structured into three **base** subsections:

1. **A Map to Vadalog's Extensions and Business Applications** giving an overview of both the research on the foundation and its extensions, as well as giving an overview of key business applications.
2. **A Gentle Introduction to Dependencies and Datalog** focusing on a gentle introduction to Datalog for readers with little background in Datalog, but some interest in logic or databases.
3. **From Datalog to Vadalog** concluding the introduction to the Vadalog language and system based on Datalog. Readers already familiar with Datalog can start here.

They are followed by four **extension** subsections:

1. **Arithmetics and Aggregation** introducing a critical extension for business applications, namely aggregating and working with numbers – quite intricate in a language that allows full Datalog recursion.
2. **Interfacing with the Real World** introducing how to access and store data from a variety of sources, including relational databases, graph stores, flat files, etc.
3. **Temporal Reasoning** introducing how to reason about the critical dimension of time, including how to manage time intervals and how to aggregate over them in various ways.
4. **Machine Learning** introducing how to interface with various machine learning methods. We are giving a particular example here on a Knowledge Graph Embedding method.

These are complemented by a number of **application** subsections:

1. **Corporate Governance** focusing on how to understand how companies control each other, and how to govern such control given the complexities.
2. **Media Intelligence** focusing on understanding how company Knowledge Graphs are important beyond the financial and economic space, but critical in media intelligence.
3. **Supply Chains** focusing on how to understand the complex network formed by supply chains and analysing the intricate dependencies and effects of events within supply chains.
4. **Collateral Eligibility** focusing on understanding when financial entities can act as guarantors for loans of other entities, and in particular, when the should *not*.

5. **Hostile Takeovers and Golden Powers** focusing on how to detect and prevent (hostile) takeovers of strategically important companies such as in the medical or energy sectors.

6. **Smart Anonymization** focusing on how to ensure the anonymity of data as required by national and international guidelines and principles.

7. **Anti-Money Laundering (AML)** focusing on how to detect money-laundering as required by Financial Intelligence Units (FIUs).

2   The Base

2.1   A Map to Vadalog's Extensions and Business Applications

The economic and financial sectors lie in the specifically positive configuration that while they are characterized by very large sets of entities with heterogeneous attributes and complex interconnections, the domain knowledge is available and often concentrated in a small set of enterprise databases or domain experts. Declarative AI is therefore a particularly effective means to provide smarter products, services, and processes that generate derived knowledge in a self-service and on-demand fashion. Machine learning solutions are complementary: whenever the domain experience and the available ground data are insufficient to generate the derived knowledge required by the applications, data mining can be effectively employed to reverse engineer the data sources at hand and extract the implicit knowledge. Extreme cases render even data mining unsuitable, and human experts need to resort to manual code analysis.

In the context of multiple projects with the Central Bank of Italy, we had the chance to explore the application of Vadalog to real-world use cases in the economic and financial realm. A driving factor has been the blossoming of *Knowledge Graphs* (KG) in the financial contexts, with many commercial data providers (e.g., Bloomberg [3], Thomson Reuters [2]), big investment banks (e.g., JPMorgan [53]), financial intermediaries, and governmental or international organizations (e.g., the United Nations [68]) using KGs to systematically capture business aspects at enterprise level. Seizing this momentum in industrial applications has been possible thanks to the parallel resurgence of logic-based reasoning systems, especially motivated by scalable processing platforms as well as the soar of expressive and tractable languages: although multiple definitions for KGs started to circulate [44] and a consensus has not been achieved yet, all of them are centered on an extensional component, composed of the ground factual data available from the data source, and an intensional component, with business rules expressed in a declarative formalism [29]. The adoption of a *Knowledge Representation and Reasoning* (KRR) language striking a balance between computational complexity (ideally with a PTIME reasoning task) and expressive power rapidly proved to be the decisive factor for the construction of effective *Knowledge Graph Management Systems* (KGMS) [32]. It is clear that this application is not restricted to the financial and economic space, but can be extended to many other applications focused around companies – such as media intelligence, for which we will later given an application developed in collaboration with Meltwater [51].

A KGMS-driven Architecture. Fostering a data-driven approach, we built our industrial applications of Vadalog around one single IT architecture, in Fig. 1, that sees KGs as a central knowledge hub connecting apps and sources.

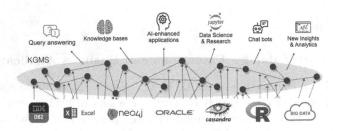

Fig. 1. IT architecture based on Enterprise Knowledge Graphs.

The KGMS plays the role of a dedicated middleware component and provides enterprise AI-driven applications with a unified information context, which includes: i. a language and a formalism for representation of and reasoning on KGs, Vadalog in this case; ii. a rich set of data sources (including big data); iii. procedural and third-party code; iv. reasoning services via a rich set of APIs.

An Applied Research Journey. Driven by the business of a central bank, we leveraged Vadalog to build enterprise KGs and inject business value into static databases, enabling the construction of smart applications, relying on a KGMS back-end. The mandates of central banks are complex and heterogeneous. The Bank of Italy, amongst many tasks, carries out economic research, oversees the financial and banking system in the Eurosystem context, operating within the *Single Supervisory Mechanism*, analyses and supervises most of the business processes operated by the commercial banks as well as their governance, hosts an internal financial intelligence unit to counter money laundering, cooperates in the definition of the monetary policy looking at the systemic financial stability. We started our applied research journey by attacking some of the mentioned business areas, fostering the construction of smart products, with the final goal of improving services and processes.

In the rest of the section, we provide the reader with a walk-through of the business context of the main application areas of Vadalog in the economic and financial setting and refer to dedicated works.

Vadalog in the Economic and Financial Setting. The presence of many interconnected entities, which interact in a complex manner, often driven by complex regulatory bodies, is extremely apparent in the realm of *corporate governance*, which very well fits KG-based solutions. A central bank looks at networks of companies from many angles: the *economic research* one, to study concentration and dispersion of control [17]; the *supervision* one, to carry out due diligence actions to assess, evaluate and decide on operations (e.g., mergers and acquisitions, changes in the board, etc.) involving banks and financial intermediaries as mandated by consolidated banking acts; *anti-money laundering*, where sophisticated shareholding constructions may be put in place to obfuscate the real ultimate beneficial owner of suspicious transactions and the financial intelligence unit is interested in unveiling them [54]; *monetary policy operations*, for instance to evaluate the risk related to the asset provided by an issuer as collateral to a specific financial arrangement favour of some other entity [1]; *credit worthiness* evaluation, i.e., to understand whether a third party is worth specific credit: its control structure is a good feature for such scoring.

A crucial application of corporate governance analysis deals with detecting, countering, and if possible preventing the so-called *hostile takovers*. Multiple countries have resorted to legal frameworks to protect strategic companies, for instance those of military, logistic and healthcare sectors, against foreign takeovers [69]. Takeovers can be studied reactively, namely, trying to understand whether a transaction underpins an undesired change of ownership, or proactively, so as to individuate cases where the corporate structure of a company as well as the features of its shareholders or branches reveal the possibility of an imminent takeover. We modeled both the scenarios with Vadalog and studied the problem in different settings: in the economic turmoil induced by the COVID-19 pandemic [22,23], and more in general, providing a hybrid reasoning and machine learning framework to pursue the determinants of takeovers [21].

Illegal or anyway undesired actions in financial networks are even more extreme in *money laundering* cases, when a perpetrator wants to inject money of illicit origin into the system in order to clean, namely, launder it, and make it suitable to enter the legit market. Money laundering is a global challenge, which involves financial and non-financial intermediaries of the private sector (banks, trusts, money transfers, casinos, securities dealers, real estate brokers, public notaries, dealers, etc.), Financial Intelligence Units and law enforcement agencies [66]. In our recent work we proposed the adoption of Vadalog to enable reasoning on complex money laundering cases [33] where sophisticated transfer pattern need to be detected to spot and counter money laundering. Vadalog, extended with the possibility to handle uncertainty in the form of probabilities [26,35], proved to be of the right expressive power to capture real-world cases of interest for a Central Bank.

In the mentioned use cases, reasoning has been used mainly to augment ground information with derived data. To achieve this goal, very often the focus is on generating relationships that are not already present in the data. As a matter of fact, Vadalog turned out to be extremely effective to model such *link prediction* settings [6,7,42], in particular, thanks to the presence of existential quantification, recursion as well as a tractable approach to the use of equality-generating dependencies [24], multiple link identification criteria could be combined together to identify clusters of connected fact nodes.

It goes without saying that the success of data-intensive initiatives often lies in the possibility to share results with the community. This is particularly relevant for a central bank, which has research as a core institutional goal, but also critical, due to the confidentiality of the data it handles, which often refer to individuals, companies, banks, intermediaries, and so on. We put into action state-of-the-art *statistical anonymization* techniques, such as k-anonimity [90], by providing a novel declarative implementation for it in Vadalog [27]: values that potentially reveal identities are replaced with null values (those introduced by existential quantification), within recursive rule evaluation processes that single out and suppress characterizing values. It is matter of current research how to optimize the suppression in such a way that the introduced values preserve the statistical properties of the original distribution.

Finally, we have used Vadalog in the Bank of Italy and with other industrial partners for many more interesting, but still initial applications, such as *fact checking* of financial claims [81] and solving industrial *blockchain challenges* [31, 84,85]. We will report about these new ares soon, in future work.

2.2 A Gentle Introduction to Dependencies and Datalog

In this section, we will give a gentle introduction to dependencies and the special kind of recursive dependencies usually called Datalog, which will be the core of what we are going to discuss. Readers familiar with TGDs, EGDs, and Datalog can skip this section if desired.

Dependencies. Let us consider the formula

$$\mathsf{PLC}(\mathsf{HSBC}, \mathsf{UK}, \mathsf{London}) \to \mathsf{Company}(\mathsf{HSBC})$$

It makes a statement about HSBC, to be precise HSBC Holdings, the largest company in the UK and one of the largest banking companies worldwide. In particular, it states that, if HSBC is a PLC ("public limited company") in the UK, registered in London, it is a company.

Questions can be asked about this formula on multiple levels. The first one may be the language. In fact, we see a formula of first-order (FO) logic. It is certainly a relatively simple such formula, as it only contains constants, and no variables. Other questions may be asked about the concrete content, or as one may call it, the modeling of the domain (e.g., should the information about a PLC contain more information, say the full name of the company, its company identifier and other information?). Although we will address this question as part of the scenario this shall not be the main focus of this section.

A very typical question may be: "is this not too specific – only about HSBC – can we not say that in general?" Let us consider a modified version of our previous formula.

$$\forall x, z\, \mathsf{PLC}(x, \mathsf{UK}, z) \to \mathsf{Company}(x)$$

This formula states that if a company is a PLC in the UK, it is also a company. Again, questions can be asked about the modeling – e.g., can it be extended to hold irrespective of the country, i.e., are all PLC considered to be companies? For example, another variant of it is

$$\forall x, y, z \, \mathsf{PLC}(x, y, z) \rightarrow \mathsf{Company}(x) \tag{1}$$

In all three formulas so far, one can see a certain form of *dependency* between data stored in the relation PLC and the relation Company. The first formula was a dependency between two very specific data items, while the second and third ones were more general statements about PLCs and companies. While we will explore a number of typical dependencies in this chapter, we have already seen a quite typical type of dependency here in Formula 1, called an *inclusion dependency*. The name "inclusion" comes from the fact that data from one relation is included in another one. The other two formulas are sometimes called *conditional inclusion dependencies*, as they have conditions, namely constants selecting only particular companies to be included.

More generally, dependencies in the field of databases and beyond have taken many different forms, some formulated in logic, some in other formalisms. Dependencies have been formulated in first-order logic or even second-order logic. This being the case, one may suggest that the term *dependency* can have no definition at all, or, in the broad sense may refer to any logical formula.

Thankfully, the vast majority of dependencies that have been developed over the years are formalized in, or can be translated into, a very clear syntactical form:

$$Q \varphi \rightarrow \psi$$

where φ and ψ are logical formulas and Q is a (possibly empty) quantifier prefix. That is, we are dealing with a (possibly quantified) logical implication with *antecedent* φ and *consequent* ψ. It is thus not completely surprising that another typical name for dependency is *rule* with the *condition* φ and *consequence* ψ. More colloquially, they are sometimes also called "if-then" statements, with φ the "if" and ψ the "then".

We shall mostly discuss dependencies of this form in what follows. Note that this is, for most purposes, still a very broad definition as it puts no constraints on quantifiers (e.g., second-order quantifiers are not ruled out) and on the formulas φ and ψ which can be arbitrary formulas. In fact, by assuming φ to be $\top$ (i.e., true) or ψ to be $\bot$ (i.e., false), one can essentially "hide" arbitrary formulas as dependencies or rules. This suggests that, and in fact it is the case that, most dependency formalisms put severe restrictions on the form Q, φ and ψ may take, and we will explore them in more detail in what follows.

Constraints and Enrichments. Let us again consider the following simple dependency, which we shall call σ:

$$\forall x, z \, \mathsf{PLC}(x, \mathsf{UK}, z) \rightarrow \mathsf{Company}(x)$$

Let us assume we are given $I = \{\mathsf{PLC}(\mathsf{HSBC}, \mathsf{UK}, \mathsf{London})\}$. Taking the logic-angle, I is a relational structure, or taking the database-angle, it is a database instance.

There are two very different views one can take on I and σ. Let us start from the perspective of logic: Does I satisfy σ, i.e., does $I \vDash \sigma$ hold? The answer is clearly no, since the antecedent of σ is satisfied by I, thus requiring

$$J = \{\mathsf{Company}(\mathsf{HSBC})\}$$

to be contained in I, but clearly $J \nsubseteq I$. This is the view of σ as a *constraint*, i.e., a description of what must hold in any "legal world".

Yet, seeing σ as describing implicit knowledge "about the world" suggests a second view of it, namely as a rule for generating new, implicit, data from already known explicit data. This view is sometimes called seeing σ as an *enrichment*. That is, σ suggests to us that if we know that HSBC is a PLC, then it also is company, i.e., that we can apply σ to I to derive $I' = I \cup J$.

These two views of logical formulas, in particular rules, is a classical topic that permeates the study of logic, databases, knowledge representation and reasoning, and adjoining areas. It is a close relative to (but separate from) a topic known as the "open world" and "closed world" assumption. While it shall not be our primary focus here, awareness of it is necessary both in terms of understanding the semantics of the considered languages and their practical implications.

Tuple-Generating Dependencies. While we have discussed that dependencies can take many forms, two kinds of dependencies have been shown as a particular "sweet spot" of expressive power and computational complexity, namely tuple-generating and equality-generating dependencies. The dependency

$$\forall x, y, z \, \mathsf{PLC}(x, y, z) \rightarrow \mathsf{Company}(x)$$

we have encountered earlier is called a *tuple-generating dependency* (tgd). It is easy to see why such a dependency is called *tuple-generating*, if we see it as an *enrichment*, i.e., a way of describing how new data should be generated: given a tuple of $\mathsf{PLC}(x, y, z)$ it requires a $\mathsf{Company}(x)$ *tuple* to be *generated*. Note that this is not the only way to view a tgd, namely as an enrichment, but it is also possible to view it as a constraint: If a $\mathsf{PLC}(x, y, z)$ tuple is present, but not a corresponding $\mathsf{Company}(x)$ tuple, the constraint is violated.

Yet, what about if our table Company should also contain the company's registered address and date of incorporation? For example, we know that in reality, HSBC's registered address and date of incorporation is as given in the following tuple t_2:

Company(HSBC, "8 Canada Square, London, E14 5HQ", "1959-01-01").

Assume that we have in addition the tuple $\mathsf{PLC}(\mathsf{HSBC}, \mathsf{UK}, \mathsf{London})$ present, which we shall call t_1, then the following dependency σ_1

$$\forall x, y, z \, \mathsf{PLC}(x, y, z) \rightarrow \exists u, v \, \mathsf{Company}(x, u, v)$$

requires that a tuple like t_2 is present. That is, the database $I_1 = \{t_1, t_2\}$ satisfies our dependency σ_1. Note that this dependency contains existential quantifiers in the conclusion, as there is no information in PLC about the address or date of incorporation about the company – the dependency simply requires the presence of *some* values there. What about the database $I_2 = \{t_1\}$? Clearly, if we view σ_1 as a constraint, it is violated, i.e., $I_2 \not\models \sigma_1$. Yet, what if we see it as an enrichment? Most likely, we would like to actually have t_2 to be generated, but there is no information in our database I_2 to know all of the information contained in t_2.

The typical answer to this dilemma in information systems is the introduction of *nulls*, values that represent unknown or missing information. The study of nulls is an important area, and in fact an active field of research, but shall not be our main focus here. We will still briefly discuss the topic here, as it deepens the understanding of dependencies considerably. In many practical systems (such as SQL-based database systems) the choice is for system-level support of a single special value NULL, with the special property that NULL $\neq$ NULL. The more general formalisation that is taken in most of the research literature is to assume a set of null values $\perp_1, \perp_2, \ldots$ different from constants. These are typically called *labelled* or *marked* nulls, as the subscripts "label" the specific null values. This allows for the usual property that equal objects are considered equal, i.e., $\perp_1 = \perp_1$, but allow for the SQL-like semantics of nulls, by assigning different "fresh" nulls whenever a null value is introduced. For example, in our case of σ_1 seen as an enrichment, the typical semantics would produce a tuple t_3

$$\mathsf{Company}(\mathsf{HSBC}, \perp_1, \perp_2).$$

As our main goal in this section is to learn to speak the language of dependencies, and not a deep exploration into their semantics, this shall conclude our discussion of nulls at this point. Formal definitions and semantics are given in Sect. 2, as well as when required in the later chapters.

So far, we have seen tgds always act on one tuple, but in fact, they also allow connecting multiple tuples. Assume we have an additional relation InScope that represents that a particular country and a particular city is in scope for the business or other problem we are trying to solve. Through the tgd

$$\forall x, y, z \, \mathsf{PLC}(x, y, z) \wedge \mathsf{InScope}(y, z) \rightarrow \exists u, v \, \mathsf{Company}(x, u, v)$$

we can express that we only want Company tuples that are PLC as well as InScope.

The same holds for the conclusion of tgds, where a particularly interesting use case is using an existential quantifier for creating an identifier, and then stating multiple atoms connected by that identifier, such as in the following example.

$$\forall x, y, z \, \mathsf{PLC}(x, y, z) \rightarrow \exists id \, \mathsf{CompanyName}(id, x) \wedge \mathsf{CompanyCountry}(id, y)$$

Altogether, the general syntactic form of a tgds is

$$\forall \boldsymbol{x}\,(\varphi(\boldsymbol{x}) \rightarrow \exists \boldsymbol{y}\,\psi(\boldsymbol{x}, \boldsymbol{y}))$$

where φ and ψ are (non-empty) conjunctions of relational atoms. Finally, let us note that tgds are sometimes also called GLAV (global-and-local-as-view) dependencies.

Equality-Generating Dependencies. Let us consider CompanyName(id, $name$) from before. How do we express that a company may only have one name? A tgd can try to detect it:

$$\forall x, y, z\ \text{CompanyName}(id, n_1) \wedge \text{CompanyName}(id, n_2) \rightarrow \text{sameName}(n_1, n_2)$$

Yet, there is no way to force sameName(n_1, n_2) to have $n_1 = n_2$ using a tgd. The solution is simple, namely allowing equality in the conclusion such as in the following dependency σ:

$$\forall x, y, z\ \text{CompanyName}(id, n_1) \wedge \text{CompanyName}(id, n_2) \rightarrow n_1 = n_2$$

Such a dependency is called an *equality-generating dependency* (egd). If we see our above egd σ as a constraint, the situation is reasonably simple. Assume we have our database $I = \{\text{CompanyName}(1, \text{HSBC}), \text{CompanyName}(1, \text{ICBC})\}$. That is, our database (probably mistakenly) expresses that the company with the identifier 1 is at the same time HSBC and ICBC (Industrial and Commercial Bank of China, the largest bank worldwide, as of 2018). Clearly, seen as a constraint, σ is violated in I, i.e., $I \not\models \sigma$. The situation is more complex once nulls are involved. Consider the following database.

$$I_2 = \{\text{CompanyName}(1, \text{HSBC}), \text{CompanyName}(1, \perp_1)\}$$

It still holds (at least in many semantics) that $I_2 \not\models \sigma$, but seen as an enrichment, we may expect that the labelled null $\perp_1$ is replaced by HSBC, yielding database $I_3 = \{\text{CompanyName}(1, \text{HSBC})\}$. This is certainly a special kind of *enrichment*, as in fact it is not the case that new tuples are added to the database, but existing tuples are modified, actually making the database contain fewer tuples in our example. It is not surprising that another name for enrichments in this context is *repairs*, as one can see our dependency σ as an instruction of how to repair our database.

This was a very simply case, where $\perp_1$ occurred just once in the entire database, but $\perp_1$ can of course occur multiple times. Assume that another tuple $t = \text{CEO}(\text{"John M. Flint"}, \perp_1)$ exists in our database (John M. Flint is the CEO Of HSBC as of 2018) and let $I_3 = I_2 \cup \{t\}$. It is fair to expect $\perp_1$ to also be replaced by HSBC in this tuple. Two observations can be made here: First, it is easy to see that such a repair may become a computationally intensive undertaking, replacing all occurrences of $\perp_1$ by HSBC. Alternatively, a system can devise more intricate storage and representation mechanisms to allow for computationally less expensive solutions. More conceptually, it is interesting to observe that while our dependency σ was applied to the two tuples in I_2, its repair actually affected another tuple t unrelated to I_2. One could say that the repair of σ had a "non-local" effect.

Given our discussion of egds as enrichments, it is easy to see why seemingly simple dependencies like egds can lead to complex considerations when using them in systems. A simply way, and a decision that most database management systems make, is to use them purely as constraints. Altogether, the general syntactic form of egds is

$$\forall \boldsymbol{x} \left(\varphi(\boldsymbol{x}) \to x_i = x_j \right)$$

where φ is a (non-empty) conjunction of relational atoms and x_i and x_j must be contained in $\boldsymbol{x}$.

Recursion and Datalog. Before going into further details about dependencies themselves, it is worth considering the relations they are based on. Let us consider a dependency we looked at before, and which we shall call σ.

$$\forall x, y, z \, \mathsf{PLC}(x, y, z) \to \mathsf{Company}(x)$$

In a single database, this can be seen simply as a dependency of two relations in that database. Another typical use is as a mapping between different schemas, a *schema mapping*. In our example dependency, one can see it as a mapping between the relation PLC in the *source* schema, and $\mathsf{Company}$ in the *target* schema. At its foundation, a schema mapping is a set of dependencies plus the designation which relations are considered to be part of the source and target schema.

The terms *source* and *target* schema are most often used in the area of *data exchange* where the goal is to transfer data from a source schema into a target schema. In *data integration* the two schemas are often called *local* and *global* schema, as the goal is to integrate local schemas into a global schema. We will see these terms return when we talk about particular types of tgds.

Assume that our source schema consists of the relation PLC and the target schema of the relation $\mathsf{Company}$, then our dependency before is called a source-to-target dependency. More generally given a dependency of the general form

$$Q\varphi \to \psi$$

if all relation symbols occurring in φ are only from the source schema, and all relation symbols occurring in ψ are only from the target schema, then the dependency is called a *source-to-target* (s-t) dependency. If both φ and ψ are over the target schema, the dependency is called a *target* dependency. Let us consider a particular dependency which we shall call σ_2.

$$\forall x, y, z \, \mathsf{SubCompany}(x, y) \wedge \mathsf{SubCompany}(y, z) \to \mathsf{SubCompany}(x, z)$$

In what we described above, and if SubCompany is part of the target schema, this is a target dependency. But more generally, the major difference between s-t dependencies and the dependency above is that σ_2 is *recursive*. Computationally, this makes a big difference.

In the remainder of this paper, we will concentrate on – in general – recursive TGDs. This concludes our gentle introduction to dependencies and Datalog. Further information on reasoning over dependencies can be found in [86–88]. More on formalism particularly suited to tree-like graphs can be found in [70,73]. More on second-order dependencies can be found in [56,57], and more generally the role of function symbols in dependencies [61]. This goes as far as that concepts such as mathematical limits can be extended to dependencies [71,72]. Query answering in the presence of inconsistency is further discussed in [5], questions on the role of updates to such queries are considered in e.g. [64].

2.3   From Datalog to Vadalog

With the previous section making clear what TGDs and recursion are, it is quite simple to define Datalog: a Datalog rule is a – in general recursive – TGD that does not contain existential quantifiers (also called *full* TGDs). A Datalog program is a set of Datalog rules.

Syntactically, one usually does not state Datalog in logic itself, but with a slightly modified syntax. Consider the formula

$$\mathsf{PLC}(x, y, z) \rightarrow \mathsf{Company}(x)$$

In Datalog, one usually exchanges left- and right-hand sides of the implication, and writes it as such:

```
Company(X) :- PLC(X,Y,Z).
```

That is, the arrow is replaced by an ASCII-art style arrow :-, and variables are typically written in upper case. Universal quantifiers are not written explicitly – any variable only on the right-hand side of the arrow is universally quantified. Vadalog and many other Datalog-derived languages adopt this typical Datalog syntax. Existential quantifiers are – so far – not allowed, we are restricted to full TGDs in Datalog.

Syntax and Semantics of Vadalog. Vadalog, and in general the Datalog$^{\pm}$ [8, 10,18,43,48–50,58] family of languages, lifts the above restriction to full TGDs and allows arbitrary, recursive TGDs again. However, as the general setting of recursive TGDs makes almost all relevant computational problems undecidable, restrictions must be defined to achieve languages that are useful in practice.

Chase and Reasoning. In this context, we recall that the semantics of a Datalog$^{\pm}$ program can be defined in an operational way via the *chase* [77]. Given a database D and a set Σ of rules, this procedure incrementally enriches D with new facts derived from the application of the rules in Σ over D into a new instance $chase(D,\Sigma)$. Such tuples may contain labelled nulls that act as placeholders for existential quantification. Note that we use the terms *tuple* and *fact* as synonyms. More formally, in the version of the chase we refer to (known as *oblivious* [48]), given a TGD $\varphi(\bar{x},\bar{y}) \rightarrow \exists \bar{z}\ \psi(\bar{x},\bar{z})$, a *chase step* can be performed over D if there exists an *applicable* homomorphism h that maps the atoms of $\varphi(\bar{x},\bar{y})$ to facts in D (i.e., $h(\varphi(\bar{x},\bar{y})) \subseteq D$). In such a case, the fact $h'(\psi(\bar{x},\bar{z}))$ is added to D (if not already present), where h' is obtained by extending h so that $h'(\bar{z})$ is a fresh labelled null, for each $z_i \in \bar{z}$. The *chase graph* $\mathcal{G}(D,\Sigma)$ is the directed graph with the facts from $chase(D,\Sigma)$ as nodes and an edge from a node n to a node m if m derives from n (and possibly other facts) via a chase step [49]. An *ontological reasoning task* consists in answering a *conjunctive query* (CQ) Q over D, augmented with a set Σ of rules. Formally speaking, given a pair $Q = (\Sigma, Ans)$, where Ans is an n-ary predicate, the evaluation of Q over D is the set of tuples $Q(D) = \{\bar{t} \in dom(D)^n \mid Ans(\bar{t}) \in chase(D,\Sigma)\}$, where $\bar{t}$ is a tuple of constants. Solving an ontological reasoning task requires finding an instance J such that: (i) $Ans(\bar{t}) \in J$ iff $\bar{t} \in Q(D)$; and (ii) for every other J' such that $Ans(\bar{t}) \in J'$ iff $\bar{t} \in Q(D)$, there is a homomorphism from J to J' [25].

Yet, we recall that reasoning on Datalog with existential quantification is in general undecidable. In fact, the chase would not terminate in such settings, due to the possible generation of infinite labelled nulls resulting from the interplay between recursion and existentials. Consider the following example.

Example 1. Let $D = \{Person(Anna)\}$ be a database instance, Σ be a set of Warded Datalog$^{\pm}$ rules with existential quantification

$$Person(x) \rightarrow \exists y\ Ancestor(y, x) \qquad (\alpha)$$

$$Ancestor(y, x) \rightarrow Person(y) \qquad (\beta)$$

and $Q = (\Sigma, Ancestor)$ be the reasoning task of finding all the Ancestor facts.

First, $Ancestor(\nu_0, Anna)$ is generated by triggering α on $Person(Anna)$. Next, $Person(\nu_0)$ derives from β, $Ancestor(\nu_1, \nu_0)$ is created by activating α, $Person(\nu_1)$ from β and so on. Due to the existential quantification in α and its interplay with the recursion in β, an infinite set $\bigcup_{i=0,...}\{Person(\nu_i), Ancestor(\nu_{i+1}, \nu_i)\}$ is generated, and the chase does not terminate.

Warded Datalog$^{\pm}$. The logic core of Vadalog is based on the powerful Warded Datalog$^{\pm}$ fragment [63]. Indeed, it encompasses both a high expressive power, capturing all SPARQL queries under OWL 2 QL entailment regime and set semantics, as well as a very good trade-off with data complexity, featuring PTIME for the reasoning [32]. To achieve this, it employs the syntactic restriction known as *wardedness*, which tames the propagation of labelled nulls in the chase by constraining the presence of body variables that can bind to such nulls and also appear in the rule head. More formally, let Σ be a set of rules and $p[i]$ a position (i.e., the i-th term of a predicate p with arity k, where $i = 1, \ldots, k$). We define $p[i]$ as *affected* if (i) p appears in a rule in Σ with an existentially quantified variable ($\exists$-*variable*) in the i-th term or, (ii) there is a rule in Σ such that a universally quantified variable ($\forall$-*variable*) is only in affected body positions and in $p[i]$ in the head. A $\forall$-variable x is *harmful*, wrt a rule σ in Σ, if x appears only in affected positions in σ, otherwise it is *harmless*. If the harmful variable also appears in *head(σ)*, it is *dangerous* [62]. Thus, Σ is *warded* if, for each rule σ $\in \Sigma$, all the dangerous variables only appear in a single body atom, called *ward*, which only shares harmless variables with other atoms in *body(σ)*. In Example 1, α is an existential rule that introduces the affected position in Ancestor[1], while β features a dangerous variable y in the ward Ancestor.

Isomorphic Chase. While in theory Warded Datalog$^\pm$ is known to be decidable and to keep the reasoning task PTIME, developing an algorithm to achieve such goals in practice is by no means trivial. Specifically, the Vadalog implementation employs a version of the oblivious chase known as *isomorphic*. It is based on a *firing condition* of the applicable homomorphisms that limits their activation and ensures chase termination. Such condition consists in performing a check of isomorphism (i.e., same predicate name, same constants in same positions and bijection between the labelled nulls) between the fact that results from the application of the current homomorphism and the ones that have already been generated at previous chase steps. If such an isomorphism occurs, the generation of this fact is suppressed, hence the chase steps starting from it are not performed and the descending portions of the chase graph rooted in it are pruned. In fact, it can be proved that the facts that would otherwise be created from such chase steps would be in turn isomorphic copies of others already in the chase—being their origins isomorphic—and therefore uninformative for query answering [40]. With reference to Example 1, we apply the isomorphic chase and we observe that the procedure terminates. Indeed, Person(ν_1) is isomorphic with Person(ν_0), therefore it is not generated and the chase graph is pruned. Algorithm 1 provides the pseudocode of the isomorphic chase. A description of the algorithm follows.

Algorithm 1. Isomorphic Chase Algorithm.

1: **function** ISOMORPHIC_CHASE(D, Σ, Q)
2:    *chase* $= D$ ▷ chase instance is initialized
3:    $H = $ init_structure(D, Σ)   ▷ structure with applicable homomorphisms
4:    **while not** H.is_empty() **do**
5:        $h = H$.poll_first()
6:        $p = $ apply(Σ, h)   ▷ apply current homomorphism and derive new fact
7:        **if** check_isomorphism($p, chase$) **then**   ▷ isomorphic facts check
8:            *chase* $= chase \cup \{p\}$
9:            $H = $ update_structure(Σ, p)
10:    **return** answer(Q, *chase*)

The algorithm takes as input a database D, a set Σ of Warded TGDs and a query Q. The output of the algorithm is the answer to Q. First of all, the chase instance *chase* that stores the facts generated during the procedure is initialized to D and corresponds to the initial chase state (line 2). A data structure H is employed to store, at each step of the procedure, all the applicable homomorphisms (line 3). While H is not empty, the next applicable homomorphism h to activate is extracted from H (line 5), and a new fact p is generated (line 6). Now the isomorphism check occurs. If p is not isomorphic with a fact already present in *chase*, then it is added to the current chase instance (lines 7–8). Finally, the new applicable homomorphisms, derived from p and Σ, are added to H (line 9). If H is empty, that is, all the applicable homomorphisms have already been triggered, then the answer to Q is evaluated and the procedure terminates (line 10).

Harmful Join Elimination. The applicability of the isomorphic chase in Vadalog is corroborated by the *reasoning boundedness* property of the Warded fragment, which states that facts derived from isomorphic origins are isomorphic, thus uninformative for the reasoning task. However, as a necessary condition to exploit this property and sustain decidability of the task while preserving correctness, it can be proved that the set of rules in the scenario is required to be in a *harmless* form, i.e., without rules featuring joins in the body between variables affected by existential quantification (namely, *harmful join rules*). A warded program not featuring harmful join rules belongs to its sub-fragment *Harmless Warded Datalog$^{\pm}$*. Indeed, during the chase, rules with such joins could activate on labelled nulls. Therefore, suppressing isomorphic facts that carry these nulls could inhibit rule activation and affect reasoning correctness. For details regarding the theory behind this section, we refer the reader to our dedicated works [9,11,12,40]. Here, we provide an intuition of such issue and its solution via the following example.

Example 2. Company merger scenario modeled with a set of warded TGDs.

$$\text{Company}(x) \rightarrow \exists c \ \text{CEO}(x,c) \qquad (\alpha)$$

$$\text{Merges}(x,y) \wedge \text{CEO}(x,c) \rightarrow \text{CEO}(y,c) \qquad (\beta)$$

$$\text{Corporation}(x,y) \rightarrow \exists c \ \text{CEO}(x,c), \text{CEO}(y,c) \qquad (\gamma)$$

$$\text{CEO}(x,c) \wedge \text{CEO}(y,c) \rightarrow \text{Corporation}(x,y) \qquad (\delta)$$

For each company x there exists a CEO c (rule α). If x merges with a company y, c also becomes CEO of y (rule β). If x and y have a common CEO, they are in the same corporation (rule δ) and vice versa (rule γ). Consider the database instance $D = \{ Company(Hsb), \ Company(Iba), \ Merges(Hsb,Iba) \}$ and the query Q: "what are all the entailed Corporations?" as ontological reasoning task.

Let us first employ the standard oblivious chase. It can be observed that, while the set of corporations is finite, the chase does not terminate. Intuitively, $\text{CEO}(Hsb,\nu_0)$ and $\text{CEO}(Iba,\nu_1)$ are generated first by triggering α on Company(Hsb) and Company(Iba), respectively. Next, $\text{CEO}(Iba,\nu_0)$ derives from β and Corporation(Hsb,Iba) is obtained via the join on ν_0 in δ. Then, $\text{CEO}(Hsb,\nu_2)$ and $\text{CEO}(Iba,\nu_2)$ are created by activating γ, β and so on. Indeed, due to the existential quantification in rule γ and its interplay with the recursions in rules β and δ, an infinite set $\bigcup_{i=0,\dots} \{\text{CEO}(Hsb, \nu_i), \ \text{CEO}(Iba, \nu_i)\}$ is generated.

On the other hand, employing the isomorphic chase is not feasible either, due to the harmful join in rule δ. Indeed, CEO(Iba,ν_0) is isomorphic with CEO(Iba,ν_1), yet it cannot be pruned without blocking the activation of the join in δ with CEO(Hsb,ν_0), essential to create Corporation(Hsb,Iba) and to answer Q correctly.

Disarming Warded Datalog$^\pm$. In presence of programs without harmful joins the isomorphic chase can be employed without affecting the correctness or the computational complexity of the reasoning. However, restricting the Warded fragment to its Harmless Warded counterpart is not a desirable solution, since it affects the expressive power available to the Vadalog system implementing it. With the goal of preventing these syntactic limitations and enabling the evaluation of reasoning settings such as the one in Example 2, we developed *Harmful Join Elimination* (HJE), a technique to solve the *disarmament problem*, that is, to rewrite a set Σ of Warded Datalog$^\pm$ rules in input to the reasoner into a set Σ' of Harmless Warded rules that is equivalent to Σ (i.e., $chase(D, \Sigma) = chase(D, \Sigma')$ modulo fact isomorphism for each database D).

HJE Algorithm. We now provide an intuition behind HJE. Please refer to our dedicated work [11] for a detailed discussion of the algorithm. Without loss of generality (as more complex joins can be broken into multiple steps [25]), let $\rho : A(x_1, y_1, h) \wedge B(x_2, y_2, h) \rightarrow \exists z\ C(\overline{x}, z)$ be a harmful join rule in a set Σ of Warded Datalog$^\pm$ rules, where A, B and C are atoms, A[3] and B[3] are affected positions, $x_1, x_2 \subseteq \overline{x}$, $y_1, y_2 \subseteq \overline{y}$ are disjoint tuples of harmless variables or constants and h is a harmful variable. The goal of HJE is to replace ρ with a set of harmless rules that cover the generation of all the facts originally derived from activating the harmful join, thus preserving reasoning correctness.

The first step of the procedure consists in determining the sequences of *causes of affectedness*, that is, the rules involved in the propagation of the *affectedness* (i.e., the labelled nulls in the chase) from the existential rules to the variables involved in the harmful join. They can be distinguished into *direct causes*, i.e., existential rules that cause a position to be affected, and *indirect causes*, i.e., rules that propagate the affectedness from a direct cause to ρ. In Example 2, the rules α and γ are direct causes of affectedness, whereas β is an indirect one. The sequences of causes for the atom CEO_k ($k \in \{1,2\}$, in order of appearance in δ) are: $\Gamma_{CEO_k1} = [\alpha]$, $\Gamma_{CEO_k2} = [\beta, \alpha]$, $\Gamma_{CEO_k3} = [\gamma]$, $\Gamma_{CEO_k4} = [\beta, \gamma]$.

Once all the sequences of causes of affectedness have been determined, the algorithm composes ρ back along each possible sequence, from the last indirect causes to the direct ones, via the well-known *unfolding* and *folding* operations [4].

The results of the compositions for ρ are modeled via the *harmful unfolding tree* (hu-tree) T, a rule-labelled tree-like structure where: (i) the root is labelled by ρ; (ii) for each sequence of causes, there exists a root-to-leaf path whose nodes are labelled by the result of unfolding (and folding, if recursive) their parent nodes with the next cause in the sequence; (iii) the leaves are harmless rules that cover the generation of all the facts derived in the chase from activating ρ on labelled nulls. Figure 2 shows the hu-tree T of Example 2. Specifically, the figure in the middle depicts the sequences of unfoldings (blue arrows) and foldings (green arrows) with the causes, from δ to the leaves with the resulting harmless rules; the left figure illustrates more in detail a single root-to-leaf path, whereas the right figure provides an application of folding over β.

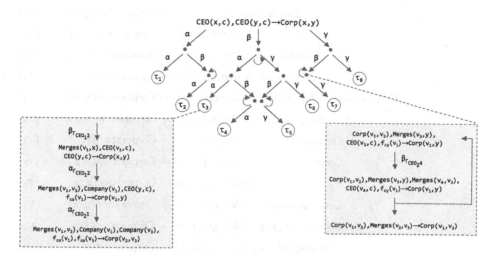

Fig. 2. Hu-tree T of Example 2, with unfolding (blue) and folding (green) compositions.

Finally, the leaves of the hu-tree are added to the new Harmless Warded set Σ', whereas the harmful join rule ρ is removed. Regarding Example 2, the full set Σ' is provided below: τs are leaves resulting from unfolding, whereas υs derive from folding. The algorithm shows an exponential behaviour with respect to the number of causes of affectedness. Intuitively, this is due to the worst-case generation of a distinct hu-path in the hu-tree for each subset of the causes. Yet, such exponential blowup in the number of generated rules is data independent and it does not affect the performance of reasoning tasks.

HJE is integrated into the *logic optimizer* of the Vadalog system, the component responsible for applying the required rewriting steps to the program before the reasoner processes it [25]. This enables reasoning termination and decidability over recursive Warded settings with harmful joins without affecting the expressive power of the Warded fragment or correctness. We close this section by listing the output facts of the query Q for Example 2: {Corporation(*Hsb,Hsb*), Corporation(*Iba,Iba*), Corporation(*Hsb,Iba*), Corporation(*Iba,Hsb*)}.

$$\text{Company}(x) \rightarrow \exists c\; \text{CEO}(x,c) \qquad (\alpha)$$

$$\text{Merges}(x,y) \wedge \text{CEO}(x,c) \rightarrow \text{CEO}(y,c) \qquad (\beta)$$

$$\text{Corporation}(x,y) \rightarrow \exists c\; \text{CEO}(x,c), \text{CEO}(y,c) \qquad (\gamma)$$

$$\text{Company}(x) \rightarrow \text{Corporation}(x,x) \qquad (\tau_1)$$

$$\text{Company}(x) \wedge \text{Merges}(x,y) \rightarrow \text{Corporation}(x,y) \qquad (\tau_2)$$

$$\text{Company}(x) \wedge \text{Merges}(x,y) \rightarrow \text{Corporation}(y,x) \qquad (\tau_3)$$

$$\text{Company}(x) \wedge \text{Merges}(x,y) \wedge \text{Merges}(x,z) \rightarrow \text{Corporation}(y,z) \qquad (\tau_4)$$

$$\text{Corporation}(x,y) \wedge \text{Merges}(x,w) \wedge \text{Merges}(x,z) \rightarrow \text{Corporation}(w,z) \qquad (\tau_5)$$

$$\text{Corporation}(x,y) \wedge \text{Merges}(x,z) \rightarrow \text{Corporation}(x,z) \qquad (\tau_6)$$

$$\text{Corporation}(x,y) \wedge \text{Merges}(x,z) \rightarrow \text{Corporation}(z,x) \qquad (\tau_7)$$

$$\text{Corporation}(x,y) \rightarrow \text{Corporation}(x,x) \qquad (\tau_8)$$

$$\text{Corporation}(x,y) \wedge \text{Merges}(x,z) \rightarrow \text{Corporation}(y,z) \qquad (\upsilon_1)$$

$$\text{Corporation}(x,y) \wedge \text{Merges}(x,z) \rightarrow \text{Corporation}(z,y) \qquad (\upsilon_2)$$

$$\text{Corporation}(x,y) \wedge \text{Merges}(y,z) \rightarrow \text{Corporation}(x,z) \qquad (\upsilon_3)$$

$$\text{Corporation}(x,y) \wedge \text{Merges}(y,z) \rightarrow \text{Corporation}(z,x) \qquad (\upsilon_4)$$

Availability. The Vadalog system has been originally developed at the University of Oxford, and is available upon request with the license depending on the use case (academic setting, commercial setting).

3 The Extensions

3.1 Arithmetics and Aggregation

In order to handle real-world data science applications, one usually requires certain aggregate functions such as *sum, min, max* or *count*. Vadalog supports a restricted notion of aggregation, namely, monotonic aggregation [40,78,91] where monotonicity w.r.t. set containment is preserved. This means, that the value of intermediate aggregation values only increase/decrease monotonicly towards the maximum/minimum value. Enforcing monotonicity is in particular useful in recursive settings as a monotonic aggregate function usually converges towards a fixpoint or towards infinity and the "final value" is the desired aggregate result (i.e., one can consider the minimum/maximum value of the produced sequence as the final value). Note however, that the derivation of the intermediary results is non-deterministic as these values depend on the sequence of the chase.

Consider the following well-studied example of counting the number of paths in a direct acyclic graph, where $\text{Subsidiary}(x,y)$ describes that x is a subsidiary of y, and $\text{PathCount}(x,y,z)$ describes the number of paths z between nodes x and y

$$\text{Subsidiary}(x, y), s = mcount(1, y) \rightarrow \text{PathCount}(x, y, s) \quad (1)$$

$$\text{PathCount}(x, y, p), \text{Subsidiary}(y, z), s = mcount(p, y) \rightarrow \text{PathCount}(x, z, s) \quad (2)$$

$$\text{PathCount}(x, y, p), s = max(p) \rightarrow \text{PathCountFinal}(x, y, s) \quad (3)$$

and the following initial dataset:

Subsidiary(A, B).   Subsidiary(A, C).   Subsidiary(D, C).   Subsidiary(C, B).

Rule 1 derives PathCount($A, B, 1$), PathCount($A, C, 1$), PathCount($D, C, 1$) and PathCount($C, B, 1$). Rule 2 derives PathCount($A, B, 2$) and PathCount($D, B, 1$). Rule 3 takes the maximum value of each of the PathCount, i.e., deriving the values PathCountFinal($A, B, 2$), PathCountFinal($A, C, 1$), PathCountFinal($D, C, 1$) and PathCountFinal($C, B, 1$) and PathCountFinal($D, B, 1$).

Carefully studying the results, one may asks oneself how these rules derive a path count of 2 between (A, B), i.e., PathCount($A, B, 2$), as one path is derived via Rule 1 and the other path via Rule 2. This is given, as an aggregation result is uniquely identified by (i) the aggregation type (e.g., count), (ii) the predicate in the head, (iii) the position of the aggregate in the head, and (iv) the group-by values that are implicitly given by co-occurrence in the head. As all of this criteria match in Rule 1 and 2, the same aggregation state is used.

It remains to discuss, why y, called a contribution value, is used in the aggregation function. While in the given example, this value has no impact, adding another edge Subsidiary(A, D) will highlight why this value is important. This contribution value tells the system that we are only interested in the maximum value in the computation of the count. This is, when computing the aggregation for the connection (A, B) instead of considering PathCount($A, C, 1$) and PathCount($A, C, 2$) in the final aggregation, always the highest value is considered only.

3.2   Interfacing with the Real World

As we have seen in the previous section, with Vadalog we are able to entail new facts based on existing facts. Today's data is usually stored in existing relational database systems, csv files, graph databases or other data structures extended with hard-coded facts in the program. Vadalog supports various storage engines and allows to combine different ones in a single program. This is, one can use for example a Cypher and SQL query in the input and output the facts of a predicate to a CSV file. The following example demonstrates the combination of the data source by merging the ownership of companies stored in different storage engines:

```
@input("own1").
@bind("own1", "postgres", "share_db", "tbl_own").
@input("own2").
@qbind("own2","neo4j", "share_graph",
```

```
        "MATCH (a)-[o:Share]->(b) RETURN a.id, b.id, o.shares").
@output("own").
@bind("own","csv","/shares","result.csv").
own3(A,T,0.7).
own3(B,T,0.3).
own :- own1.
own :- own2.
own :- own3.
```

In total, this example uses four different kind of annotations: @INPUT, @OUTPUT, @BIND, and @QBIND. The annotations @INPUT and @OUTPUT mark a predicate as input/output, telling the system that the entry should be read/written to the given source in the @BIND/@QBIND annotation. The "q" in @QBIND stands for query bind, so accessing the storage engine by a query, while the @BIND annotation access the full "table". In summary, the syntax can be described as

```
@bind("atomName", "dataSource", "outerContainer", "innerContainer").
@qbind("atomName","dataSource", "outerContainer", "query").
```

and is heavily used in all of our real-world applications to interact with the data sources.

3.3   Temporal Reasoning

Reasoning over temporal phenomena is one of the crucial tasks identified while using Vadalog in industrial applications. Reasoning over changes in shareholding settings, monitoring systems for a certain time-period after an event and many more tasks turned out to be of important interest. This is, why we recently worked on a native temporal extension for Vadalog [28,37–39]. Our implementation is based on DatalogMTL [47,95] and uses the operators from the metric temporal logic in the Vadalog system.

In detail, each fact is equipped with a rational interval of the form $\varrho = \langle t_1, t_2 \rangle$, where $t_1, t_2 \in \mathbb{Q} \cup \{-\infty, \infty\}$ and $\langle$ and $\rangle$ either denote open "()" or closed "[]" intervals. For example, to say that an suspicious event was ongoing for five time units starting at time point 3, one writes the fact SuspiciousEventDuration@$[3, 8)$.

In order to manipulate the intervals of facts in rules, Vadalog support the $\boxminus_\varrho$, $\boxplus_\varrho$, $\diamondsuit_\varrho$, $\diamonddsuit_\varrho$, $\mathcal{S}_\varrho$ and $\mathcal{U}_\varrho$ operators in the body of the rule, where ϱ is a non-negative interval. The $\boxminus_\varrho$ and $\boxplus_\varrho$ require that a fact is valid for each relative time point in the interval ϱ in the past/future, while the $\diamondsuit$ and $\diamonddsuit$ operator requires that some point in that interval is valid. For example, to express the given suspicious event duration with a rule, where the suspicious event fires at time point 3, i.e., one has a fact SuspiciousEventFired@3, the corresponding rule would be given as follows

$$\diamondsuit_{[0,5)} \text{SuspiciousEventFired} \rightarrow \text{SuspiciousEventDuration}$$

and to say that when there was a contiguous duration for a suspicious event of five time units, then there is an operational investigation ten time units later, one would write a rule as follows:

$$\boxminus_{[10,15)}\mathsf{SuspiciousEventDuration} \rightarrow \mathsf{OperationalInvestigation}$$

Note, that is presented in Sect. 2.3, the rule in Vadalog would look as follows:

```
OperationalInvestigation :- [-][10,15) SuspiciousEventDuration
```

DatalogMTL itself has been extended in several directions, such as stratified negation, existentials, monotonic aggregation, tractable fragments and so on. While each of these topics is interesting by its own, the goal of this section is to provide a general overview of the temporal capabilities of the temporal extension of Vadalog. However, we want to note that each extension of DatalogMTL shares similar characteristics as the non-temporal counterpart with some additional extras to handle the temporal domain (e.g., different kinds of temporal aggregations, whether existentials along the timeline should be treated equivalent, etc.). For details of the language and each of these extensions we refer the reader to one of the many DatalogMTL papers.

3.4 Machine Learning

As has been seen in the previous sections KGs allow us to represent and reason about knowledge in many different ways. Yet, most real-world KGs such as Freebase [45], WordNet [80], and YAGO [76] are inherently incomplete, which poses an obstacle for their immediate utilization in many applications. For instance, the nationality of approximately 75% of the people captured in the Freebase KG [98] is missing. Thus, much research has been invested in the task of *knowledge graph completion* (KGC), i.e. in automatically predicting these missing facts. KG embedding models have recently become a very popular technique for completing KGs, achieving promising results on KGC tasks [97]. In general, KG embedding models embed entities and relations as vectors over some field $\mathbb{K}$ and define a scoring function over these embeddings to quantify the plausibility of a fact to be true. To become more familiar with KG embedding models, their components and inner workings, we will investigate a simple KG embedding model called TransE [46] in more detail.

Before we can introduce TransE [46], we will in the following briefly introduce a simplified definition of KGs that is commonly used in the KG embedding community and in particular by TransE. Specifically, TransE defines a KG as a set of triples $r(h,t)$ over the set of relations $r \in \boldsymbol{R}$ and over the set of entities $h, t \in \boldsymbol{E}$. Typically, we refer to the entity h in a triple $r(h,t)$ as its head entity and we refer to the entity t as the tail entity of the triple. Of course there are more complex KG embedding models that can take KGs into account that consider facts of higher arities than two, but for simplicity we will stay with these definitions for now.

TransE. TransE [46] is the pioneering translational KG embedding model. Specifically it embeds each entity $e \in \boldsymbol{E}$ and each relation $r \in \boldsymbol{R}$ as a d-dimensional vector $\boldsymbol{e}, \boldsymbol{r} \in \mathbb{R}^d$. TransE embeddings capture a triple $r(h,t)$ to be true if $\boldsymbol{t} \approx \boldsymbol{h} + \boldsymbol{r}$, i.e. if the embedding of the head entity $\boldsymbol{h}$ translated by the embedding of the relation $\boldsymbol{r}$ is approximately equal to the embedding of the head entity $\boldsymbol{t}$. To be able to quantify the error of this approximation a scoring function is introduced. Specifically the scoring function $s : \mathbb{R}^d \times \mathbb{R}^d \times \mathbb{R}^d \to \mathbb{R}$ of TransE is defined as $s(h,r,t) = |\boldsymbol{t} - \boldsymbol{h} - \boldsymbol{r}|_p$, where $|.|_p$ represents the p-norm. Furthermore, to be able to optimize the score function the training data needs to be defined, which needs to consist of true and false facts. Typically, KGs specify solely positive knowledge, thus negative triples are generated by corrupting positive triples utilizing most commonly the local closed world assumption. Specifically, triples are corrupted by replacing the head h or tail t entity of the triple $r(h,t)$ with an entity $e_c \in \boldsymbol{E}$ such that the corrupted triple does not occur in training, validation, or testing data. Finally, the scoring function is typically optimized using gradient descent such that positive triples have a high score and such that negative triples have a low score. For the optimization process, commonly the margin-based ranking loss together with some strategy that samples corrupted triples in each iteration (called negative sampling strategy) is applied.

KG Embeddings in Vadalog. Next, we will investigate how we can apply and combine KG embedding models in Vadalog [93]. In the following code example a KG embedding model is loaded into Vadalog, trained on incomplete ownership information contained in our KG, and then used to predict missing ownership triples that could be enhanced with logical knowledge down the pipeline:

```
@library("KGE:", "tensorflow", "", "<path_to_KGE_model>").

training_set(["own", H, T], 1) :- own(H, T, Share).
training_set(["own", H, T], 0) :- own(H, _, _),
                                  own(_, T, _),
                                  not own(H, T, _).

training_size(name, C) :- training_set(In, Out),
                          C = KGE:fit(ID, In, Out)

to_predict(["own", H, T]) :- own(H, _, _),
                             own(_, T, _).

threshold(0.8).

KGE_own(H, T) :- to_predict(["own", H, T]),
                 Out = KGE:predict(["own", H, T]),
                 threshold(T),
                 Out > T.
```

Specifically, the annotation @library loads a KG embedding model written in Tensorflow into Vadalog, by providing the name of the model as the first argument, "tensorflow" as the second argument and the path to the KG embedding model as the fourth argument. Next, we need to define the data the model should train on. Therefore, we create a predicate called "training_set", containing the triple converted into a list as its first argument and the likelihood of the triple to be true, as its second argument (in this case 1 for true and 0 for false). We calculate the set of corrupted triples similarly to the description of the previous paragraphs. Yet, instead of corrupting triples with arbitrary entities we can exploit Vadalogs rules to constrain corrupted triples to plausible cases. Specifically, in the second training_set rule, we exclusively select head and tail entities for creating corrupted triples that have already occurred at least once in the considered predicate at the respective position. Of course, we can apply more complex logic at this point to restrict our set of corrupted triples to even more plausible cases.

Next, we fit the KG embedding by using the "KGE:fit" predicate, specifying the input to the KG embedding model with the *In* variable and the output of the KGE embedding with the *Out* variable. Next, we specify for which head and tail entity pairs we want to compute predictions for using the "to_predict" predicate. Specifically, in our code example we want to predict for any entity pair (h, t) that occurs either as the head or tail of an ownership triple whether (h, t) should be in an ownership relation. The predicate "threshold" then specifies the threshold of the normalized score, such that a triple should be predicted to be true. We have set the threshold in this example to 0.8. Finally, we predict for each of the entity pairs contained by "to_predict" whether they should be in an ownership relation. Specifically, we use the "KGE:predict" function, which takes as its argument the input to the KG embedding model and outputs the score "Out". If the score is greater than the threshold, then we want to predict the triple and since the predicted triples are uncertain we save them in the "KGE_own" predicate for future processing such as consistency checking.

Thereby, we have shown how KG embedding models can be integrated into Vadalog and we have briefly mentioned how Vadalog rules can be used to enhance the input (such as the corrupted triples) and the output (the predicted triples) of the KG embedding model. Extensive discussion of the use of embeddings in KGs can be found in [82,83] in particular a dedicated workshop series [89], and in particular in combination with logic-based reasoning in Vadalog [94]. Further information in general on Vadalog and Knowledge Graphs can be found in [67] and the reasoning [41] and embedding-focused [42] chapters. Challenges on parallelization are discussed in [52,65]. Further information on the overall VADA architecture can be found in [74].

4   The Applications

4.1   Corporate Governance

A first group of applications of Vadalog we developed on real-world use cases concerns the realm of *corporate governance*, i.e., *company control* and *ultimate controller* [36,75]. This realm is characterized by many entities (i.e., people and companies) that are highly interconnected (e.g., shareholding relationships) and well suited to be modeled in the form of a graph where nodes are shareholders and subsidiaries. At the same time, edges represent ownership relationships among them. This graph, also known as *company ownership graph*, constitutes the extensional component of our Financial Knowledge Graph. As company controls and ultimate controllers are central to many of other applications, the extracted information is used to enrich the Financial Knowledge Graph itself.

Company Control. Understanding the concentration and dispersion of control plays a crucial role in several contexts in which the Central Bank of Italy operates, e.g., economic research, banking supervision, monetary policy operations, and many more. According to a widely adopted assumption [60], corporate governance (or, company control) relates to the ability of a shareholder x to exert decision power on a subsidiary y by controlling the majority of its shares and, therefore, the voting power.

A company x controls a company y if: (i) x direcly owns more than 50% of the total equity of y; or, (ii) x controls a set of intermediary companies that joinly (i.e., summing their shares), and possibly together with x itself, own more that 50% of y.

In order to derive control edges, we formalized the definition with the two following Vadalog rules.

$$\mathsf{Company}(x) \rightarrow \mathsf{Control}(x,x) \quad (2)$$

$$\mathsf{Control}(x,y) \wedge \mathsf{Own}(y,z,w) \wedge v = sum(w, \langle y \rangle) \wedge v > 0.5 \rightarrow \mathsf{Control}(x,z) \quad (3)$$

We make the assumption that that every company controls on itself (Rule 2)[1]. Then, inductively, we define the control of x on z by summing the shares of z held by companies y, over all companies y controlled by x (Rule 3).

Ultimate Controller. It happens that a shareholder x is able to push decisions to company y through a controlled intermediary z which in turn owns more than the majority of the total equity of y and so directly controls y. In this case, z does not independently exert the decision power on y because it depends on x. In chains of control, the only investor able to act independently on the underlying firms is the one that resides on top of the chain. In the economic literature [92], this subject is defined as *ultimate controller* and is the one who actually takes decisions.

---

[1] This formalization of the base case is slightly different from the natural definition but commonly assumed in the literature as it is more compact and formally equivalent.

Given a company y, an investor x (either a firm or an individual) is said to be the ultimate controller of y if: (i) x directly or indirectly controls y; and, (ii) x is not controlled by any other investor.

$$\text{Control}(x, y) \rightarrow \text{Controlled}(y) \qquad (4)$$

$$\text{Control}(x, y) \land not\ \text{Controlled}(x) \rightarrow \text{UltimateController}(x, y) \qquad (5)$$

Rule 4 collects all the companies controlled (either directly or indirectly) by at least one other firm. Then, the ultimate controller x of a company y is the one that controls it but, in turn, it is not controlled by any other firm (Rule 2).

4.2 Media Intelligence

Knowledge Graphs play a key role in the space of media intelligence, as is the case for Meltwater, innovation leader in the space of media intelligence. Similar to the case of corporate governance and central bank-level applications, the core entities in the graphs are *companies*. Key to such a knowledge graph is to provide *enrichments* to internal and external users which give added value through either defining signals to users of the platform, or enabling other AI tasks in the system.

While we cannot here show the exact details of the Knowledge Graph enrichments in this space, we can show analogous ones derived together with Meltwater as basis of recommender systems [51]. The key challenge here is that recommender systems typically are based on "low-level" features contained in the data, which works well if the low-level features are highly indicative of recommendations, but not so well if discriminative low-level features are not present, or highly-complex, domain-knowledge dependent combinations of low-level features are needed to understand a particular domain.

High-Level Features. Declarative languages, and in particular Vadalog are well-suited to capture high level features as it allows to express complex domain requirements as knowledge including (1) aggregation, (2) graph traversal, (3) integration of different data sources, and (4) exisential rules to reason about previously unknown information.

Let us consider such a high level feature in the abstracted space of movies, and in particular those of award-winning casts.

```
feature(User, "AwardWinningCast", Movie, Score) :-
    user(User),
    hasAwardWinningActor(Movie, Person, Award),
    awardScore(Award, AwardScore),
    Score = max(AwardScore).

hasAwardWinningActor(Movie, Person, Award) :-
    crew(Movie, PersonID, "Cast"),
    hasWonPrestigiousAward(Person, Award).

hasWonPrestigiousAward(Person, "Oscars") :-
```

```
oscarsAward(Nomination, Person, Movie, Year).

hasWonPrestigiousAward(Person, "BAFTA") :-
    baftaAward(Nomination, Person, Movie, Year).
```

We see combinations of defining high-level features, including aggregates, and including specific domain knowledge that is of high significance to the user of the knowledge graph. Further examples can be found in [51].

We conclude by the comment that while this represented a very simply, abstracted example, in the space of media intelligence, many advanced and very complex high-level features are used, but can highly exploit features such as (i)–(iv) mentioned above.

4.3 Supply Chains

Supply chains are one of the most critical networks underlying the function of modern society. The JRC Live, FH OÖ, Logistikum, Steyr, is one of the leading research and development centers in the area of logistics and supply chains. Knowledge Graphs can support many aspects of supply chains, including real-time visibility, detection and prediction of bottlenecks, crisis management, disaster response, sustainability, resilience, and many other aspects [19,20]. Some recent graph-based analyses include the connection between network central measures and supply chain performance [96].

A good example is structurally very similar to analysing company networks in other situations – showing both the use of Knowledge Graphs and the added value. Assume the following:

- Supplier S is dependent on buyer B when
  1. buyer is responsible for more than 25% of the sales volume or
  2. more than 25% of sales goes to a set of buyers each of which is dependent on B
- Buyer is dependent on supplier, if the supplier is single supplier

Note that the value of 25% is picked arbitrarily in this case, and can be adjusted – or may be provided from other information in the Knowledge Graph itself. Formulated as KG knowledge, we have:

$$\text{Sells}(S, B, P) \wedge P > 0.25 \rightarrow \text{Depends}(S, B) \quad (6)$$

$$\text{Sells}(S, B', P') \wedge \text{Depends}(B', B) \wedge V = msum(P', < B' >) \wedge V > 0.25$$
$$\rightarrow \text{Depends}(S, B) \quad (7)$$

What we see in the above example is in the first rule the direct dependence established established above the threshold, and in the second rule indirect dependence if the total of indirect contributions is above the threshold.

Another interesting aspect is concerned with temporal information. For example, consider a (simplified) example of transport paths: predictions of times taken for a transport paths depend on the starting times and mean times of particular sections of the path in the past:

$$\mathsf{Start}(X, T0) \wedge \mathsf{Section}(X, Y) \wedge Time = T0 + stat : mean(X, Y)$$
$$\rightarrow \mathsf{Path}(X, Y, Time) \quad (8)$$
$$\mathsf{Path}(X, Y, T1) \wedge \mathsf{Section}(Y, Z) \wedge Time = T1 + stat : mean(Y, Z)$$
$$\rightarrow \mathsf{Path}(X, Z, Time) \quad (9)$$

The first rule expresses that the initial section of a transport path's time can be estimated from previous statistical means. The second rule expresses that for further sections, the time can be computed from the previous sections' time and the statistical mean of the new section. We restrict ourselves to such a simple, illustrative example here and note that much more complex temporal relationships can be explored and formulated using temporal reasoning.

4.4   Collateral Eligibility

In the complex financial context, companies can not be considered as standalone entities but they are part of articulated ownerships structures, sometimes referred as *corporate groups*. The notion of *Integrated Ownership* has been introduced to help quantifying the ownership involvement of companies in such economic structures. Indeed, the simple shareholding information identifies a direct connection between two companies, in contrast, the Integrated Ownership encompasses the total ownership accumulated via multi-path and multi-hop shareholding relationships from company x to y.

Since the information related to the accumulated ownerships is crucial in many financial applications, such as the collateral eligibility, we formalized and encoded the Integrated Ownership computation task as a set of reasoning rules in the Vadalog language.

$$\mathsf{Own}(x, y, q) \wedge p = [x, y] \wedge v = msum(q) \rightarrow \mathsf{IOwn}(x, y, v, p) \quad (10)$$
$$\mathsf{IOwn}(x, z, q_1, p_1) \wedge \mathsf{IOwn}(z, y, q_2, p_2) \wedge p = p_1|p_2 \wedge v = msum(w_1 \times w_2, z)$$
$$\rightarrow \mathsf{IOwn}(x, y, v, p) \quad (11)$$

Close Links. The concern of collateral eligibility assumes particular importance when it comes to the assessment of creditworthiness. It entails estimating the risk of granting a loan to a company x guaranteed by securities issued by another company y. The Eurosystem only provides credits in qualified cases and only for adequate collateral [15]. Regulations for monetary policy of the European Central Bank [16] specify a set of standards that National Central Banks must follow when determining whether assets are eligible. For example, to access the credit, the National Central Banks of the Eurosystem do not permit a counterparty to provide collateral issued by a guarantor entity to whom it is linked via a *close links* relationship.

A counterparty x and its guarantor y are in a close link relationship if: (i) the total, either direct or indirect, ownership of y (resp. x) held by x (resp. y) is above 20% of the equity of y (resp. x); or (ii) a common third entity z owns, either directly or indirectly, 20% or more of the equity of both the counterparty and the guarantor.

To support the evaluation of the collateral eligibility, we employed an encoding of the given definition as a set of deductive rules in the Vadalog language [13,14,75], and let the KGMS automatically derive all the existing close link relationships among firms in the Financial Knowledge Graph of the Bank of Italy.

$$\mathsf{IOwn}(x,y,q) \wedge q \geq 0.2 \rightarrow \mathsf{CLinks}(x,y) \wedge \mathsf{CLinks}(y,x) \tag{12}$$

$$\mathsf{IOwn}(z,x,q) \wedge \mathsf{IOwn}(z,y,w) \wedge q \geq 0.2 \wedge w \geq 0.2$$
$$\rightarrow \mathsf{CLinks}(x,y) \wedge \mathsf{CLinks}(y,x) \tag{13}$$

In Rule 12, we derive the existence of a close links relationship between x and y (resp. y and y) if the total accumulated ownership of y held by x (resp. x held by y) is equal or greater than 20%. Finally, Rule 13 considers the last case of the definition in which a common third party z owns (still in terms of accumulated ownership) more than 20% of both.

4.5   Hostile Takeovers and Golden Powers

During the COVID-19 outbreak and, generally, in crisis times, the lowered share price may bait market players to pursue takeovers that may affect the public control of national companies of strategic relevance. A takeover is a typical corporate event in which the public control of a company moves from one shareholder to another; typically, it is a consequence of a share acquisition operation.

Many European countries have developed legal frameworks to protect national strategic companies from acquisitions that would bring the control of such companies outside national or European borders. Italy has the "Golden Powers" (GP) framework, allowing the Government to veto specific individual share acquisition operations. The application of the framework is far from trivial. Indeed, how can we tell whether a share acquisition operation is hiding a takeover attempt? Will an acquisition lead to a takeover? How can the Government intervene in order to proactively secure a strategic company acquiring or increasing its participation in it (technically, *investment beef-up*)? Furthermore, how to protect national assets against coordinated, collusive behaviors aiming at a hidden takeover?

We shown how these problems can be modeled as a rich set of reasoning tasks to analyze both reactive and proactive measures against takeover attempts, however intricate the setting where they take place. Specifically, such reasoning tasks are design to: (i) detect takeover attemps; (ii) suggest limits within which the framework may be exercised; (iii) show options for proactively secure companies.

While a full-detail description of all the scenarios we analyzed can be found in [22], we present here the one addressing the crucial problem of timely detecting a takeover.

Golden Power Check. Let T be a set of target companies (i.e., strategic national companies to be protected), V a set of attacking actors (e.g., companies operating outside national or European borders), and N a set of neutral companies. Let t be a acquisition operation issued by a market player x to buy an amount s of shares of a company y, with $x \in V$, $y \in T \cup N$.

The goal of this reactive scenario is to check whether the share acquisition operation t causes any company in V to gain control of any company in T. If it does, the framework suggests to consider the possibility to block t employing the Golden Power framework.

We formalized the scenario with the following Vadalog rules:

$$V(x) \wedge \neg V(y) \wedge \mathsf{Tx}(x, y, w) \rightarrow \mathsf{Own}(x, y, w) \tag{14}$$

$$V(x) \wedge \mathsf{T}(y) \wedge \mathsf{Control}(x, y) \rightarrow \mathsf{GPCheck}(x, y) \tag{15}$$

We first consider the transaction to be virtually applied and thus consolidating an ownership relationship over the strategic company y (Rule 14). Then, computing all companies in V that control at least one company in T, the reasoning process returns a list of takeovers caused by the single acquisition. If the list is empty, there is no need to employ Golden Power.

4.6 Smart Anonymization

Reasoning on Knowledge Graphs produces valuable business knowledge that could be shared to different stakeholders, both internal or external to the company, and with different visibility profiles. For instance, bank supervision data are required to be in full detail to be analyzed by supervisory bodes while an anatomized form can be publicly disseminated for statistical purposes.

In the context of data anonymity in surveys about families and individuals, the Bank of Italy has adopted the guidelines defined by the Italian national statistical office (ISTAT) in recent dissemination initiatives. Indications in the guidelines have been operationalized in the intensional component of the Knowledge Graph: a set of Vadalog rules are used to determine the confidentiality level of the data and allow to prevent identity disclosure and to intervene with ad-hoc anonymization.

We show a sample of the Vadalog rules used for increasing the anonymity of a dataset on a subset of its features, i.e., the Italian *fiscal code* (f), *age* (a), *region* (r) and *education* (e). The feature l represents the data anonymity level obtained during the process. Despite introducing the features addressed during the anonymization process, we recall that, as the variable scope is within each rule, given the same predicate in two distinct rules, the same feature is referenced by its position and not by the used variable names.

$$\text{Person}(f, a, r, e) \rightarrow \exists i \ \mathsf{P}(i, a, r, e, 0) \tag{16}$$

$$\mathsf{P}(i, a, r, e, l) \wedge 0 < a \leq 20 \rightarrow \mathsf{P}(i, 10, r, e, l + 1) \tag{17}$$

$$\mathsf{P}(i, a, r, e, l) \wedge f = mcount(i)/N \rightarrow \mathsf{FreqR}(a, r, f) \tag{18}$$

$$\mathsf{P}(i, a, r, e, l) \wedge \mathsf{FreqR}(a, r, f) \wedge f < F \rightarrow \exists x \ \mathsf{P}(i, a, x, e, l + 1) \tag{19}$$

Rule 16 generates a unique id for each input data replacing the *fiscal code* identifier. Rule 17 applies a value-normalization step for the feature *age* by setting a specific value for a whenever the condition $0 < a \leq 20$ is met. In Rule 18, the occurrence frequency f is derived for each pair *age-region*. Finally, in Rule 19, if the frequency f is below the safety threshold F (i.e. the data is not "statistically safe"), the feature r is dropped and replaced with the anonymized value x, increasing by one unit the anonymity level of the data. Features i and x are, therefore, generated within the program and are returned in replacement of *fiscal code* and *region* to reduce the overall confidentiality level of the data. These rules just show a partial combination of criteria; in the full Knowledge Graph, many more criteria can be combined together.

Let us consider another example, in which, for a firm, we collect information such as the *fiscal code* (f) and the *profit* (p). For a CEO, we know the *unique id* (i), day (d), month (m) and year (y) of birth, the company's *anonymized id* and the actual anonymity level (l).

$$\text{Firm}(f, p) \rightarrow \exists x \ \mathsf{F}(x, p, 0) \tag{20}$$

$$\mathsf{F}(x, p, l) \wedge p < P_0 \rightarrow \mathsf{F}(f, \text{``LOW''}, l + 1) \tag{21}$$

$$\mathsf{F}(x, p, l) \wedge P_0 \leq p < P_1 \rightarrow \mathsf{F}(f, \text{``MEDIUM''}, l + 1) \tag{22}$$

$$\mathsf{F}(x, p, l) \wedge p \geq P_1 \rightarrow \mathsf{F}(f, \text{``HIGH''}, l + 1) \tag{23}$$

$$\text{CEO}(i, d, m, y, x, l) \wedge \mathsf{F}(x, p, l) \wedge p = \text{``HIGH''} \rightarrow \exists k \ \mathsf{C}(i, k, m, y, x, l + 1) \tag{24}$$

In Rule 20, we drop the *fiscal code* strong identifier and generate a new unique id x. With Rules 21–23, we replace the numeric feature *profit* with a category (i.e., *low, medium* or *high*) depending on its value w.r.t. the thresholds P_0 and P_1; and we increase the anonymity level. Finally, we hide the day of birth for the CEO of a company having an "high" profit (Rule 24).

4.7   Anti-Money Laundering (AML)

The money laundering process is an activity that makes illegally-gained money appear legal by obfuscating its actual and illegal origin. Several stakeholders, such as central banks, financial intelligence units (FIUs), law enforcement agencies, and financial intermediaries, are involved in countering such a phenomenon. For instance, FIUs constantly collect and analyze suspicious transaction reports (STR) from those other actors and decide whether a financial transaction meets a definition of *suspicious* provided by some regulatory body. If so, the case goes for further legal follow-up.

We recently analyzed a comprehensive set of AML use cases and introduced our vision on a rule-based reasoning approach to AML.

While more complex use cases are described in [34], we propose here a one common use case which requires to evaluate the *suspiciousness scoring* of a STR s and then, if the case, explain why it is suspicious.

A well known money laundering pattern regards a person x that requests a fake load to a controlled bank by in order to justify illegally gained money: *A person x who is requesting a loan to a bank b of which he/she is the ultimate beneficial owner, i.e., a person who ultimately owns or controls the entity on whose behalf a transaction is being conducted (the bank in this case), may intend to launder unclean money via the bank.*

This pattern can be formalized and encoded in the Knowledge Graph with a single Vadalog rule.

$$\mathsf{STR}(x, b, s) \wedge \mathsf{Loan}(s) \wedge \mathsf{Family}(x, f) \wedge \mathsf{Control}(f, b) \rightarrow \mathsf{Suspicious}(s) \qquad (25)$$

In Rule 25, *STR(x,b,s)* is the suspicious transaction report about a loan s (whence *Loan(s)* requested by x to bank b; *Family(x, f)* models the fact that a person x is part of the family f; finally, *Control(f, b)* states that the family f controls the bank b.

Countless other applications could be presented here, more than there is available space. We just mention here the use for data acquisition, such as for DBLP [79] (also discussed in [30,55]), or for modelling of enterprise architecture [59].

Acknowledgements. This work has been funded by the Vienna Science and Technology Fund (WWTF) [10.47379/VRG18013], [10.47379/NXT22018], the Raison Data Royal Society grant, and the Christian Doppler Society (CDG) Josef Ressel Centre for Real-Time Value Network Visibility, Logistikum, University of Applied Sciences Upper Austria.

References

1. Guideline (eu) 2011/14 of the ecb. https://www.ecb.europa.eu/ecb/legal/pdf/l_33120111214en000100951.pdf
2. Thomson reuters launches first of its kind knowledge graph feed allowing financial services customers to accelerate their ai and digital strategies (2017). https://www.thomsonreuters.com/en/press-releases/2017/october/thomson-reuters-launches-first-of-its-kind-knowledge-graph-feed.html. Accessed 21 Sep 2022
3. Understanding news using the bloomberg knowledge graph (2019). https://speakerdeck.com/emeij/understanding-news-using-the-bloomberg-knowledge-graph. Accessed 21 Sep 2022
4. Afrati, F., Gergatsoulis, M., Toni, F.: Linearisability on datalog programs. Theor. Comput. Sci. **308**(1–3), 199–226 (2003)

5. Arming, S., Pichler, R., Sallinger, E.: Complexity of repair checking and consistent query answering. In: Martens, W., Zeume, T. (eds.) 19th International Conference on Database Theory, ICDT 2016, Bordeaux, France, March 15–18, 2016. LIPIcs, vol. 48, pp. 21:1–21:18. Schloss Dagstuhl - Leibniz-Zentrum für Informatik (2016). https://doi.org/10.4230/LIPIcs.ICDT.2016.21

6. Atzeni, P., Bellomarini, L., Iezzi, M., Sallinger, E., Vlad, A.: Augmenting logic-based knowledge graphs: the case of company graphs. In: KR4L@ ECAI, pp. 22–27 (2020)

7. Atzeni, P., Bellomarini, L., Iezzi, M., Sallinger, E., Vlad, A.: Weaving enterprise knowledge graphs: the case of company ownership graphs. In: EDBT, pp. 555–566 (2020)

8. Baget, J.F., Leclère, M., Mugnier, M.L.: Walking the decidability line for rules with existential variables. KR **10**, 466–476 (2010)

9. Baldazzi, T., Atzeni, P.: Warded datalog+/- reasoning in financial settings with harmful joins. In: Ramanath, M., Palpanas, T. (eds.) Proceedings of the Workshops of the EDBT/ICDT 2022 Joint Conference, Edinburgh, UK, 29 March 2022. CEUR Workshop Proceedings, vol. 3135. CEUR-WS.org (2022). http://ceur-ws.org/Vol-3135/EcoFinKG_2022_paper13.pdf

10. Baldazzi, T., Bellomarini, L., Favorito, M., Sallinger, E.: On the relationship between shy and warded datalog+/-. arXiv preprint arXiv:2202.06285 (2022)

11. Baldazzi, T., Bellomarini, L., Sallinger, E., Atzeni, P.: Eliminating harmful joins in warded datalog+/-. In: Moschoyiannis, S., Peñaloza, R., Vanthienen, J., Soylu, A., Roman, D. (eds.) RuleML+RR 2021. LNCS, vol. 12851, pp. 267–275. Springer, Cham (2021). https://doi.org/10.1007/978-3-030-91167-6_18

12. Baldazzi, T., Bellomarini, L., Sallinger, E., Atzeni, P.: Reasoning in warded datalog+/- with harmful joins. In: Amato, G., Bartalesi, V., Bianchini, D., Gennaro, C., Torlone, R. (eds.) Proceedings of the 30th Italian Symposium on Advanced Database Systems, SEBD 2022, Tirrenia (PI), Italy, June 19–22, 2022. CEUR Workshop Proceedings, vol. 3194, pp. 292–299. CEUR-WS.org (2022). http://ceur-ws.org/Vol-3194/paper35.pdf

13. Baldazzi, T., Benedetto, D., Brandetti, M., Vlad, A., Bellomarini, L., Sallinger, E.: Datalog-based reasoning with heuristics over knowledge graphs (2022)

14. Baldazzi, T., Benedetto, D., Brandetti, M., Vlad, A., Bellomarini, L., Sallinger, E.: Heuristic-based reasoning on financial knowledge graphs. In: EDBT/ICDT Workshops (2022)

15. Bank, E.C.: The use of credit claims as collateral for eurosystem credit operations, June 2013. https://www.ecb.europa.eu/pub/pdf/scpops/ecbocp148.pdf

16. Bank, E.C.: Guideline (eu) 2015/510 of the european central bank of 19 december 2014 on the implementation of the eurosystem monetary policy framework (ecb/2014/60), June 2014. http://data.europa.eu/eli/guideline/2015/510/oj

17. Barca, F., Becht, M.: The control of corporate Europe. Oxford University Press, European corporate governance network (2001)

18. Barceló, P., Pichler, R. (eds.): LNCS, vol. 7494. Springer, Heidelberg (2012). https://doi.org/10.1007/978-3-642-32925-8

19. Baru, C., et al.: Open knowledge network roadmap - powering the next data revolution (2022). https://nsf-gov-resources.nsf.gov/2022-09/OKN%20Roadmap%20-%20Report_v03.pdf

20. Baru, C., et al.: Open knowledge network roadmap - powering the next data revolution - appendix a (2022). https://nsf-gov-resources.nsf.gov/2022-09/OKN%20Roadmap%20-%20Appendix%20A$_v03$.pdf

21. Bellomarini, L., et al.: Reasoning on company takeovers: from tactic to strategy. Data Knowl. Eng. **141**, 102073 (2022)
22. Bellomarini, L., et al.: Reasoning on company takeovers during the COVID-19 crisis with knowledge graphs. In: RuleML+RR (Supplement). CEUR Workshop Proceedings, vol. 2644, pp. 145–156. CEUR-WS.org (2020)
23. Bellomarini, L., et al.: COVID-19 and company knowledge graphs: assessing golden powers and economic impact of selective lockdown via AI reasoning. CoRR abs/2004.10119 (2020). https://arxiv.org/abs/2004.10119
24. Bellomarini, L., Benedetto, D., Brandetti, M., Sallinger, E.: Exploiting the power of equality-generating dependencies in ontological reasoning. Proc. VLDB Endow. **16** 3967–3988 (2022)
25. Bellomarini, L., Benedetto, D., Gottlob, G., Sallinger, E.: Vadalog: a modern architecture for automated reasoning with large knowledge graphs. Inf. Syst. **105** 101528 (2020)
26. Bellomarini, L., Benedetto, D., Laurenza, E., Sallinger, E.: A framework for probabilistic reasoning on knowledge graphs. In: Building Bridges between Soft and Statistical Methodologies for Data Science . SMPS 2022. AISC, vol. 1433, pp. 48–56. Springer, Cham (2023). https://doi.org/10.1007/978-3-031-15509-3_7
27. Bellomarini, L., Blasi, L., Laurendi, R., Sallinger, E.: Financial data exchange with statistical confidentiality: a reasoning-based approach. In: EDBT, pp. 558–569. OpenProceedings.org (2021)
28. Bellomarini, L., Blasi, L., Nissl, M., Sallinger, E.: The temporal vadalog system. In: RuleML+RR. p. to appear (2022)
29. Bellomarini, L., Fakhoury, D., Gottlob, G., Sallinger, E.: Knowledge graphs and enterprise AI: the promise of an enabling technology. In: ICDE, pp. 26–37. IEEE (2019)
30. Bellomarini, L., et al.: Data science with vadalog: bridging machine learning and reasoning. In: Abdelwahed, E.H., Bellatreche, L., Golfarelli, M., Méry, D., Ordonez, C. (eds.) MEDI 2018. LNCS, vol. 11163, pp. 3–21. Springer, Cham (2018). https://doi.org/10.1007/978-3-030-00856-7_1
31. Bellomarini, L., Galano, G., Nissl, M., Sallinger, E.: Rule-based blockchain knowledge graphs: declarative AI for solving industrial blockchain challenges. In: RuleML+RR (Supplement). CEUR Workshop Proceedings, vol. 2956. CEUR-WS.org (2021)
32. Bellomarini, L., Gottlob, G., Pieris, A., Sallinger, E.: Swift logic for big data and knowledge graphs. In: IJCAI, pp. 2–10. ijcai.org (2017)
33. Bellomarini, L., Laurenza, E., Sallinger, E.: Rule-based anti-money laundering in financial intelligence units: experience and vision. In: RuleML+RR (Supplement). CEUR Workshop Proceedings, vol. 2644, pp. 133–144. CEUR-WS.org (2020)
34. Bellomarini, L., Laurenza, E., Sallinger, E.: Rule-based anti-money laundering in financial intelligence units: experience and vision. In: RuleML+ RR (Supplement) (2020)
35. Bellomarini, L., Laurenza, E., Sallinger, E., Sherkhonov, E.: Reasoning under uncertainty in knowledge graphs. In: Gutiérrez-Basulto, V., Kliegr, T., Soylu, A., Giese, M., Roman, D. (eds.) RuleML+RR 2020. LNCS, vol. 12173, pp. 131–139. Springer, Cham (2020). https://doi.org/10.1007/978-3-030-57977-7_9
36. Bellomarini, L., Magnanimi, D., Nissl, M., Sallinger, E.: Neither in the programs nor in the data: mining the hidden financial knowledge with knowledge graphs and reasoning. In: Bitetta, V., Bordino, I., Ferretti, A., Gullo, F., Ponti, G., Severini, L. (eds.) MIDAS 2020. LNCS (LNAI), vol. 12591, pp. 119–134. Springer, Cham (2021). https://doi.org/10.1007/978-3-030-66981-2_10

37. Bellomarini, L., Nissl, M., Sallinger, E.: Monotonic aggregation for temporal datalog. In: RuleML+RR (Supplement). CEUR Workshop Proceedings, vol. 2956. CEUR-WS.org (2021)
38. Bellomarini, L., Nissl, M., Sallinger, E.: Query evaluation in datalogmtl - taming infinite query results. CoRR abs/2109.10691 (2021)
39. Bellomarini, L., Nissl, M., Sallinger, E.: iTemporal: an extensible generator of temporal benchmarks. In: ICDE, pp. 2021–2033. IEEE (2022)
40. Bellomarini, L., Sallinger, E., Gottlob, G.: The vadalog system: datalog-based reasoning for knowledge graphs. VLDB **11**(9), 975–987 (2018)
41. Bellomarini, L., Sallinger, E., Vahdati, S.: Chapter 2 Knowledge graphs: the layered perspective. In: Janev, V., Graux, D., Jabeen, H., Sallinger, E. (eds.) Knowledge Graphs and Big Data Processing. LNCS, vol. 12072, pp. 20–34. Springer, Cham (2020). https://doi.org/10.1007/978-3-030-53199-7_2
42. Bellomarini, L., Sallinger, E., Vahdati, S.: Chapter 6 Reasoning in knowledge graphs: an embeddings spotlight. In: Janev, V., Graux, D., Jabeen, H., Sallinger, E. (eds.) Knowledge Graphs and Big Data Processing. LNCS, vol. 12072, pp. 87–101. Springer, Cham (2020). https://doi.org/10.1007/978-3-030-53199-7_6
43. Berger, G., Gottlob, G., Pieris, A., Sallinger, E.: The space-efficient core of vadalog. ACM Trans. Database Syst. **47**(1), 1:1–1:46 (2022). https://doi.org/10.1145/3488720
44. Bergman, M.K.: A common sense view of knowledge graphs (2019)
45. Bollacker, K.D., Cook, R.P., Tufts, P.: Freebase: a shared database of structured general human knowledge. In: Proceedings of the Twenty-Second AAAI Conference on Artificial Intelligence, 22–26 July 2007, Vancouver, British Columbia, Canada, pp. 1962–1963. AAAI Press (2007)
46. Bordes, A., Usunier, N., García-Durán, A., Weston, J., Yakhnenko, O.: Translating embeddings for modeling multi-relational data. In: Burges, C.J.C., Bottou, L., Ghahramani, Z., Weinberger, K.Q. (eds.) Advances in Neural Information Processing Systems 26: 27th Annual Conference on Neural Information Processing Systems 2013, pp. 2787–2795. Proceedings of a meeting held, 5–8 December 2013, Lake Tahoe, Nevada, United States (2013)
47. Brandt, S., Kalayci, E.G., Kontchakov, R., Ryzhikov, V., Xiao, G., Zakharyaschev, M.: Ontology-based data access with a Horn fragment of metric temporal logic. In: AAAI, pp. 1070–1076. AAAI Press (2017)
48. Calì, A., Gottlob, G., Kifer, M.: Taming the infinite chase: query answering under expressive relational constraints. J. Artif. Intell. Res. **48**, 115–174 (2013)
49. Calì, A., Gottlob, G., Lukasiewicz, T.: A general datalog-based framework for tractable query answering over ontologies. J. Web Semant. **14**, 57–83 (2012)
50. Calì, A., Gottlob, G., Lukasiewicz, T., Marnette, B., Pieris, A.: Datalog+/-: a family of logical knowledge representation and query languages for new applications. In: 2010 25th Annual IEEE LICS, pp. 228–242. IEEE (2010)
51. Clearman, J., et al.: Feature engineering and explainability with vadalog: a recommender systems application. In: Alviano, M., Pieris, A. (eds.) Datalog 2.0 2019–3rd International Workshop on the Resurgence of Datalog in Academia and Industry co-located with the 15th International Conference on Logic Programming and Nonmonotonic Reasoning (LPNMR 2019) at the Philadelphia Logic Week 2019, Philadelphia, PA (USA), 4–5 June 2019. CEUR Workshop Proceedings, vol. 2368, pp. 39–43. CEUR-WS.org (2019). http://ceur-ws.org/Vol-2368/paper4.pdf
52. Csar, T., Lackner, M., Pichler, R., Sallinger, E.: Winner determination in huge elections with mapreduce. In: Singh, S., Markovitch, S. (eds.) Proceedings of the

Thirty-First AAAI Conference on Artificial Intelligence, 4–9 February 2017, San Francisco, California, USA, pp. 451–458. AAAI Press (2017). http://aaai.org/ocs/index.php/AAAI/AAAI17/paper/view/14894

53. Ding, W., Chaudhri, V.K., Chittar, N., Konakanchi, K.: JEL: applying end-to-end neural entity linking in jpmorgan chase. In: AAAI, pp. 15301–15308. AAAI Press (2021)

54. FATF: Transparency and Beneficial Ownership (2016). http://www.fatf-gafi.org/media/fatf/documents/reports/Guidance-transparency-beneficial-ownership.pdf. Accessed 17 Jan 2020

55. Fayzrakhmanov, R.R., Sallinger, E., Spencer, B., Furche, T., Gottlob, G.: Browserless web data extraction: challenges and opportunities. In: Champin, P., Gandon, F., Lalmas, M., Ipeirotis, P.G. (eds.) Proceedings of the 2018 World Wide Web Conference on World Wide Web, WWW 2018, Lyon, France, 23–27 April 2018, pp. 1095–1104. ACM (2018). https://doi.org/10.1145/3178876.3186008

56. Feinerer, I., Pichler, R., Sallinger, E., Savenkov, V.: On the undecidability of the equivalence of second-order tuple generating dependencies. In: Barceló, P., Tannen, V. (eds.) Proceedings of the 5th Alberto Mendelzon International Workshop on Foundations of Data Management, Santiago, Chile, 9–12 May 2011. CEUR Workshop Proceedings, vol. 749. CEUR-WS.org (2011). http://ceur-ws.org/Vol-749/paper5.pdf

57. Feinerer, I., Pichler, R., Sallinger, E., Savenkov, V.: On the undecidability of the equivalence of second-order tuple generating dependencies. Inf. Syst. **48**, 113–129 (2015). https://doi.org/10.1016/j.is.2014.09.003

58. Furche, T., Gottlob, G., Neumayr, B., Sallinger, E.: Data wrangling for big data: towards a lingua franca for data wrangling. In: Pichler, R., da Silva, A.S. (eds.) Proceedings of the 10th Alberto Mendelzon International Workshop on Foundations of Data Management, Panama City, Panama, 8–10 May 2016. CEUR Workshop Proceedings, vol. 1644. CEUR-WS.org (2016). http://ceur-ws.org/Vol-1644/paper20.pdf

59. Glaser, P., Ali, S.J., Sallinger, E., Bork, D.: Model-based construction of enterprise architecture knowledge graphs. In: Almeida, J.P.A., Karastoyanova, D., Guizzardi, G., Montali, M., Maggi, F.M., Fonseca, C.M. (eds.) Enterprise Design, Operations, and Computing - 26th International Conference, EDOC 2022, Bozen-Bolzano, Italy, 3–7 October 2022, Proceedings. LNCS, vol. 13585, pp. 57–73. Springer, Cham (2022). https://doi.org/10.1007/978-3-031-17604-3_4

60. Glattfelder, J.B.: Ownership networks and corporate control: mapping economic power in a globalized world. Ph.D. thesis, ETH Zurich (2010)

61. Gottlob, G., Pichler, R., Sallinger, E.: Function symbols in tuple-generating dependencies: expressive power and computability. In: Milo, T., Calvanese, D. (eds.) Proceedings of the 34th ACM Symposium on Principles of Database Systems, PODS 2015, Melbourne, Victoria, Australia, 31 May–4 June 2015, pp. 65–77. ACM (2015). https://doi.org/10.1145/2745754.2745756

62. Gottlob, G., Pieris, A.: Beyond SPARQL under owl 2 QL entailment regime: rules to the rescue. In: IJCAI (2015)

63. Gottlob, G., Pieris, A., Sallinger, E.: Vadalog: recent advances and applications. In: Calimeri, F., Leone, N., Manna, M. (eds.) JELIA 2019. LNCS (LNAI), vol. 11468, pp. 21–37. Springer, Cham (2019). https://doi.org/10.1007/978-3-030-19570-0_2

64. Guagliardo, P., Pichler, R., Sallinger, E.: Enhancing the updatability of projective views. In: Bravo, L., Lenzerini, M. (eds.) Proceedings of the 7th Alberto Mendelzon International Workshop on Foundations of Data Management, Puebla/Cholula,

Mexico, 21–23 May 2013. CEUR Workshop Proceedings, vol. 1087. CEUR-WS.org (2013). http://ceur-ws.org/Vol-1087/paper6.pdf

65. Gulino, A., Ceri, S., Gottlob, G., Sallinger, E., Bellomarini, L.: Distributed company control in company shareholding graphs. In: 37th IEEE International Conference on Data Engineering, ICDE 2021, Chania, Greece, 19–22 April 2021, pp. 2637–2648. IEEE (2021). https://doi.org/10.1109/ICDE51399.2021.00294

66. International Monetary Fund: World economic outlook, April 2019. https://bit.ly/3cKyuzL. Accessed 22 Sep 2022

67. Janev, V., Graux, D., Jabeen, H., Sallinger, E. (eds.): LNCS, vol. 12072. Springer, Cham (2020). https://doi.org/10.1007/978-3-030-53199-7

68. Joshi, A., et al.: A knowledge organization system for the united nations sustainable development goals. In: Verborgh, R., et al. (eds.) ESWC 2021. LNCS, vol. 12731, pp. 548–564. Springer, Cham (2021). https://doi.org/10.1007/978-3-030-77385-4_33

69. Kinnear, M., Shan, W.: The legal protection of foreign investment: a comparative study (with a Foreword by Meg Kinnear, Secretary-General of the ICSID). Bloomsbury Publishing (2012). https://books.google.it/books?id=RyvcBAAAQBAJ

70. Kolaitis, P.G., Pichler, R., Sallinger, E., Savenkov, V.: Nested dependencies: structure and reasoning. In: Hull, R., Grohe, M. (eds.) Proceedings of the 33rd ACM SIGMOD-SIGACT-SIGART Symposium on Principles of Database Systems, PODS 2014, Snowbird, UT, USA, 22–27 June 2014, pp. 176–187. ACM (2014). https://doi.org/10.1145/2594538.2594544

71. Kolaitis, P.G., Pichler, R., Sallinger, E., Savenkov, V.: Limits of schema mappings. In: Martens, W., Zeume, T. (eds.) 19th International Conference on Database Theory, ICDT 2016, Bordeaux, France, 15–18 March 2016. LIPIcs, vol. 48, pp. 19:1–19:17. Schloss Dagstuhl - Leibniz-Zentrum für Informatik (2016). https://doi.org/10.4230/LIPIcs.ICDT.2016.19

72. Kolaitis, P.G., Pichler, R., Sallinger, E., Savenkov, V.: Limits of schema mappings. Theory Comput. Syst. **62**(4), 899–940 (2017). https://doi.org/10.1007/s00224-017-9812-7

73. Kolaitis, P.G., Pichler, R., Sallinger, E., Savenkov, V.: On the language of nested tuple generating dependencies. ACM Trans. Database Syst. **45**(2), 8:1–8:59 (2020). https://doi.org/10.1145/3369554

74. Konstantinou, N., et al.: VADA: an architecture for end user informed data preparation. J. Big Data **6**(1), 1–32 (2019). https://doi.org/10.1186/s40537-019-0237-9

75. Magnanimi, D., Iezzi, M.: Ownership graphs and reasoning in corporate economics. In: EDBT/ICDT Workshops (2022)

76. Mahdisoltani, F., Biega, J., Suchanek, F.M.: YAGO3: a knowledge base from multilingual wikipedias. In: Seventh Biennial Conference on Innovative Data Systems Research, CIDR 2015, Asilomar, CA, USA, 4–7 January 2015, Online Proceedings (2015). https://www.cidrdb.org/

77. Maier, D., Mendelzon, A.O., Sagiv, Y.: Testing implications of data dependencies. ACM Trans. Database Syst. (TODS) **4**(4), 455–469 (1979)

78. Mazuran, M., Serra, E., Zaniolo, C.: Extending the power of datalog recursion. VLDB J. **22**(4), 471–493 (2013)

79. Michels, C., Fayzrakhmanov, R.R., Ley, M., Sallinger, E., Schenkel, R.: Oxpath-based data acquisition for dblp. In: 2017 ACM/IEEE Joint Conference on Digital Libraries, JCDL 2017, Toronto, ON, Canada, 19–23 June 2017, pp. 319–320. IEEE Computer Society (2017). https://doi.org/10.1109/JCDL.2017.7991609

80. Miller, G.A.: Wordnet: a lexical database for English. Commun. ACM **38**(11), 39–41 (1995)
81. Mori, M., Papotti, P., Bellomarini, L., Giudice, O.: Neural machine translation for fact-checking temporal claims. In: Proceedings of the Fifth Fact Extraction and VERification Workshop (FEVER), pp. 78–82. Association for Computational Linguistics, May 2022
82. Nayyeri, M., Vahdati, S., Sallinger, E., Alam, M.M., Yazdi, H.S., Lehmann, J.: Pattern-aware and noise-resilient embedding models. In: Hiemstra, D., Moens, M.-F., Mothe, J., Perego, R., Potthast, M., Sebastiani, F. (eds.) ECIR 2021. LNCS, vol. 12656, pp. 483–496. Springer, Cham (2021). https://doi.org/10.1007/978-3-030-72113-8_32
83. Nayyeri, M., et al.: Fantastic knowledge graph embeddings and how to find the right space for them. In: Pan, J.Z., et al. (eds.) ISWC 2020. LNCS, vol. 12506, pp. 438–455. Springer, Cham (2020). https://doi.org/10.1007/978-3-030-62419-4_25
84. Nissl, M., Sallinger, E.: Modelling smart contracts with datalogmtl. In: Ramanath, M., Palpanas, T. (eds.) Proceedings of the Workshops of the EDBT/ICDT 2022 Joint Conference, Edinburgh, UK, 29 March 2022. CEUR Workshop Proceedings, vol. 3135. CEUR-WS.org (2022). http://ceur-ws.org/Vol-3135/EcoFinKG_2022_paper4.pdf
85. Nissl, M., Sallinger, E., Schulte, S., Borkowski, M.: Towards cross-blockchain smart contracts. In: IEEE International Conference on Decentralized Applications and Infrastructures, DAPPS 2021, Online Event, 23–26 August 2021, pp. 85–94. IEEE (2021). https://doi.org/10.1109/DAPPS52256.2021.00015
86. Pichler, R., Sallinger, E., Savenkov, V.: Relaxed notions of schema mapping equivalence revisited. In: Milo, T. (ed.) Database Theory - ICDT 2011, 14th International Conference, Uppsala, Sweden, 21–24 March 2011, Proceedings, pp. 90–101. ACM (2011). https://doi.org/10.1145/1938551.1938566
87. Pichler, R., Sallinger, E., Savenkov, V.: Relaxed notions of schema mapping equivalence revisited. Theory Comput. Syst. **52**(3), 483–541 (2013). https://doi.org/10.1007/s00224-012-9397-0
88. Sallinger, E.: Reasoning about schema mappings. In: Kolaitis, P.G., Lenzerini, M., Schweikardt, N. (eds.) Data Exchange, Integration, and Streams, Dagstuhl Follow-Ups, vol. 5, pp. 97–127. Schloss Dagstuhl - Leibniz-Zentrum für Informatik (2013). https://doi.org/10.4230/DFU.Vol5.10452.97
89. Sallinger, E., Vahdati, S., Nayyeri, M., Wu, L. (eds.): Proceedings of the International Workshop on Knowledge Representation and Representation Learning co-located with the 24th European Conference on Artificial Intelligence (ECAI 2020), Virtual Event, September 2020, CEUR Workshop Proceedings, vol. 3020. CEUR-WS.org (2021). http://ceur-ws.org/Vol-3020
90. Samarati, P.: k-anonymity. In: van Tilborg, H.C.A., Jajodia, S. (eds.) Encyclopedia of Cryptography and Security, 2nd ed., pp. 663–666. Springer, Boston, MA (2011). https://doi.org/10.1007/978-1-4419-5906-5_754
91. Shkapsky, A., Yang, M., Zaniolo, C.: Optimizing recursive queries with monotonic aggregates in deals. In: ICDE, pp. 867–878. IEEE Computer Society (2015)
92. Staff, O.: OECD handbook on economic globalisation indicators. OECD (2005)
93. Vlad, A., Vahdati, S., Nayyeri, M., Bellomarini, L., Sallinger, E.: Towards hybrid logic-based and embedding-based reasoning on financial knowledge graphs. In: EDBT/ICDT Workshops (2022)
94. Vlad, A., Vahdati, S., Nayyeri, M., Bellomarini, L., Sallinger, E.: Towards hybrid logic-based and embedding-based reasoning on financial knowledge graphs.

In: Ramanath, M., Palpanas, T. (eds.) Proceedings of the Workshops of the EDBT/ICDT 2022 Joint Conference, Edinburgh, UK, 29 March 2022. CEUR Workshop Proceedings, vol. 3135. CEUR-WS.org (2022). http://ceur-ws.org/Vol-3135/EcoFinKG_2022_paper8.pdf

95. Walega, P.A., Cuenca Grau, B., Kaminski, M., Kostylev, E.V.: Datalogmtl: computational complexity and expressive power. In: IJCAI, pp. 1886–1892 (2019). https://www.ijcai.org/

96. Wallmann, C., Gerschberger, M.: The association between network centrality measures and supply chain performance: the case of distribution networks. In: Longo, F., Affenzeller, M., Padovano, A. (eds.) Proceedings of the 2nd International Conference on Industry 4.0 and Smart Manufacturing (ISM 2020), Virtual Event, Austria, 23–25 November 2020. Procedia Computer Science, vol. 180, pp. 172–179. Elsevier (2020). https://doi.org/10.1016/j.procs.2021.01.153

97. Wang, Q., Mao, Z., Wang, B., Guo, L.: Knowledge graph embedding: a survey of approaches and applications. IEEE Trans. Knowl. Data Eng. **29**(12), 2724–2743 (2017)

98. West, R., Gabrilovich, E., Murphy, K., Sun, S., Gupta, R., Lin, D.: Knowledge base completion via search-based question answering. In: Proceedings of the 23rd International Conference on World Wide Web, pp. 515–526. WWW 2014, Association for Computing Machinery, New York, NY, USA (2014)

Cross-Modal Knowledge Discovery, Inference, and Challenges

Meng Wang[1] and Ningyu Zhang[2(✉)]

[1] Southeast University, Nanjing, China
meng.wang@seu.edu.cn
[2] Zhejiang University, Hangzhou, China
zhangningyu@zju.edu.cn

Abstract. In recent years, multimodal knowledge has become a popular research topic in many fields, such as knowledge graphs and natural language processing. Multimodal knowledge involves multimodal knowledge graphs, multimodal pre-trained language models, multimodal knowledge inference, etc.; from online shopping to medical care, whether it is theoretical research or engineering application, the knowledge representation, discovery, and inference of multimodal knowledge have become the core technologies of the academic and industrial concern. This tutorial focuses on the state of the art of cross-modal knowledge discovery and inference and presents future research opportunities and challenges.

Keywords: Multimodal Knowledge · Knowledge Graph · Natural Language Processing

1 Multimodal Knowledge Graph

1.1 What is Multimodal Knowledge?

"Multimodal" can be intuitively regarded as different types of multimedia data, and the main point of distinguishing modality can be regarded as whether the data is heterogeneous[1]. For instance, as shown in Fig. 1, the fact that "the weather in Hangzhou is fine and there is a short rainfall in the afternoon" can have different knowledge expressions, mainly including: spoken and visual knowledge, symbol and temperature knowledge, gestural and linguistic knowledge, geography knowledge, and weather specific knowledge. Therefore, multimodal knowledge is an awareness or understanding of someone or something in different modalities [34, 60].

1.2 Why Do We Need Multimodal Knowledge?

In the perspective of the cognitive science [17, 24], multimodal knowledge is in line with the "two systems" of the information processing in the human brain,

---

[1] https://en.wikipedia.org/wiki/Multimodality.

© The Author(s), under exclusive license to Springer Nature Switzerland AG 2023
L. Bertossi and G. Xiao (Eds.): Reasoning Web, LNCS 13759, pp. 199–209, 2023.
https://doi.org/10.1007/978-3-031-31414-8_6

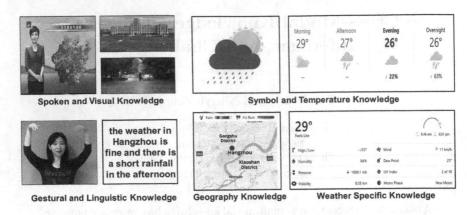

Fig. 1. Instance of multimodal knowledge about Hangzhou's weather.

the complementarity between different modalities helps the individual to the depth of understanding complex things, break through the limitations of single modality in information perception, fusion and reasoning, and effectively improve the efficiency of knowledge acquisition, analysis and cognition [27]. From the perspective of the application, first of all, multimodal knowledge, especially cross-modal semantic relations, can help us better discover more details and answers in many multimodal applications [10,16,42]. Secondly, multimodal knowledge can help us deal with cross-modal disambiguation problems better, including visual entity disambiguation [59], textual entity disambiguation [25], coreference resolution [12,15], syntactic parsing [18], and question answering [1].

1.3   Multimodal Knowledge Graph Construction

The multimodal knowledge graph construction can be achieved by fusing graphs of different modalities (such as text graphs and visual graphs), or it can make full use of the existing knowledge graphs with multimodal extensions [34,51]. Usually, multimodal knowledge graph construction consists of many sub-tasks, including multimodal named entity recognition [56] and relation extraction [58], multimodal entity linking [37], multimodal knowledge graph completion [46] and so on. Multimodal knowledge graphs can play a role in other tasks like cross-modal entity linking as shown in Fig. 2.

2   Multimodal Knowledge Discovery

Multimodal knowledge discovery - the ability to automatically retrieve specific entities and relations from both textual and visual data - holds an important place in multimodal knowledge graph construction [55], and can serve various downstream tasks such as question answering [45], search engines [52], cross-discipline [10,50], and so on. For example, as shown in Fig. 3, given the text "Loris

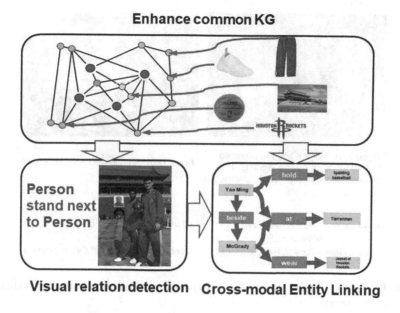

Fig. 2. Multimodal knowledge graph construction and application.

Karius is reported to feel let down by the signing of Alisson and wants to leave Liverpool" with a relevant image, the model aims to extract the entities "Loris Karius[PER]", "Alisson[PER]" and the relation "Person/Person/Peer" between them.

The critical aspect of multimodal named entity recognition and multimodal relation extraction lies in how to obtain good visual representations and integrate them into the textual features for better performance. Note that there exist many noisy visual clues, such as irrelevant objects in images which may lead to negative effects on multimodal knowledge discovery [46]. Intuitively, it is labor-intensive and challenging to obtain all relevant visual-text pairs. Thus, effective models should be developed to obtain good visual features as well as mitigate the noisy effect of irrelevant visual clues for multimodal knowledge discovery.

To address the above-mentioned issues, in the early stage, [25,56] investigates how to integrate the feature of the visual information into the textual representation. [48,49,58] empirically finds that object-level visual fusion may be more necessary for multimodal knowledge discovery. [32] proposes to train a classifier of whether the "visual integrates to the text" before multimodal entity recognition. [47] proposes a new model MAF (matching and alignment framework) for multimodal named entity recognition. [39] proposes to identify and highlight some task-salient features to refine the cross-modal attention. [46] proposes a general data splitting strategy for multimodal knowledge discovery. [38] proposes to utilize entity-related prompts for multimodal entity extraction. [19] illustrates that the current methods may not take full advantage of visual information. [19] further introduces a strong baseline called IFAformer based on Transformer to

Fig. 3. Examples of the multimodal entity and relation extraction for multimodal knowledge discovery.

implicitly align fine-grained multimodal information. Recently, [8] proposes a hierarchical visual prefix fusion network (HVPNeT) for multimodal entity and relation extraction. Specifically, HVPNet regards images as the visual prefix for the corresponding textual inputs, and the visual prefix is a pluggable operation and doesn't require relevance annotations which can help mitigate the error sensitivity of irrelevant object images. Different from HVPNet, [7] proposes a hybrid transformer with multi-level fusion, namely MKGformer, for multimodal knowledge discovery.

3 Inference

Multimodal knowledge graph inference aims to perform knowledge graph completion and link prediction. As shown in Fig. 4, multimodal knowledge graph inference aims to infer the target tail entity given the head entity "Superman Returns" with visual clues and the relation "Film Crew Role". Usually, multimodal knowledge graph inference utilizes to encode entities and relations into continuous embeddings [4,54], which can be used for multimodal reasoning. Note that the major challenges of multimodal knowledge inference lie in the projection and fusion of heterogeneous multimodal features into a common space.

To address the above-mentioned issue, [44] proposes to integrate visual embeddings into the vanilla knowledge graph embeddings for knowledge graph inference. Moreover, [30,41] proposes to joinly encode structureal and visual embedding via concatenation and auto-encoder. [58] proposes to utilize a scene graph for multimodal alignment. [49] proposes to fuse textual and visual features via co-attention. [35] further proposes to encourage or filter the influence

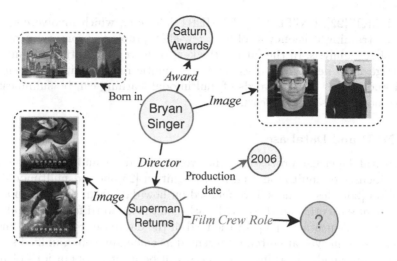

Fig. 4. Examples of multimodal link prediction for multimodal knowledge inference.

of visual information for multimodal knowledge graph inference. Besides, [7] proposes MKGformeer, a hybrid transformer for multimodal knowledge inference which can obtain better performance on both benchmark datasets FB15K-237 and WN19, and also yield promising performance on real-world multimodal knowledge graph OpenBG-IMG[2] [11,29] More recently, [57] proposes a modality split representation learning and ensemble inference framework for multimodal knowledge inference. [53] proposes a new task of multimodal analogical reasoning over knowledge graphs, which needs multimodal reasoning ability with the help of background knowledge.

4 Future Research Opportunities and Challenges

4.1 Knowledge Representation and Multimodal Learning

The traditional representation work in multimodal knowledge is LSCOM [26], which defines an ontology with thousand related multimedia concepts, mainly for use in the broadcast. On the basis of LSCOM, COMM [2] provides a more unified and comprehensive definition of multimodal ontology, but it requires high-quality annotation from domain experts. Benefiting from large-scale open encyclopedia and structured knowledge graphs such as Conceptnet [31], COMET [6], WordNet [23], many works extend the data types in existing knowledge graphs to enrich multi-modal information, such as IMGPedia [13], MMKG [21], KgBench [5], Richpedia [34], etc. In the field of multimodal learning [3], the current main research focuses on multimodal pre-trained language models, such

---

[2] This work is part of the OpenBG Benchmark in https://github.com/OpenBGBenchmark/OpenBG, a large-scale open business knowledge graph evaluation benchmark based on OpenBG (https://kg.alibaba.com/).

as ViLBERT [22], UNITER [9], LXMERT [33], etc., which involve contrastive learning, training efficiency problem, few-shot problem, prompt learning and modal effect analysis. In the future, the key to the representation of multimodal knowledge is to define and discover the semantic relationships between cross-modal knowledge. The keywords of multimodal learning can be summarized as fine-grained representation learning.

4.2 NLP and Database

For natural language processing, the work related to multimodal knowledge mainly focuses on multimodal entity recognition [25,56] and multimodal event extraction [20]. Researchers have focused on how data from different modalities complement each other in these NLP tasks, so the keyword for multimodality in NLP is "complementary" [36]. In the field of the database, researchers find that text, videos or images are often represented as embeddings in a unified semantic space by multimodal learning, and there will be a lot of operations of nearest neighbor search over the embeddings for downstream tasks, which is called the querying embeddings or query vectors [28]. This will face many challenges, such as in the semantic space, the distribution of multimodal embeddings is not uniform, in this case, how to effectively build indexes and query vectors are very challenging, so "querying embeddings" is the key to the future of the database domain.

4.3 IoT and Human-Computer Interaction

In the field of the Internet of Things, researchers pay more attention to the non-visual multimodal information collection, preprocessing, and model-level generalization ability [14,40]. Future research keywords are temporal data segmentation, self-supervised model, few-show learning, and transfer learning. Similar to the IoT field, the human-computer interaction field also pays more attention to the annotation and preprocessing of multimodal data, especially for fine-grained alignment information between different modal data [43]. On this basis, segmentation and Spatio-temporal are keywords for future research.

4.4 Challenges

The challenges and key core issues of multimodal knowledge research are as follows:

1) Data: to engage in the research of multimodal knowledge discovery or engineering application, multimodal data must be available first.
2) Representation of multimodal knowledge: how to break through the existing symbolic knowledge representation and model multimodal, spatial-temporal, event and dynamic knowledge is a difficult problem.
3) Multimodal knowledge graph inference: how to leverage neural networks for symbolic reasoning or how to improve the efficiency of traditional symbolic reasoning is a difficult problem.

4) Effectiveness of multimodal information: how to fully explore and play the effect of different modal information for the knowledge graph itself and downstream tasks, and realize adaptive modal information selection of the model is a difficult problem.

Acknowledgements. This work was supported by the National Key Research and Development Program of China (No. 2021ZD0113202), National Natural Science Foundation of China (Nos. 61906037, 62276063 and 62206246), Natural Science Foundation of Jiangsu Province (No. BK20221457), Zhejiang Provincial Natural Science Foundation of China (No. LGG22F030011), Ningbo Natural Science Foundation (2021J190), and Yongjiang Talent Introduction Programme (2021A-156-G).

References

1. Antol, S., et al.: VQA: visual question answering. In: Proceedings of the IEEE International Conference on Computer Vision, pp. 2425–2433 (2015)
2. Arndt, R., Troncy, R., Staab, S., Hardman, L., Vacura, M.: COMM: designing a well-founded multimedia ontology for the web. In: Aberer, K., et al. (eds.) ASWC/ISWC -2007. LNCS, vol. 4825, pp. 30–43. Springer, Heidelberg (2007). https://doi.org/10.1007/978-3-540-76298-0_3
3. Baltrušaitis, T., Ahuja, C., Morency, L.P.: Multimodal machine learning: a survey and taxonomy. IEEE Trans. Pattern Anal. Mach. Intell. **41**(2), 423–443 (2018)
4. Bi, Z., Cheng, S., Zhang, N., Liang, X., Xiong, F., Chen, H.: Relphormer: relational graph transformer for knowledge graph representation. arXiv preprint arXiv:2205.10852 (2022)
5. Bloem, P., Wilcke, X., van Berkel, L., de Boer, V.: kgbench: a collection of knowledge graph datasets for evaluating relational and multimodal machine learning. In: Verborgh, R., et al. (eds.) ESWC 2021. LNCS, vol. 12731, pp. 614–630. Springer, Cham (2021). https://doi.org/10.1007/978-3-030-77385-4_37
6. Bosselut, A., Rashkin, H., Sap, M., Malaviya, C., Celikyilmaz, A., Choi, Y.: COMET: commonsense transformers for automatic knowledge graph construction. In: Proceedings of the 57th Annual Meeting of the Association for Computational Linguistics, pp. 4762–4779 (2019)
7. Chen, X., et al.: Hybrid transformer with multi-level fusion for multimodal knowledge graph completion. In: Amigó, E., Castells, P., Gonzalo, J., Carterette, B., Culpepper, J.S., Kazai, G. (eds.) The 45th International ACM SIGIR Conference on Research and Development in Information Retrieval (SIGIR 2022), Madrid, Spain, 11–15 July 2022, pp. 904–915. ACM (2022). https://doi.org/10.1145/3477495.3531992
8. Chen, X., et al.: Good visual guidance make a better extractor: hierarchical visual prefix for multimodal entity and relation extraction. In: Carpuat, M., de Marneffe, M., Ruíz, I.V.M. (eds.) Findings of the Association for Computational Linguistics (NAACL 2022), Seattle, WA, United States, 10–15 July 2022, pp. 1607–1618. Association for Computational Linguistics (2022). https://doi.org/10.18653/v1/2022.findings-naacl.121
9. Chen, Y.-C., et al.: UNITER: universal image-text representation learning. In: Vedaldi, A., Bischof, H., Brox, T., Frahm, J.-M. (eds.) ECCV 2020. LNCS, vol. 12375, pp. 104–120. Springer, Cham (2020). https://doi.org/10.1007/978-3-030-58577-8_7

10. Cheng, S., Liang, X., Bi, Z., Zhang, N., Chen, H.: ProteinKG65: a knowledge graph for protein science. arXiv preprint arXiv:2207.10080 (2022)
11. Deng, S., et al.: Construction and applications of open business knowledge graph. arXiv preprint arXiv:2209.15214 (2022)
12. Eisenstein, J., Davis, R.: Conditional modality fusion for coreference resolution. In: Proceedings of the 45th Annual Meeting of the Association of Computational Linguistics, pp. 352–359 (2007)
13. Ferrada, S., Bustos, B., Hogan, A.: IMGpedia: a linked dataset with content-based analysis of Wikimedia images. In: d'Amato, C., et al. (eds.) ISWC 2017. LNCS, vol. 10588, pp. 84–93. Springer, Cham (2017). https://doi.org/10.1007/978-3-319-68204-4_8
14. Gao, N., Shao, W., Rahaman, M.S., Salim, F.D.: n-gage: predicting in-class emotional, behavioural and cognitive engagement in the wild. Proc. ACM Interact. Mob. Wearable Ubiquitous Technol. **4**(3), 1–26 (2020)
15. Guo, D., et al.: GraVL-BERT: graphical visual-linguistic representations for multimodal coreference resolution. In: Proceedings of the 29th International Conference on Computational Linguistics, pp. 285–297 (2022)
16. He, Y., Jia, Q., Yuan, L., Li, R., Ou, Y., Zhang, N.: A concept knowledge graph for user next intent prediction at Alipay. CoRR abs/2301.00503 (2023). https://doi.org/10.48550/arXiv.2301.00503
17. Kahneman, D.: Thinking, fast and slow. Macmillan (2011)
18. Kojima, N., Averbuch-Elor, H., Rush, A.M., Artzi, Y.: What is learned in visually grounded neural syntax acquisition. In: Proceedings of the 58th Annual Meeting of the Association for Computational Linguistics, pp. 2615–2635 (2020)
19. Li, L., Chen, X., Qiao, S., Xiong, F., Chen, H., Zhang, N.: On analyzing the role of image for visual-enhanced relation extraction. CoRR abs/2211.07504 (2022). https://doi.org/10.48550/arXiv.2211.07504
20. Li, M., et al.: Cross-media structured common space for multimedia event extraction. In: Proceedings of the 58th Annual Meeting of the Association for Computational Linguistics, pp. 2557–2568 (2020)
21. Liu, Y., Li, H., Garcia-Duran, A., Niepert, M., Onoro-Rubio, D., Rosenblum, D.S.: MMKG: multi-modal knowledge graphs. In: Hitzler, P., et al. (eds.) ESWC 2019. LNCS, vol. 11503, pp. 459–474. Springer, Cham (2019). https://doi.org/10.1007/978-3-030-21348-0_30
22. Lu, J., Batra, D., Parikh, D., Lee, S.: ViLBERT: pretraining task-agnostic visiolinguistic representations for vision-and-language tasks. In: Wallach, H.M., Larochelle, H., Beygelzimer, A., d'Alché-Buc, F., Fox, E.B., Garnett, R. (eds.) Advances in Neural Information Processing Systems 32: Annual Conference on Neural Information Processing Systems (NeurIPS 2019) (December), pp. 8–14. Vancouver, BC, Canada, pp. 13–23 (2019). https://proceedings.neurips.cc/paper/2019/hash/c74d97b01eae257e44aa9d5bade97baf-Abstract.html
23. Miller, G.A.: WordNet: a lexical database for English. Commun. ACM **38**(11), 39–41 (1995)
24. Minsky, M.: Society of mind. Simon and Schuster (1988)
25. Moon, S., Neves, L., Carvalho, V.: Multimodal named entity recognition for short social media posts. In: Proceedings of the 2018 Conference of the North American Chapter of the Association for Computational Linguistics: Human Language Technologies, vol. 1, pp. 852–860. Association for Computational Linguistics, New Orleans, Louisiana (2018). https://doi.org/10.18653/v1/N18-1078
26. Naphade, M., et al.: Large-scale concept ontology for multimedia. IEEE Multimedia **13**(3), 86–91 (2006)

27. Qiao, S., et al.: Reasoning with language model prompting: a survey. arXiv preprint arXiv:2212.09597 (2022)
28. Qin, J., Wang, W., Xiao, C., Zhang, Y., Wang, Y.: High-dimensional similarity query processing for data science. In: Proceedings of the 27th ACM SIGKDD Conference on Knowledge Discovery and Data Mining, pp. 4062–4063 (2021)
29. Qu, Y., et al.: Commonsense knowledge salience evaluation with a benchmark dataset in e-commerce. CoRR abs/2205.10843 (2022). https://doi.org/10.48550/arXiv.2205.10843
30. Sergieh, H.M., Botschen, T., Gurevych, I., Roth, S.: A multimodal translation-based approach for knowledge graph representation learning. In: Nissim, M., Berant, J., Lenci, A. (eds.) Proceedings of the Seventh Joint Conference on Lexical and Computational Semantics, *SEM@NAACL-HLT 2018, New Orleans, Louisiana, USA, 5–6 June 2018, pp. 225–234. Association for Computational Linguistics (2018). https://doi.org/10.18653/v1/s18-2027
31. Speer, R., Chin, J., Havasi, C.: ConceptNet 5.5: an open multilingual graph of general knowledge. In: Thirty-first AAAI Conference on Artificial Intelligence (2017)
32. Sun, L., Wang, J., Zhang, K., Su, Y., Weng, F.: RpBERT: a text-image relation propagation-based BERT model for multimodal NER. In: Thirty-Fifth AAAI Conference on Artificial Intelligence (AAAI 2021), Thirty-Third Conference on Innovative Applications of Artificial Intelligence (IAAI 2021), The Eleventh Symposium on Educational Advances in Artificial Intelligence (EAAI 2021), Virtual Event, 2–9 February 2021, pp. 13860–13868. AAAI Press (2021). https://ojs.aaai.org/index.php/AAAI/article/view/17633
33. Tan, H., Bansal, M.: LXMERT: learning cross-modality encoder representations from transformers. In: Proceedings of the 2019 Conference on Empirical Methods in Natural Language Processing and the 9th International Joint Conference on Natural Language Processing (EMNLP-IJCNLP), pp. 5100–5111. Association for Computational Linguistics, Hong Kong, China (2019). https://doi.org/10.18653/v1/D19-1514
34. Wang, M., Wang, H., Qi, G., Zheng, Q.: Richpedia: a large-scale, comprehensive multi-modal knowledge graph. Big Data Res. **22**, 100159 (2020)
35. Wang, M., Wang, S., Yang, H., Zhang, Z., Chen, X., Qi, G.: Is visual context really helpful for knowledge graph? A representation learning perspective. In: Shen, H.T., et al. (eds.) ACM Multimedia Conference, Virtual Event, China (MM 2021), 20–24 October 2021, pp. 2735–2743. ACM (2021). https://doi.org/10.1145/3474085.3475470
36. Wang, W., et al.: Visually-augmented language modeling. arXiv preprint arXiv:2205.10178 (2022)
37. Wang, X., et al.: WikiDiverse: a multimodal entity linking dataset with diversified contextual topics and entity types. In: Proceedings of the 60th Annual Meeting of the Association for Computational Linguistics, vol. 1, pp. 4785–4797 (2022)
38. Wang, X., et al.: PromptMNER: prompt-based entity-related visual clue extraction and integration for multimodal named entity recognition. In: Bhattacharya, A., et al. (eds.) Database Systems for Advanced Applications (DASFAA 2022). LNCS, vol. 13247, pp. 297–305. Springer, Cham (2022). https://doi.org/10.1007/978-3-031-00129-1_24
39. Wang, X., et al.: CAT-MNER: multimodal named entity recognition with knowledge-refined cross-modal attention. In: IEEE International Conference on Multimedia and Expo (ICME 2022), Taipei, Taiwan, 18–22 July 2022, pp. 1–6. IEEE (2022). https://doi.org/10.1109/ICME52920.2022.9859972

40. Wang, Z., Jiang, R., Xue, H., Salim, F.D., Song, X., Shibasaki, R.: Event-aware multimodal mobility nowcasting. In: Proceedings of the AAAI Conference on Artificial Intelligence, vol. 36, pp. 4228–4236 (2022)
41. Wang, Z., Li, L., Li, Q., Zeng, D.: Multimodal data enhanced representation learning for knowledge graphs. In: International Joint Conference on Neural Networks (IJCNN 2019). Budapest, Hungary, 14–19 July 2019, pp. 1–8. IEEE (2019). https://doi.org/10.1109/IJCNN.2019.8852079
42. Wu, Q., Shen, C., Wang, P., Dick, A., Van Den Hengel, A.: Image captioning and visual question answering based on attributes and external knowledge. IEEE Trans. Pattern Anal. Mach. Intell. **40**(6), 1367–1381 (2017)
43. Wu, Z., Jiang, Y., Liu, Y., Ma, X.: Predicting and diagnosing user engagement with mobile UI animation via a data-driven approach. In: Proceedings of the 2020 CHI Conference on Human Factors in Computing Systems, pp. 1–13 (2020)
44. Xie, R., Liu, Z., Luan, H., Sun, M.: Image-embodied knowledge representation learning. In: Sierra, C. (ed.) Proceedings of the Twenty-Sixth International Joint Conference on Artificial Intelligence (IJCAI 2017), Melbourne, Australia, 19–25 August 2017, pp. 3140–3146 (2017). https://doi.org/10.24963/ijcai.2017/438
45. Xie, X., et al.: PromptKG: a prompt learning framework for knowledge graph representation learning and application. CoRR abs/2210.00305 (2022). https://doi.org/10.48550/arXiv.2210.00305
46. Xu, B., et al.: Different data, different modalities! reinforced data splitting for effective multimodal information extraction from social media posts. In: Calzolari, N., et al. (eds.) Proceedings of the 29th International Conference on Computational Linguistics (COLING 2022), Gyeongju, Republic of Korea, 12–17 October 2022, pp. 1855–1864. International Committee on Computational Linguistics (2022). https://aclanthology.org/2022.coling-1.160
47. Xu, B., Huang, S., Sha, C., Wang, H.: MAF: a general matching and alignment framework for multimodal named entity recognition. In: Candan, K.S., Liu, H., Akoglu, L., Dong, X.L., Tang, J. (eds.) The Fifteenth ACM International Conference on Web Search and Data Mining (WSDM 2022), Virtual Event/Tempe, AZ, USA, 21–25 February 2022, pp. 1215–1223. ACM (2022). https://doi.org/10.1145/3488560.3498475
48. Yu, J., Jiang, J., Yang, L., Xia, R.: Improving multimodal named entity recognition via entity span detection with unified multimodal transformer. In: Proceedings of the 58th Annual Meeting of the Association for Computational Linguistics, pp. 3342–3352. Association for Computational Linguistics, Online (2020). https://doi.org/10.18653/v1/2020.acl-main.306
49. Zhang, D., Wei, S., Li, S., Wu, H., Zhu, Q., Zhou, G.: Multi-modal graph fusion for named entity recognition with targeted visual guidance. In: Thirty-Fifth AAAI Conference on Artificial Intelligence, (AAAI 2021), Thirty-Third Conference on Innovative Applications of Artificial Intelligence (IAAI 2021), The Eleventh Symposium on Educational Advances in Artificial Intelligence (EAAI 2021), Virtual Event, 2–9 February 2021, pp. 14347–14355. AAAI Press (2021). https://ojs.aaai.org/index.php/AAAI/article/view/17687
50. Zhang, N., et al.: OntoProtein: protein pretraining with gene ontology embedding. In: The Tenth International Conference on Learning Representations (ICLR 2022), Virtual Event, 25–29 April 2022 (2022). https://openreview.net/forum?id=yfe1VMYAXa4
51. Zhang, N., Gui, T., Nan, G.: Efficient and robust knowledge graph construction. In: Proceedings of the 2nd Conference of the Asia-Pacific Chapter of the Association for

Computational Linguistics and the 12th International Joint Conference on Natural Language Processing: Tutorial Abstracts, pp. 1–7. Association for Computational Linguistics, Taipei (2022). https://aclanthology.org/2022.aacl-tutorials.1

52. Zhang, N., et al.: AliCG: fine-grained and evolvable conceptual graph construction for semantic search at Alibaba. In: Zhu, F., Ooi, B.C., Miao, C. (eds.) The 27th ACM SIGKDD Conference on Knowledge Discovery and Data Mining (KDD 2021), Virtual Event, Singapore, 14–18 August 2021, pp. 3895–3905. ACM (2021). https://doi.org/10.1145/3447548.3467057

53. Zhang, N., Li, L., Chen, X., Liang, X., Deng, S., Chen, H.: Multimodal analogical reasoning over knowledge graphs. CoRR abs/2210.00312 (2022). https://doi.org/10.48550/arXiv.2210.00312

54. Zhang, N., Xie, X., Chen, X., Deng, S., Ye, H., Chen, H.: Knowledge collaborative fine-tuning for low-resource knowledge graph completion. J. Softw. **33**(10), 3531 (2022). https://doi.org/10.13328/j.cnki.jos.006628

55. Zhang, N., et al.: DeepKE: a deep learning based knowledge extraction toolkit for knowledge base population. arXiv preprint arXiv:2201.03335 (2022)

56. Zhang, Q., Fu, J., Liu, X., Huang, X.: Adaptive co-attention network for named entity recognition in tweets. In: McIlraith, S.A., Weinberger, K.Q. (eds.) Proceedings of the Thirty-Second AAAI Conference on Artificial Intelligence (AAAI-18), The 30th Innovative Applications of Artificial Intelligence (IAAI-18), and The 8th AAAI Symposium on Educational Advances in Artificial Intelligence (EAAI-18), New Orleans, Louisiana, USA, 2–7 February 2018, pp. 5674–5681. AAAI Press (2018). https://www.aaai.org/ocs/index.php/AAAI/AAAI18/paper/view/16432

57. Zhao, Y., et al.: MoSE: modality split and ensemble for multimodal knowledge graph completion. CoRR abs/2210.08821 (2022). https://doi.org/10.48550/arXiv.2210.08821

58. Zheng, C., Feng, J., Fu, Z., Cai, Y., Li, Q., Wang, T.: Multimodal relation extraction with efficient graph alignment. In: Shen, H.T., et al. (eds.) ACM Multimedia Conference (MM 2021), Virtual Event, China, 20–24 October 2021, pp. 5298–5306. ACM (2021). https://doi.org/10.1145/3474085.3476968

59. Zheng, Q., Wen, H., Wang, M., Qi, G.: Visual entity linking via multi-modal learning. Data Intell. **4**(1), 1–19 (2022)

60. Zhu, X., et al.: Multi-modal knowledge graph construction and application: a survey. CoRR abs/2202.05786 (2022). https://arxiv.org/abs/2202.05786

Author Index

Printed in the United States
by Baker & Taylor Publisher Services